HONOLULU CHINATOWN

200 YEARS of RED LANTERNS & RED LIGHTS

GARY R. COOVER

Rollston Press

Honolulu Chinatown: 200 Years of Red Lanterns & Red Lights
by Gary R. Coover

All rights reserved. No part of this book may be reproduced, scanned, transmitted, or distributed in any printed or electronic form without the prior permission of the author except in the case of brief quotations embodied in articles or reviews.

Copyright © 2022 Gary R. Coover

ISBN-13: 978-1-953208-01-9

All images are in the public domain unless otherwise noted.

Recent photographs are by the author.

Front Cover Photograph: Wo Fat Chop Sui Restaurant (2021), by Gary R. Coover

Back Cover Photographs: James J. Williams (1886) and Board of Health Photographers (1899/1900)

ROLLSTON PRESS
1717 Ala Wai Blvd #1703
Honolulu, HI 96815
USA
info@rollstonpress.com

CHINATOWN

A thousand lights illume the crowded pave,
    Blanching the faces that the narrow sidewalks throng;
The sights—the sounds! it might be Foochow Road,
    Or some street in Hongkong.

The Orient's spices mingle on the breeze
    With scents unspeakable, filched from the swelt'ring East
Of ties that bind the exile to his home,
    These nowise are the least.

Quaint carvings deck the windows by the road,
    Rare wares, that tell a tale of centuries agone,
Bespeak the notice of the passing crowd
    Which hurries ever on.

Almost one sees the rickshaws on the streets—
    Almost one sees the sing-song girls pass gaily by,
When the ear senses some shrill instrument,
    Or a street-vendor's cry.

The cafes hold their throngs of silk-clad guests,
    The soup-shops echo with the coolie's ribaldry,
And sometimes lanterns light the pilgrim's path
    When the New Year is nigh.

The street-cars clang along a nearby street—
    Great cars, with dazzling gleam, dash ever up and down,
While curious ones seek tokens of Cathay
    Amid a new world town.

The lights die out, the poppy's drowsy breath
    Steals like a sick'ning blight o'er each deserted street,
And night keeps watch o'er an enchanted spot
    Where past and future meet.

                —By Herbert M. Ayres.

Honolulu Advertiser, April 30, 1925

HONOLULU'S CHINATOWN

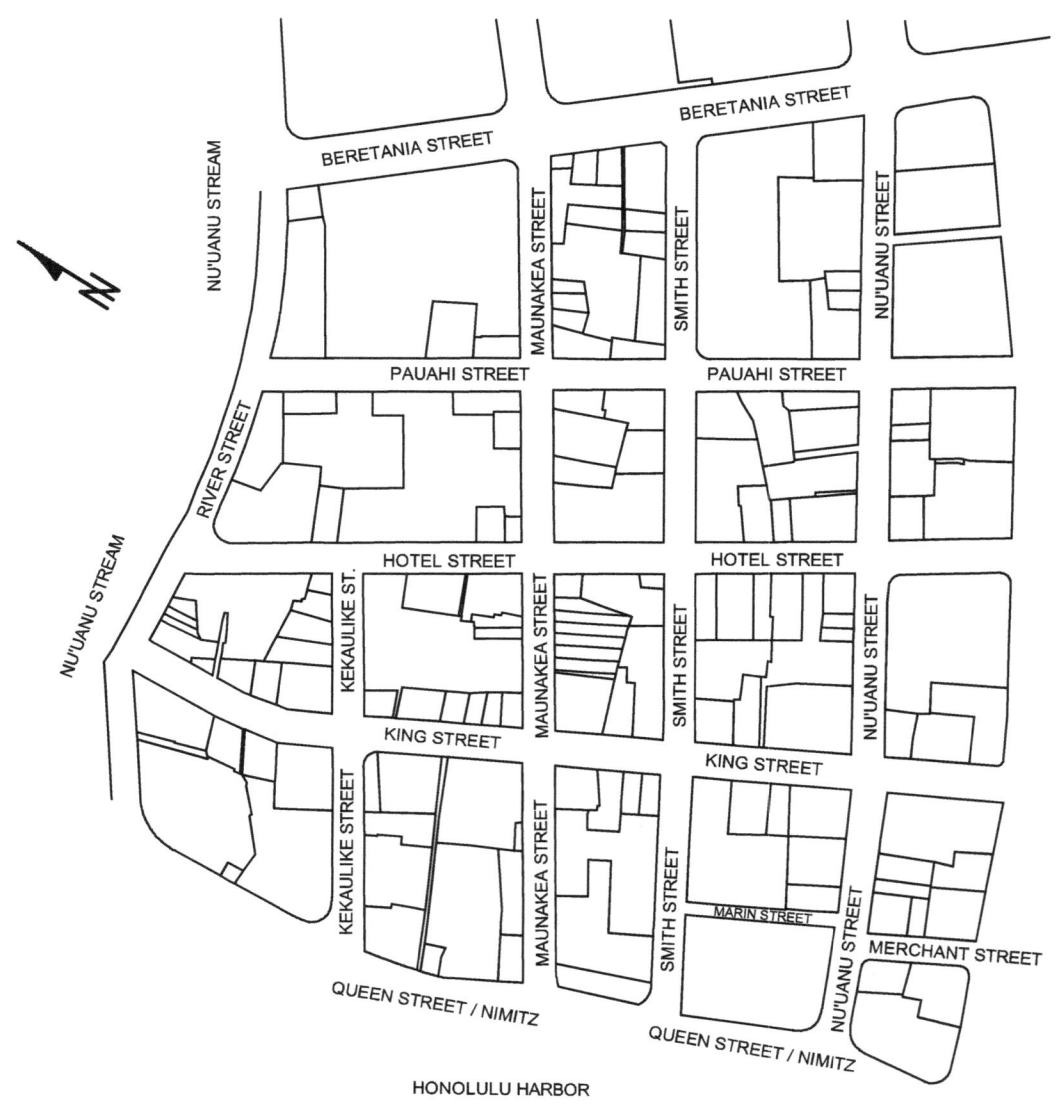

TABLE OF CONTENTS

PREFACE 8
INTRODUCTION 9
EARLY DAYS 10
ECONOMIC WAVES 12
WAVES OF IMMIGRATION 16
PIDGIN 24
BENEVOLENT SOCIETIES 25
CHINESE NAMES 26
CHINATOWN FOOD 28
PAI GOW, FAN-TAN, CHE-FA, PAKAPIO 29
CHASING THE DRAGON 30
THE FIRST GREAT CHINATOWN FIRE 31
BUBONIC PLAGUE 40
THE FIRES OF 1900 41
EARLY 20th CENTURY 51
CLIMBING THE STAIRS 52
BURLESQUE, NUDES, PORN, & DRUGS 54
ALMOST LOST 55
HISTORIC PRESERVATION 56
BUILDING RESTORATION 58
URBAN RENEWAL 59
ENDURING TRADITIONS 61
THE FUTURE? 62
ARCHITECTURAL STYLES 63
ARCHITECTS & BUILDERS 68
STREETS – "ALANUI" 89
STREET SCENES THEN & NOW 91

BERETANIA STREET 121
   Honolulu Auto Supply Building 122
   Honolulu Tower 123
   Roberts Building 126
   Arita Building 127
   Hai On Tong Building 128
   Chinatown Cultural Plaza 129
   Hale Pauahi (Hale Lahui, Hale O'Pili) 131
   Fong Building 132

HOTEL STREET 133
   Empire Saloon / Hoffman Café (site) 134
   Smith's Union Bar 136
   Bickerton Block / Hubba Hubba 137
   Mendonça & Selig Building 140
   Independent Theater 141
   Risque Theatre / Buffum's Hall (site) 142
   The Swing Club 146
   42 N. Hotel 152
   50 N. Hotel 153
   1913 Mendonça buliding 154
   Joseph P. Mendonça Building 155
   Araujo Building 160
   Chinatown Police Station 162
   Siu Building 163
   Yee Yee Tong Building 165
   Wo Fat Restaurant 166
   Colusa Building (site) 171
   Lum Yip Kee Building 172
   Chinese Theatre (site) 174
   Maunakea Marketplace 176
   Kekaulike Courtyards 177
   Glade Show Club (site) 179
   Lung Doo Building 182
   Yew Char Building 183
   Chinatown Manor 184
   Winston Hale 185

KEKAULIKE STREET 189
   Sperry Flour Building 190
   City Mill (Site) 191

Service Cold Storage Building 194

928 Kekaulike 197

Holau Market 198

1011-1015 Kekaulike (site) 202

Ying Leong Look Funn Buliding 204

Sam Chew Lau Building 205

KING STREET 207

Robinson Building / 1 N. King 208

Hocking Building / 2 N. King 218

Honolulu Trust Company 221

United Chinese Society Building 222

Hawaii National Bank 226

Central Pacific Bank 229

Mendonça Makai / Sumitomo Bank 232

Yim Quon Building 234

Lum Yip Kee Building 236

Yuen Chong Building 237

Liberty Bank 238

Y. Anin Block (King St.) 243

C.Q. Yee Hop Plaza 245

C.Q. Yee Hop Market 250

Hop Sing Building 252

Yee Hop Market 253

L. Ah Leong Building 254

Shun Lung Building 256

Oahu Market 257

Tanaka Brothers Building 259

Arrow Hardware Building 261

Lee Let Building (site) 262

E.C. Winston Block 264

Armstrong Building 266

Ching Lum Block 269

MAUNAKEA STREET 271

M. Kawahara Building 272

J.H. Schnack Building 274

C.Q. Yee Hop Cold Storage & Dormitory 276

Hawaiian Mercantile Building 277

Lee & Young Building 279

Kwai Chan Trust Building 283

Kekaulike Courtyards 287

Chee Wo Tong Building 288

Y. Anin Block (Maunakea) 291

Maunakea Marketplace 292

Maunakea Marketplace 293

Wing Sing Wo Building 295

Lum Yip Kee Building 296

Pang Lum Mow / Aloha Hotel (site) 298

Sumida Building 299

Pang Lum Mow Building (site) 302

Hawaii Hochi / Y. Anin Building 303

T. Sumida building 305

K.C. Siu Building 307

Asahi / Oahu Theater (site) 308

Tsung Tsin Association Building 311

Loo Chow Building 312

K.C. Wong Building 313

1168-1172 Maunakea (site) 314

1171-1187 Maunakea (site) 315

Tom's Grill (site) 316

Maunakea Hale (site) 317

NUʻUANU Street 319

Nuʻuanu Court (Queen's Court) 321

802-830 Nuʻuanu (Site) 323

Oahu Hotel (Site) 326

Royal Saloon 327

T.R. Foster Building 330

Irwin Block (Nippu Jiji Building) 332

Wing Wo Tai Building 337

Wing Wo Tai / Wing Wo Chan (site) 338

Anchor Saloon (site) 339

Flores Building (Pacific Saloon) 340

Aseu Building 342

National Hotel (site) 345
Aswan Building 347
Uyeda Building 350
Cosmopolitan Saloon 352
Perry Block 354
Mendonça / Encore Saloon 358
Paiko Block / Lai Fong Building 361
McLean Block 366
Love's Bakery 368
Pantheon Bar 371
Novelty Theater/Chinese Bazaar 372
C. Ahi Building 374
Kimura Building 377
Marks Building (Marks Garage) 378
Pegge Hopper Gallery 383
Holt Block / Brown Derby (site) 384
Kokusai Theatre / Empress Theater 388
Queen Emma Hall / Ye Liberty Theater (site) . 390
The Commercial Hotel (site) 395
Honolulu Park Place 397

PAUAHI STREET 399
L.L. McCandless Block 400
Biltright Shoe Repair 401
Wing Coffee Company 402
Wang Building 404
Char Hung Sut 405
Pauahi Hale 406
Gum Chew Lau Building (site) 407
Pauahi Kupuna Hale 408
Pauahi Recreation Center 409

RIVER STREET 411
Harbor Village Apartments 412
Komeya Apartments 414
River-Pauahi Apartments 416

SMITH STREET 419
Marin Tower 420
Honolulu Iron Works (site) 424
Sailor Jerry's Tattoo Shop 425
Mendonça Makai 426
Little Village Noodle House 427
Sun Yun Wo (site) 428
Tan Sing Building 429
1125-1141 Smith / 45 N. Pauahi (site) 431
1130 Smith (site) 433
1143-1151 Smith / 46-50 Pauahi (site) ... 434
Golden Harvest Theatre 436
1153-1155 Smith (site) 438
1159 Smith (site) 439
Be Bop Hotel 440
Honolulu Auto Supply Service Station 442

BUILDINGS BY DATE 443
SOURCES & ACKNOWLEDGEMENTS 447
THE AUTHOR 449
INDEX 451
GEOGRAPHICAL INDEX 457

PREFACE

Through this research I have met some of the most interesting people – immigrants, ship captains, saloon owners, shopkeepers, architects, builders, gamblers, opium dealers, merchant princes, kings, queens, exotic dancers – and it is my distinct pleasure to be able to introduce you to them, their buildings, their stories. It is indeed an honor to be able to recognize and celebrate their lives, their achievements, and the buildings they designed and built.

Original research included going down countless rabbit holes, poring through thousands of newspaper pages, studying hundreds of historical photographs, historical maps, and land records, and then connecting millions of dots – a huge jigsaw puzzle with the added element of different things being in different places at different times.

Added to this was the challenge of multiple street name and address number changes, plus the many different ways Chinese names are notated and translated into English.

And there's also contending with the inevitable gaps, inaccuracies, misspellings, mistakes, biases, and lapses of information that often accompany printed historical accounts.

Funny thing about historical research – two buildings that I initially thought were uninteresting and unworthy of even being included in the walking tour turned out to have the richest and most noteworthy histories. The moral of the story? Always keep looking, you never know what you might find if you dig deep enough.

In addition to the snippets of social history this original research establishes exact building construction dates and rediscovers the identities of many of the architects and builders. Original building names are shown where possible, but names often change through successive generations and owners. For the most part, modern businesses are not included – their history is still being written.

Many corner buildings have frontages and addresses on both streets, so decisions had to be made where to put them in the street listings. if you are looking for a particular building, check both streets.

For many this will be a stroll down memory lane. For others, a reference or perhaps a revelation or two. At the very least, some entertaining narratives about this most unique place.

No one book can tell all the stories of Honolulu's Chinatown – this is just a starting point. Not everything could be included lest the book run to several thousand pages. Many more stories are still waiting to be discovered. I hope it inspires you to explore further on your own to learn even more about the many hard-working people (and interesting characters) who have made Honolulu's Chinatown into the incredibly diverse and fascinating place that survives today and hopefully tomorrow.

Gary R. Coover
Honolulu, Hawaii

INTRODUCTION

There was a time when Chinatown wasn't Chinatown.

And it's never been 100% Chinese.

It might be more correct to call it Foreignertown or Immigranttown or Workingclasstown, but the huge wave of Chinese immigration beginning in the 1850's resulted in over 50% of its population being Chinese, giving it the name by which it has been known ever since. But there were also many others here including English, Irish, Scottish, American, German, French, Russian, Japanese, Okinawan, Portuguese, Puerto Rican, Korean, Filipino, Lao, Vietnamese, and of course, Native Hawaiian. A land of red lanterns, red lights, and so much more.

For over 200 years it has been in a constant state of change and metamorphosis, sometimes gradual, sometimes drastic, and sometimes catastrophic, in a process that continues to the present day.

Honolulu's Chinatown is a residential area, a business center, a shopping place, an eating and drinking place, a place with temples and churches, and a place with brothels and nightclubs. It has survived immigration, plagues, fires, strikes, riots, opium dens, drunken sailors, toppled governments, prostitution, adult bookstores, exotic dancers, transvestite hookers, drug busts, Urban Renewal, homeless vagrants, and even an earthquake.

Surprisingly, for such a fascinating place, there has never been a comprehensive history of Honolulu's Chinatown – until now.

The first part of this book provides a historical summary of the early settlement and economic forces that impacted the development of Chinatown, plus detailed accounts of the major events in its history. It also includes short biographies of the architects and builders who built Chinatown over the years, and includes many historical photographs never before published. Comparative street views show how scenes have changed over the years, and a detailed gazetteer by street presents a brief history of every building currently in Chinatown.

Sprinkled throughout the book are stories of early Chinatown residents, noteworthy visitors like Billie Holiday, Louis Armstrong, Dame Clara Butt, and Muhammed Ali, and unusual historical connections to George Washington, Marquis de Lafayette, George Custer, Mao Zedong, Napoleon, and famous fictional characters like Charlie Chan, Captain Peasley, and Mamie Stover. Also included are many filming locations for *Hawaii 5-0*, *Magnum P.I.*, *Lost*, and movies like *Kong: Skull Island*, *Godzilla vs. Kong*, and a 1953 award-winning film that won 8 Oscars.

There are even bizarre things like a cat with a gold earring, an exotic dancer with flaming butt tassels, and a report of spontaneous human combustion – all par for the course in the multi-national and multi-cultural Hawaiian mixed plate that is Honolulu's Chinatown.

A WORD ABOUT HAWAIIAN DIRECTIONS: The cardinal directions of north, south, east, and west do not make much sense in an island setting, so these are the directions commonly used in Hawaii, and specifically in Honolulu:

Mauka (MAU-ka)	=	toward the mountains
Makai (ma-KAI)	=	toward the ocean
Ewa (EV-uh)	=	toward Ewa Beach
Waikiki (WAI-kee-KEE)	=	toward Waikiki (1800's and early 1900's)
Diamond Head (or DH)	=	toward Diamond Head (in current use)

EARLY DAYS

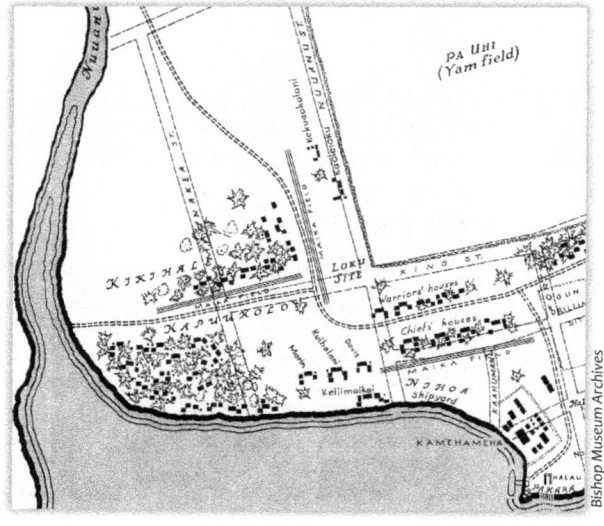

The area we now call Chinatown was initially a small fishing community with a handful of grass houses that had been there since ancient times.

The very first immigrants to Hawaii were the seafaring Polynesians who initially discovered the islands, traveling the nearly 3,000 miles across open water from Tahiti approximately 1,500 years ago.

By the late 1700's, Keali'imaika'i, the brother of Kamehameha I, lived along the beach at the foot of Nu'uanu Street.

King Kamehameha moved his royal court in 1809 to a place called Kou along the Honolulu Harbor between Nu'uanu Street and the point of land called Pākākā.

Two of the king's closest European advisors lived just ewa of Nu'uanu Street – Isaac Davis and Don Francisco de Paula Marín.

By 1810 the area housed a mixture of Native Hawaiians and Europeans trusted by King Kamehameha I, and part of the area that would become Chinatown was known as Kapu'ukolo – the area "where white men and such dwelt."

And yes, some of those early "and such" were Chinese. Others were British, American, German, French and Portuguese. Honolulu and Lāhainā were the two deepwater harbors in Hawaii that could accommodate the large European sailing ships – Hawaiian ocean-going craft only needed a sandy beach.

The local geographical place names were Kapu'ukolo for the area near the water (makai), Kikihale was a little further mauka (toward the mountains) and named after a stream in the area, Kaumakapili was the area closer to present-day Beretania Street, Kalanikāhua was at Smith and Hotel streets, and Pololewa was in the area of King and Nu'uanu streets. These descriptive names were used in land titles and early newspaper accounts well into the late 1800's.

The earliest houses in Honolulu were thatched, made of wooden poles covered with pili grass. A writer in 1828 described the town as:

> "A mass of brown huts, looking like so many hay-stacks in the country; not one white cottage, no church spire, not a garden nor a tree to be seen save the grove of coconuts."

The first solidly constructed building in Hawaii was a coral block storehouse built by Don Francisco de Paula Marín in 1809 for Kamehameha I, and Don Francisco subsequently built a coral stone house for himself in 1810 which he called "America" that was located where Marin Tower is today. European-style frame house construction slowly began to take hold, and many New England-style houses were imported in pieces, but thatched houses were used well into the mid 1800's.

By the 1830's there were about 600 Hawaiian houses, most being the traditional "grass shack". They were spaced apart to minimize fire hazards, and were susceptible to high winds that "scalped, twisted or even demolished them". Most of the foreigners lived in adobe houses made by mixing soil with dry grass and molding into blocks roughly 18" x 12" x 8" in size, which were then covered with a plaster of lime and sand.

The unofficial lanes between houses became the first streets in 1837, and by 1838 there were about 6,000 people in Honolulu proper and 3,000 or so in the surrounding area. There were 350 to 400 foreigners including 200 to 250 Americans, 75 to 100 British, and 30 to 40 Chinese, with the rest being French, Spanish, Portuguese, and other nationalities. This is where the melting pot, or mixed plate, of cultures began in Hawaii.

On January 9, 1847, *The Polynesian* reported 1,386 buildings in Honolulu which included:

```
Residences (1,337)
    Grass                875
    Adobe                345
    Stone (coral)         49
    Wood                  39
    Stone/adobe/ wood     29

Stores and warehouses (40)
    Stone                 15
    Adobe                 15
    Wood                  10

Public Buildings (9)
    Churches               4
    Palace & Government    5
```

All land ownership was originally vested in the king and the chiefs. In 1848 King Kamehameha III introduced a system of private property ownership that was called the Great Māhele (*māhele* means "division") whereby a special Land Court established existing ownership through detailed boundary surveys and multiple interviews.

Two years later, foreigners were allowed to purchase land, and by 1890 more than 75 percent of the lands originally granted to the chiefs were owned by non-Hawaiians. Many Native Hawaiians had simply cashed in, or forfeited the lands due to over-extended credit, or not realized that being nice and allowing foreigners to live on their land would lead to later claims of ownership.

Chinatown was never officially platted into surveyed lots and blocks – most of the lot lines date back to the original 1848 Great Māhele distribution of private land and before. The street pattern was overlaid across these old traditional property lines, leaving some unusually shaped lots as well as many remnants of ancient lanes and pathways.

The Chinatown side of town was the working-class area of Honolulu – the main business district was centered around Merchant Street and Fort Street. The first newspaper reference of the name "Chinatown" occurs in 1876, and it was called "Old Chinatown" by 1909.

ECONOMIC WAVES

SANDALWOOD

The Chinese called Hawaii 檀香山 (Tánxiāngshān) – The Sandalwood Mountains.

To the ancient emperors, sandalwood (*Santalum*) symbolized power and status, and its aromatic wood was prized throughout China for incense, medicine, and furniture. Believe it or not, ancient Hawaii was once covered in huge forests of native sandalwood trees.

Sandalwood was first collected in Kaua'i in 1791 by Captain John Kendrick of the *Lady Washington*. From 1810 to 1830 the sandalwood trade with China was at its height, and it is estimated that over 13 million pounds of sandalwood were harvested in Hawaii, as much as 1,400 tons per year.

> "There were between two and three thousand men, carrying each from one to six pieces of sandal wood, according to their size and weight. It was generally tied on their backs by bands made of ti leaves, passed over the shoulders and under the arms, and fastened across their breast." – William Ellis, 1823

The sandalwood trade drastically changed the Hawaiian economy from self-sufficiency to commercial trading. It also created the desire for Eastern and Western goods like fabrics, furniture, tools, and imported household goods.

King Kamehameha I even tried to get in on the action by buying a brig which he renamed *Ka'ahumanu*, hiring Captain Alexander Adams to sail it to China.

American and British merchants extended massive amounts of credit to the government and the chiefs simply signed promissory notes with little regard to the debt they were incurring. The national debt increased every year and by the reign of Kamehameha III the kingdom was in debt by $500,000. As a result, Hawaii's first written law in 1826 was a tax requiring every man to provide 67 pounds of sandalwood annually. And this was when the hillsides were already being rapidly deforested.

Although Kamehameha I had imposed a kāpu (restriction) on sandalwood harvesting, it was ignored after his death and the subsequent greed and willful denuding of the hillsides severely damaged the natural environment and shortsightedly brought a quick end to the once lucrative sandalwood trade.

WHALING

On September 29, 1819, the sailing ships *Equator* and *Balena* from New England were the first whaling ships to arrive in Hawaii. In 1820, the Nantucket whaling ship *Maro* under the command of Captain Joseph Allen was the first whaling ship to enter Honolulu Harbor. Captain Allen soon discovered the rich whaling ground off the coast of Japan.

Two years later there were approximately 60 whaling ships operating out of Hawaii, growing to nearly 600 ships wintering in the islands by 1846 at the two main ports of Honolulu and Lāhainā.

> **ODD NAMED LOCALITIES.**
>
> AN EARLY instrument of record, conveying certain property in the town of Lahaina, Maui, locates it by terms of a decidedly nautical flavor, no doubt well known then when it was so frequented by whaleships, but now lost and forgotten.
>
> Like names were applied to various locations in Honolulu, along in the "early fifties," which are recalled by the above incident and clearly indicates, like Lahaina's, their source of origin.
>
> BLACK SEA was that portion of Honolulu lying back of King and Maunakea streets, toward the stream.
>
> JAPAN SEA comprised the upper part of Maunakea street toward the Nuuanu stream.
>
> YELLOW SEA lay back of the Commercial Hotel, corner of Nuuanu and Beretania streets up to Kukui lane.
>
> CHINA SEA was that portion of the town which lay on both sides of Smith street, between Hotel and Beretania streets.
>
> CAPE HORN comprised the Kaumakapili block.
>
> COW BAY was off Maunakea street and extended to the stream, and was reached by a lane leading by Liberty Hall, known to some as *Bugle Alley*.
>
> MOSQUITO BAY lay in the rear of Dudoit's (later Dickson's) premises, reached by a lane off Beretania street.
>
> 6 Known also as Keoua Lelepali.

The whalers were mostly interested in sperm whales since the oil from their blubber was worth three times more than oil from humpback whales.

Conveniently located halfway between the West Coast and Japan, whaling had a huge impact on the Hawaii economy that more than made up for the dwindling sandalwood trade.

There were numerous shops along the Honolulu waterfront catering to cargo operations and provisions, along with ship repair workshops, sailmakers, iron workers, foundries, carpenters, ship's chandlers, and commission agents.

A block or two farther inland were the boarding houses, saloons, shops, residences, and sundry businesses catering to the workers.

The posh folks lived near the Palace while the working folks lived near the docks in what would later become known as Chinatown.

The local economy was bolstered greatly by the "dissipation expenses" of the thousands of ship's crew members, spent freely in the local saloons and in the company of willing native women.

In 1843, a sailor on the whale ship *Charles and Henry* abandoned his post and was caught and tried for mutiny but escaped and made his way to Lāhainā and then Honolulu. He briefly worked as a pinsetter in a bowling alley that was probably located somewhere along Nuʻuanu Street. In 1851 he wrote a best-selling novel based on his whaling experiences – his name was Herman Melville and the book was titled "Moby Dick".

In 1859, the discovery of oil in Titusville, Pennsylvania, marked the beginning of the end of the whaling business. Whales were rapidly disappearing anyway due to over-hunting, and the early Arctic freezes in 1871 and 1876 that destroyed the North Pacific whaling fleet essentially ended Hawaii's whaling days.

SUGAR

Sugar cane is a "canoe plant" brought to Hawaii with the first Polynesian settlers over a thousand years ago. The first sugar mill was started on the island of Lanai in 1802 by Wong Tze-Chun using a boiler and stone mill shipped from China. But Lanai proved to be too dry for sugarcane and he returned to China in 1803.

The first commercial sugar plantation was established in Koloa, Kaua'i, in 1835 by Ladd & Company. By 1850 the Hawaiian sugar industry exported over 750,000 pounds of sugar.

The Great Māhele of 1848, followed by the 1850 amendment allowing foreigners to buy and lease land led to the creation of large plantations.

The American Civil War created a massive sugar shortage, resulting in the price of sugar rising 525% to 25 cents per pound by 1864.

Sugar became even more profitable when the Reciprocity Treaty of 1875 meant Hawaii could sell products like sugar to the United States without any duties or taxes in exchange for the use of Pearl Harbor as a naval base by the United States.

By 1880 there are 63 sugar plantations in Hawaii, most of which are controlled by the "Big Five": Theo H. Davies & Co., Amfac, C. Brewer & Co., Alexander & Baldwin Inc., and Castle & Cooke.

In 1906, Thomas Edison filmed a sugarcane harvest which can be viewed here:

Growing and harvesting sugarcane is a very labor-intensive process and working conditions were incredibly grueling. Workers were subjected to a variety of hardships and often brutal lunas (overseers).

The first recorded sugar strike was by Native Hawaiian workers in 1841 and lasted two weeks.

At the urging of the plantation owners in 1850 the Hawaiian government approved the use of mass importation of workers and the government brought in the first contract workers from China in 1852.

The owners became increasingly concerned about the growing number and potential political power of so many Chinese workers, so they brought in other laborers from the Madeira Islands, Japan, Puerto Rico, Korea, Philippines and even Russia. But the strikes continued, with the largest being in 1909 and again in 1920, both organized by Japanese workers. Many workers quit after their initial contract, and instead of returning many stayed in Hawaii.

After a peak in 1933 of more than 250,000 acres dedicated to sugar cane, Hawaii's last sugar mill (in Puunene, Maui) closed in 2016.

RICE

Although no rice is currently grown commercially in Hawaii, at one time it was second only to sugar.

The Royal Hawaiian Agricultural Society was the first to promote the growing of rice in 1850, and the subsequent introduction of thousands of Chinese laborers created a substantial demand since most Chinese did not care for poi. With the concurrent decline in the Native Hawaiian population many former taro ponds were converted into rice production.

Many of the rice farmers were former sugar plantation laborers who had served out their contract and elected to stay, and many in the established Chinese business community became owners of the rice farms. The first rice mill was established in Honolulu in 1862 by the Steam Flour Mill Company.

By 1889 only Louisiana and South Carolina produced more rice. But oddly enough, the importation of Japanese workers did not result in higher demand for Hawaiian rice as Chinese grew long grain rice and Japanese preferred the short grain varieties. Around 1920, cheaper California rice, as well as the removal of the embargo on Japanese rice, resulted in rice production being no longer profitable in Hawaii.

PINEAPPLES

Ananas comosus, better known as pineapple, was first recorded in Hawaii as being planted by Don Francisco de Paula Marín on January 21, 1813. By 1820 pineapples were growing wild as well as in small plots and gardens.

Annexation in 1898 plus the revocation of a 35% tariff inspired a group of California homesteaders to start the pineapple export business, and after the arrival of James D. Dole (second cousin to Sanford Dole) in 1899 the first profitable canned pineapples were produced by Dole's Hawaiian Pineapple Company. By 1903 Hawaii was the world's top producer of canned pineapples.

In 1906 Dole built the world's largest fruit cannery in Iwilei on the site of the former red-light district known as the "Iwilei Stockade" featuring a water tower shaped and painted to resemble a pineapple. By 1946 there were 9 pineapple companies with canneries in Hawaii, and 13 plantations covering 60,000 acres. It was the second-largest industry in Hawaii and it employed nearly 20,000 workers.

Pineapple production peaked in 1957 and declined afterwards due to competition from Del Monte's pineapple plantations and canneries in the Philippines.

TOURISM

Starting with the interest in Hawaii sparked by the Panama-Pacific International Exhibition in 1915, Hawaiian tourism was heavily promoted by Matson Lines and took a massive leap forward with statehood in 1959 and the increased availability and affordability of air travel to Hawaii. And for the very first time, Chinatown became a tourist destination.

WAVES OF IMMIGRATION

After the early Polynesian migration and later haphazard European immigration, there were several periods in Hawaiian history where mass immigrations were officially organized to provide much-needed plantation labor.

Comparative Table of Nationality of Population of Hawaiian Islands at Various Census Periods since 1853.

NATIONALITY	1853	1866	1872	1878	1884	1890	1896
Natives	70,036	57,125	49,044	44,088	40,014	34,436	31,019
Part Hawaiians	983	1,640	1,487	3,420	4,218	6,186	8,485
Chinese	364	1,206	1,938	5,916	17,937	15,301	19,382
Americans	692		889	1,276	2,066	1,928	2,263
Haw'n-born Foreigners	309		849	947	2,040	7,495	13,733
British	435		619	883	1,282	1,344	1,538
Portuguese	86		395	436	9,377	8,602	8,232
German	81	2,988	224	272	1,600	1,434	912
French	60		88	81	192	70	75
Japanese					116	12,360	22,329
Norwegian	8				362	227	216
Other Foreigners	80		364	666	416	419	424
Polynesian	4				956	588	409
Totals	73,138	62,959	56,897	57,985	80,578	89,990	109,020

There was no complete division of nationalities noted in the census of 1866.

Chinese

The first Chinese seen in Hawaii were two or three cooks who prepared food for the ship captains in the sandalwood trade in 1789. In China, Hawaii was called 檀香山 (Tánxiāngshān) which translates to "Sandalwood Mountain".

After that initial encounter, most of the Chinese who came to Hawaii were not cooks or laborers – they were ship captains and businessmen. *The Polynesian* published a "Register of Foreigners Residing in Honolulu" on January 9, 1847, and out of the 350 names listed at least twelve were obviously Chinese.

They did not settle exclusively in Chinatown but were mixed in with the general population, and many were married to Hawaiian women. By the 1830's several had already set up shop in Honolulu, including Wong Tai Hoon who owned a store at the ewa/makai corner of Hotel and Nu'uanu streets.

These early Chinese businessmen were mostly Punti from the Canton (Guangzhou) area while many of the laborers imported later were Hakka from Fukien. Although they had a common written language, the spoken languages were very different and many subsequently used spoken Hawaiian to communicate.

China was known as the Celestial Empire 天朝 (Tiāncháo), "heavenly dynasty", and the Chinese in Hawaii were often referred to as "Celestials".

On January 3, 1852, the *Thetis* arrived from China with 195 contract laborers – the first ever imported by the government of Hawaii and the first of what would become a tidal wave of immigration to Hawaii.

Between 1855 and 1867, the Punti and Hakka groups in China were engaged in horrific clan wars that left roughly a million dead, and the Taiping Rebellion from 1850 to 1864 killed another 20 million. Consequently, many Chinese were more than eager to start a new life elsewhere when the Hawaiian planters began searching for workers.

The first mention of the word "Coolie" appears in the Hawaiian newspapers in 1847, referring to the Chinese laborers being imported to the west coast of America after the worldwide movement to abolish slavery. Considered dated and offensive today, the term originated in India and was later applied to any unskilled and uneducated low-wage Asian laborer. In Chinese the word 苦力 (Kŭli) literally translates as "bitter strength".

Fortunately, Hawaii did not experience the many abuses of the "Coolie Trade" and the hope was the imported workforce would be "intelligent, industrious and self-respecting workmen" and not "ignorant, brutish and servile". By the late 1800's many Chinese came to Hawaii as free immigrants and not contract laborers.

The Chinese men were hard workers, but they did not like the working conditions and most quickly abandoned the hard existence of the plantations when their contracts expired. Instead of returning to China they moved to town to become merchants. It has been estimated that 60 percent of the stores in Honolulu were Chinese-owned by 1880.

The rapid expansion of the Chinese presence in America and Hawaii caused great concern and some animosity, and in 1882 the US Congress passed the Chinese Exclusion Act. It had exceptions for merchants, students, teachers, diplomats, and travelers, but was not repealed until 1943. Hawaii followed suit in 1886 with the Hawaiian Kingdom Chinese Exclusion Act halting the importation of Chinese laborers.

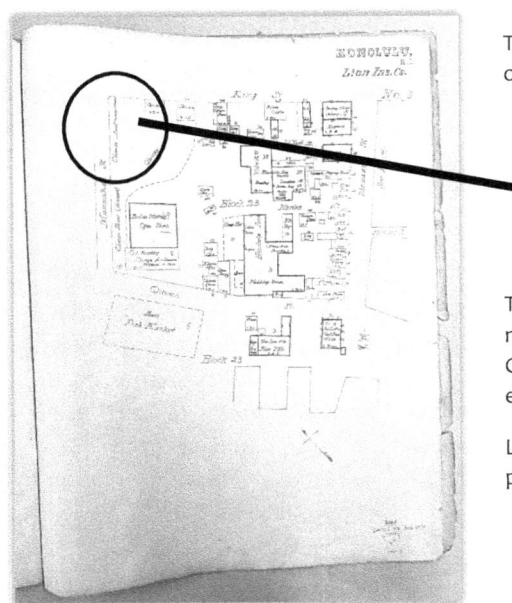

There is an astonishing note in the upper left corner of Sheet 6 of the 1879 Lion Fire Insurance Map of Honolulu:

The delineator of the 1879 fire insurance maps also deliberately neglected to map the many buildings in the Chinese area of Chinatown, instead just drawing a dashed line and labeling everything on the other side as "Chinese".

Let's hope the mapmaker just didn't want to insure these properties as opposed to expressing any blatant xenophobia.

The Chinese in Hawaii were not confined to Chinatown, in fact, far from it. There were Chinese houses and businesses all over town and across the other islands. But the rapid influx of laborers that began in the late 1870's required massive new housing and wooden apartments and barrack-like dwellings were quickly constructed and packed into existing spaces in Chinatown. Conditions were often less than ideal, and the local newspapers were more than eager to report on the unsanitary and decrepit living conditions they blamed were caused by the Chinese.

It was this sudden large population of Chinese in this part of Honolulu that gave it the name "Chinatown".

On March 22, 1883, the Hawaiian Chinese News Company was founded by Loo Chit Sam, A. Conchook, C. Winam, Lam Kam Cheun, Tam Ting and Tang Yung.

In 1884 the United Chinese Society of Hawaii was created:

> "To further friendly relations among the Chinese and various Chinese societies in the State of Hawaii; to promote projects of benevolence, charity, and cultural awareness; and to promote the welfare of the Chinese community."

It represented over 100 Chinese societies, organizations, and clubs, and worked hard to create harmony between Punti and Hakka divisions while representing and supporting the Chinese community within the greater Hawaiian community.

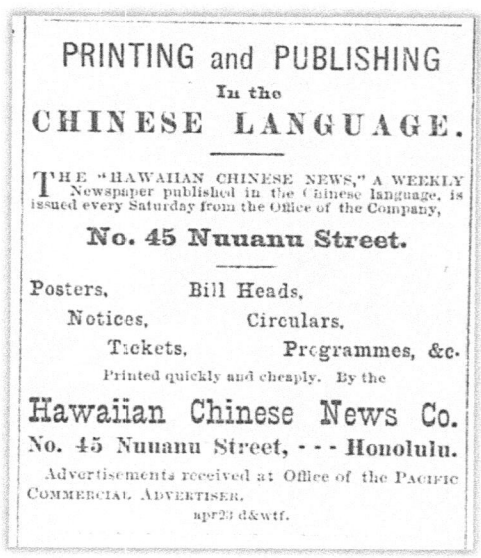

One downside of the labor trade was that fact that only men had been brought in to work the fields. Consequently, many Chinese men intermarried with Hawaiian and Portuguese women.

To better assimilate into the community and to build better relations, many Chinese embraced the Christian religion and joined local churches, and even founded a Chinese Christian Church. Goo Kim and Luke Aseu were two of the most prominent early Chinese Christians.

"Chinatown is a place for entrepreneurship. People do basic business here they get their start and they move on. It's been a good place for immigrant groups to start, new businesses to start, and as they get successful, they broaden beyond." – Warren Luke, CEO, Hawaii National Bank.

Japanese

Like China, Japan was previously closed off to foreign travel for decades. The first Japanese seen in Hawaii were 8 fishermen from the *Inawaka Maru* which was found adrift in 1806 by Captain Cornelius Sole. He brought them to Kamehameha I in Honolulu and provided money for their keep until they could find passage to Canton (Guandong). A second drifting ship made it to Waialua Bay in 1832 with 4 survivors who later found passage to Kamchatka.

In 1839 Captain Cathcart of the whaleship *James Loper* found the *Choajamur* (*Choja Maru*?) with 7 fisherman who had been floating adrift in the Pacific Ocean for over 6 months. Like before, they were of great interest and curiosity to the local citizens and were treated with all hospitality while in Hawaii despite the language barrier. The fishermen had never heard the word "Japan", instead calling their largest island "Nipon" (nee-PON). Unfortunately, the boat's captain and owner died and was buried in Honolulu before the others eventually found passage back to Japan via Kamchatka.

On Friday, June 19, 1868, Captain Reagan's British ship *Scioto* landed in Honolulu with 140 men, 6 women who accompanied their husbands, and 2 teenagers from Yokohama, Japan, after a voyage of 33 days. They were the first Japanese immigrants and they were known as the *gannen-mono* – the "first-year people" since they came to Hawaii in the first year of the reign of Emperor Meiji.

Through the efforts of Eugene Miller Van Reed, the Hawaiian Consul at Yokohama, their travel was fully paid and their contract called for a salary of $4 per month including room and board for 3 years. The Japanese government was initially reluctant, but this first group was finally allowed to depart. Most were craftsmen and not farmers, and they were not accustomed to the hard life on a sugar plantation and subsequently complained to the point where more than 40 returned to Japan and the Japanese government banned all further emigration.

It was not until King Kalākaua's tour of Japan in 1881 and following treaty in 1885 that promised better pay, medical care, and a food allowance, that emigration was permitted again.

On February 8, 1885, the steamship *City of Tokio* brought 943 Japanese immigrants – 676 men, 159 women, and 108 children to Honolulu. Most were from Hiroshima and Yamaguchi prefectures, and they were met at the dock by King Kalākaua himself along with hula dancers. Three days later the newcomers organized a sumo wrestling and kendo fencing exhibition, along with celebratory sake and the singing of traditional Japanese folk songs.

Instead of only bringing single men like the planters had done with the Chinese, this time they had encouraged families to emigrate, hoping it would result in a more stable workforce. By 1900 there were over 60,000 Japanese in Hawaii – 40% of the total population of the islands.

In 1900, Japan lifted the ban on emigration from Okinawa and by 1920 there were nearly 20,000 Okinawans in Hawaii.

But all did not go well on the plantations – after numerous protests and confrontations the Japanese organized devastating labor strikes in 1909 and 1920. And as before with the Chinese, few stayed on the plantations past their 3-year contracts, preferring instead to move to town and open businesses or start their own farms. Many settled in the mauka area of Chinatown around Beretania Street and in the Moiliili area.

The Federal Immigration Act of 1924 put an end to immigration from Japan. By that time over 180,000 Japanese had moved to Hawaii.

The first generation were called = *Issei* 一世

Second generation = *Nisei* 二世

Third generation = *Sansei* 三世

Fourth generation = *Yonsei* 四世

By 1912 there were three Japanese banks in Honolulu, including a branch of the Yokohama Specie Bank, and a well-established Japanese fishing fleet. The Japanese consulate noted that there were 300 barbers, 200 tailors, 500 carpenters and 500 farmers. There were also 40 geisha, 18 Shinto priests, 19 Buddhist priests, 77 bathhouse workers, 38 missionaries and 18 photographers.

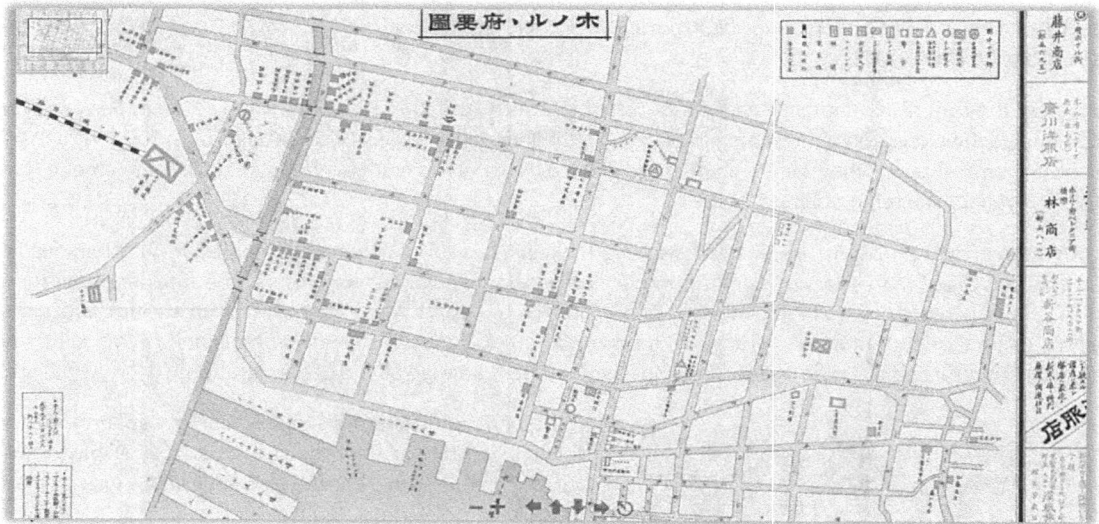

The plantation strikes created a fair amount of anti-Japanize sentiment, but it was nothing like the reaction to the Japanese bombing of Pearl Harbor on December 7, 1941. Hundreds were arrested, businesses were shut down, and many were sent to the internment camp at Honouliuli on Oahu and to camps on the US mainland.

Many of the Nisei, born in Hawaii as American citizens, worked hard to prove their loyalty in spite of overwhelming wartime suspicions. Initially prevented from serving in the US military, Japanese-Americans were finally accepted and trained as military specialists and soldiers.

The most famous Nisei unit was the 100th Battalion which later became the 442nd Regimental Combat Team that was decorated for their efforts in the war in Europe. President Harry Truman told them, *"You fought not only the enemy, but you fought prejudice and you have won"*.

Japanese leaders, many born in Hawaii, worked very hard to repair and restore relations during and after the war.

Portuguese

The first Portuguese who came to Hawaii arrived as sailors on board whaling ships in the mid 1800's.

Concerned about the growing numbers of Chinese being brought into the islands, the government looked to other countries to provide laborers and decided to focus on the Portuguese island territories of Madeira and the Azores.

Jason Perry (Jacinto Pereira), the Portuguese Consul to Hawaii, had suggested in 1876 that the Madeira and Azores Islands might be good places to find reliable workers since the climate was similar and they also grew sugar cane.

On September 30, 1878, the bark *Priscilla* brought the first 120 immigrants from Madeira, arriving after a voyage of 120 days around Cape Horn. British ship *Ravenscrag* arrived on August 23, 1879, with the second contingent of Portuguese, consisting of 135 men, 110 women, 178 children between 2 and 12 years old, for a total of 423, plus 4 stowaways. Unlike the Chinese laborers who were all men, the government made sure to bring in families this time.

There were three luthiers on board the *Ravenscrag* – Manuel Nunes, José do Espírito Santo, and Augusto Dias – and they inspired the creation of Hawaii's most-famous musical instrument – the ukulele.

Adapted from a small Portuguese guitar-like instrument called a *braguinha*, "ukulele" is Hawaiian for "jumping flea", and the name was in common usage by 1888. Nunes claimed credit for inventing the ukulele in 1879 and had the largest shop.

The store of Dias & Gonsalves first advertised guitars in 1883 along with a variety of other Portuguese goods from Madeira. Augusto Dias opened a shop "jammed in between Chinese stores" on King Street in 1886.

Kamaka Ukulele

In 1878 there were only 438 Portuguese residents in Hawaii. There were by 5,000 in 1902, that number grew to 16,000 by 1911, and at that time they made up approximately 10% of the Hawaiian population.

Many of the Portuguese family names from those first ships are still around today: Andrade, Cabral, Camacho, Camara, Carvalho, Castro, Coelho, Correa, Cunha, Dias, Fernandez, Ferreira, Freitas, Gomes, Gonsalves, Gouveia, Medeiros, Mendonça, Nobrega, Nunes, Olivera, Pereira, Santos, Silva, Souza, Teixeira, and Vieira.

The San Antonio Society (Sociedade Portugueza de St. Antonio Beneficente de Hawaii) was founded in 1877 by John Gaspar "for purposes consistent with the promotion of charity, friendship, goodwill and mutual benefit" for the Portuguese in Hawaii. It was named after Saint Antony of Padua, the famous 13th century Portuguese Confessor, and lasted 78 years until 1955. During its heyday it had over 3,000 members.

There was also the Lusitana Society (Sociedade Lusitana Beneficente de Hawaii) founded in 1882 as a welfare and mutual aid organization for Portuguese. It had a peak membership of over 2,500 until it closed in 1943.

The two societies teamed up in 1922 to create the Union Trust Company as an investment vehicle for their members and hired Emory and Webb to build a large 2-story building on Alakea Street in 1923.

Caesar L. Brito built a large 1-story stone hall at the ewa-mauka corner of Smith and King streets in 1890 that became known as the Portuguese Hall.

The first Portuguese language newspaper began in 1884, *O Luso-Hawaiiano*, managed by Luiz M. Gonzaga Da Silva. In 1896 two Portuguese newspapers, *Sentinella* and *Lusitana*, consolidated to become *O'Luso*, edited by J.M. Vivas, J.S. Ramos and Camillo Pereira with the stated policy being "the defense of the interests and rights of the Portuguese colony". In business for 30 years, the last weekly issue was printed on March 27, 1924, admitting the older generation had passed and "the younger generation is thoroughly Americanized".

In addition to the ukulele, there are many other lasting and popular legacies of the Portuguese immigrants in Hawaii: malasadas (deep-fried sugar-coated pastries originally made for Fat Tuesday), pão doce (sweet bread), bean soup,

The Native Hawaiians called the Portuguese "pukiki".

In addition to the ukulele, the Portuguese also brough guitars and other stringed instruments, and two weeks after the arrival of *Ravenscrag* the newspaper reported:

"During the past week a band of Portuguese musicians, composed of Madeira Islanders recently arrived here, have been delighting the people with nightly street concerts. The musicians are fine performers on their strange instruments, which are a kind of cross between a guitar and banjo, but which produce very sweet music in the hands of the Portuguese minstrels."

Puerto Rican

Two hurricanes in Puerto Rico in August of 1899 led to a shortage of sugar which only increased the demand for Hawaiian sugar. Consequently, many Puerto Rican sugar laborers emigrated to Hawaii, with the first 56 contract laborers arriving on the SS *City of Rio de Janeiro* on December 23, 1900. By 1910 there were almost 5,000 Puerto Ricans in Hawaii including men, women and children, and there were over 30,000 by the year 2000.

One lasting and very noisy result of Puerto Rican immigration is the invasive and incredibly loud little coqui tree frog. Another much more melodious and world-famous musical Hawaiian of Puerto Rican lineage is pop singer Bruno Mars (born Peter Gene Hernandez).

Korean

On January 13, 1903, the RMS *Gaelic* landed in Honolulu with the first large group of Korean immigrants. There were 56 contract laborers plus 21 women and 25 children. In 1902 there were 16 Koreans in Hawaii, and by 1905 there were over 7,000.

The laborers were initially recruited in response to the Japanese worker strikes, with their passage paid through a money-laundering scam that also violated existing US contract laborer emigration laws.

The Korean Christian Church was founded in 1918, and in 1938 hired architect Y.T. Char to design their large building at 1832 Liliha Street that is still in excellent condition today.

One of the more famous Koreans associated with Hawaii is actor/producer Daniel Dae Kim who played Jin-Soo Kwon in the *Lost* TV series and Chin Ho Kelly in the 2010 reboot of *Hawaii 5-0*.

Filipino

There were a handful of Filipinos in Hawaii in the 1800's, known as "Manila Men".

The first 15 Filipino contract laborers were brought to Hawaii by Albert F. Judd on the O & O steamship SS *Doric* which arrived in Honolulu on December 20, 1906, after a voyage of 32 days. Known as "sakadas" they were recruited to replace striking Japanese workers and mostly came from the Ilocos and Visayas regions of the Philippines.

There were 120,000 Filipino workers in Hawaii by 1931, and by 2010 they were the second largest ethnic group in Hawaii with a total population of over 342,000.

Russian

Although a group of Russians had tried to colonize Hawaii in the early 1800's and even built a couple of forts on Kaua'i (and almost in Honolulu), it wasn't until October 21st of 1909 that 103 Russian workers and their families arrived on the Pacific Mail steamship *Siberia*. Before their arrival only two people in Honolulu could speak Russian.

In the late 1900's many immigrants from Vietnam and Laos moved into the Chinatown area and they now run many of the small shops and restaurants.

Census Data for the State of Hawaii

POPULATION	1878		1884		1900	
Natives	47,508	59%	44,232	55%	63,221	41%
Chinese	5,916	7%	17,937	22%	25,767	17%
Portuguese	436	1%	9,377	12%		
Japanese	---	---	---	---	61,111	40%
Other Foreigners	4,128	5%	9,032	11%		
TOTAL	57,988		80,578		154,001	

In 1900, of the 25,767 Chinese, 22,296 were males (87%) and 3,471 were females (13%), including 782 children between 5 and 20 years of age. Compare this to 61,111 Japanese in 1900 with 47,508 males (78%) and 13,603 females (22%), with 9,947 children between 5 and 20 years of age.

With so many single males immigrating to Hawaii, intermarriages with local and Native Hawaiian women were commonplace. The phrase "half-caste" was often used to describe those of mixed races, and "hapa haole" was used to describe those who were children of Caucasian and Hawaiian parents.

By 1980, the population of Chinatown looked like this:

Filipino	47.7%
Chinese	19.0%
Hawaiian	10.0%
Caucasian	9.6%
Japanese	7.5%
Other	6.3%

PIDGIN

There is a unique hybrid language that developed in Hawaii in response to the mixing of so many foreign cultures and languages, a creole-style language known as Hawaiian pidgin.

It developed primarily in the plantations as a way to communicate between many different nationalities, and then spread into the mainstream with many of the words are still in common usage today.

Pidgin is loosely based on English but consists of bits and pieces of words and phrases and grammar borrowed from Hawaiian, Cantonese, Japanese, and Portuguese, with additions from later arrivals from Okinawa, Puerto Rico, Korea and the Philippines. Some of the words are close to the originals but most have been altered and adapted as early speakers heard and mis-heard the foreign words they were unfamiliar with.

Used primarily in casual conversations, and at one time looked down upon as uneducated broken English, it was officially recognized by the US Census Bureau in 2015 as an official language in Hawaii.

BENEVOLENT SOCIETIES

In addition to churches and temples accommodating the different faiths of the immigrants, a large number of fraternal and benevolent societies were established to attend to the needs of the various immigrant populations.

For the early European immigrants:

    1847 – Lodge of Free Masons

    1850 – International Order of Odd Fellows (I.O.O.F.)

    1852 – Stranger's Friend Society, British Club, Hawaiian Missionary Society

    1853 – Sailors' Home Society

    1856 – German Benevolent Society, Mechanics' Benefit Union

    1858 – Ladies' Benevolent Society

    1860 – British Benevolent Society

    1876 – San Antonio Benevolent Society

    1879 – Ka Lima Kokua

    1882 – Portuguese Mutual Benevolent Society of Hawaii

    1885 – Portuguese Ladies' Benevolent Society

    1891 – Sons of St. George, Scottish Thistle Club

There are reportedly over 100 Chinese societies in Chinatown – political, benevolent, and family. Many of these societies built or bought buildings and met upstairs with ground floor rents generating income.

Many of the political societies (known as "tongs") were once considered to be secret societies since many were active in the political struggle to overthrow the Qing Dynasty on the Chinese mainland. Secrecy was a must as the penalty for membership could result in death.

The Chinese benevolent societies were typically geographically based and were often from specific areas or villages. Since new immigrants couldn't borrow from banks, often spoke different dialects of Chinese, and knew no English, these societies provided a welcome place to interact with their fellow countrymen and learn how to adapt to living in the Honolulu community. Many also provided burial and savings plans for their members.

The third type of Chinese societies were made up of extended local families who shared the same last name and wanted to keep their family together to honor their ancestors and preserve their family and cultural histories.

Each Chinese society typically sponsored a large seven- or nine-course banquet every year where they also invited the presidents of the other societies to attend. Many of these societies are still active today over 100 years later.

In more recent times, there are societies who specialize in teaching self-improvement and teamwork through martial arts training, many of whom provide public demonstrations and also field lion dance teams for the many Chinese holiday celebrations.

CHINESE NAMES

Most, if not all of the Chinese who came to Honolulu in the 1800's were from the Guangdong area near Hong Kong. They spoke either Cantonese or Fukienese languages, not Mandarin. Luckily, the languages all used the same Chinese characters with the same meanings and Chinese speakers of either language can understand the written text, but the spoken languages are completely different and mutually exclusive.

Written Chinese is character-based whereas English is a kit of parts composed of 26 letters arranged to form various words. Many Chinese sounds do not translate well into written English, resulting in a wide variety of English attempts at spellings for the same Chinese word or name.

And where Mandarin has four distinct tones which can completely change the meaning of the same syllable, Cantonese has up to nine tones.

Unlike Western culture, Chinese names always present the family name first, followed by the individual's given name.

Take the name "Ching Sing Wo" for example. He was the founder of the well-known Honolulu furniture and home furnishings company called C.S. Wo. But there was no Mr. Wo – the family name was Ching. Sing Wo was his first name.

This can be very confusing for Westerners, not knowing if a Chinese name should be in Chinese or Westernized order. In the 1950's the Ching family surrendered to public perception and officially changed their last name to Wo.

If Franklin Delano Roosevelt were Chinese, his name would be Roosevelt Franklin Delano, and the Americanization of that would result in him being called Mr. R.F. Delano!

> **AH FAMILY IN PILIKIA.**
>
> Last night was a bad night for the Ah family. Twenty-three of them were arrested for gambling, and carted off to the police station. There was Ah Mo, Ah Fat, Ah Chong, Ah Ching, Ah See, Ah Man, Ah Leong, Ah Hoi, Ah Ping, Ah Num, Ah Chan, Ah Sing, Ah Sam, Ah Chan, Ah Hoy, Ah Hung, Ah Chung, another Ah Leong, Ah Cheong, Ah Lum, Ah Hee, Ah Chee and another Ah Sam. Chung Hee, in some way or other, got mixed up with the Ah family and he also went to the police station to have his name booked opposite a gambling charge.—Advertiser.

In Cantonese it is a sign of familiarity to add "Ah" (阿) before a person's first name, so this often morphed into various new names like this:

Western:	Mr. Fong Chun
Cantonese-1:	Chun Fong
Cantonese-2:	Chun Ah Fong
Hawaiianized:	Afong

Or, sometimes into numerous versions of the same name: Achun was also known as Achona, Akana, Ah Chon and Achung. Wong Tai-hoon became Tyhune, Tyhoon, Tihune, Tyhoun, Tihoon, Tyhung, Taihoun, or the Hawaiianized Taihuna.

Without seeing the Chinese characters, there is no way to know the original pronunciations or names of people and of businesses, or even how to tell them apart. Consequently, many Chinese names became altered into more Western-sounding names and some Chinese adopted new English names that they used in addition to their original Chinese names. Some had "milk names", married names, and business names, and often went by nicknames too.

Many of the early Chinese settlers in Hawaii were fluent in Hawaiian as they found it easier to learn than English.

From the 1888 *Hawaiian Directory* published by the McKenney Directory Company:

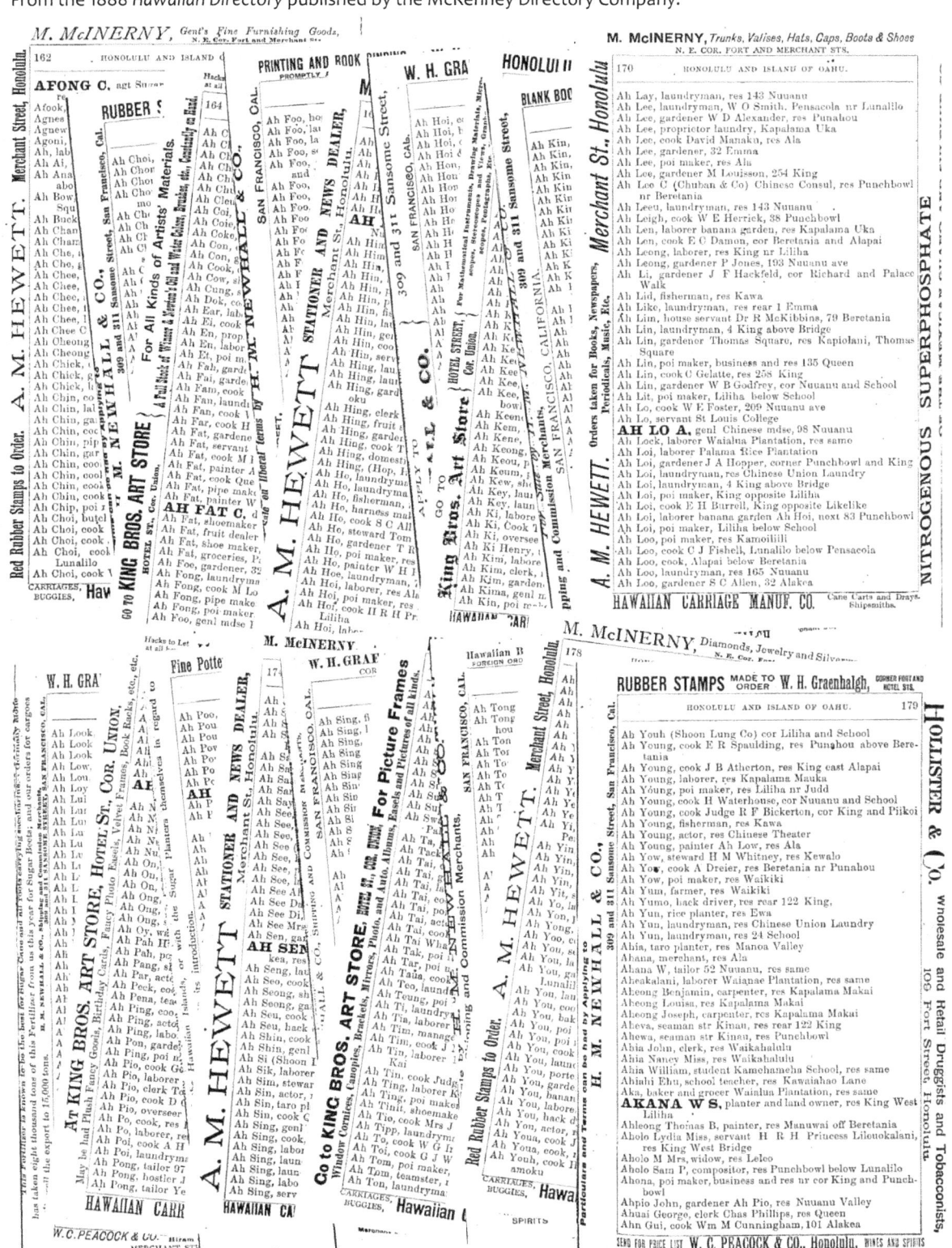

HONOLULU CHINATOWN

CHINATOWN FOOD

The many waves of immigration have introduced an amazing variety of different foods to Hawaii, served in their traditional form or sometimes combined into "Asian Fusion cuisine" – all contributing to the "mixed plate" that is Hawaiian food today. The shops and markets in Chinatown carry an amazing variety of unusual and ethnic foods.

Some of the more popular foods that can be found in Chinatown (and elsewhere in Hawaii) listed by nationality:

Hawaiian

Haupia
Kalua Pork
Lau Lau
Loco Moco
Poi
Poke
Saimin
Spam

Chinese

Char Siu (Manapua)
Chop Suey
Chow Mein
Dim Sum
Gyoza
Har Gow
Moon Cakes
Roast Duck

Japanese

Bento
Furikake
Katsu
Manju
Miso Soup
Mochi
Musubi
Ramen
Sake
Sashimi
Shoyu
Sukiyaki
Sushi
Tepanyaki
Teriyaki
Tako

Portuguese

Malasada
Pão Doce (Portuguese Sweet Bread)
Portuguese Sausage
Bean Soup

Puerto Rican

Arroz con Gandules
Pasteles
Tres Leches

Korean

Banchan
Bulgogi
Bibimbap
Kalbi (Korean BBQ)
Kim Chee
Meat Jun
Shik Hae
Soju
Soodubu

Filipino

Adobo Fried Rice
Kare Kare
Kinilaw
Lechon
Lumpia
Pork Adobo
Sarciado
Sari Sari

PAI GOW, FAN-TAN, CHE-FA, PAKAPIO

When a culture highly values both money and luck, there will undoubtedly be gambling. And there was a lot of gambling in Chinatown.

The two most common gaming and gambling activities in early Chinatown were a domino game called Pai Gow, sometimes spelled "Pai kau" and translating to "card nine", and a game of pure chance known as Fan-Tan ("repeated divisions").

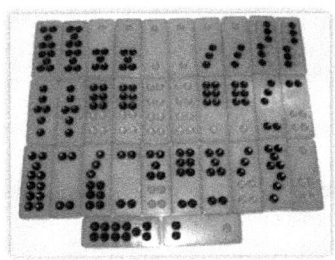

Pai Gow is an ancient Chinese game that is still played in casinos today. It consists of seven players betting against the dealer using 32 special Chinese dominoes. There are two hands of two tiles each, and the player only wins the bet if both beat the dealer.

The maximum score for a hand is nine, unless one has double-one or double six tiles, which combined with an eight is a 10-point "Gong" or an 11-point "Wong" if combined with a nine. The 1-2 and 2-4 tiles are called "Gee Joon" tiles and can act as wild cards.

Fan-Tan is an ancient game dating back about 2,000 years and was originally called Yanqian ("covering coins"). It was very popular in Canton and spread quickly during the mid-1800's Chinese emigration. It starts with a large square in the center of table with each side numbered 1-4. A handful of coins or buttons or beans are dumped in the middle and then covered with a metal bowl.

After all the bets are made the dealer removes the bowl and then removes four of the objects at a time with a small bamboo stick. The winner is the one who correctly guessed whether 1, 2, 3 or 4 objects would remain at the end, and the payoff is 3 for 1.

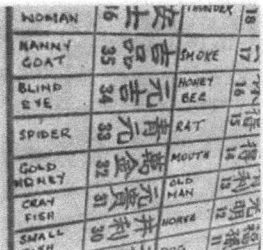

Another very popular lottery game was Che-Fa, a banking game with 36 characters on a ticket, each representing a familiar object like a lion, tiger, moon, silver money, box, dog, rat, etc. To play the game one had to locate an agent, pay at least five cents, and select one character on the ticket. Once the tickets were all in via various runners, the result would be announced and the person who guessed the right word would win 30:1 on their money with the agent getting 10%. One of the characters on the ticket was always "kapu" which meant the bank would win every bet if that one was pre-selected.

Some of the banks utilized as many as 48 agents for selling tickets, and the largest operation in 1905 took in $1,000 a day. Drawings were held in the morning and another in the afternoon, and one bank on Smith Street ran three games a day. In theory, each bank would draw its own individual words to be sealed up in an envelope before the bets came in, but in practice they would often wait until the agents' returns were received and then select the least-played word. Huge crowds would gather in the streets awaiting the results to be posted on the "Maunakea flagpole" and runners on bicycle would fan out through Chinatown to announce the winning word and to sell tickets for the next game.

Che-Fa was easy to run and did not need anything other than "a man with some money, some fools who think they can win it from him, and a number of scraps of paper".

Pakapio (Pak kop piu) was a very similar game, theoretically originating in 187 BC, where one selected 10 characters out of 80 from the "Thousand Character Classic" (Chian Ji Mun) poem in which no two characters are repeated.

CHASING THE DRAGON

While the haole population in early Honolulu preferred "spiritous liquors" as their vice of choice, for the Chinese it was opium. "Chasing" meant keeping the liquid moving to avoid overheating as well as chasing the smoke to inhale.

Officially available only for medical purposes, it was often referred to as "the Chinese Problem", and in the early 1900's there were at least 20 opium dens in Chinatown. It has been estimated that about 25-30 percent of the Chinese population indulged, mostly men, and many addictively.

The *Pacific Commercial Advertiser* wrote in 1908:

"There is nothing attractive about an opium dive. Dark, stinking with the exhalations of those who overcrowd the little rooms, floors and windows dirt begrimed and filthy, and everywhere the reek and gurgle of the opium, there is nothing to remind the casual visitor of the fairy tales that are sometimes related of the palaces of Nirvana, where amid Oriental splendor the white slaves of the drug indulge themselves in vice.

This place was in the rear of the row of dirty tenements facing mauka on Pauahi street, near River. Every room in the back of that building on the ground floor except one is an opium joint and on the day of the visit was crowded with Chinese, many of whom were busily inhaling the white fumes from the burning dope or sleeping off their debauches.

Tucked away in the corners of bunks, laid out on mats on the floor and even slid out of the limited way under the bunks were poppy-soaked figures, pallid-faced, and in many instances bare-footed and ragged, deep in sleep, dreaming of Elysium, while over and about them swarmed the teeming other patrons and proprietors of the dives. Throughout Chinatown there is scarcely a tenement in which at any time of the day or night some opium smoking is not going on, more or less publicly."

Although there were efforts to curb the use of opium, it was erratically regulated since the Chinese were an important labor source and opium was a major Chinese cultural indulgence. The opium trade was also very, very profitable for the dealers and for the government that licensed it. An embarrassing bribery scandal over opium licenses involving King Kalākaua led to the 1887 Bayonet Constitution and the disenfranchisement of Honolulu's Chinese residents.

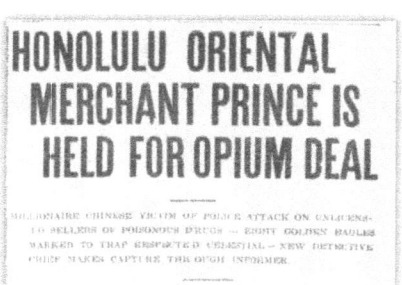

In 1898 a Senator from Maui, Alfred Hocking, announced he would support a bill for the licensing of opium:

"I have had considerable to do with Chinese, and in my opinion it is almost a crime to keep this stuff away from them. I have seen Chinese laborers come in from a half day's labor almost completely exhausted. They have taken this drug during the noon hour and have gone back to the fields and done strong work during the remainder of the day." He also said, *"Our Island government might just as well derive some revenue from the importation of opium as to expend thousands of dollars each year endeavoring to keep it out. It is my judgment that the Hawaiian people will not become any more addicted to the habit under a system where opium is imported legally than under the present conditions."*

But that never happened, and police busts were an all-too-common occurrence in Chinatown for many years.

THE FIRST GREAT CHINATOWN FIRE

Ruins of the United Chinese Society building on King Street, still smoldering

By the 1880's, Chinatown was densely packed with mostly 2-story wooden tenements and stores in large blocks with overhanging balconies on both sides of narrow streets. There might have even been a few thatched houses still within those blocks. Many of these buildings contained cooking fires, kerosene, and other flammable goods.

On November 25, 1871, the *Pacific Commercial Advertiser Supplement* featured a full-page story that imagined in great detail a massive Chinatown fire that would prove to be alarmingly prophetic.

On April 18, 1886, a fire started in a large Chinese restaurant at the waikiki/mauka corner of Hotel and Smith streets.

From the official report to His Majesty the King:

> *"The Chinese examined state as their belief that a gambling game or lottery, in which a large number of tickets were used, was in progress. A dispute arose, and the tickets were seized by one of those present and thrust into a fire, which was burning in the room. A scuffle then ensued, during which the fire was scattered over the floor, and in a moment the room was in a blaze. Some twenty or more Chinamen were seen running out from the upper story when the fire broke out."*

The fire quickly spread, causing about $1.5M in damage in Chinatown, burning the homes of 7,000 Chinese and 350 Hawaiians, and coming very close to burning the whole of Honolulu.

Extents of the 1886 Fire

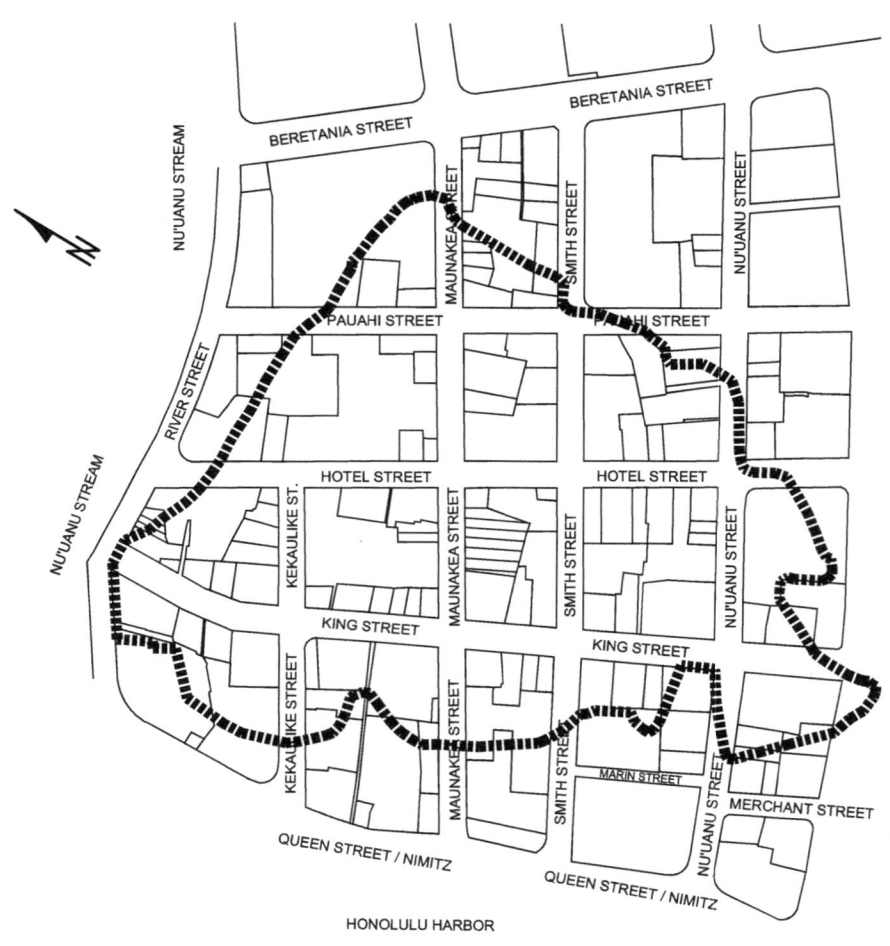

PROGRESS OF THE FIRE.

By 5 o'clock the fire had spread along Hotel street near Maunakea, and the fine three story building, of Sun Hang Far Co., corner of Maunakea and Hotel streets, was enveloped in flames. It was evident by this time that the fire was beyond control. The flames from this structure ignited the Hop Chong Market and Hing Kee Laundry on the opposite side of the street, which were soon ablaze. From this corner, it marched steadily forward in opposite directions towards Beretania and King streets, the firemen fighting it at every step, but the odds were against them. At the same time, the flames kept steadily advancing towards Nuuanu and Beretania street corner, taking possession of a lot of small wooden buildings in the rear of Love's bakery and the store formerly occupied by Hollister & Co. These buildings being of brick and stone proved excellent towers of defence to the opposite side of the street. The Hollister building within was a great burning cauldron, bursting out occasionally in fierce jets round the iron shutters. A vacant lot between this and the bakery proved a valuable neighbor to that establishment, the bakery suffering but little damage, being at work again next morning. The well-directed exertions of the firemen, aided by a number of active citizens, among whom were noticed ex-Marshal Parke, Mr. J. A. Hassinger and Mr. F. W. Damon, were crowned with success in arresting the conflagration's further march in this direction.

At the same hour, 5 o'clock, Meek and Maunakea streets were blazing on both sides, and the forward march of the flames was making steady progress, being then about halfway down Meek, towards King street. On Maunakea street, the American House, at 5:20, was a mass of flame. On the opposite side of the street, a couple of warehouses were being rapidly consumed, giving forth a series of loud explosions as the oil and other inflammable stock within were reached by the devouring element. It was becoming more and more evident every minute that unless further progress was soon arrested in this direction, the Kaumakapili church was doomed. Suggestions were urged by the BULLETIN reporters and other spectators to prominent persons supposed to be in authority to make a gap ahead of the fire by demolishing a few of the small buildings on the river side, after which the firemen and other workers would have their hands free to prevent the flames getting hold of a long row of two-story buildings on the Waikiki side and which extended clear back to Beretania opposite the church, but the invariable answer was "I have no authority." At this juncture, His Majesty the King accompanied by Captain Hayley walked round the corner, and at once took in the situation, and gave orders forthwith to tear down the structures referred to, and the job was done. About half an hour later, the tug of war here reached a climax. A body of men on the top and within the building at the end of the row already mentioned, were tearing the fabric to pieces, while the hosemen on the opposite side surrounded by the blistering heat were playing upon the flames with a steady stream. The fire fiend was happily baffled in the struggle, and the conflagration at this point was under control.

All this time, the conflagration was rapidly spreading in other directions. Maunakea, Meek and Nuuanu streets were all but cleaned out.

King street, by 6 o'clock, presented an awful scene. The flames, having marched down, in three solid, double columns by Maunakea, Meek and Nuuanu streets, raged on both the seaward and mountain sides of King, all the way from Maunakea to Mossman's corner. Great volumes of smoke, in pink, purple, orange, black and yellow rolled skyward, while, in every direction, columns of flame and showers of sparks contributed to the advancing shades of evening a lurid and terrible glare. From the upper rear verandah of the Sailor's Home, a fair view of the whole scene was obtained. The flames from the burning Anchor Saloon rose high in the air; a body of men were at work desperately trying to demolish the building on the corner of Nuuanu and King streets, occupied by Wolfe & Co., grocers, when, on the opposite corner, a dense grey cloud of smoke covered the roof of the Chinese store. The Chinese store was in a few minutes a mass of blazing timbers. Wolfe's store was at once ignited and axemen and others, engaged in tearing it down, were driven off, and the building soon met the fate of the day. Adjoining this was a fine brick building, the Merchant's Exchange, part of which was occupied by the Merchant's Exchange Saloon. Windows, doors and all other removable woodwork were torn out, and flung into the street. By this means, the building was saved, and the adjoining store of Castle & Cooke received but little damage. However, in case of emergency, Messrs. Castle & Cooke had removed all powder and inflammable stock from the premises. The Police Station was now enveloped in flame from the ground to the cupola. The officials had, early in the progress of the fire, removed the prisoners from the premises, as well as all records of value, leaving the stock of opium, confiscated from time to time, to be smoked out by the fire fiend. However, the old Station, where many a woful tale was told; where Judge Bickerton daily sat and frowned on the inebriates arraigned before him, and where McKeague gracefully reposed with his feet on the window sill, will not disappear in oblivion, for Mr. J. Williams, on the morning before the fire photographed the building and the officers grouped in front. At precisely 6:57, the bell and cupola tumbled into the blazing debris.

The interior of the Chinese Club House, the grand opening of which was reported in the BULLETIN on the third of February, was being licked up by the flames, its iron shutters next morning presenting a sadly warped and battered appearance. From the Anchor Saloon to the Bethel Vestry, the blaze rose upward in a mighty volume, and was bent over in a threatening manner towards the roof of the Sailors' Home, three stories high. At this stage, the old historic Bethel church around which clustered many sacred associations of the past and the present, was given up for lost. The movables were quickly taken in charge by friendly hands, and by 8:30 o'clock all that was left of this grand landmark in the history of Hawaiian civilization was the bare stone walls of the lower half of the building. On the Bethel and King street corner, the shop occupied by S. M. Johnson as a harness and saddlery store was torn down, and also C. C. Coleman's blacksmith and machine shop, on the opposite side of King street. The equipments and lease of this shop were advertised to have been sold at auction, Monday. Several buildings had been pulled down, at other points, during the evening.

From the Anchor Saloon, the fire entered the brick and cement store of Wing Wo Tai, and was thence communicated to the large three-story brick building of Wing Wo Chan. With the burning of the Bethel Church and the Wing Wo Tai and Wing Wo Chan buildings, the crisis of the conflagration was reached. It was an hour of terrible suspense. Merchant and Fort streets were in imminent danger. Thirty minutes would decide whether only the Chinese quarters or the whole city of Honolulu would next morning be a weird wilderness of charred and smoking ruins.

The phenomenally perfect calm which had prevailed all the evening now changed to a barely perceptible southwest breeze, turning the flames and flying fragments in the direction of the quarters already hopelessly on fire. Several umbrageous giants, in the rear of the Bethel Church lot, interposed their widespreading arms, between the flames and the two-story fabric behind the Post Office on one side of Bethel street, and the Sailors' Home on the other. Connecting sheds were speedily torn down by the British tars with axes and hawser, aided by a body of the household troops, firemen and others. The Punabou College boys, with a number of the sailors and citizens, set to work on Mr. W. E. Herrick's shop with buckets of water from the tank on the premises for supplying the engine of the machine shop, and thus did good service in confining the fire to the opposite side of Bethel street. Captain Alington stood on a table opposite Castle & Cooke's during the fire, issuing orders to his British boys. When through there, he started on the double quick, followed by his men bearing the hawser, across through the sea of fire in the rear of the Bethel, to pull down the shed on the lower side of Wing Wo Chan's. A number of the officers and marines got on the top of the shed and wouldn't come down until the shed fell under them. The Wing Wo Chan building, stocked with a ship's cargo of goods, burned internally like the crater of a volcano, while explosions from burning kerosene sounded like discharges from a battery of artillery. Happily for the city, the conflagration did not get across Bethel street or into the Sailors' Home building, and the crisis had passed in safety so far as Fort, Merchant and Queen streets were concerned.

A hard fought battle was maintained for three long hours, up to 9 o'clock, in the vicinity of the Foundry. Only the outbuildings of this establishment were destroyed. Meanwhile, the flames were working along King street, on both sides, towards the bridge. The long rows of two-story shops, nearly all Chinese, closely packed together, presented a most inviting field for the operations of the fire fiend. From the foundry to the bridge, lay one of the worst areas, from a sanitary point of view, in the city. Dwelling houses, pig-sties, privies, fowl yards, cesspools and accumulations of all sorts of refuse were huddled together with a degree of ingenuity that was simply wonderful. This formed the principal part of the areas explored some months ago by a representative of the BULLETIN under convoy of a medical man, and described at that time. By 9 o'clock, all that was left of it was a field of ashes, firebrands and a grove of rapidly falling timbers.

At 11:20 precisely, the wall of the last building, on the seaward side, next the bridge, fell in; the second last house directly across the street being then well ignited. These two houses, strange to stay, were saved; and next morning stood, in grim isolation, on the corner of full thirty acres of a black waste of smoking debris.

The number of persons, made houseless by this terrible calamity, is variously stated from 5,000 to 8,000.

THE BRITISH SAILORS.

The gaps made by the tearing down of buildings were effected by the assistance of detachments of sailors and marines from H. B. M.'s steamships Heroine and Satellite, some of whom were ashore on leave, and others had been sent from the ships immediately on the outbreak of the fire. The jolly naval heroes worked with tremendous energy and enthusiasm, and their splendid order and discipline caused their efforts to tell. At whatever point their services were engaged, results were at once apparent.

THE FIRE COMPANIES.

According to the arrangements of the Fire Department, two of the four companies are placed on active duty, in rotation, each month, and are required to be first at a fire, the other companies being in reserve until called. Nos. 2 and 5 have their turn this month, and were first to respond to the alarm, the volunteer boys of No. 2 being first to get water on the fire. Nos. 1 and 4 responded promptly when the whole force was called out. It is highly creditable to the vigilant efficiency of the Survey Engineer, Mr. J. C. White, who has supervision of the fire engines and apparatus, that every engine, hose reel, and hose was in perfect trim and ready for instantaneous service. Each engine is furnished with the usual complement of axes, but when it became apparent that buildings would need to be torn down, and that the ordinary supply of axes was insufficient for the quantity of chopping to be done, His Excellency Minister Gulick of the Interior Department, purchased $360 worth of axes, crowbars and hammers, and gave them out with orders to use them subject to the direction of the Chief Engineer.

Engine No. 1, with Mr. Alex. Flohr, engineer, and Mr. James Hiton, stoker, was first placed at the corner of King and Maunakea streets, where she got 100 lbs. water pressure to the square inch on the pump. Driven from there, after an hour's hard fighting, by the advance of the flames, the engine was moved down to Ames's Wharf, near the Fish Market, and took water from the bay. From this position, two streams were played, through 1,500 feet of hose, towards King-street bridge, and 800 feet to the buildings in the rear of the foundry, their efforts being crowned with success in this direction, by saving the foundry from destruction. In this fierce fight, lasting for several hours, the firemen's efforts were ably seconded by the employees of the establishment, the sailors and others, with Mr. Theo. H. Davies, President of the company, and Mr. Young, manager, who were on the ground rendering all the assistance in their power. The engine, while here, had 200 lbs. water pressure to the square inch on the pump, and the streams were delivered through 7-8ths and 1 inch nozzles. At 1 o'clock A. M., the engine returned to its first position to play upon the burning debris, where she worked with 30 lbs. pressure until towards 9 o'clock in the morning. The foreman of the company is Mr. Robert More, who worked like a giant during the whole progress of the conflagration.

Engine No. 2, Mr. E. B. Hopkins, engineer, and Mr. George Townsend, stoker, was placed at a cistern in the rear of the Empire Saloon. The cistern was full at first, but gave signs of weakening, when Mr. Frank Hustace, the efficient foreman of the company, ran a line of hose from the hydrant opposite Horn's bakery to keep up the supply in the cistern. Two lines of hose were run out, one on each side of Hotel street, and were doing good service, but it became apparent that another base of operations must be found owing to the water becoming low, the engine beginning to suck air about 7 o'clock. She was then moved to the corner, at Mr. James Dodd's, where the cistern supplied all the water she could take. The water pressure obtained was 195 lbs. to the square inch with two pumps. From this point, two streams were carried, one through 900 feet of hose, to the Paiko Block and vicinity, the other, through 1,400 feet of hose to the Empire Saloon, and through Rose Lane to Castle & Cooke's, on King street. By the first mentioned stream the Waikiki side of Nuuanu street, above Hotel, was saved, and by the second, the fire was stopped at Castle & Cooke's building. On the seaward side of Hotel street, the progress of the flames was arrested by the tearing down of the Chinese coffee saloon, next the Empire, a job in which the British tars rendered effective aid; and on the mountain side, the fire was intercepted in its forward march, after the Paiko Block went down.

Junior Mechanic Co. No. 2, better known as the Volunteer Boys, 15 in number, on hearing the first alarm, took their hose cart to the hydrant, corner Hotel and Nuuanu streets, ran their hose up Hotel street, through a stable yard to the origin of the fire on Smith street, and if they had obtained pressure enough of water, would have stayed the fire, at least until the engine hose was got under way. The low pressure was due to the smallness of the water pipes at the place. The Boys, though driven back, continued to work like Trojans, joining in with No. 2 engine, where they gave a good account of themselves, at other points. The Boys are to be recommended for their pluck, and Engine Co. No. 2 may well be congratulated on so fine a corps of effective allies.

Engine No. 4, William Kapela, engineer, and William Kapela, Jr., stoker, was taken to the hydrant at the head of Maunakea street, next to the corner of Maunakea and Beretania, where the water pipes were found to be too small to supply the engine properly, upon which she was moved by the survey engineer to the corner of Beretania and Nuuanu streets. Running one line of hose down Nuuanu, and carrying it in through an alleyway between Ahi's carpenter shop and the Beehive, and over the roof of three buildings, a 1¼ inch stream was turned on the buildings in the rear of Love's bakery, and with such splendid effect as to turn the direction of the fire, when it took a diagonal course towards Smith street, across which it was followed up with length after length of hose to Maunakea and down to the river, until 1,500 feet of hose were out. Through some accident, several lengths of new hose, used for the first time, were lost in the fire. The engine had 150 lbs. water pressure; but the pressure fluctuating, she was moved down to the bay at Brewer's wharf, and assisted the other engines in their operations between the foundry and King street. She was last moved to the hydrant next King street bridge. The foreman of the company, Mr. James Boyd, commanded his men with marked efficiency, and was assisted by 2nd Assistant Engineer of the Fire Department, Mr. Julius Asch.

China Engine Company No. 5, engineer Akana, stoker Atim, commenced taking water from the hydrant, corner Nuuanu and Hotel streets, and speedily had the hose playing on the buildings around where the fire started. Forced to retreat from this point, she took up a position at the hydrant between Hotel and King streets, whence 750 feet of hose were carried by the side of Ah Swan's block over roofs, and threw water through a 1¼ inch nozzle. A second hose of 300 feet, with 1 inch nozzle, was attached, and was directed towards the Waikiki side of Nuuanu street. The engine was **again driven back and took a new stand at Mossman's corner.** The next position taken was at the Old Corner, whence a well directed stream was delivered at the Anchor Saloon, Wing Wo Tai's and Wing Wo Chan's buildings. Here Mr. Fred. Wundenberg rendered good assistance in holding the nozzle, despite the blistering heat of the locality. This company's services were lastly engaged at Mossman's corner, to throw water on the burning ruins along King street.

The water pressure at different points varied from 100 to 125 lbs. The foreman of this company is Mr. Wong Kim.

Pacific Hose Co. No. 1, did excellent service, distributing their hose among the different companies, and dividing the members into parties to work wherever their services could be of most avail. The foreman of the company is Mr. C. K. Miller, and assistant, Mr. J. Macdonald.

The Hook & Ladder Company did effective work with ladders, hooks and poles, assisting the firemen to climb verandah, and roofs with their hose. Foreman, Mr. C. Winchester; assistant foreman, Mr. George Norton.

Altogether 6,800 feet of hose were out. Chief Engineer Nott, First Assistant Engineer J. M. Monsarrat and the secretary and treasurer of the Fire Department, Mr. Henry Smith, distinguished themselves by the activity they displayed in directing operations at every point. The plan of the battle was well arranged so that every man on the force knew his duty, and the whole strength of the department was utilized to the best advantage. The engines were under steam 17 hours. During all this time, the men worked with the most heroic perseverance. The enterprising ingenuity of the Chinese in storing their shops with kerosene oil, contrary to law, was being proclaimed in unmistakable tones from every direction. Cans were flying in the air like rockets, all the evening, while the boom, boom of exploding oil was a source of consternation both to workmen and spectators. On proceeding to pull down one Chinese store at an important strategic point, the tearing off of the outer covering disclosed a stock of kerosene cases piled from the ground floor to the second story, over an area of some four or five feet square. It is needless to add that both sailors and firemen got out of that building without much delay. A fireman says that on entering a store on Maunakea near King street, he found a stock of 140 cases of kerosene; and an estimate has been made from the ruins of kerosene tins in the Chinese Club House, that at least 400 cases must have been stored there. Judging from the fierceness of the blazes that burst instantaneously from many buildings almost before the pine and redwood was fully ignited, it was apparent that the illegal storing of kerosene were the rule and not the exception in Chinatown. Under these circumstances, it is no matter of surprise that during the first few hours of the battle, the firemen were driven back from point to point, and were unable to cope with the conflagration until it had pursued them to the outer limits of Chinatown. As remarked to a BULLETIN reporter by Survey Engineer White, "Firemen can fight burning timber, but they can not fight blazing kerosene."

SCENES AND INCIDENTS.

As the fire advanced along the streets, it was preceded by and often overtook an indescribable scene. Through the throng of spectators, the occupants of threatened tenements and shops broke their way, carrying their movable effects to places of safety. Many had wheelbarrows and hand carts; more improvised hand barrows out of doors, blinds, reversed tables, and the like; bulky articles were carried or dragged according to their weight; drays were hurrying after loads or moving away heavily laden; from windows and verandahs household goods were thrown into the streets, often striking with the sound of crashing glass or other fragile material. Above all the roar of the flames and an almost constant fusillade of exploding kerosene, ammunition and fireworks, of one or all of which nearly every shop seemed to carry a large stock.

Down on the Waikahalulu stream, from Smith's bridge, very sad, though sometimes ludicrous scenes were presented while the flames were still on the conquering march toward Beretania street and the water. The left bank was swarming with natives and Chinese, in the midst of piles of household effects. Men, women and children were wading and swimming back and forth across the stream, propelling every imaginable sort of float, piled with goods or returning after discharging freight on the opposite flats. There were boats, canoes, reversed tables, rafts made of pieces of furniture, and trunks, all employed in the work of salvage. In one case a native lad was seen swimming over, propelling what looked like a kneading trough, with a lively little dog for a passenger. Furniture and utensils were hurled from the top of the bank to those engaged in the ferriage service below, leaving the latter to take all the care of not being struck with the flying chattels. On the large marsh opposite were heaps of effects in numberless array, surrounded by groups, of every age and sex, in a picturesque variety of costumes. The whole formed a scene peculiarly inviting to an artist, but the pencil was never wielded that could adequately transfer it to canvas.

The sandbar and flats at the head of the harbor, toward the Oahu Jail, presented an equally striking picture when the approaching flames drove out the inhabitants of that densely populated region—so recently described, to show up its unsanitary condition, in several of the local papers—between King street and the harbor. In the light of the blazing houses, dimming the radiance of the moon, a numerous array of human faces could be seen regarding with dismay the advancing ruin of their recently sheltering roof trees. These unfortunate people were grouped in canoes and on rafts, with their effects heaped about them and on adjacent canoe stages. There was one pile of three trunks, surmounted by a rocking chair, standing right up out of the water.

THE LOSS.

The following is the valuation of the property destroyed, as given by the assessment books, from which it is inferred that the disaster involves a loss of at least one million five hundred thousand dollars ($1,500,000):—

Block 18	$150,000
Block 37	95,000
Block 14	80,000
Block 15	165,000
Block 10	450,000
Block 7	135,000
Block 5	130,000
Block 9	150,000
Total assessment	$1,355,000

The Daily Bulletin Summary, April 30, 1886

King Street, looking ewa from Nuʻuanu Street (Robinson Building on the left, United Chinese Society on the right)

King Street, looking waikiki from River Street (Hoʻoliliamanu house behind tree on the left)

Looking toward the ruins of Liberty Hall from Honolulu Iron Works, with the remains of the Chinese bakery (former Isaac Montgomery house and Fred Horn bakery) on the left.

Maunakea Street, looking makai from near Beretania Street, ruins of Liberty Hall on the right.

Maunakea Street, mauka from Honolulu Iron Works, ruins of Charles Vincent's former shop on the left.

Many people have incorrectly stated that after the fire, builders ignored the building codes and built new wooden buildings anyway. This is not the case. There was a tremendous amount of discussion immediately afterwards about how and where to establish a Fire Limit line to protect the downtown area from any future conflagration.

Although some called for everything to be built back in brick or stone between downtown and Nuʻuanu Stream, not everyone could afford this expensive construction so a Fire Limit line was drawn through Chinatown and around downtown that required fire-proof construction within its limits, and this was largely adhered to by all.

The city also expanded and widened the street network since narrow streets with rows of wooden buildings with overhanging balconies were much too likely to spread fires across streets and from block to block.

The 1886 Fire Limit Line

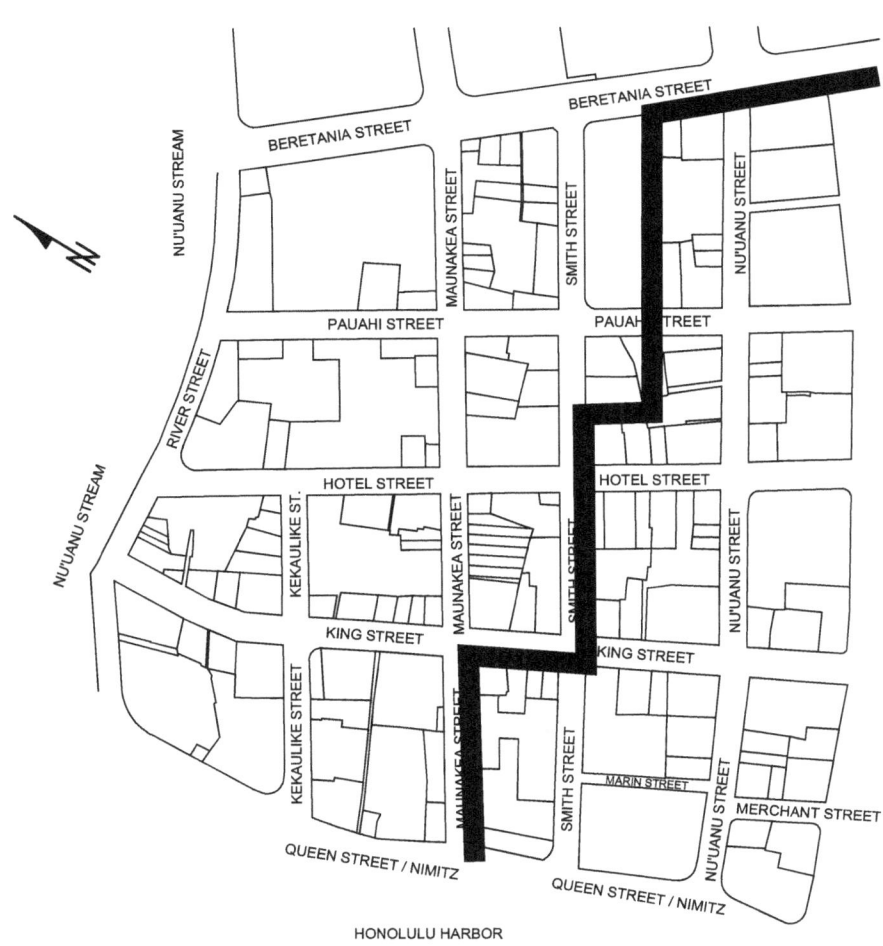

BUBONIC PLAGUE

On December 12, 1899, at 5:00 a.m., 22-year-old You Chong, a bookkeeper with the Wing Wo Tai Company, died of bubonic plague, the first official plague death in Honolulu. Three more died later that same day, sending the population and the government into a panic. Bubonic plague had been ravaging through Asia in the late 1890's but it had not yet appeared in Hawaii.

The *Nippon Maru* had landed in Honolulu in June 1899 with a Chinese passenger who had died at sea, and they were required to quarantine for 7 days on Quarantine Island (now Sand Island) when Dr. Luis Alvarez determined he had died of plague. With no further outbreaks, the ship was allowed to continue to San Francisco.

No one at the time knew that fleas from infected rats were responsible for spreading "*Yersinia pestis*", and it was perhaps a rat from the *Nippon Maru*, or maybe the steamship *Manchuria*, that escaped and made its way onshore. By late fall, residents near the harbor noticed unusually large numbers of dead rats, and within the Chinese community there were rumors of a deadly new disease that Chinese healers were powerless against.

Hawaii (and Chinatown) had previously experienced outbreaks of cholera, measles, whooping cough, and deadly smallpox, but this was obviously something different.

The Board of Health was given extraordinary powers to deal with the plague, and they concluded that fumigation along with destruction by fire was the best policy. All of Chinatown was fenced off with many residents trapped inside while the Board systematically responded to plague cases and reacted with fire and fumigation.

DR. N. B. EMERSON,
Government Physician.

DR. WALTER HOFFMAN,
Government Bacteriologist.

DR. F. R. DAY,
Member of Board of Health.

DR. GEORGE HERBERT,
Government Physician at Insane Asylum.

The last plague victim died on March 31, 1900, marking the end of one of the most extraordinary times in Honolulu's history. All totaled there had been 71 confirmed cases of plague, with 61 of those being fatal.

Plague cases by nationality:

Nationality	Cases
Chinese	35
Hawaiian	15
Japanese	13
Haole	7
South Sea Islander	1

Fifty-eight were male and thirteen were female.

For further reading: James C. Mohr's well-researched book, *Plague and Fire*, Oxford University Press, 2005.

THE FIRES OF 1900

There was not just one Chinatown fire in 1900 – there were 10 of them. They started on December 31, 1899 and included the big out-of-control fire on January 20, 1900.

All of the fires were started by the Honolulu Fire Department under the direction of the Board of Health.

Where outbreaks of plague had occurred, buildings of brick or stone were closed up and fumigated, but wooden structures could not be made airtight so they were ordered to be burned. And sometimes not just single buildings but entire blocks were condemned to be burned.

The standard procedure was to select a day with calm winds, place fire-fighting equipment at strategic locations around the perimeter, and then start the fire on the downwind side and let it slowly burn against the wind while maintaining steady flows of water on adjacent structures intended to be spared.

Most of these controlled burns occurred in Chinatown, but they were also done in various other locations throughout the city but not to quite the same extent.

Residents were given short notice to pile their belongings in the street, to be burned or sent for fumigation, and they were then forcibly evacuated while their residences and businesses were put to the torch.

The Board of Health conducted these controlled burns in Chinatown:

- December 31, 1899 – part of Block 18 (waikiki side of Nuʻuanu Street)
- January 1, 1900 – part of Block 8 (corner of Maunakea & Pauahi streets)
- January 4, 1900 – part of Block 2 (Joss house on Pauahi street between Maunakea and River streets
- January 4, 1900 – part of Block 5 (ewa side of block along Kekaulike Street)
- January 6, 1900 – part of Block 13/14 (Nuʻuanu Street at Merchant Street)
- January 12, 1900 – Block 10 (between Smith, Beretania, Nuʻuanu and Pauahi streets)
- January 15, 1900 – part of Block 18 and part of Block 19 (waikiki side of Nuʻuanu Street)
- January 16, 1900 – Block 9 (between Maunakea, Beretania, Smith, and Pauahi streets)
- January 19, 1900 – part of Block 11 (along Pauahi and Smith streets)
- January 20, 1900 – part of Block 15 – (mauka of Beretania Street)

It was this last burning that led to the second Great Fire in Chinatown.

On January 20, the fire department was burning infected buildings behind Kaumakapili Church when the wind suddenly changed direction and began to blow with great force. They tried valiantly to keep sparks away from the church but burning embers hit the roof of one of the steeples and it caught fire out of reach of their hoses.

The steeple burned like a giant sparkler with the wind sending flaming cinders downwind all across Chinatown. People tried in vain to put out fires on their buildings and rooftops, but they were no match for the wind and the sparks and the rapidly spreading fire.

Fire-protection engineer Sam Dannaway gave an excellent presentation on the 1900 Chinatown fire to the Engineers and Architects of Hawaii on October 23, 2020. You can watch it here: (https://youtu.be/qQIaE6jGems)

Personal belongings destined for fumigation

Mauka side of N. Pauahi Street, between River and Maunakea streets, January 1900

Waikiki side of Kekaulike Street, between King and Queen (Nimitz) streets, January 1900

First fire: December 31, 1899

Quarantined residents and curious spectators gathered on Pauahi Street between Nuʻuanu and Smith streets.

> Police ropes had been stretched across all the street approaches to Nuuanu street, against which many hundreds were gathered craning their necks to witness the first official fire during the present crisis. The mili-

The crowd in the photograph is watching this exact scene – the first Board of Health deliberate burning of part of a block in Chinatown, located at the intersection of Nuʻuanu and Pauahi streets.

HONOLULU CHINATOWN

January 20, 1900 – photographs by Brother Bertram, Principal of St. Louis College

HONOLULU CHINATOWN

The troubles on January 20th were compounded by the fact that Chinatown and all the people in it were under strict quarantine and the entire area was cordoned off with wooden fences under armed guard.

King Street, looking ewa from Bethel Street

As the fire started to spread, panicked residents were initially prevented from leaving the area. Large groups massed at Kukui Street near River Street and on King Street between Maunakea and Nuʻuanu streets.

Sensing a potentially dangerous situation verging on a near-riot, the guards finally relented and directed everyone along King Street to temporary quarantine facilities on the grounds of Kawaiahaʻo Church.

Fearing uncontrolled spread of the plague, local citizens and guardsmen lined King Street on both sides, many of whom carried axe handles and baseball bats to ensure no one escaped. It's hard to imagine the indignity perpetuated on those poor fire victims (Chinese, Japanese, Hawaiian, etc.), many of whom could speak no English, who were already under virtual house arrest in a plague-infected area, and who had lost everything in the fire started by the Board of Health.

The fire spread all the way to Nuʻuanu Stream and the harbor, but the fire department along with volunteers and sailors from the S.S. *Iroquois* and the tug *Eleu* were able to stop it from destroying the Honolulu Iron Works. Due to the previous burnings and the brick buildings within the Fire Limit line, the downtown area was not threatened.

The fire was essentially over by 4 p.m., and although writers at the time claimed it had destroyed 60 acres it actually burned an additional 29 acres.

No fire deaths were reported. But it was estimated there were 4,000 to 7,000 homeless victims and about $2.5M in property damage. Surprisingly, the Board of Health conducted at least 20 more burnings around town after this.

The insurance companies at the time fought many of the claims, saying they were caused by government action.

The ruins of Chinese Engine House No.5 as seen from Beretania Street

The burned-out shell of Kaumakapili Church

After most of the debris was cleared, only the brick walls of Kaumakapili Church, Chinese Engine House No.5, a small storehouse, the John F. Colburn building, and the Sing Chong & Company building were still standing.

The Board of Health had previously burned 5.7 acres of Chinatown, and an additional 29 acres were burned on January 20, making for a total of nearly 35 acres of Chinatown completely destroyed by fire.

From the map below showing burned and targeted areas in gray, it looks like they were planning on burning about half of Chinatown anyway.

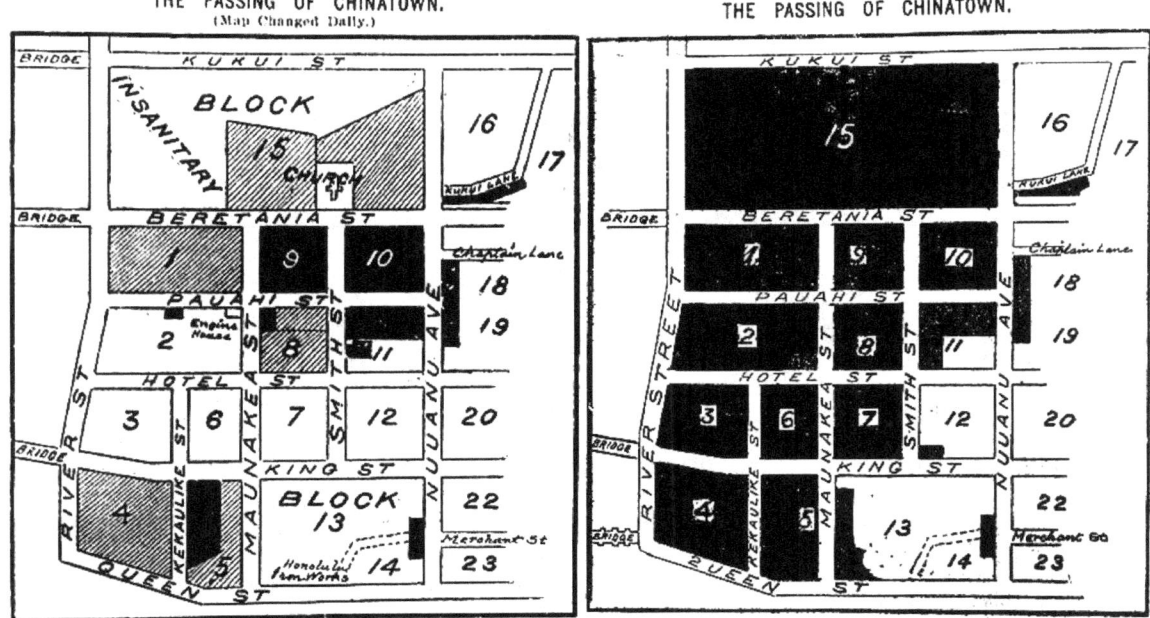

HONOLULU CHINATOWN

The Burning of Chinatown

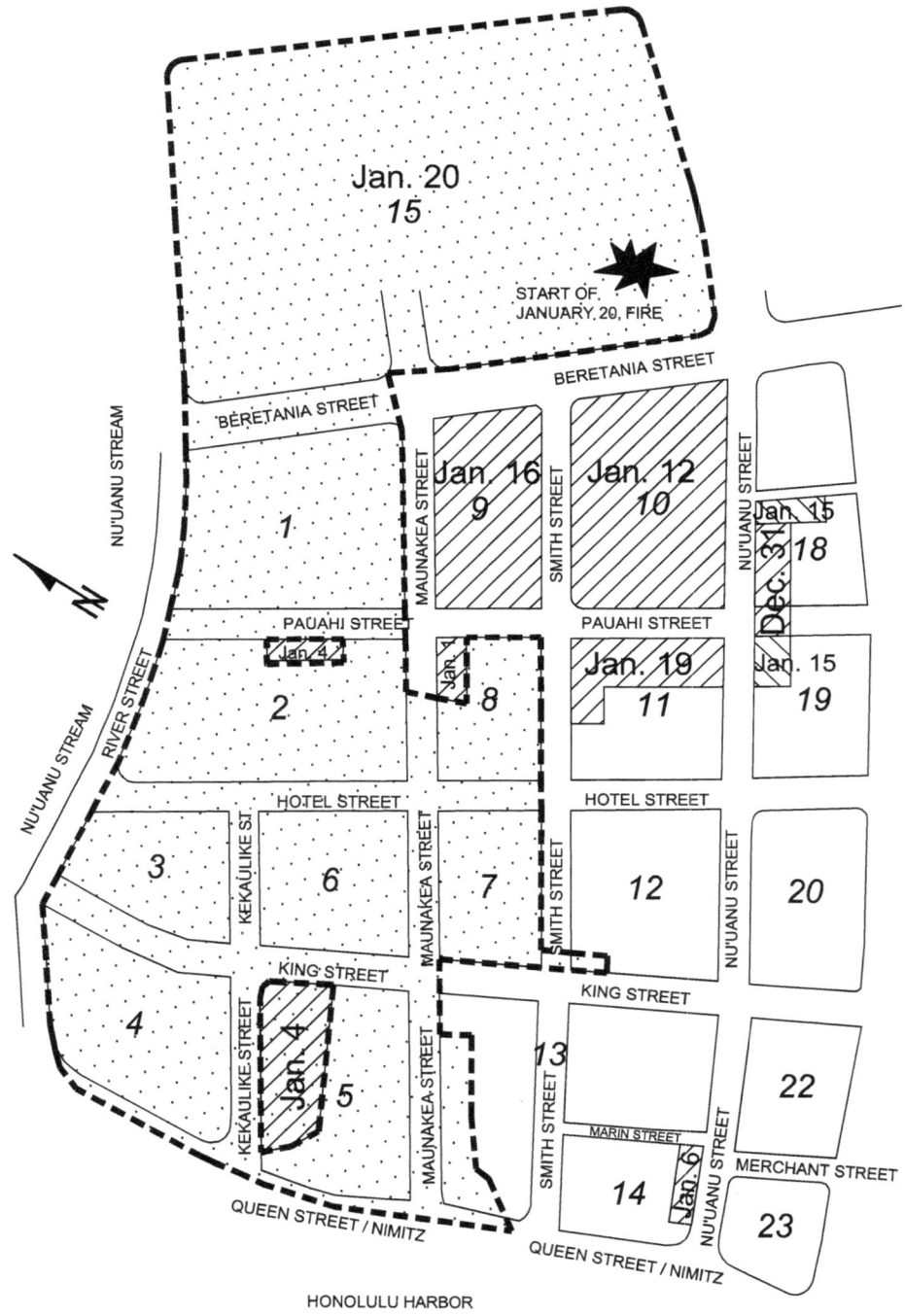

Although there was much talk afterwards of extending the official Fire Limits to Nuʻuanu Stream, it never happened due to several reasons: the Board of Health was essentially running the government, the Legislature was not scheduled to meet until August or September, they were in the middle of a bubonic plague outbreak, and there were too many refugees needing immediate housing to put Chinatown construction on hold.

EARLY 20TH CENTURY

The early 1900's were primarily a time of rebuilding and rapid growth, especially given the clean slate left after all the 1900 fires. New business stores sprang up along the streets with apartments and tenements packed into the interior of the blocks.

The hustle and bustle of the city were perfectly captured in 1906 by cameraman Robert K. Bonine. Working for Thomas A. Edison, Inc., he mounted a 35mm moving picture camera on the front of a streetcar going down King Street. Now part of the George Kleine Collection in the Library of Congress, you can view the video with this link:

https://youtu.be/ICsli_sKmMM , or by scanning the QR code:

The scenes in Chinatown start about one minute into the film.

Here are a few representative screenshots:

CLIMBING THE STAIRS

As with many seaports of its day, Honolulu had no shortage of houses of prostitution. The first customers were whalers, then imported male laborers, and then hordes of sailors and servicemen between the two World Wars.

In 1860 the Hawaiian government passed "The Act to Mitigate the Evils and Diseases arising from Prostitution" requiring all female sexworkers to be registered – 170 women signed up.

Before the 1900 fire, the area around Pauahi Street was infamous for its "Yoshiwara women" – Japanese prostitutes. It was the subject of an exposé in 1896 identifying nearly a dozen houses of "vice and immorality" which ironically let customers know where to go!

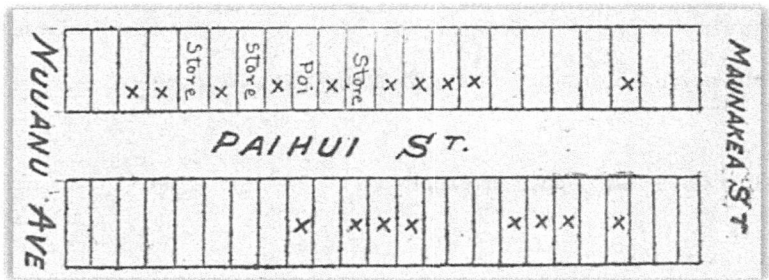

The women were named after Yoshiwara (吉原), the famous red-light district in Tokyo established in 1617, and were easily recognized since they wore the traditional Japanese obi (silk sash belt) in front instead of in back.

After the 1900 fire, and like many cities in the US about this same time, certain citizens of Honolulu created a special "restricted district" that was located away from the city proper, past the train station and the jail and at the end of Iwilei Road beside a rice mill and fertilizer plant. It was enclosed with a wooden fence and was known as the Iwilei Stockade and housed for over 200 women. The Dole Cannery buildings are on the site today.

After the stockade was officially closed in 1917, the sex businesses moved back into the Chinatown area and became really big business by the 1930's.

The houses were highly regulated by the local police, endorsed and supported by the military, and even tolerated and welcomed by many in local government and society. Well, except for the moralist and religious community – the strong missionary movement here had always fought hard to apply their Western morality values to the greater Honolulu population.

The massive influx of wartime sailors created an enormous demand for sex services and local officials thought that by allowing and containing such businesses to one area (Chinatown) that would somehow protect their local women and daughters from all those lusty males. For the military, it was also a way to better control off-hours movements and minimize contagious disease.

The sex workers had to be registered with the Chief of Police, undergo regular health checks, and were not to be seen outside of Chinatown (and certainly not in the "more respectable" areas like Waikiki).

Called "boogie houses" by the customers, they were nothing like the Old West saloons and whorehouses – there was no alcohol, no drugs, and no piano players. At this point in time most of the women were Caucasian from the US Mainland, and since most brothels were on the second floor, the phrase "climbing the stairs" was the going euphemism.

The sailors in this photo are waiting to do just that, at the New Bungalow Hotel at 1166 Smith Street.

In the 1940's the going rate was $3 for 3 minutes. The madams got $1 off the top and the women paid for their room and board out of the remaining and pocketed the difference. The local "kama'aina" (local) discount was $2.

Everyone involved made an unbelievable amount of money – the girls, the madam, the landlord, and the local jewelry and finery shops who courted their business. It is estimated the tax office made $200,000 a year from the girls and madams. The police made money too, with official fees and very likely a few under-the-counter payments.

A Navy engineer typically made $2,000 per year – a boogie house worker could easily make 10 times that amount. The local luxury goods stores welcomed their business.

> "These girls have always been big spenders for jewelry and expensive clothes, cosmetics and other luxury items. One girl, and she isn't even a madam, I know spends more from $200 to $500 a month in my place. Last Christmas she laid $3,000 on the line for a ring to give to her boyfriend. Why, I know one dress shop up the way which has practically lived off these girls."

The houses went by a variety of names: The New Senator Hotel, Pacific Rooms, Rex Rooms, New Bungalow Hotel, Lark Rooms, Service Hotel, Camp Rooms, Mirror Room, Modern Hotel – these were all in Chinatown, mostly in the Hotel and Pauahi street area.

Hotel Street Harry and the Honolulu Harlot, Greystone Productions, 2002:

The houses were finally ordered to close on September 21, 1944.

> "I see here that this paper says we can't practice prostitution any more. Heck, I don't practice, I'm an expert."

Honolulu Historian Richard Greer asked:

> "What were the results of closing the houses? Did it end prostitution? No. Did it trigger unrest and a big morale crisis in the military? No. Did it fill the streets with bug-eyed rapists and assorted sex fiends? No. Did it abolish venereal disease? No. Did it compromise the imaginary virgin purity of the city? No.
>
> Well, then, what did it do? It closed the houses and presumably protected society from itself by excising the foul tumor of the red-light district. It also raised Honolulu to the moral eminence already occupied by other large American cities."

Undoubtedly the trade continued in more clandestine ways after the official closure, but for Chinatown the next big sex-related business was burlesque, first appearing in the late 1940's.

BURLESQUE, NUDES, PORN, & DRUGS

After World War II, Chinatown became a bit of a backwater. The post-war boom in housing and business occurred elsewhere, leaving this older part of town less and less relevant.

There were still bars and restaurants, but in 1947 the Beretania Theater was the first to feature burlesque and striptease performances. Other clubs in Chinatown quickly followed suit.

The mid 1960's brought go-go girls to Chinatown, and yes, they often danced on elevated platforms or in cages with lights synchronized to the music or with strobe lights.

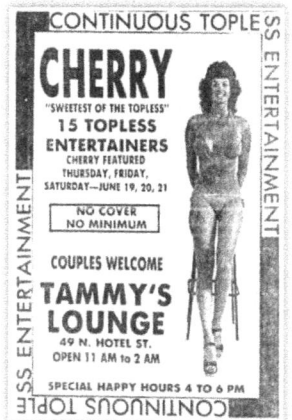

But like a lot of places throughout the US at this time, the free-wheeling 1960's turned into the hardcore 1970's with topless female dancers and performance acts becoming more and more sexual. Erotica was now X-rated, community-offending, and law-breaking pornography. Legendary porn star John Holmes started out doing live shows at the Swing Club on Hotel Street.

So-called "adult movie houses" and "adult bookstores" also appeared and congregated in Chinatown, accompanied by an ever-growing drug trade and all the types of crime that comes with it.

By the mid 1990's, the corner of Hotel and Smith streets was called "the worst corner in Honolulu" and was the site of numerous drug raids and building forfeitures.

ALMOST LOST

By the 1960's, Chinatown's buildings were in big trouble.

- Much of the land was leased from absentee landlords who had little interest or incentive in maintaining the old out-of-date buildings.

- Tenants were unlikely and unwilling to undertake major repairs if their leases were about to expire.

- The automobile was creating havoc with its voracious need for parking.

- There were development pressures to build more high-rise office buildings adjacent to downtown.

- And something of colossal impact had appeared halfway toward Diamond Head...

On August 13, 1959, the Ala Moana Center opened outside of downtown in what had previously been a flat empty coral plain. It was one of the largest shopping centers in America with 80 stores and free parking. It cost $60M and was so new and exciting and successful that it literally sucked the retail out of Honolulu's downtown. On that first day only 13 of the 80 stores were open but over 10,000 shoppers eagerly awaited the opening and the 5,000-car parking area was completely full. The mall was an immediate success.

That left Chinatown with crumbling buildings, little customer base, scant parking, and indifferent landlords. *Literally crumbling* – a large section of the once-mighty Y. Anin block on Maunakea Street collapsed in 1964, as did the King Market that same year. Most of the wooden structures in Chinatown had been built immediately after the 1900 fire so they were sixty years old and aging fast, with many in very poor condition.

Buildings became difficult to rent and often went vacant for months at a time. Consequently, rents were low but that left little if any for building maintenance or improvements.

The population in the area deteriorated as well and Chinatown was plagued with an almost critical mass of drugs, vagrancy, gambling, pornography and violent crime which became the hallmarks of Chinatown nights.

The businesses that remained in Chinatown clamored for more parking, thinking that would help them compete with the new mall. Many of the wooden buildings were torn down for surface parking lots. To try to address the parking needs in the greater downtown business district, nearly an entire block of Nu'uanu street from near King Street to Hotel Street was condemned in 1969 by the city who then demolished all the brick buildings to make way for what was proposed to be a multi-level parking structure but turned into another surface lot instead.

Triggered by several fires in the late 1950's, in 1960 the city stepped up building inspections and began condemning and demolishing dozens of wooden tenements deemed unsafe throughout Chinatown.

In 1968, the *Honolulu Advertiser* predicted:

> "Except for the most recent buildings – and a few which may be declared historic landmarks – Chinatown's 36 acres will be bulldozed and rebuilt as small businesses and moderate-income housing."

And there was plenty of money to do just that – the 1960's and 1970's saw staggering amounts of federal money being allocated for "slum removal" and "urban renewal" projects, with the city specifically targeting Chinatown.

Luckily, there was one voice in the 1960's calling for preservation of Chinatown's architectural and cultural heritage – an activist firecracker named Nancy Bannick.

HISTORIC PRESERVATION

"Why do you want to save that old stuff? We couldn't wait to get out of there."

Although there was usually a voice or two lamenting the impending or actual loss of a beloved building in years past, there were no organized efforts or groups advocating historic building preservation in Honolulu until the establishment of the Historic Hawaii Foundation in 1974.

In 1959, Julius S. Rodman wrote a two-page spread titled "Our Vanishing Past... A Heritage to be Saved?" in the *Honolulu Star-Bulletin* Saturday Edition, but there was no mention of any Chinatown buildings.

On May 20, 1963, the editor of *Sunset Magazine* and member of the Honolulu Chamber of Commerce City Beautification Committee, **Nancy Bannick**, began a six-part series in the *Honolulu Advertiser* that strongly urged building and community preservation in response to recent government-funded and sponsored slum clearance projects in the Chinatown area.

In her first article titled "Quaint Kukui Landmarks Live on Borrowed Time" she charged, "we are wiping out the city's character" and bemoaned "the gradual obliteration of picturesque Old Honolulu". Not one to mince words, she fought tirelessly against redevelopment plans that were "heartless, unfitting, insensitive, sterile, unimaginative, without character and perhaps economically unsound" and also railed against "government secrecy and public default".

And her concern was not just for the "quaint old buildings" but also for the people and institutions who were being displaced by the radical redevelopment plans calling for unsympathetic concrete high-rises.

Bannick's articles stirred up a great amount of public debate and led to Dr. Andrew Lind and photographer Francis Haar documenting many of the sites, and surprisingly, the support of the manager of the Honolulu Redevelopment Agency.

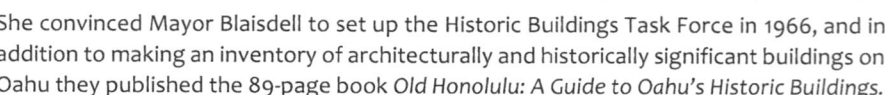

She convinced Mayor Blaisdell to set up the Historic Buildings Task Force in 1966, and in addition to making an inventory of architecturally and historically significant buildings on Oahu they published the 89-page book *Old Honolulu: A Guide to Oahu's Historic Buildings*.

Various surveys and inventories were conducted in Chinatown: University of Hawaii (1969), Jacobsen (1970), J.M. Neil (1971), DMJM (1972), Aotani & Hartwell Associates (1974).

The Chinatown Historical District (SIHP #50-80-14-9986) was officially listed on the National Register of Historic Places on January 17, 1973. It was Hawaii's first historic district.

In April 1991 the Chinatown Special District Design Guidelines were created by the city's Department of Land Utilization "to illustrate how development can be shaped to the context of the historic character of Chinatown".

Historic Buildings Task Force

In 1966, Mayor Neal Blaisdell set up a 22-member task force with Nancy Bannick as chairman that was part of the Mayor's Action for Beautification Committee (ABC). They were tasked with making a methodical inventory of all architecturally and historically significant buildings on Oahu that were worth saving.

The University of Hawaii helped by providing students from the Architecture History 171 class. Every reviewer was given an Evaluation Sheet to judge each building by these 12 criteria:

1. Historical Significance
2. Cultural Contribution
3. Educational Merit
4. Appropriateness to Environment
5. Architectural Interest
6. Uniqueness of Design
7. Integrity of Original Materials
8. Apparent Soundness of Structure
9. Practical to Preserve or Restore
10. Possible Future Use
11. Contribution to Flavor of City
12. Accessibility to the Public

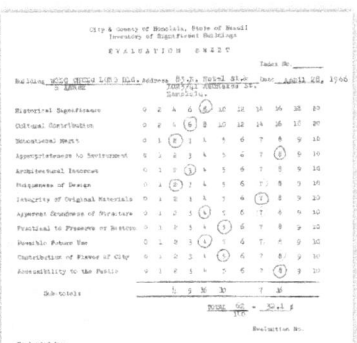

The numbers were tabulated, divided by 140, with the result shown as a percentage. The rankings were accompanied by a Significant Buildings Inventory Work Sheet that collected and documented details, comments, maps, photographs, and sources of information. Some of the more unusual comments from the Work Sheets:

- *"There is nothing worth knowing or preserving about the place. Sorry." (1901 Mendonça Building)*
- *"He knows all there is to know about the building: nothing." (1913 Mendonça Building)*
- *"The Perry Building… has no characteristics which set it apart from other buildings in Honolulu built during this time period."*
- *"The building taken over-all isn't really unique." (Royal Saloon)*
- *"Like most of the buildings in Chinatown, this one is nothing spectacular architecturally nor does it have a noteworthy history… being by no means unique." (McLean Block)*
- *"It is a representation of modern man's attempts to recapture a famous past."*
- *"Thus it has and has not withstood the test of time as far as the design goes."*
- *"These 2 structures that I have been researching seem to be a waste of time." (Aseu, Aswan buildings)*
- *"Other significant features of the second floor is its fluorescent lights and its hollow tile floor."*
- *"It is historical because it was built before the Second War and still remains standing after the Pearl Harbor attack"*
- *"The fire escape in the front of the building in plain view surely doesn't add to the beautiful architecture of the building, if we are to say that this building is beautiful" (Hocking Building)*
- *"The building, as it is, is little more than a fire hazard."*
- *"This building radiates aesthetical architectural form and at the same time, emits a spirited tradition and heredity."*
- *"No real historical import" (the first Chinese Chamber of Commerce Building)*
- *"The building stands out today as a symbol of endurance, from which a feeling of historical data is presented."*
- *"The building seems almost out of place in its site, but it adds greatly to the dignity of the street."*
- *"Poor example of Bastardize Greek Revival". (Pantheon Bar)*

The construction dates they came up with are wildly inaccurate, but at least it was a commendable effort that resulted in snapshots of the buildings as they existed in 1966, including many of which are no longer extant. Involving student evaluators was a great way to increase community participation and awareness, and it was an important forerunner to the 1973 National Register of Historic Places application.

BUILDING RESTORATION

The establishment of the Chinatown National Register Historic District in 1973 was perhaps the single most monumentally positive event in Chinatown's history. Not only did it effectively prevent the use of federal funds for demolitions (still allowed but only after an extensive and lengthy review process), but it also gave owners and developers access to historic preservation grants and a 25% tax credit for restoring historic buildings to their original state. This was huge.

The first developers to take advantage of this were **Bob Gerell** and **Peter Smith**, two former AMFAC executives who appreciated Chinatown and recognized an opportunity. Working closely with preservation architect **Robert Fox** and contractor **Mickey Thielen** of Mouse Builders, their first project was a big one, the largest historic building in Chinatown – the 1901 Mendonça Building on Hotel Street – which they began restoring in 1976.

> *"It's a bet. You're betting the second floors will rent and the first floors (rent) will increase. If you don't have deep pockets to take it through the browning stages, then the second guy reaps the benefits."* – Mickey Thielen

By 1988, Gerell and Smith were responsible for these renovation/preservation projects in Chinatown:

- Mendonça Block, Hotel Street
- Tan Sing Building, Smith Street
- Mendonça Building, Smith Street
- King Kekaulike Building, King Street
- L. Ah Leong Building, King Street
- Chang Block, King & River Street
- Lum Yip Kee Building, Maunakea Street
- Lum Yip Kee Building, Hotel Street
- Schnack Building, Maunakea Street
- 1029 Maunakea, Maunakea Street
- 1145 Maunakea, Maunakea Street
- Maunakea Marketplace, Maunakea Street
- Pauahi St. Block A, Pauahi Street
- Hinode Building, Beretania Street
- Nippu Jiji Building, Nuʻuanu Street
- Central Pacific Building, King & Smith streets
- Encore Building, Nuʻuanu and Hotel streets
- Sumida Building, Maunakea and Pauahi streets
- Minatoya Building, Maunakea and Pauahi streets

Other developers and building owners over the years have followed Gerell's lead, and today many of Chinatown's historic buildings have been saved from demolition and restored.

But it is safe to say that without the colossal efforts of Nancy Bannick in the 1960's and Bob Gerell and Peter Smith in the 1970's there would be no historic Chinatown today. Nominations for sainthood, anyone?

URBAN RENEWAL

Starting in the 1960's, there was a concerted effort to remove all ramshackle wooden houses and tenements in the Chinatown area. Many had been built crammed in tightly together immediately after the 1900 fire and due to landlord neglect were more than showing their age.

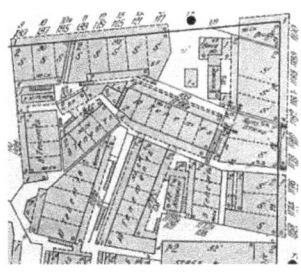

And there was a tremendous amount of federal dollars available at the time for "slum clearance" in the name of Urban Renewal. This money was accompanied by extraordinary legislation that provided sweeping powers of condemnation and demolition to local government authorities, in this case the Honolulu Redevelopment Agency.

Combined with the Housing Authority's goal of creating more affordable housing, the city created General Neighborhood Renewal Plans (GNRP) that unleashed such a wave of destruction that it galvanized concerned citizens like Nancy Bannick and led to the designation of Chinatown as a National Register Historic District in 1974.

Most of the initial clearances were in the congested area mauka of Beretania Street, and when it began in Chinatown it also triggered a mass movement against evictions that was known as the People Against Chinatown Evictions (PACE) wielding significant grassroots power that resulted in a government office sit-in and a dramatic standoff with the police at the Aloha Hotel (remainder of Pang Lum Mow Building) at 1133 Maunakea Street.

Some concessions were eventually agreed upon but the city continued to remove dilapidated structures and build high-rise affordable housing complexes. Several of these projects were built on former surface parking lots owned by the city and included parking garages with spaces for tenants and shoppers.

To date, these are the projects owned and developed by the City and County of Honolulu:

    1965 – Winston Hale, 1055 River Street, 94 units

    1975 – Kukui Plaza, 1255 Nuʻuanu Street, 908 units

    1982 – Pauahi Hale, 126 N. Pauahi Street, 77 units

    1983 – Smith Beretania Apartments, 1170 Nuʻuanu Street, 164 units

    1985 – Pauahi Kupuna Hale, 167 N. Pauahi Street, 48 units

    1987 – Hale Pauahi, 155 N. Beretania Street, 396 units

        Hale Lahui ("house of many people of all races", 111 N. Beretania

        Hale O'Pili ("house of people gathering together"), 155 N. Beretania

    1987 – Maunakea Marketplace, 1120 Maunakea Street

    1990 – Chinatown Gateway Plaza, 1031 Nuʻuanu Street, 200 units

    1991 – Harbor Village, 901 River Street, 90 units

    1995 – Chinatown Manor, 175 N. Hotel Street, 89 units

    1994 – Marin Tower, 60 N. Nimitz Highway, 236 units

    1995 – Kekaulike Courtyards, 1016 Maunakea Street, 76 units

These private developments were built with city participation:

> 1974 – Chinatown Cultural Plaza, 100 N. Beretania Street
>
> 1982 – Honolulu Tower Condominium, 60 N. Beretania Street, 396 units
>
> 1991 – Honolulu Park Place Condominium, 1212 Nuʻuanu Street, 437 units

A corruption scandal involving the misuse of millions of dollars of federal funds put an end to the city's 100-person Housing Department in 1998.

Private developers argued at the time that the city was unduly competing with them, and that affordable housing could be built by the private sector. Twenty years later, the city is still struggling with the issue of providing sufficient affordable housing.

The entire area of Chinatown is approximately 34 acres, and the City of Honolulu currently owns well over half (approximately 55%) of the parcels, excluding streets. Time will tell if this is good or bad for Chinatown.

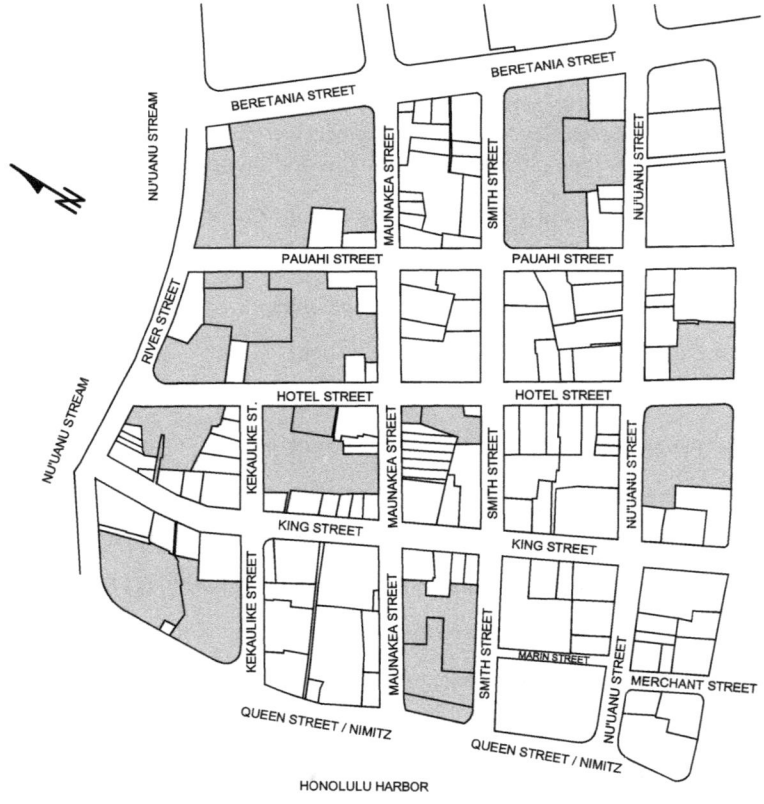

City-owned parcels in Chinatown

ENDURING TRADITIONS

Chinese New Year

Honolulu's Chinatown has celebrated Chinese New Year for nearly 200 years, and in its current manifestation it is an astonishing sight to behold. In addition to a parade with dragons and beauty queens, the real action is in the evening with roving clubs of musicians and lion dancers traveling from business to business to welcome the New Year.

This is no genteel celebration – with the cacophonous beating of drums and clanging of cymbals, the furious prancing and dancing of the 2-person lions, the crowds feeding money into the lion's mouth, and the dozens of strings of loud firecrackers with accompanying smoke filling the air it more resembles a full-scale war, especially when there are several different groups performing along the same street.

Vibrant, exhilarating, primal, entertaining – it's a phenomenon that must be experienced.

Tony Grillo, Artistic Mindz Photography

KUNG HEE FAT CHOY!

THE FUTURE?

Honolulu's Chinatown has never been a static place. Far from it. But where will it be in the next 200 years?

There have been many attempts over the years to "save Chinatown" and/or redefine it, with varying degrees of success. And it has gone through many cycles of ups and downs through the years.

Most recently, the city has struggled to adequately address the plague of homelessness and vagrancy that has hurt businesses, residents, and tourism in the Chinatown area. There are many unusual sights and smells in Chinatown, but stale urine and the antics of the mentally disturbed detract mightily.

It remains to be seen what the effect will be of the City of Honolulu owning over half of the land in Chinatown. Stability? Perhaps. Bureaucracy and politics? No doubt about that. Will private landowners be incentivized to restore and maintain their properties? Let's hope so.

Regardless of ownership, it will ultimately be the people who live and pass through Chinatown who will define it for generations to come, as its shopkeepers, business owners, customers, residents and visitors.

While first generation immigrants often strive hard to preserve vestiges of their home cultures and traditions, subsequent generations tend to assimilate and move on. New immigrants move in and bring their own new customs and traditions, and the cycle repeats as it has for the past 200 years.

As long as there is sustained public, community, and political support, the buildings and businesses and activities will continue to evolve hopefully within a framework that recognizes and respects the multi-faceted historic and cultural resources.

Chinatown should never become a theme park or historic building "petting zoo" tied to any particular time in history – but it will be an interesting and delicate challenge for all to find ways to value and incorporate its past into its future.

There are many who are hopeful – I recently met a senior Japanese businessman having lunch at Murphy's and he sees a bright future for Chinatown and especially for Nuʻuanu Street with its direct makai/mauka connection from the sea to the mountains, from the busy harbor to the Royal Mausoleum, with consulates, botanic gardens, cozy restaurants, chic boutiques, art galleries, and friendly bars in between.

The current mayor, Rick Blangiardi, has made Chinatown a priority of his administration.

Chinatown has always been a place of many different types of opportunities for many different types of people. As long as there is a healthy curiosity and respect for its people, its buildings, and its past, Honolulu's Chinatown will thrive.

"Curiosity is an essence of humanity, so there is a future." – Mike Sata

ARCHITECTURAL STYLES

19th Century Victorian Commercial

Eastlake Victorian

Richardsonian Romanesque

Portuguese Revival

Classical Revival

Art Deco

Chinese Revival

Mid-Century Modern

International Style

Modern High-Rise

Brutalist

Faux Victorian Commercial

And then there is this category. A large number of buildings in Chinatown have been made to look old, to mimic earlier architectural styles. This started with the Chinatown Special District Design Guidelines in April 1991 in an attempt to create a more harmonious and homogenous streetscape. In addition to new buildings, many other buildings had their façades deliberately altered.

These buildings are not old – they were built/altered less than 30 years ago:

ARCHITECTS & BUILDERS

Thomas J. Baker

Originally from Australia, Thomas Baker came to Honolulu in 1876 after working as a bricklayer and builder in San Francisco for several years. His first newspaper ad appeared in October 1876.

In 1877 he built a 2-story brick building that was faced with concrete at the corner of Fort & Hotel streets for C. Brewer, "the finest looking and perhaps most substantially built structure in Honolulu (aside from the Government House)".

That same year he also built a 63' x 112' brick building at the corner of Fort and King streets for grocery firm H.E. McIntyre & Bro., and in September he demolished the old William French coral stone building at Ka'ahumanu and Merchant streets and built a new 2-story brick bank for Bishop & Co.

In 1878 he built a "splendid two-story brick mansion" on Beretania Street near Punchbowl Street for Henry May, and a 50' x 82' 2-story brick building on Fort Street near Merchant Street for T. Cummins for the Dillingham & Co. store. It had the first elevator in Hawaii – "by this contrivance three men can easily raise three tons weight".

He built a large 30' x 40' "fireproof" 2-story brick building for Mr. Aswan on Nu'uanu Street near King Street in 1878, and in 1879 a 2-story brick addition on the northwest side of the main Queens Hospital building.

But his really big commission was in 1879 when he was one of two architects asked to draw plans for King Kalākaua's new palace. The King preferred his plan, in the ornate style called as "American Florentine". The plans called for a 4-story building, 120' x 140', with a central 80' tower plus towers at each corner, and the cornerstone was laid on the King's birthday, December 31, 1879. The brick masonry was by noted local contractor E.B. Thomas.

But all did not go well. The Minister of the Interior, Samuel C. Wilder, was supposed to be in charge of purchases and contracts, but he also claimed that he and not Baker should control the work. Baker responded saying that would be "a procedure unprecedented in the history of Architecture".

It went rapidly downhill from there, aspersions were cast on the accuracy of the foundation plans, His Majesty's Cabinet Council passed a resolution supporting Wilder, and Baker's response was said to be "insulting in tone".

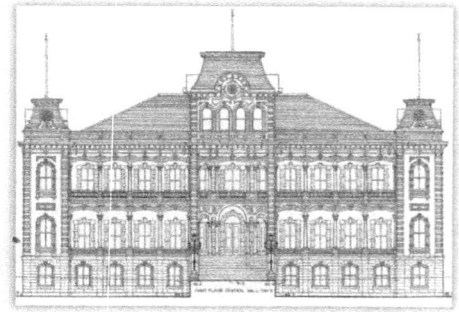

Baker was paid $1,000 for plans and services on January 17, 1880, and it was announced on February 11 that he had been succeeded by Charles J. Wall, an architect from San Francisco. Baker sailed for Australia on February 25 and apparently never came back.

S.D. Burrows

Born in Lāhainā in 1840, contractor and builder S.D. Burrows was half-Hawaiian. At age 16 a friend took him to Brockton, Massachusetts where he spent 6 years learning carpentry and stone masonry.

Burrows built the Emma Street mansion for Princess Ruth Keʻelikōlani (the largest and richest landowner in Hawaii) as well as the 1881 Chinese Church, and he had a planing mill and lumber yard on Fort Street.

Well-loved and well-respected, he was supposed to be the superintendent for the brick Kaumakapili Church on Beretania Street but heart disease caused an early death in 1881 at the age of 41.

Century Construction

Founded in 1956 by Everard Quan Sun Au, William Chun Ming, and Francis H. Chung, Century Construction built three buildings that we know of in Chinatown: Kwai Chan Trust Building (1956), Lee & Young Building (1957), and the Lee Building at 1170 Maunakea Street (1962).

Y.T. Char

Yuk Tong Char was born in Waipahu in 1890 to Char Fat who had immigrated from the Bao On district in Kwangtung (Guangdong), China.

He graduated from Mills School in 1910 and received a degree in architecture from Cornell University in 1915. He had previously worked for H.L. Kerr, and spent two years with Ripley & Davis.

One of his first commissions was an auto stand on N. King Street next to the Robinson Building in 1916.

In Chinatown he designed the Chinese Chamber of Commerce addition to the United Chinese Society Building (1928), the Wo Fat Building (1938) at the corner of Hotel and Maunakea streets, the Wing Sing Wo Building on Maunakea Street (1938), the major remodel of the Yuen Chong Building at 89 N. King Street (1938), and the modernizing remodel of the Robinson Building for Oahu Furniture (1939).

Other Y.T. Char designs include: Waikiki Lau Yee Chai restaurant addition (1932), Mun Lun Chinese School (1932), New Deal Market Building (1934), Palolo Chinese Home Dormitory (1936), Aliiolani School Auditorium (1937), Hilo Chinese Church (1937), Korean Christian Church (1938), Chun Hoon Market (1939), Kaimuki Bowling & Amusement Center (1941), Empire Building at Hotel and Bethel (1949), See Dai Doo Building (1950), University Baptist Church (1951), Hiram L Fong house (1961), and the Kailua Village Condominium (1970).

He was active in the Chinese YMCA, was a director of the Nyin Fo Fui Kon, and was a vice-president of the King Street First Chinese Christian Church. He had three sons and two daughters with very American-sounding names: Adeline, Bernice, Norman, Albert, and Bernard.

Pang Chong

A foreman at City Mill, Pang Chong was president of the Pacific Land and Improvement Company that was created immediately after the 1900 fire, and he likely built many of the new wooden buildings in Chinatown.

In November 1901, he bought the ruins of Kaumakapili Church for $2,725, which he then used to construct several brick buildings nearby.

> **PANG CHONG,**
> Nuuanu Street, opposite Emma Hall.
>
> Contractor, Carpenter, Painter, Paper Hanger. A very nice line of wall papers on hand.

In 1902 he built a 3-story building on Beretania Street that might have been the Hai On Tong Building. That same year he built a building on the corner of Nu'uanu and Beretania streets that fell into the street during construction, which prompted the city to create the first-ever position of building inspector.

In 1903 he built a 2-story brick building for Sin Sing Kee at Beretania and Nu'uanu streets, plus the Honolulu Auto Supply Building at the corner of Beretania and Smith streets.

He built the Yee Hop Market for C.Q. Yee Hop in 1906, and he was also president of the King Market Company.

Chong was also vice-president of Sun Chung Kwock Bo Ltd, with C.Q. Yee Hop was president.

Charles W. Dickey

One of Hawaii's most renowned architects, Charles William Dickey was the grandson of missionary William Alexander, the nephew of the founders of Alexander and Baldwin. He was born in Alameda, California in 1871, grew up in Haiku, Maui, and graduated with a degree in architecture from M.I.T.

in 1894 after briefly working in California he came back to Hawaii and partnered with Clinton B. Ripley from 1895 to 1900, and then with E.A.P. Newcomb from 1901 to 1904.

His designs with Ripley included Pauahi Hall (1894-96), the Bishop Estate Building on Merchant Street (1896), the Irwin Block (1896), the Progress Block on Fort Street (1897), and the Stangenwald Building (1900). With Newcomb he designed the Royal School on Emma Street in 1904.

Dickey moved to Oakland, California in 1904 but still worked for clients in Hawaii and partnered with Hart Wood in 1920 and moved back to the islands in 1924.

He designed Farrington High School, Kamehameha Boy's School, Kodak Hawaii Building, Waikiki Theater Building, Aala Theater, Varsity Theater, Hilo Theater, Halekulani Hotel, Naniloa Hotel in Hilo, Kona Inn, Alexander & Baldwin Building, Castle & Cooke Building, Montague Hall at Punahou, Wilcox Hospital in Lihue, Kula Sanatorium on Maui, Honolulu Immigration Station, Volcano House Hotel, George Vanderbilt house, Paul I. Fagan house, and was an associate designer for the Honolulu City Hall and Central Fire Station.

Dickey was an early proponent of large open spaces and fewer walls, and one of his trademark designs was a double-pitched hip roof with wide projecting eaves that is known locally as a "Dickey roof".

Walter Emory & Marshall Webb

Originally from North Dakota and Pennsylvania respectively, Walter L. Emory and Marshall J. Webb both came to Hawaii independently in the early 1900's. Emory was the Assistant Superintendent of Construction on the Alexander Young Hotel, and after meeting up with Marshall Webb they opened an architectural practice together in 1909.

In addition to the J.H. Schnack Building (1916), they were the architects for the Hawaii Theatre (1922), Blaisdell Hotel (1913), Union Trust Building (1923), Castle Hall Dormitory, Cooke Art Building, Honpa Hongwanji Temple, Masonic Temple, Palama Theatre, and buildings at St. Louis College.

Emory

Webb

Hego Fuchino

Born in Saga prefecture in Japan in 1888, Hego Fuchino came to Honolulu in 1907 to study at the University of Hawaii. He graduated with a degree in civil engineering but taught himself architecture by studying traditional Japanese design.

Fuchino was the architect for the Oahu Theater, the B.K. Yamamoto Building, Holau Market, Aala Market, the Maikiki Christian Church, Kuakini Hospital, Sodo Mission, Shinto Temple in Palama, Park Theater, Kaimuki Theater, YMBA Building, Holau Market, and many of the Japanese shrines throughout Honolulu.

Ernest Hara

Born in 1909, Ernest Hideo Hara was one of the first Asian architects in Hawaii. He first worked with Claude Stiehl and then C.W. Dickey before opening his own office in 1945.

He designed at least 43 schools, 36 apartments/hotels, and 32 commercial projects, including Robert Louis Stevenson School (1950), Central Pacific Bank (1955), Lee & Young Building (1957), Waikiki Grand Hotel (1962), Queen Kapiolani Hotel (1968), Waikiki Shopping Plaza (1975), Hilo Hawaiian Hotel (1976), and the new Central Pacific Bank (1981). He was a founding member of the bank and served on its board from 1954 to 1980.

Fred Harrison

Fred Harrison was born in Sneinton, Nottingham, England in 1859, and came to Honolulu in 1879 with his father Samuel who was also a contractor and builder.

He was one of the most prolific building contractors in Honolulu and was the first to use cut lava blocks in construction. It was said "he mixed reputation with his mortar".

Harrison was arrested in 1895 and exiled for two years for his part in the Wilcox Rebellion to restore the monarchy.

In addition to several sugar mills, Harrison built the second brick tower on the Kaumakapili Church (1885), Chinese Engine House No.5 (1889), Lower Nuʻuanu Stream bridge (1889), Custom House (1889), Oahu Railway Depot (1889), A.L. Smith Building (1890), Cummins Building (1891), Progress Block (1897), Judd Building (1898), J.B. Castle's palatial "Kainalu" residence (1899), Elite Block (1899), Brewery addition (1901), O'Neill Building (1902), Odd Fellows Building (1903), McLean Block (1903), Harrison Block (1906), and the Central Building (1908).

Hawaiian Ballasting Company

Founded in 1899 by Captain Harry L. Evans of the waterfront police and Rudolph M. Duncan formerly in the express business. The *Jessie Minor* was the first ship they provided ballast for, and this led immediately to 11 more orders. They had exclusive arrangements with quarries in Liliha, Kapalama and Kamoliili.

The Pearl City Cemetery was their first big development project where they provided 90 men, twenty teams and four "carloads of stuff" for the site layout and grading in October 1901. About this same time, Captain Evans inherited a half-million-dollar estate in Wales and he sold the company including the schooner *Alice Kimball*, to Kikutaro Matsumoto, Shoichi Yokomizo and George M. Yamada who called themselves the Hawaiian-Japanese Ballasting Company. The name was changed back to Hawaiian Ballasting Company in 1905.

They specialized in basalt curbing, black sand, concrete work, white sand, coral, crushed rock, and material hauling. Their new offices were located at 1018 Smith Street in the new large Mendonça Building constructed after the 1900 fire.

In 1908 they won the contract to build the Sacred Heart Academy in Kaimuki for $55,750. In 1910 they built the Alice MacIntosh Memorial Tower for St. Andrew's Episcopal Church and bought the old City Library and Brewer buildings at auction to be demolished and removed.

Hawaiian Ballasting built the Lee Let Building on King Street in 1906, numerous houses and cottages on the mauka side of Beretania near the site of the old Kaumakapili Church, the Hocking Building on King Street in 1914, the Honpa Hongwanji Mission in 1916, and the Love's Bakery Building on Nuʻuanu in 1917. In 1919 they did the renovation work for the Sumitomo Bank on the Mendonça Building at King Street and Smith Street.

Kikutaro Matsumoto was Hawaii's first Japanese millionaire, acquired through much hard work after starting with almost nothing. At the age of 24, he and his wife immigrated to Hawaii in 1891. His first job was as a laborer for the Guano Fertilizer Company in Kalihi while living with a part-Hawaiian family in return for house, yard, and maid work.

His wife developed a severe mental illness that required him to care for her and take her to his work, but they eventually divorced and she went back to Japan to live with his parents. Originally named Kisaburo, he changed it to Kikutaro after his two older brothers died, believing this new name was more suitable for a first son. He took a new job as a yard man at Kamehameha Schools where he learned to raise honeybees and leased some land in Moiliili from a Native Hawaiian woman to start a bee farm.

In 1899 he married the woman's daughter, Kalei Kaimana Kelii Kiaaina Leleiohoku, and as a wedding present was given an acre of land with a house where the Varsity Building now stands on University Avenue. He broke up a large boulder on the property took it to the harbor to sell for ballast, giving him the idea that would lead to buying Hawaiian Ballasting from Captain Evans.

Matsumoto returned to Japan in 1918. An astute businessman to the end, he had been working on acquiring a fleet of Japanese schooners and steamers to carry supplies between the various South Sea Islands. It was said that he never learned to read or write but could do mathematical and financial calculations with the aid of an assistant.

Hawaiian Engineering & Construction Company

Incorporated March 11, 1901, with Charles Atherton (president), William R. Castle Jr., (secretary/treasurer), and manager Frederick J. Amweg who had formerly been the chief engineer for the Honolulu Rapid Transit and Land Company. Other incorporators included Clarence H. Cooke, Philip M. Lansdale, and Philip L. Weaver.

They built the two large Mendonça Buildings in Chinatown (1901), Oregon Block (1901), Waity Block (1902), Egan-Frear Building (1902) and the Hilo Dock (1903).

In 1903 they became the American-Hawaiian Engineering & Construction Company with Charles H. Gilman as president and with F.J. Amweg as manager, with offices in Honolulu and San Francisco.

In California they built the Carnegie Library in Vallejo, CA, the courthouse in Redwood, and the Red Men's Hall in San Francisco in 1903.

In Honolulu they built the Royal School building and Brewer's Wharf in 1904, and State Archives Building on the Palace and Capitol grounds in 1905. They almost built the Insane Asylum in 1905 but were involved in a very public dispute with the Superintendent of Public Works over irregularities in the contract, including the requirement to make concrete blocks with a specific machine that had not been invented yet.

They left Honolulu in 1906 to concentrate on projects in San Francisco and were in the process of constructing the 10-story Monadnock Building when the Great Earthquake struck. Luckily it was only slightly damaged and still survives today as the Beaux Arts-style 685 Market Street next to the Palace Hotel.

Hawaiian Dredging & Construction Company

Founded in 1901 by Walter F. Dillingham, Hawaiian Dredging & Construction Company is the oldest and largest construction firm in Hawaii. Initially focused on dredging activities, they later expanded into full-service construction.

They dredged the entrance to Pearl Harbor and built much of the waterfront infrastructure in Pearl Harbor. They also built the Ala Wai Canal in Waikiki.

After World War II they merged Hawaiian Dredging and Hawaiian Contracting into Hawaiian Dredging & Construction Ltd. Some of their more notable projects include Ala Moana Shopping Center, King Kalākaua Building (US Post Office), Honolulu Museum of Art, Hawaii Prince Hotel, Four Seasons Wailea Hotel, Ritz Carlton Mauna Lani (Fairmont Orchid), Manele Bay Hotel, Hualalai Resort, John A. Burns School of Medicine, Ala Wai Boat Harbor Floating Docks, Moana Pacific Condominium, and the Halawa end of the H-3 tunnel.

In Chinatown, Hawaiian Dredging & Construction Company built the Sperry Flour Building (1919), Chinatown Cultural Plaza (1974), Chinatown Gateway Plaza (1990), Harbor Village (1991), Chinatown Manor (1994), and Kekaulike Courtyards (1997).

Peter Hsi

Peter Hsi was born in Shanghai, China, and started as a civil engineer but changed to architecture with degrees from Rensselaer Polytechnic Institute and the University of Michigan. After working 9 years in Detroit, he came to Honolulu in 1962 and opened his own office. Hsi was the first architect to use tilt-wall construction in Hawaii.

He designed and developed the Magellan Condominium, the C.Q. Yee Hop Plaza, the King Market, the Franklin Towers in Salt Lake, and the Gold Bond Building on Ala Moana Boulevard.

Theodore C. Heuck

"Truly I would not like anything better than to work as an architect; it is one of the most beautiful and elevating professions I can think of." (personal letter, September 22, 1861)

Born in Hamburg, Germany in 1830, Theodore Heuck was trained as an architect and came to Hawaii in 1850. He worked as a commission agent with Herman Von Holt until King Kamehameha IV noticed his drawings in his store and subsequently asked him to design the first Queens Hospital building in 1860.

He designed a large stone and brick fireproof store at King Street and Bethel Street for Castle & Cooke in 1861, "which for spaciousness and comfort is unsurpassed in town".

Heuck designed the Robinson Building and the Royal Mausoleum in 1863, and the 'Iolani Barracks in 1870. He was the German and Danish Consul, member of the legislature and the Privy Council, and Director of Public Works. He returned to Germany in 1874 and died there in 1877 at age 47.

Paul D. Jones

Born in Powell, Wyoming in 1921, Paul D. Jones was a graduate of the University of Washington School of Architecture and came to Honolulu in 1950 after serving in the Navy aboard the USS *New Jersey*. He initially worked for the architectural firm of Wimberly & Cook, and in 1957 became a partner in Lemmon Freeth Haines & Jones.

He was known as "the Church Architect" and designed about 50 churches throughout the state. He also designed the Hale Koa Hotel, Kona Surf Hotel, First Presbyterian Church, and the Pohai Nani Retirement Home in Kaneohe.

He designed the Yee Yee Tong Building (1957) at 110-112 N. Hotel Street, and it is possible he was involved in the design of Winston Hale (1964) and the Bishop Insurance Building (1964). Jones was active in Free Masonry and was a Past Master of the Lodge le Progres de l'Oceanie that was founded in Hawaii in 1843.

C. Kavanagh

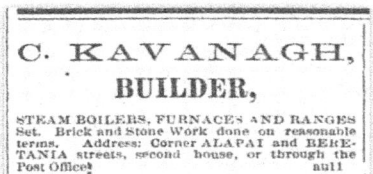

Not much is known about C. Kavanagh (sometimes spelled "Cavanagh") other than he came to Hawaii from Los Angeles. He is first mentioned in the newspaper as one of the bidders for the widening of Queen Street in 1881, and his last newspaper ad is in 1887. He built the Aseu Building (1886), Collins Harness Shop (1886), and the Mendonça & Selig Building (1886). Claus Kavanagh was listed in the city directories as a bricklayer in 1902 and 1903.

Solomon F. Kenn

Born 1877 in Honolulu, Solomon Fukumura Kenn was the son of Fukumura Toyo who came to Hawaii in 1868 with the first group of 148 plantation laborers known as the *Gannenmono* (people of the first year of the Meiji period). His mother was Hawaiian, and he graduated from Kamehameha School for Boys in 1894 and became an architect.

He supervised the new building for Sperry Flour in Hilo in 1919 and designed an incinerator for medical waste in 1924. He designed the Sumida Building in 1926.

From 1927 to 1931 he was the architect inspector of the city and county building department. During that time, he designed the Kakaako Fire Station (1928) and its twin the Makiki Fire Station (1929).

In 1934 Kenn became the Acting Secretary and later Chief Inspector for the Liquor Commission. He later designed the Kauluwela School Classroom (1938) and interior of Johnny Welch's Porthole at 49 N. Hotel (1950).

Harry L. Kerr

Born in Port Ewen, NY, in 1863, Harry Livingston. Kerr attended a private architectural school and worked for 2 years in New York City. In 1887 he moved to San Diego, then 3 years later to the state of Washington, and finally to Portland, Oregon, where he opened his own architectural office in 1892.

Kerr arrived in Honolulu on December 7, 1897, just one month after Minnesota architect Oliver Traphagan.

In addition to his architectural work, in 1900 he formed the Honolulu Clay Company with three partners to make local bricks.

It is said he designed over 1,000 buildings in Honolulu, including the Orpheum Block (1899), JR Wilson/ WH Shipman House in Hilo (1899), Sachs Building (1901), Y. Anin Block (1901), Hustace Building (1901), Hawaiian Electric Building (1901), C. Ahi Building (1901), United Chinese Society Building (1903), McCandless Building (1906), Yokohama Specie Bank (1908), L.L. McCandless Block (1910), Mendonça Building (1913), Moana Hotel Expansion (1917), Sumitomo Bank renovation (1919), Tan Sing (Mendonça) Building (1920).

In 1919 he promoted Edwin C. Pettit to partner, and the firm became Kerr & Pettit.

After 1920 he specialized in apartment buildings, mostly in Waikiki, and was the owner of the Kerr Apartments at Kalākaua and Liliʻuokalani streets.

Norman Lacayo

Called by some "the most influential architect of the late 20th century in downtown Honolulu", Jose Norman Lacayo was born in Los Angeles to parents who had immigrated from Nicaragua. He started as a draftsman and later graduated from Southern California University's School of Architecture in 1960.

He briefly worked for Charles Luckman and Associates in New York City before moving to Hawaii in 1966 to work with John Russell Rummell on Henry Kaiser's Hawaii Kai development.

Lacayo opened his own office in 1969 and designed luxury residences as well as high-rise projects.

Four of his projects are in Chinatown: Honolulu Tower (1982), Irwin Block Addition (1981), Chinatown Gateway Plaza (1990), and Honolulu Park Place (1991).

He also designed the Nuʻuanu Craigside Condominium in 1985, and the towering Harbor Court Condominium at Queen and Bethel streets in 1993.

Lacayo is known for his use of space and unusual angles, and many of his tower projects were built with the relatively new technology known as slip-form concrete.

> "His dramatic residences and sculptural like towers stand out amongst the many banal box-shaped high rises in Honolulu."

He now lives and work in Mexico and continues to design award-winning properties.

George W. Lincoln

Born in New York in 1832, and said to be a great nephew of Abraham Lincoln, George Walter Lincoln was a Civil War veteran who came to Hawaii about 1874.

His first newspaper ad in 1881 offered contracting and building services as well as being the sole agent for the Housekeeper's Kitchen Cabinet, plus offering reconditioning and retoothing of saws. He built the Clark Building in 1879 and the Cunha Saloon on Merchant Street in 1881, followed by the 2-story brick Lincoln Block on King Street in 1884.

1885 was a particularly busy year – he built a large icehouse for James Campbell, the new mansion for Judge McCully at "Pawaa-on-the-plains", and the Pacific Commercial Advertiser Building on Merchant Street. He built the S.M. Maguin Building at 941 Nuʻuanu Street in 1886, plus the Quong Sam Kee Building at King and Maunakea streets in Chinatown.

Lincoln built the Von Holt Building in 1895 and the new Opera House in 1896 with Thomas B. Walker and Archie Sinclair as subcontractors. He ran his last newspaper ad in 1905. Married to Maleana Kina Lincoln, he lived to the ripe old age of 92.

Robert Lishman

Born in Horsely, Northumberland, England in 1831, Robert Lishman was living in Australia when he was summoned by King Kamehameha V to come to Hawaii in 1874 as the supervising architect and builder of the Judiciary Building known as Aliiolani House.

In 1875 he designed and supervised the construction of the Lunalilo Mausoleum in the Kawaiahaʻo Church yard, and at the request of the British government in 1878 he was put in charge of the construction of the Captain Cook Obelisk at Kealakekua Bay. He was briefly Superintendent of the Water Works in 1877, and he was the superintending architect for the Lunalilo Home in 1881.

Lishman went to England in 1884 to personally select the stone for St. Andrew's Cathedral that was delivered later that year by the bark *Ophelia* from Liverpool. He also designed and built the Empire Saloon at the corner of Nuʻuanu and Hotel streets in 1886.

He did the stonework for the Central Union Church (1890-92) and was the supervisor for the chancel of St. Andrew's Church. He was superintendent of the stonework for the Bishop Museum (1892) that was designed by San Francisco architect William F. Smith.

Lishman teamed with John Ouderkirk in 1896, "for the purpose of carrying on the business of erecting buildings and contracting for the erection of brick and stone buildings, and also the selling and quarrying of stone".

He also ran a dairy in the Maikiki area but met his end in 1902 at age 71 when he was tossed over a fence by an angry Jersey bull. The Lishman House was in the Makiki District Park and on the National Register of Historic Places but was demolished anyway in 1985 by the city. Irwin Lane with the Department of Parks and Recreation said, "IT IS SO unattractive, it would require at least a half acre of heavily landscaped land to obscure it".

George Lucas

George Lucas was born in County Clare, Ireland in 1821. His father was one of the English guards who watched over Napoleon during his banishment to St. Helena. Lucas's parents later moved to Australia where he met and married Sarah Williams.

He and his wife spent three weeks in Honolulu in 1849 on their way to the California Gold Rush. Not having much luck as a miner, he turned to carpentry and worked in San Francisco for six years.

They moved to Hawaii in 1856 and he founded the Honolulu Steam Planing Mill in 1859 on the newly reclaimed land called the Esplanade in front of the former fort. The mill employed 20 people and was housed in a "shapely stuccoed brick structure" that was also famous for its clock tower which was used by mariners as an official timepiece and also as a range marker for ships entering and leaving the harbor.

In addition to running the planing mill, Lucas was also one of the most active and most respected builders in Honolulu.

Lucas provided all the carpentry, cabinetry, and woodwork for Iolani Palace, using imported woods like American walnut and white cedar, plus Hawaiian woods like koa, kou, kamani and ohia.

He also built the Campbell Block, YMCA Hall, Knights of Pythias Hall, the old Gazette Building, the Pantheon Block, the Brewer Block and the Hawaiian Hotel. He also built a stone bridge on Nu'uanu Street.

In Chinatown, we know he built these buildings: Cosmopolitan Saloon (1886), Bickerton Block/Club Hubba Hubba (1886), Holt Block (1886), Yim Quon Building (1886), Mendonça/Encore Saloon (1886/87), Honolulu Iron Works Storage Building (1888).

Lucas was a proud and active member of the Honolulu Volunteer Fire Department and was their chief engineer for many years. He was also one of the leading originators of the Honolulu Library and Reading Room.

His funeral in 1892 was one of the largest seen in Honolulu, with large musters of firemen and members of benevolent societies he had helped, plus the Royal Hawaiian Band. Over 60 carriages followed the hearse to the cemetery.

> "No citizen was better known than he. He could count his friends by the score, and when he made a friend it was a friendship that would last forever."

> "There are few individuals in Honolulu who have done more in the way of charity and benevolence in proportion to their means than Mr. Lucas."

Three of his sons – Thomas, Charles, and John – carried on the business as the Lucas Brothers.

Edward E. Mayhew

Not much is known about carpenter E.E. Mayhew – he first appears in 1878 coming to Honolulu from Kauaʻi. In 1885 he introduced a 4-person patent adjustable swing that could be seen at the houses of J.H. Paty, B.F. Dillingham, E.C. McCandless, and at the Casino.

In 1885 he built the Kapiolani Home on the Kakaako Branch Hospital grounds, the house on King Street for Attorney General Paul Nueman, and the dwelling house for the Honolulu Lighthouse keeper. After the 1886 fire he won the bid to rebuild the ruins of the United Chinese Society club house on N. King Street.

Mayhew was in a very brief partnership with architect W. Crewes in 1886, and they did the carpenter work on the new Aseu Building at the corner of N. King and Nuʻuanu streets.

Said to have experience in stage carpentry, built a new stage for the Hawaiian Opera House in 1887. That same year he also built a dispensary and residence at the Insane Asylum. He is listed as a "machinist" in an ad for the 1890 Opera House and is also referred to as the stage carpenter.

In the 1892 *Directory and Hand-Book of the Kingdom of Hawaii*, published by F.M. Husted, the listing for E.E. Mayhew says "*gone to San Francisco*". His wife had contracted leprosy in 1891 and was being treated in the City Hospital in San Francisco, and he apparently never returned to Hawaii.

Risuke Miyata

Not much is known about Japanese contractor Risuke Miyata. His first building permit was in 1903, and by 1907 he was regularly advertising construction services partnering with Zenkichi Sugihara.

In 1909 he built a new 2-story brick building at King and Kekaulike streets for L. Ah Leong, replacing an earlier 1-story building that had been built immediately after the 1900 fire.

In 1915 Miyata teamed up with I. Kodama in the Poi Factory & Merchandise Store.

In April 1915, shortly before Miyata's death, Zenkichi Sugihara bought the business and renamed it Z. Sugihara & Company.

Mouse Builders

Paul Michel Thielen went by the name of "Mickey" so of course he playfully named his construction company "Mouse Builders". He was born in 1931 and graduated from Claremont Men's College in California as class president.

In the 1980's he teamed up with Bob Gerell and Peter Smith and restored and built many buildings in Chinatown, including the 1913 Mendonça Building, Maunakea Marketplace, J.H. Schnack Buildling, 1147 Maunakea, Tan Sing Building, and the 1988 police station remodel in the Perry Block.

Thielen was a longtime resident of Hawaii and was perhaps best known for his restoration of the Stangenwald Building on Merchant Street which won a national Renaissance Award.

William Mutch

Born in Scotland in 1845 and Superintendent of Buildings for the Bishop Estate, Mutch designed the new wing to the Bishop Museum, and he was also the head carpenter at Kamehameha Schools. He provided the woodwork for the original Bishop Museum in 1892.

Mutch built the Moana Hotel, Armstrong Building, Colusa Building, and the Alexander Young Hotel which at that time was the largest construction project ever undertaken in Hawaii. He was the first foreign-born naturalized American citizen in the Territory of Hawaii.

Vladimir Ossipoff

Born in 1907 in Vladivostok, Russia, Vladimir Nicholas Ossipoff grew up in Tokyo and came to Hawaii in 1932 shortly after graduating from the University of California at Berkeley. He initially worked with Charles W. Dickey and founded his own firm in 1936.

He was Hawaii's foremost Modernist architect, mixing Modernism with Japanese and Hawaiian Territorial elements. Many of his houses and buildings incorporated large informal indoor/outdoor living spaces through open walls and multiple lanais.

His buildings include the University of Hawaii Administration Building (1949), Hawaiian Life Insurance Building (1951), the Liljestrand house (1952), Liberty Bank (1952), The Pacific Club (1959), IBM Building (1962), and the Outrigger Canoe Club (1963). Described as both "charming and cantankerous", he waged a "War on Ugliness" against Hawaiian architecture that was neither regional nor climate-friendly. Ossipoff bequeathed 66 boxes of drawings and papers to the University of Hawaii at Manoa.

Isaac A. Palmer

Born in St. Clairsville, Ohio in 1835, Isaac A. Palmer served in the Wisconsin 30th Regiment as Principal Musician in the Civil War. He moved to Seattle, Washington in 1871, and by April of 1872 was advertising as an "Architect and Builder". He designed the county courthouse and jail, several houses and commercial buildings, plus the towering 12-room 1883 Central School on Sixth Street with French mansard roof, clock tower and tall central belfry.

By 1887 he was in Honolulu and was the architect of the new Perry Block on Nuʻuanu Street. He also designed the Hoffschlaeger Building (1888), the T.H. Davies Building (1888), the Cartwright Building (1889), the Honolulu Dispensary (1889), the J.A. Cummins Building (1891), the British Club (1891), the Hawaiian Hotel Lanai (1891), and the Daily Bulletin Building on Merchant Street (1892).

In 1891 Palmer teamed up with former USS *Benecia* ship's carpenter W.W. Richardson to form Palmer & Richardson, advertising "Eastlake, Queen Anne, Renaissance, Gothic, Italian, Classic and Norman" styles of architecture in "stone, brick, iron or wood". Based on stylistic similarities with the Perry Block, along with his interest in Eastlake architecture, he was very likely the architect for the Royal Saloon (1890), T.R. Foster Building (1891), the Chilton Block (1891), the Robinson Block on Hotel Street (1891), and the E.S. Cunha "Republic Building" (1894).

Apparently catching "gold fever", Palmer was in Medford, Oregon, by 1896 where he designed at least 20 downtown buildings and houses there and in Grants Pass until 1908.

Clinton B. Ripley

Clinton Briggs Ripley was born in Peru, Maine in 1849. He worked in Chattanooga, Nashville, and Los Angeles before moving to Hawaii in 1890.

He initially worked as the architect for contractor Peter High of the Enterprise Planing Mill. In 1891 he teamed up with architect Arthur Reynolds and designed the Masonic Temple, new Sailor's Home, and Queen's Hospital Addition in 1893.

Ripley partnered with Charles W. Dickey in 1896 and they designed the Irwin Block, Bishop Estate Building, Central Fire Station, and Pauahi Hall at Punahou School that same year, the Progress Block in 1897 and the Stangenwald Building in 1900. Ripley developed a strong interest in concrete buildings and started The Concrete Construction Company after investigating techniques on the mainland and returning with specialized machinery.

He was in Manila doing concrete construction from 1902 to 1907, and then back to architecture in Oakland before returning to Hawaii in 1910 when he got the contract for the YMCA Building. In 1912 he teamed with Louis E. Davis, and they designed the Honolulu Iron Works warehouse (1912), Hocking Building (1914), Methodist Parsonage (1917, and Love's Bakery (1917).

Louis E. Davis was born in Oregon in 1884 and was known for his work in the Spanish Colonial/Mission Revival style. He designed the Princess Theatre (1922), McKinley High School (1924), New Pawaa Theatre (1929), New Palama Theatre (1930), Waipahu Theatre (1930), Territorial Board of Agriculture and Forestry Building (1930), Honolulu Police Station (1931), Lihue Theatre (1932), several homes in Kahala, and the private residence in Waimanolo known as Pahonu that was featured in the original Magnum PI television series.

Saiki & Davenport

Masataro Saiki was born in Hiroshima-ken, Japan, in 1878, and came to Honolulu in 1889 when he was 11 years old.

He later teamed up with Richard Davenport as Saiki & Davenport, and during their brief partnership built the Fong Building (1923), the Siu Building (1926), Lum Yip Kee Building on Maunakea Street (1926), the Sumida Building (1927), and the Oahu Theater (1927).

They were big promoters of hollow concrete building tile, and their offices were in the Fong Building at the corner of Beretania and River streets.

Archibald Sinclair

Archie Sinclair was an expert stone mason and builder born in Glasgow, Scotland, in 1837. In the late 1860's he was working in New York, and he went to help rebuild Chicago after the great fire in 1871.

From there he moved on to San Francisco and in 1879 accepted the position as foreman for E.B. Thomas for the construction of 'Iolani Palace where he laid the first stone. He also built the first Hawaiian Opera House.

He was arrested on June 23, 1893, along with T.B. Walker and E.C. Crick and charged with conspiracy to seize the palace and overthrow the Provisional Government. Their attorney, Charles Creighton, compared their arrest to the Spanish Inquisition. But all they could come up with was Sinclair saying, "I am for annexation, but not for making a missionary government solid". The case was dismissed.

E.B. Thomas

Born in Liverpool, England in 1850, contractor and builder Edwin B. "Ted" Thomas came to Hawaii in 1877 on the steamship *Zealandia* as a tourist to see the volcano and decided to stay.

In 1878 he teamed up with Alfred Foster for one year as Foster & Thomas. They obviously parted on friendly terms as E.B. Thomas was the best man at Foster's wedding in 1881.

Thomas quickly became one of the most prominent and respected builders in Honolulu.

He provided the brickwork for 'Iolani Palace (1880-1882), the Music Hall (1880), Lunalilo Home (1881), Wilder & Co. Building (1881), Honolulu Library (1883), Love's Bakery (1884), Bishop Hall of Science (1884), and the Police Station House on Merchant Street (1885).

1886 was a particularly busy year for Thomas: United Chinese Society Building, John F. Colburn Building, Aswan Building, brickwork for Quong Sam Kee Building, Uyeda Building, Sing Chong Building, Anchor Saloon, Maguin Building, a 300' breakwater in Waikiki for C. Afong, and the new building for sewing machine and firearms dealer Mrs. Thomas Lack.

In November of 1886 the bark *Forest Queen* from San Francisco delivered to Thomas 400 barrels of lime and 83,240 hard bricks plus iron and wood mill work.

In 1887 he built the McInerny Block, Pacific Saloon Building, W.E. Foster Building, Hoffschlaeger Building, the brickwork for the Judd Building, plus a new front the King's Court (Yat Loy) Building. In 1888 he built the T.H Davies Building and the Perry Block, followed by the Cartwright Building in 1889.

He built his own brick office and yard at King and Smith streets in 1891, plus the British Club Building and the Wong Kwai Building on Nu'uanu Street, and he built the T.R. Foster Building on Nu'uanu Street in 1892.

Thomas also built the Hawaiian Hotel Music Pavilion and Masonic Temple in 1892, laid some of the granite sidewalk on King Street below Maunaukea Street, and did the brickwork for the Von Holt Block (Hawaiian Gazette Building) in 1895. He laid the foundation for the Central Fire Station (1896) and developed and built the Katsey Block (1900).

He was known as "Kamaki" to the Hawaiians and was described as a man of "a genial and sociable nature, though a man of firm opinions and outspoken expression", he was certainly no fan of Asian immigrants. In 1892 he wrote:

> "Something must be done about Chinese competition or other mechanics will go to the wall... Did you ever know me to hire Chinese or Japanese? No. I think there is no money in them. We don't want the Chinese here; all they do is to bring old clothes, old cabbages, cholera and smallpox."

Thomas also held very strong political beliefs which became even more pronounced after a few drinks. He was called "a pronounced and ardent Royalist and hostile to this government" and felt the present government had "stolen the country from the natives".

On January 7, 1895, he was arrested along with John Bowler, A.J. Testa, F.H. Redward, A.P. Peterson, E. Norrie, Harry Von Werthern, Henry Derie, and George Markham for conspiracy in the Wilcox Rebellion. In his case, it was something do with 50 pounds of gunpowder he had hidden on the *Haleakala*. Given the option to leave the country, Thomas, Norrie and Henry Poor preferred to remain in jail, but "Thomas says if the Government will give him $20,000 he will call it even and depart". He was imprisoned for 3 months until finally pardoned.

On October 30, 1900, Thomas left for South Africa via Liverpool on a steamship appropriately named S.S. *Queen*, saying "there is nothing for me here. I am a Republican where National politics are concerned, but I cannot agree with the local party's treatment of local issues... South Africa is my destination, and I am going there to assist in the founding of a nation." Queen Lili'uokalani gave him a departure gift of a large cluster of green oranges and maidenhair ferns as a token of her esteem and friendship. But after being there one year and nine months he wrote that South Africa was "the most awful country" he had ever visited and intended to return to Hawaii but he died there in 1907.

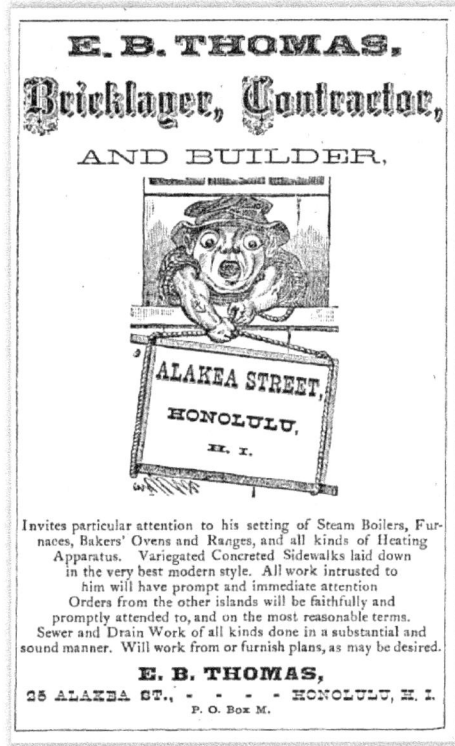

Town Construction Company

Masami Yamauchi

Owned by **Masami Yamauchi** and **Toshio Ansai**, Town Construction Company was one of Honolulu's most prolific post-war construction contractors, active from 1947 to 1986. Yamauchi was from Kealia, Kaua'i, and Toshio Ansai was from Wailuku, Maui and was state senator and member of the decorated 442nd Regimental Combat Team.

In addition to buildings all over Hawaii, they built these buildings in Chinatown: Central Pacific Bank (1955), C.Q. Yee Hop Plaza (1965), Winston Hale (1965), Yee Hop Market (1966), Lum Yip Kee Building (1968), Loo-Chow Building (1968).

Oliver Traphagen

Born in Tarrytown, New York, in 1854, Oliver Green Traphagen moved with his parents to St. Paul, Minnesota in the 1870's and became a carpenter and later an apprentice with architect George Wirth.

O. G. TRAPHAGEN, ARCHITECT.

223 MERCHANT ST., HONOLULU.
Between Fort and Alakea.
Telephone 743.

He moved to Duluth in 1882 and worked on his own as well as partnering with Wirth and Francis Fitzpatrick and built a number of prominent public and private buildings in Duluth: First National Bank, Turner Hall, Wieland Block, City Hall and Jail, Fire Station No. 1, First Presbyterian Church, Duluth Central High School, and the landmark Oliver G. Traphagen House called Redstone. Many of his designs were in the Richardsonian Romanesque style.

Traphagen moved his family to Hawaii in 1897 due to his daughter's health and he quickly became "the most prolific and highly regarded architect in town". He designed the Judd Building (1898), James B. Castle House (1899), Peacock Block in Hilo (1899), Kakaako Pumping Station (1900), Moana Hotel (1901), Palama Fire Station (1901), local architect for Alexander Young Building (1901), Senator George Carter House (1901), Odd Fellows' Building (1901), Collins Building (1901), Hackfeld Building (1902), Hilo Jail (1904), Hawaiian State Archives Building (1906), and Punahou School president's home (1907).

In Chinatown he designed the two large Mendonça Buildings (1901) on Hotel and Smith streets, and was the supervising architect for the McLean Block (1903) on Nuʻuanu Street.

Traphagen moved to Alameda, California in 1907 and retired in 1925.

James K. Tsugawa

Architect James Kumato "Jimmy" Tsugawa, AIA, was born in Papaikou, Hawaii, and graduated from Hilo High School. He received his degree in architecture from the University of Oregon in 1953 under the G.I. Bill and as Corporal Tsugawa worked as a draftsman for G-2 Headquarters IX Corps in Sendai, Japan. He spent five years in California before opening his own office in Honolulu in 1965.

His first major project was the 192-unit high-rise Hale Kilohana apartments, followed by the 150-unit Kalanihuia Elderly Apartments (1969) at Beretania & Aala streets.

> **JAMES K. TSUGAWA & ASSOCIATES**
> (ARCHITECTS)
> Announce the opening of their new office at
> 1232 Waimanu Street
> Penthouse
> Honolulu, 96814
> Phone 512-964

Other projects included: Foster Tower condo conversion (1972), Aiea Heights Townhouses (1974), Kona Hospital (1975), Kinau Lanais Condominium (1976), Kawaiahaʻo Plaza (1978), Stangenwald Building restoration (1980), City Bank Makiki Branch (1983), Punahou Cliffs (1984), Hilo Hattie Fashion Center in Kailua-Kona (1985), Kahuku Village Center (1986), The Lodge at Wailuna (1986), Windward Town & Country Plaza (1989), The Knolls at Waikaloa (1991), Halewili gated community (1992), and the Na Lei Hulu Kupuna Apartments in Kakaako (1992).

In Chinatown, Tsugawa bought and restored the Pacific Saloon (Flores Building) in 1977, restored the Mendonça Building on Hotel Street in 1978, restored the Encore Saloon Building in 1979, and designed all the new buildings in the Maunakea Marketplace built in 1989. He also designed the 1-story Wang Building (1995) at 65 N. Pauahi Street.

Charles W. Vincent

Not much is known of the early life of Charley Vincent, one of Honolulu's first builders. Reportedly a native of New York, he first appears in the newspapers in 1844, and is listed as a house carpenter in the 1847 Register of Foreigners.

Vincent employed a sizable workforce and was the premier builder in town in the 1840's and 1850's in stone, brick, adobe, wood, or thatch. He built the Robert Wyllie house and the Sailors' Home and was also known for several house-moving projects. In 1847 he took out an ad for 4,000 coral stones, perhaps for the construction of Liberty Hall.

In addition to being a contractor and carpenter, he was also a dealer in lumber, hardware, paint, and builder's supplies. His lumberyard was located on Maunakea Street just mauka of King Street, and at one time he stocked as much as 140,000 feet of Astoria pine timber, plus a huge stock of windows, sashes, doors, nuts, bolts, etc.

Vincent founded Honolulu's first theater, The Thespian, in 1847, and married a Hawaiian woman named Mauli in 1848. In 1849 he teamed up with his neighbor across the street, Isaac Montgomery, in the Puuloa Salt Works.

The last newspaper reference to C.W. Vincent in Honolulu is in 1864 where he is listed as a "foreign juror".

The *Pacific Commercial Advertiser* on September 9, 1865, reported: *"By the Polynesian, particulars of the death of C.W. Vincent, Esq., were received. It appears that he was murdered at Guaymas"*. There are no clues as to what or how or why he would have been in Mexico.

Thomas B. Walker

Born in Norfolk, England, in 1847, Thomas Beresford Walker came to Hawaii in 1877 after serving with the British Army in Afghanistan and Abyssinia in 1868. Stopping in Cheyenne, Wyoming, on his way to San Francisco in 1875 he helped build the Inter-Ocean Hotel. He met Wild Bill Hickock and General George Custer and fought with the Third Cavalry against the Sioux. He was wounded at the Battle of Powder River in 1876.

In San Francisco he met E.B. Thomas who convinced him to come to Hawaii. By 1880 he was a bricklayer teamed up with W.K. Metcalfe and by 1883 with H.G. Treadway. Insolvent by 1884, he worked at the Keystone Saloon and was manager of the Royal Saloon in 1886 when he was arrested in a highly publicized burglary of a safe at the post office. The trial captivated the town and he was eventually acquitted by the Hawaii Supreme Court.

In 1888 he teamed up with fellow Englishman Fred H. Redward as Walker & Redward and they built the new Royal Saloon at Merchant and Nuʻuanu streets in 1890. By 1891 the firm was Bertelmann & Walker, building the Brewer Block on Fort Street for $12,200. Walker also built the 200' tall smokestack at the Makaweli sugar mill.

A staunch royalist, he was arrested in 1893 with Archibald Sinclair for conspiracy to overthrow the Provisional Government and spent 2 months in jail before being acquitted. He was arrested again in the 1895 Rebellion and was pardoned after being sentenced to 30 years imprisonment and a $5,000 fine for organizing and making hand grenades.

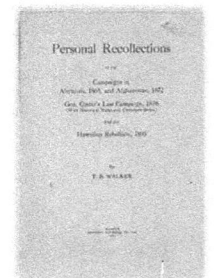

Described as "a very popular but at times erratic man", he was an accomplished performer on the English concertina, but one day in 1897 he also took a rifle and shot at building owner John Emmeluth in broad daylight, apparently upset over the construction schedule.

As Sinclair & Walker he worked on the Von Holt Building in 1895 in 1929 at 82 years old he rehabilitated the smokestack at the Waianae plantation. He wrote a 100-page book in 1931 titled "Personal Recollections" that was published by Advertiser Publishing Company.

Charles J. Wall

Born in Dublin, Ireland in 1827, Charles John Wall first arrived in New York in 1848, and came to Honolulu via Santa Barbara, California, in 1879.

His first job was to "make the detail drawings from the first architect's plans" for Iolani Palace (1880) and to also be the supervising architect. In 1880 he also prepared the plans for Kaumakapili Church and the Music Hall / Opera House.

That same year he also designed a large hall for the St. Louis School, but when the roof collapsed in 1881, killing a young native boy, Wall and the Rev. W.J. Larkin were arrested and charged with manslaughter.

Wall also designed the C.M. Cooke residence on Beretania, Victoria Ward's "Old Plantation" house, and the first Lunalilo Home (1881) in conjunction with Robert Lishman.

George M. Yamada

Born in Kanagawa-ken, Japan in 1878, George M. Yamada came to Hawaii in 1885 with his parents. He attended the Royal School on Emma Street and was a graduate of Honolulu High School. Early in his career he was the official Japanese interpreter in the circuit and federal courts of Honolulu.

In 1901 he teamed up with Kikutaro Matsumoto and Shoichi Yokomizo to form the Hawaiian-Japanese Ballasting Company when Captain Henry Evans left the Hawaiian Ballasting company. Yamada later opened his own contracting business and first advertised in 1910.

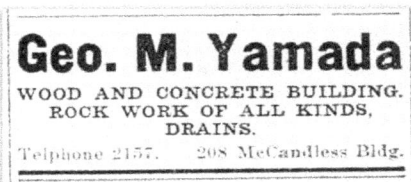

He built the "mini" Mendonça Building (1913), perhaps the S.M. Iida Store (1912), Aala Market (1919), Sperry Flour Building in Hilo (1920), and he also demolished the old Opera House (c.1921).

Clifford Young

Clifford Fai Young was born in Honolulu in 1917 and earned degrees in architecture from the University of Michigan and M.I.T. He initially worked with McAuliffe & Young and Alfred Preis, and opened his own office in 1953. Young designed the United Chinese Society Building remodel (1954), the United Church of Christ (1955), Pearl Harbor Memorial Community Church (1958), and the Kuan Yin Temple (1961). He also worked with I.M. Pei on the East-West Center at the University of Hawaii.

Young served in World War II, Korea and Vietnam, and was a military observer at Yenan in China in 1946 where he often dined with Mao Zedong.

James C.M. Young

Born in Honolulu, "Jimmy" C.M. Young was a graduate of St. Louis High School and the University of Illinois, and was the president of Park Associates, Inc. He designed the impressive gateway and main pavilion at the Manoa Chinese Cemetery, the Lung Doo Building (1965), and the remodels in 1994 of the Ying Leong Look Funn and Sam Chew Lau buildings on Kekaulike Street.

John Mason Young

John Mason Young was born in Tennessee in 1874, and after serving in the Spanish American War he earned two masters degrees in engineering from Cornell University. In 1908 he came to Hawaii to be professor of engineering at what would become the University of Hawaii, and at the same time he also started the Pacific Engineering Company. When he retired from the university in 1940 he was the last of the original thirteen faculty members.

In addition to planning and engineering buildings on the university campus, Young built Castle Hall at Punahou School, the Theo H. Davies block, the Empire Theatre, the S.M. Damon Building, the Christian Science Church on Punahou Street, and designed the 1930 remodel of the Mendonça Building on Smith Street.

Z. Sugihara & Company

Zenkichi Sugihara was born in Hiroshima-Ken, Japan, and went to Kaua'i in 1890 with his wife Taki to work on a sugar plantation near Kapaa. When their three-year contract was finished, they moved to Honolulu where he partnered with Risuke Miyata in the contracting firm of R. Miyata & Company. In April 1915, shortly before Miyata's death, he bought the company and renamed it to Z. Sugihara & Company.

In addition to this building plus many houses, he also built the Japanese Hospital in 1917, known today as the Kuakini Medical Center. He was also president of the Honolulu Building and Lumber Company, Ltd. In 1925 he retired from the Z. Sugihara Company and turned it over to his son Edwin.

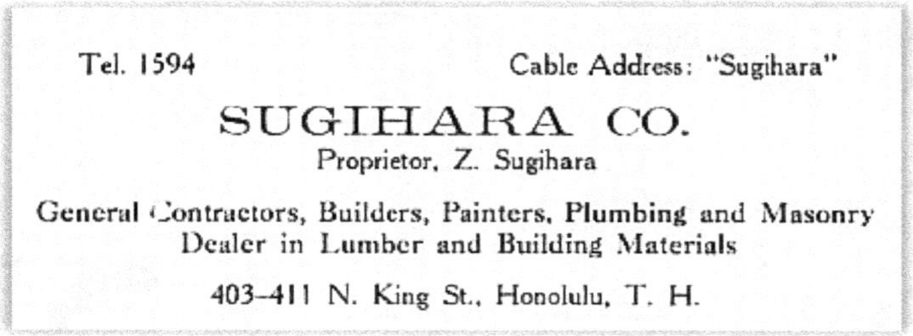

Tel. 1594   Cable Address: "Sugihara"

SUGIHARA CO.
Proprietor, Z. Sugihara

General Contractors, Builders, Painters, Plumbing and Masonry
Dealer in Lumber and Building Materials

403–411 N. King St., Honolulu, T. H.

BUILDING and General Contracting
Dealers in Building Materials.
Labor furnished by day or week.

Z. SUGIHARA & CO.
Store and office at
Palama Jct.   Phone 1594

STREETS – "ALANUI"

Chinatown was never officially platted or laid out as a subdivision – streets were first superimposed on the existing jumble of ancient land ownership in 1838, with major additions and realignments added after the 1886 fire.

Andrew Bloxam, the naturalist on the HMS *Blonde* remarked in 1825,

> "The streets are formed without order or regularity. Some of the huts are surrounded by low fences or wooden stakes ... As fires often happen the houses are all built apart from each other. The streets or lanes are far from being clean ...".

The early streets were known as "Alanui" which translates as "large path".

Toward the end of 1837 the *Hawaiian Gazette* newspaper began campaigning for proper streets and the government responded in late January of 1838. Kīnau declared "I shall widen the streets in our city and break up some new places to make five streets on the length of the land, and six streets on the breadth of the land". She tasked her husband, Governor Mataio Kekūanāoʻa, to straighten and widen the paths into streets.

But it was not without controversy, as many fences, walls, and even houses had to be torn down to make way for the new roads. English residents mostly opposed the new roadwork and Americans mostly supported it, but the gangs of Hawaiian laborers seemed to take "a little too much delight in the destruction of foreigners' property".

After the staking of the Pearl River Road (which would later be known as Chapel Street, Church Street and finally King Street) took out a long string of buildings owned by foreigners, missionary leader Hiram Bingham got involved as did Captain John Meek and Eliab Grimes, and they argued and assisted in minimizing further destruction.

At this time the boundaries of Honolulu were the harbor, Nuʻuanu Stream, Beretania Street, and Alakea Street. The rock walls along the large 30-acre Pa Uhi yam field determined the alignments of Nuʻuanu, King, Beretania and Alakea streets.

These first streets were dirt streets, and if there were sidewalks they were made of wooden planks. Beretania Street between "Smith's Bridge" on Nuʻuanu Stream and Richards Street was first macadamized in 1882.

The streets were officially named by the Privy Council on August 30, 1850. At that same meeting they also officially named the City of Honolulu and made it the capital of the kingdom.

After the 1886 fire the city realized they needed more streets and wider streets.

- Hotel Street was extended towards Nuʻuanu Stream from Maunakea Street.
- Kekaulike Street was created between Queen (Nimitz) and Hotel streets, and although there was talk of extending it to Beretania Street it never happened.
- Nuʻuanu Street was widened from Hotel Street to Beretania Street in 1902.
- Pauahi Street was created between Nuʻuanu Street and River Street.
- Queen Street (Nimitz) was extended along the waterfront from Nuʻuanu Street.
- River Street was created in 1896 after the re-alignment and channelization of Nuʻuanu Stream.
- Smith's Lane was straightened and widened from Beretania to King streets.

During the 1960's there was talk of major widening of King and Nuʻuanu streets, but luckily it never happened.

1896 Land Ownership Map (before the re-alignment of Nuʻuanu Stream)

STREET SCENES THEN & NOW

Nuʻuanu Street mauka from Hotel Street

1883

Nuʻuanu Street mauka from Hotel Street

c.1902

2021

Hotel Street ewa from Nuʻuanu Street

1899

2021

Nuʻuanu Street makai from Beretania Street

1900

2021

Maunakea and Pauahi streets, ewa/makai corner

1900

2021

Maunakea Street mauka from King Street

c.1890

2021

Nu'uanu Street near Pauahi Street

1900

2021

Maunakea Street from Beretania Street

c.1899

2021

Maunakea and Pauahi streets, makai/waikiki corner

1899

2021

Nuʻuanu Street makai at Hotel Street

c.1885

2021

Smith Street mauka from Pauahi Street

1890

2021

Beretania Street ewa from Nuʻuanu Street

1900

2021

Pauahi Street at Nuʻuanu Street

1900

2021

HONOLULU CHINATOWN

Hotel Street at Nuʻuanu Street

1888

2021

River Street and Pauahi Street, mauka/waikiki corner

1899

2021

Smith and Pauahi streets, mauka/ewa corner

1899

2021

Smith Street mauka from Hotel Street

1900

2021

Hotel Street ewa from Nuʻuanu Street

1877

1900

Hotel Street ewa from Nuʻuanu Street

2021

Nuʻuanu Street above Hotel Street

1900

2021

Pauahi Street from River Street

c.1920's

2021

Maunakea Street mauka at Beretania Street

1900

2021

Hotel Street ewa from Smith Street

c.1885

2021

Pauahi Street between Nuʻuanu and Smith streets

December 31, 1899

2021

Nuʻuanu Street mauka at King Street

1881 / 1903

Nuʻuanu Street at King Street

1957

2021

Maunakea Street makai from near Pauahi Street

c.1906

2021

Smith Street at Beretania Street

1900

2021

Maunakea from Hotel Street

c.1890

2021

BERETANIA STREET

The Hawaiianized spelling of "Britain".

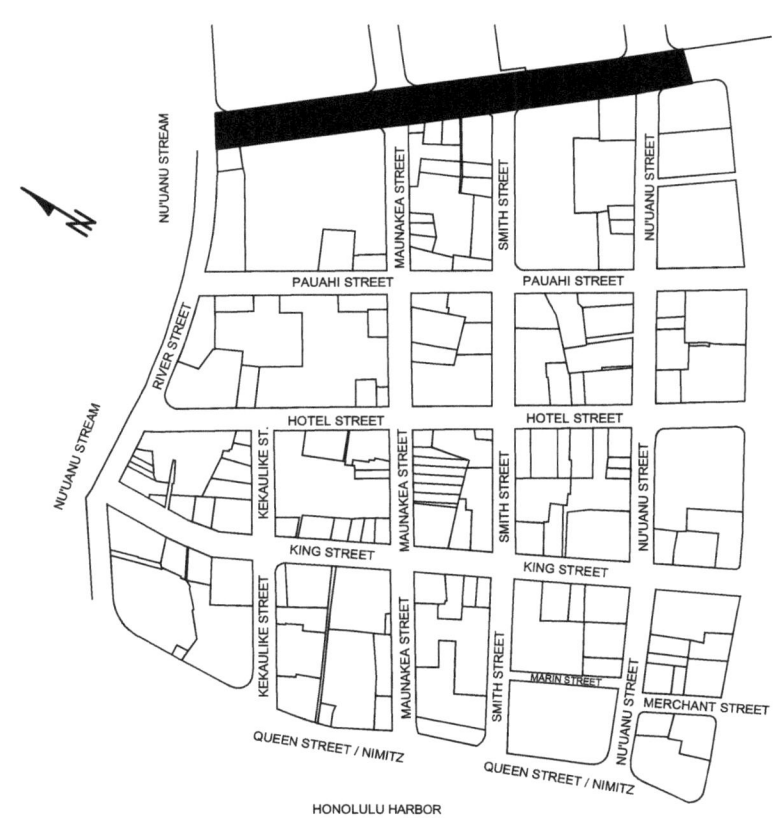

HONOLULU AUTO SUPPLY BUILDING

59-63 N. Beretania / 1198 Smith
1903
Architect / Builder: Pang Chong

c.1917

Chinese building contractor Pang Chong took out a 40-year lease on this corner from Reverend R. Maka and the Board of the Hawaiian Evangelical Association on November 21, 1902 and hired bricklayer Jacob Schuermann to build this building in 1903. Pang Chong had just purchased the ruins of Kaumakapili Church, so this building is very likely built with bricks salvaged from the church which was right across the street.

But he didn't hold it long – the property was sold in a Sheriff's auction in March 1903 along with his interest in the Yee Sing Tai Company for non-payment of rent, and Scheurmann had to file a mechanics lien for his unpaid work. Early tenants included a Japanese Macaroni Factory and a plumbing shop. In 1917, dentist D.H. Kurisaki rented upstairs.

From 1917 to 1943 it was home to the Honolulu Auto Supply Company, with Kaoru Fujiwara as company president. They were the local agent for Chandler cars and Dunlop tires and provided a full range of automobile accessories.

Before the 1900 fire, the building on the corner was a coffee shop in 1891 and a general merchandise store in 1899, and in 1899 the building next to it on Beretania sold tin merchandise.

In 1851 the office of Honolulu's first permanent dentist – Dr. John Mott-Smith – was on this corner.

HONOLULU TOWER

60 N. Beretania
1982
Architect / Builder: Norman Lacayo, James K. Tsugawa / Charles Pankow Associates

This 41-story, 395-unit condominium project was built in 1982 by CAP Development Corporation and included "nearly an acre of lush landscaping". It was part of Block F of the Kukui Redevelopment Urban Renewal Project.

Previously this site was a jumbled collection of tenements constructed after the 1900 fire that filled the block bounded by Nuʻuanu, Beretania, River, and Kukui streets. Maunakea Street did not extend mauka of Beretania Street until 1970.

Here is what the streetscape looked like in January 1900, right before the big fire:

On the left, the building housed a Japanese massage business, and it is located right in the middle of the future Maunakea Street. The twin spires of Kaumakapili Church are barely visible in the photograph on the far right.

Kaumakapili Church

This was the first location of Kaumakapili Church, known as "The Native's Church".

Shortly after the start of construction of Kawaiahaʻo Church near the Royal Palace and the Mission Houses in 1836 there was a petition to Hiram Bingham to establish a second church or mission "in the village" for the common people of Honolulu.

Chief Abner Pākī and his wife, Kōnia (the parents of Princess Bernice Pauahi Bishop, the founder of Kamehameha School) granted the land for the church at the western end of town in the Kaumakapili area since there were approximately 13,000 people living there.

Reverend Lowell Smith moved across the street in December 1837 and opened a school where he initially held church services. With the assistance of the new congregation he built a huge 60' x 125' adobe church building with 3-foot-thick walls, a high-pitched thatched roof, and a 7-foot wide veranda all around the outside, at a cost of $3,000.

They had big plans – it was built to accommodate 2,500 people while the congregation numbered about 400 when the building was dedicated on August 29, 1839. Reverend Smith administered the sacrament using a ball of taro and sweetened water as substitutes for bread and wine.

The old adobe church was torn down in 1881 to make way for the new brick church. King Kalākaua suggested an impressive building with two steeples, saying "a man has two arms, two eyes, two ears, two legs, therefore, a church ought to have two steeples."

It was designed by Charles J. Wall, and the cornerstone was laid on September 2, 1881, by Princess Liliʻuokalani on her birthday.

The first steeple was completed in October 1884, and Fred Harrison completed the second steeple in September 1885. It took 7 years and $65,000, and the church was finally dedicated on Sunday June 10, 1888.

During the bubonic plague in 1900 many people stored their valuables in the church basement while various buildings and blocks were being burned by the Board of Health.

On January 20, the fire department was burning some infected buildings behind the church when the wind suddenly changed direction and began to blow with a ferocious intensity.

Although they tried valiantly to keep sparks away from the church, one of the steeples caught fire out of reach of their hoses. The steeple burned like a giant sparkler and the wind sent flaming embers all across Chinatown. People tried in vain to put out all the fires on the building rooftops, but they were no match for the wind and the rapidly raging fire.

Much to everyone's dismay, the church was quickly engulfed in flames and was a total loss, as was much of Chinatown.

The church bells were later found in the ruins "utterly broken, melted and destroyed".

After standing for nearly two years, in November 1901 the ruins were sold to Chinese contractor Pang Chong for $2,735, to be removed and hauled away within four months.

The land was traded to the Bishop Estate for a new church lot in Palama, and C.Q. Yee Hop and K. Matsumoto quickly built wooden tenements and cottages on the old church site.

One of the many casualties of the 1900 fire was this magnificent Bevington & Sons (London) pipe organ with 26 ranks, 1274 pipes, two rows of keys, 32 stops and a full set of pedals.

It was completed in London May 16, 1887, with a test recital by Dr. J. Frederick Bridge, the organist of Westminster Abbey, with Queen Kapiolani in attendance.

The organ cost the congregation the enormous sum of $4,500. It arrived on the bark *Min* on January 13, 1888, and the first public performance was on April 7, 1888.

The organist was Wray Taylor and the first piece played was one of his compositions – "The Kaumakapili March in F".

ROBERTS BUILDING

65-69 N. Beretania
1991
Architect / Builder: Gilman K.M. Hu / Command Construction Co.

1900

This building, completed in 1991, was designed by Gilman K.M. Hu. It replaced a 2-story wooden store built c.1906, which in turn replaced a 2-story wooden store housing a tailor and a barber that was deliberately burned along with the entire block on January 16, 1900 by the Board of Health.

The c.1906 building originally housed a carpenter and a barber, with residences above and a kitchen behind. In 1935 it was the Boston Liquor Store owned by Philip N. Sing, and in 1940 it became the long-time home of the Naturotone Radio Mart owned by T.C. Lee.

In the 1970's, Gifts International, a Mexican curio store was located here, and in the 1980's it was the United Home Video Center which was busted for pirating Cantonese-dialect movies.

The ad on the right came out on December 7, 1941, and that radio was likely one of many broadcasting the attack on Pearl Harbor and its aftermath.

Architect **Gilman K.M. Hu** was born in China and graduated with a degree in architecture from St. Louis University. He partnered with Arthur A. Kohara and designed the Governor Cleghorn condominium in Waikiki. He was also President of the local chapter of the Construction Specifications Institute (CSI).

ARITA BUILDING

73-77 N. Beretania
1914
Architect / Builder: unknown / Saiichi Arita?

1900

This blue stone building was constructed in 1914 by Saiichi Arita and Henrietta Fishel. She and her husband Charles owned a general merchandise store in the Irwin Block on Nuʻuanu Street, and they bought this property in 1897 and likely built the 2-story frame building in the photograph taken in 1900. The stone building was completed in June 1914 with materials from City Mill. Arita was from Kumamoto-ken, Japan, and he had been burned out of his previous location at 1178-1180 Maunakea Street. In 1924, despondent over business losses, Arita committed hari-kari.

From 1914 to the mid 1930's the upstairs was a bath house operated by Saiichi Arita and later Hiroshi Sato, plus the photography studio of M. Takamiya. In 1915 the first floor housed the grocery store of Seu Tin Chong and a taxi and auto stand.

ROOMS in the Arita Bldg., just completed. Beretania St., near Maunakea. 9928

The Ideal Shop was here in the 1920's, advertising it was "the place to buy your fruit ice cream". In 1933 it became the Sing Sing Meat Market, and Yee's Market in 1938 owned by Yee Leong Foon formerly with C.Q. Yee Hop & Co.

Wimpy's Café relocated here in 1949 after 15 years at 127 N. Beretania. Owned by Satoyoshi "Henry" Shumizo and his wife Janet, it was likely named after J. Wellington Wimpy, the cartoon character who loved hamburgers and was first introduced in the popular "Popeye" comic strip in 1929. Like many of the restaurants in the 1930's and 1940's they actively sponsored a local baseball team. They also sponsored a bowling team and trophy tournaments at the Honolulu Japanese Golf Club. Wimpy's Restaurant was here for over 30 years.

BARMAID WANTED
Japanese preferred.
Apply in person.
WIMPY'S CAFE
79 N. Beretania

In 1979 it housed Club Hanako with Hawaiian pupus and entertainment, and in the 1980's became Club Hinode with "beautiful girls" and live entertainment. The building was rehabilitated in 2010 and was designed with the option of adding a stepped-back third floor at some point in the future.

HAI ON TONG BUILDING

83-89 N. Beretania
c.1902
Architect / Builder: Pang Chong??

1900

"Ocean Safe Hall"

The longtime home of Sharon's Maunakea Leis, this building was the clubhouse for the Hai On Tong, the Chinese Seamen's Guild, a benevolent society for Chinese steamship workers.

In 1906 it housed a tailor on the first floor, rooms on the second, and a joss house (Chinese temple) on the third floor. It was built on the site of a general merchandise store that was burned when the Board of Health torched the entire block on January 16, 1900.

One of the few 3-story buildings in early Chinatown, a notable feature is the tall flagpole on top. But it wasn't for flying the Hawaiian flag or American flag – this was very likely the "the Maunakea flagpole" used for announcing Che-Fa gambling results.

In 1977 the building was purchased and restored by Sharon and Howard Lum using federal restoration funds channeled through the State Historic Preservation Office. They received a Historic Hawaii Preservation Award for their efforts in 1980. It has been Sharon's Maunakea Lei shop since 1974.

Sharon's is one of many lei shops in Chinatown with workers stringing flowers within sight of the sidewalk. Someone once asked about the secrets of making a lei last more than a few hours, and they were told "don't try - a lei is a gift to honor a person or an occasion, meant to be temporary and enjoyed for the moment."

CHINATOWN CULTURAL PLAZA

100 N. Beretania
1974
Architect / Builder: Daniel Mann Johnson & Mendenhall, Peter Hsi Associates, Park Associates, Wong & Wong Associates, Au Cutting Smith & Haworth, Cannell & Chaffin / Hawaiian Dredging & Construction Company

In 1962 the city began planning for a central Chinese cultural site for the 27 Chinese societies impacted by the Kukui Redevelopment Project. The stated goal was:

"To provide sufficient land and opportunity for the return of the cultural, fraternal and religious institutions necessary to serve the residential population. The societies have real historical significance which at present is quite strongly supported. All indications are that with a modernization of their programs they can play a significant and positive role in the community.

Clarence T. C. Ching was the chairman of the Joint Committee on Chinatown Renewal. The United Chinese Society, the Chinese Chamber of Commerce, and the five largest societies hired nationally known architect John Carl Warnecke in 1965 to plan the Cultural Plaza on Block E of the Kukui Redevelopment Area which mostly consisted of 1-story and 2-story wooden tenements, a few society halls, and the Mun Lun Chinese School.

Warnecke's plan proved too expensive at over $40M, so a $11M plan was created for the 4.4-acre site by the local office of Daniel Mann Johnson & Mendenhall (DMJM). The new plan included 70 shops and restaurants, two Chinese schools and four Chinese societies – Kuo Ming Tan, Leong Doo, Chee Kung Tong, and Lung Doo – plus a 5-story public parking garage. Groundbreaking was July 1, 1972.

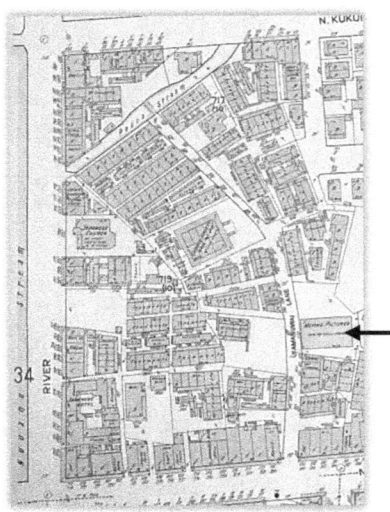 

Dotted lines show site of Cultural Plaza development in Downtown Honolulu.

About half of the project is built on reclaimed land. Before 1896, Nuʻuanu Stream ran through the site and "Smith's Bridge" would have been located about 150' ewa of the intersection of Maunakea and Beretania streets.

After the 1900 fire, the block quickly filled up with a maze of 1-story and 2-story wooden tenements that were all condemned by the city in 1961. Kamanuwai Lane, only 20' wide, was located about 70' ewa of present-day Maunakea Street before it was removed when Maunakea Street was extended to Kukui Street in 1970.

As early as 1914 there was a 1-story metal building with "moving pictures" at 1229 Kamanuwai Lane (indicated by the arrow). From 1947 to 1961 the Beretania Theater was the site of Honolulu's first burlesque theater, the Beretania Follies, owned by William C. Ferreira.

It had 300 seats and at its peak had 5 "girlesque" shows a day. Featured performers included "Tempest Storm", the "Queen of Quiver", and "The Original Sweater Girl".

The Beretania Follies had a large flashing neon sign with a "lewd and lascivious" nude that could be seen from as far away as the harbor.

After condemnation in 1961 the theater continued to show art movies until 1967. The building was finally demolished in 1969.

HALE PAUAHI (HALE LAHUI, HALE O'PILI)

101-163 N. Beretania
1987
Architect / Builder: Kajioka Okada & Partners / Pacific Construction Corp.

Built by the city through the Pauahi Block A Non-profit Housing Corporation with Community Development Block Grant Funds from the US Department of Housing and Urban Development (HUD). This was a $33M project with 396 rental units plus a 593-space parking garage and two towers: "Hale Lahui" translates to "house of many people of all races", and "Hale O'Pili" is "house of people gathering together". Here is what was along the street in 1900:

In the 1930's, the Reno Dance Hall with the Ritz Rooms brothel upstairs was located where the left half of the parking garage sits today. It later became the Caliente Ballroom, the Paradise Club, the Ligaya Ballroom, and the New Crystal Ballroom.

FONG BUILDING

171-175 N. Beretania, 1197 River
1923
Architect / Builder: Saiki & Davenport

Before 1896, this site was part of the mudflats on the far side of the Nu'uanu Stream. Built on land reclaimed after the straightening of the stream in 1896, the first building here housed the Wing Wo Sang Coffee Saloon and the store of Mow Lung in 1899.

Saiki & Davenport (Richard Davenport and Masataro Saiki) built this building in 1923, replacing a 3-story wooden building built after the 1900 fire. They also officed here until 1927 and were big promoters of hollow concrete building tile.

Saiki & Davenport also built the Siu Building (1926), Lum Yip Kee Building on Maunakea Street (1926), the Sumida Building (1927) and the Oahu Theater (1927).

This building was later the offices of the Cooperative Finance Company which specialized in loans to Japanese. It has also housed the Kyodo Finance Company, the Charm Beauty Shop, Asato Insurance, and United Furniture.

The city purchased the building as part of the Pauahi Redevelopment Project and sold it to Beatrice Ng Oka with conditions in 1980.

HOTEL STREET

Named for the Warren Hotel opened in the 1820's by Major William K. Warren on the mauka side of Hotel Street where Bethel Street crosses today. Major Warren came to Hawaii before the missionaries arrived and left for California in February 1838.

The section ewa of Maunakea was a small lane called Theater Lane until Hotel Street was extended in 1887.

For much of the 1900's Hotel Street was the main entertainment street in Honolulu.

Hotel Street was converted to a bus-only transitway in 1982 as a temporary measure toward the eventual creation of the Hotel Street Mall which was to be a permanent pedestrian mall with street furniture as part of Mayor Eileen Anderson's Downtown Revitalization Program. It is still a bus-only street today.

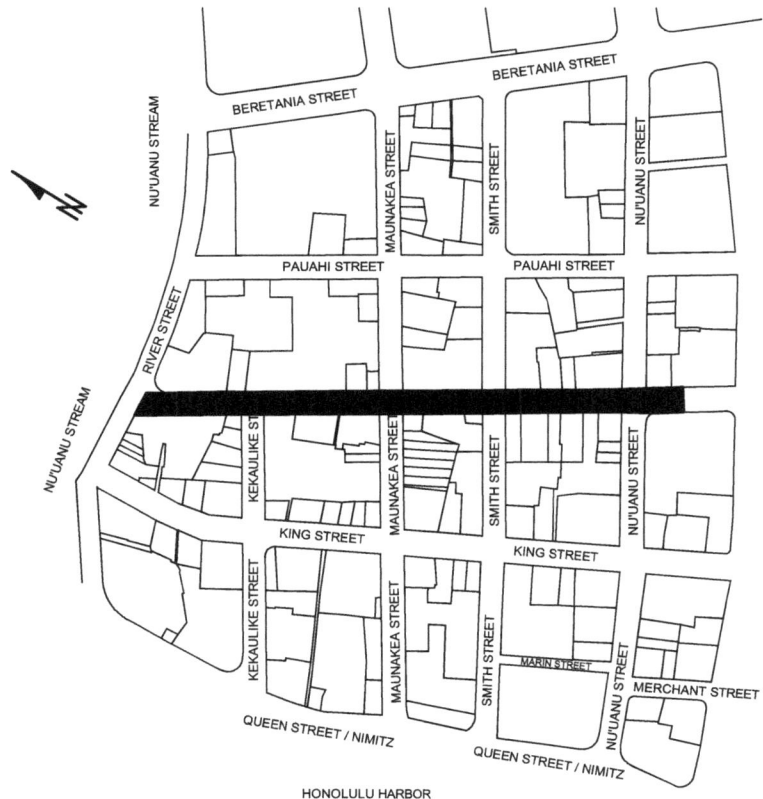

EMPIRE SALOON / HOFFMAN CAFÉ (SITE)
1 S. Hotel
(1886)
(Architect / Builder: Robert Lishman)

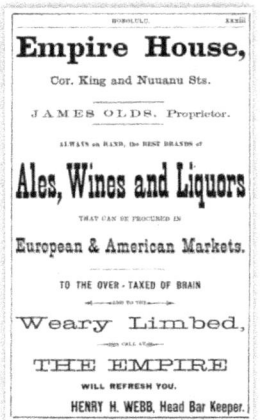

The Hawaiian Gazette newspaper first mentions the Empire Saloon on this corner in 1870. A favorite hangout of sailors, its specialty was "pineapple cocktails".

It burned in the 1886 fire and proprietor James Olds hired architect and builder Robert Lishman, the supervising architect for Ali'iolani Hale in 1874, to build a new 1-story brick building on the corner (pictured on the right).

From 1899 to 1908 it was known as the Hoffman Saloon, serving Bavarian Beer and Olympus Beer on tap, adding the Hoffman Chop House in 1907 to serve food. In 1908 they renovated the bar and hired the manager of the saloon on the opposite corner who brought the name "Encore Saloon" with him.

In 1911, Little Sing opened the Hoffman Café on Hotel Street next to the saloon. It was open all night with "Best Meal in City, 25¢". It was purchased by Fu Wah and Chin Hoy in 1914 and lost its Red Cross safety certification in 1916 when it was deemed "the worst conducted and most insanitary" of the 23 restaurants in Honolulu.

By the late teens it was owned by Ching Hin-Yee and was subsequently owned by three generations of the Ching family. Ching Hin-Yee came to Honolulu in the 1880's from On-Ding village, Nam-Long, Chungshan district, Kwangtung province in China. Under his ownership the Hoffman Café became one Honolulu's top restaurants.

The interior was remodeled and modernized in 1938 in seven different shades of green. It had one of the largest wooden bars in the Territory, built by the K. Fujii Carpenter Shop, and it featured live Hawaiian music every night.

In the 1930's they sponsored a champion softball team, and The Hoffman was also the home of Joseph Doyle's Bartending School with a diploma guaranteed in three months. The Hoffman's signature cocktail was the Waldorf Gin Fizz. Eddie Ching Wan was also owner of South Seas Restaurant in Waikiki from 1939 to 1960.

The Hoffman Café building was purchased by the city in 1969 and demolished for a parking lot in 1970.

The photograph on the left is from 1888 and shows the brand new Perry Block with the 1886 Empire Saloon on the right. The photograph on the right shows that same corner c.1880, before the 1886 fire, looking makai.

(You'll just have to imagine the seven shades of green).

HONOLULU CHINATOWN

SMITH'S UNION BAR

15-19 N. Hotel
c.1904
Architect / Builder: Z. Yashida?

This building is not in a 1903 photograph of Hotel Street but does appear on the 1906 Dakin Fire Insurance Map, so it was built sometime in between, possibly by Z. Yashida who took out a building permit in 1904 for a 1-story brick building on Hotel Street.

In 1885 there were two 2-story wooden tea stores on the site that were burned in the 1886 fire. Vacant in 1891, by 1899 there was a small stone barber shop on the left and a wooden building housing a shooting gallery on the right. There was a shooting gallery in this brick building until at least 1927. Targets were 40' away and a bell rang when a bullseye was hit.

The Germania Shooting Gallery was owned by T.H. Thone, described as "a big husky fellow" who obviously enjoyed shooting – on April 29, 1901, he fired four shots at his quarrelsome father-in-law. Thone was arrested and fined and put on probation, but later that same year he threatened to shoot G.W. Ahoy affiliated with the Chinese store next door.

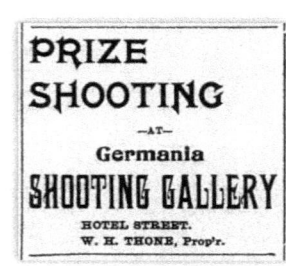

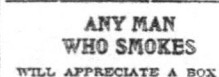

A cigar shop, the Nam Chong Company, was on the left side from 1922 to 1928, and that space was United Jewelers for 45 years, from 1939 to 1984.

The right side was briefly Max Finkel's clothing store, and from 1934 to 1939 was Joe Holley's Café. Joe Holley was originally from West Virginia and was a US Army sergeant in World War I. He later came to Hawaii, married Virginia Ornellas in 1919, and worked as a "motorman" with the Honolulu Rapid Transit & Land Company.

Holley opened his café in 1934, and in February, 1939, Antone Henriques and Joseph S. Ornellas became the owners. Three months later Ralph C. Smith replaced Henriques as co-owner and it was renamed Smith's Union Bar. By 1943 the partnership was Joseph S. Ornellas and James S.B. Ing. Holley's son, Leroy, later owned the bar and was married to one of the bartenders.

Smith's Union Bar is a favorite watering hole for merchant seamen and survivors of the USS Arizona, and claims to be Honolulu's oldest bar.

BICKERTON BLOCK / HUBBA HUBBA

21-25 N. Hotel
1886
Architect / Builder: George Lucas

The most famous business in this building started off as a sandwich shop and quickly devolved into a showplace – from live cowboy hillbilly music to "strippers galore". But the buildings early tenants were far less exotic.

This 2-story brick building was built by George Lucas in 1886 for Supreme Court Judge Richard Bickerton, replacing the 2-story wooden buildings here that were destroyed in the 1886 Chinatown fire. It housed two general merchandise stores in 1891 and 1899.

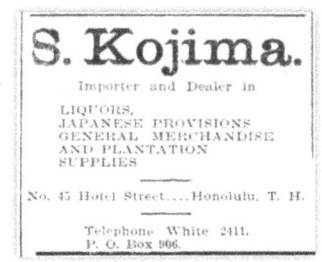

From 1900 to 1905 the S. Kojima store was at 25 N. Hotel on the right. They were one of the largest dealers in Japanese provisions and general merchandise and specialized in plantation orders and importing rice from Japan. K. Yamamoto, the manager, bought the business in 1905 and continued here until 1910.

On the left side, 21 N. Hotel Street was the Lee Choy photography studio from 1929 to 1932, the King's China Jade Mart in 1941, and the Diamond Barber shop from 1943 to 1949 which also included photo shops and arcade amusements. In a harbinger of things to come, they were fined in 1946 for having "Panoram" machines that showed indecent photographs.

In the 1940's, upstairs were the offices for the Bartenders' Union & Culinary Alliance, the Hotel, Restaurant Employees and Bartenders Association, and the Marine Fireman, Oilers, Watertenders and Wipers Association.

From 1933 to 1938, 25 N. Hotel Street was the Green Front Café, owned by Clyde C. Hopkins and later William A. Mulcahey, and then Herbert Lyle Bloemen. It was called Frank's Place (for J.D. Frank Baynard) in 1938.

In 1939 "Buck" Buxton opened Buck's Mickey Mouse café, featuring "Bunny Ranch" triple-decker sandwiches. By 1943, Buxton's plant on Keawe Street made 80,000 sandwiches a day.

In 1935, John Riuichi "Jack" Matsuoka from Hiroshima opened the Aloha Café at 221 N. Queen Street near the train station, and he relocated it to 25 N. Hotel Street in 1940.

In addition to the Aloha Café, the space also hosted the Indoor Gift & Curio shop, followed by the New Indoor Gift & Curio shop (owned by Peggy J. Brandon and Rachel K.C. King), the Rainbow Foto Shop, and June's Sweet Shop owned by family members Shigeru and June Matsuoka.

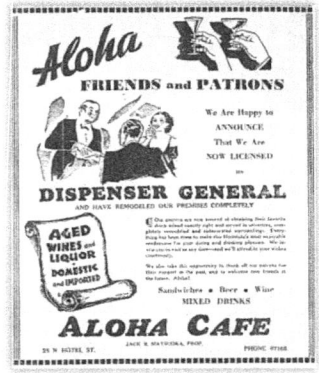

Although the phrase "hubba hubba" had been in circulation for a few years, it was made popular by American servicemen and Bob Hope during World War II, and also by the singing of Perry Como and Martha Stewart in the 1945 movie *Doll Face*.

You can hear and see their dance routine here:

In 1946, Jack Matsuoka took out a building permit for $5,000 and renamed his new restaurant Café Hubba Hubba.

There was a major renovation in 1950 inside and out that also added a much larger room and dance hall in back, and in 1954 he added his children, Shizuko, Takeo and Tadami, to the license and renamed it Club Hubba Hubba.

The café had featured full meals with live music, often by cowboy bands, but the club featured live dancers and quickly went fully into burlesque.

By 1953 there were evening shows at 9, 10:30, 12 and 1:30, with Wilma Wescott as the "femcee". There was dancing between shows and until closing at 3am, with music by George Burgie's Trio. No cover, no minimum.

In 1962 one of the exotic dancers shot and killed her former cop ex-husband at the club. The bar stayed open, and everyone continued drinking.

The inside of the club was red and black with a large semi-circular stage with a Plexiglas catwalk lit underneath with lights. A dancer once asked the night manager for a glass of water and got the reply, "get a customer to buy it for you."

Episodes of the original *Hawaii 5-0* and *Magnum PI* TV series were filmed at the club, plus the movie *Byrds of Paradise*.

In the latter days the club was described as "grossly accented with the miasma of stale beer, cigarette smoke, roach spray, cheap perfume and Pine-Sol". Many of the dancers lived upstairs in small rooms with a shared shower and a small kitchen that had "an old stove, a washing machine and tar-paper flooring".

Club Hubba Hubba finally closed in 1996, and after years of being vacant the building was restored by Mason Architects in 2010. The neon sign, originally made by Robert "Bozo" Shigemura was restored by Von Monroe and given special planning permission to remain on the building. Shigemura was the "bender" who also made the neon signs for the Hawaii Theater Marquee and the Wo Fat Chop Sui Restaurant.

What would Judge Bickerton have thought of dancer Tanya Tata's "Biggest Chest in the Midwest" at 60KK-24-36?

The evolution of Café/Club Hubba Hubba in four ads:

1949

1954

1955

1960

MENDONÇA & SELIG BUILDING

24-26 N. Hotel
1886
Architect / Builder: C. Kavanagh

This building was built by C. Kavanagh and it closely matches the George Lucas buildings on the right. Joseph P. Mendonça and S. Selig owned the lot, and the building was completed in late 1886, slightly before the buildings on the right.

S. Selig was associated with M.S. Grinbaum & Company, the first Jewish business to open in Hawaii, established in 1856 as an import export company.

In 1899 it housed the Harng Lung Kee general merchandise store which suffered a bad fire in 1899. By 1906 it was the warehouse for the Sayegusa store, and was later split up into two storefronts, 24 N. Hotel and 26 N. Hotel Street.

On the left side, City Contracting & Building Company was here in 1912, and from 1922 to 1925 it was the Tin Wo Cong On jewelry manufacturing company. There was a big opium den bust upstairs in 1922 in the room of a Chinese named Lai Tuck.

Chew Yow & Company was here in 1932, and from 1937 to 1946 it was the Lum Yun Store, a tailor shop owned by Chang Hin Lum.

From 1948 to 1955 it was the Robert & Company pawnshop, and there were gypsies operating out of the stairwell in 1965.

The history of this location took a big turn when it became the My Way Lounge in 1982 and then the Club Sahara in 1987. Club Sahara was owned by Helen Adachi, and it was fined $4000 in 1988 for lewd behavior between an exotic dancer and a customer, fined for selling liquor to minors on numerous occasions, and the hostess and manager were arrested for marijuana sales in 1990 at which time the license was revoked.

But it gets worse. The next occupant was the Paradise Lost club from 1991 to 2004, owned by Angeline Sung. In 1999 alone there were 150 police complaints for drugs, robberies, assaults, and sexual assaults. It was said to be "the hub of all drug distribution in the area", "a trash magnet", and "a classic nuisance establishment".

In 2004 Ms. Sung asked the Liquor Commission to cancel her license, saying she was "sick of it" and they agreed. But shortly thereafter she changed her mind and asked for the request to be rescinded. The commission said no.

The right side was much tamer, home to City Mercantile Company in 1915, owned by K.O. Kam, the offices of John Chong, OD, and from 1933 to 1947 it was The Pennant Shop who also made military chevrons.

INDEPENDENT THEATER

29-31 N. Hotel
1911
Architect / Builder: unknown

2021

After the 1886 fire this parcel was vacant until at least 1899, and from 1911 to 1927 it was the Independent Theatre owned by Isaac Crockett, Henry De Fries and John Froelicher.

Opening night featured a Wild West drama, a story about a shipwrecked man, and two "most laughable" farces, all shown on a special aluminum-coated screen. The show was attended by hundreds, lasted for one hour, and was "a good ten cents' worth from start to finish".

They also sponsored a contest to win a $850 Ford runabout that was displayed out front, with music by the Marine Band.

During the 1940's it was California Amusements, and later Maria-Ella Photos owned by Maria Yandell and Ella Freitas.

It was Brock's Amusements in 1954, and two years later when it was Al's Amusement the US Treasury Department raided and seized a Bally Ice Frolics pinball machine

In 1961, when it was Bartlett and Chang Amusements, William Sing Chang was arrested for a "pay off" in a pinball machine game. The amount of the payoff? 50 cents.

RISQUE THEATRE / BUFFUM'S HALL (SITE)

32-36 N. Hotel
c.1902
Architect / Builder: unknown

c.1880

This site has seen all types of entertainment over the years, high and low, from a future Supreme Court justice reading poetry to pornographic peepshows, in a place that at one time was frequented by Kamehameha IV, Queen Emma and other members of the royal family.

This is possibly the site of the c.1845 Robert Boyd grog shop called L'Ambuscade, but the first structure we know for sure was a large 2-1/2 story wooden building called Buffum's Hall that was here for 17 years from 1869 to 1886.

In the Sacramento Daily Union in 1866, Mark Twain wrote that **Dr. A.C. Buffum** had a growing practice in Honolulu, having recently come from San Francisco. Buffum was originally from New York state and had previously established a private hospital in California at Magalia for miners and as a mountain resort for invalids from the Valley.

After accumulating "a snug little fortune" he put it up for sale in 1865 and came to Hawaii and opened up a private practice serving mostly Native Hawaiians while serving as the Port Physician with the Board of Health.

Described as a "tall, sallow-looking man" who always rode a white horse, he bought this property in August 1869 and constructed Buffum's Temperance (or Templar) Hall which quickly became a premier venue for high-brow, cultured and refined entertainment with local and touring performers.

Events and performances included lectures, parlor magic, prestidigitation, escamotage, recitations, tableaux, dioramas, panoramas, minstrel shows, masquerade balls, elocutions, pantomimes, "tricks of legerdemain", quadrilles, dissolving views, church choirs, firemen's balls, Lancashire bell ringers, even "educated birds and mice". At one of the YMCA lecture nights, Sanford B. Dole, future Supreme Court Justice and President of the Republic of Hawaii, did a reading Irving's *Rip Van Winkle* which was unfortunately described as "rather lengthy and tedious".

On April 18, 1871, Dr. Buffum's medical license was revoked. He left for San Francisco three days later and never returned. He began to exhibit signs of general paralysis and a "cerebral disorder" and in 1874 was placed in the Insane Asylum in Stockton where he died a short time later on July 24, 1875, at about 40 years of age.

In May 1871, two gentlemen by the names of Williams and Wallace leased Buffum Hall on the off-nights for the Honolulu Skating Rink. Taking advantage of the recent invention of parlor skates and the current mainland craze, this was the first roller skating rink in Hawaii.

> "Old men, remembering the feats on ice of their boyhood days, now on rollers again feel the magical exhilaration of rapid motion, and ladies glide swiftly and gracefully about like sylphs."

After a month of practice runs, opening night was July 22, 1871, with Queen Emma in attendance, and it included a Grand March, Plain Quadrille, Lancers, Queen's Quadrille and Virginia Reel – *danced on skates!*

The last known performance in Buffum's Hall was Madame Cora in 1884.

In 1880 the building was owned by Achee and portrait painter Kin Hing had a studio here. A Chinese merchant named Apaii owned the building in 1881.

From 1884 to the 1886 fire, it was the Chinese grocery store of Sing Chong & Co. They also had a store at Nuʻuanu and Beretania streets, and after the fire built a large brick building at Maunakea and King streets in 1886.

In 1887 the empty lot was owned by Hermann Kockmann (Bishop of Olba) who sold the site at auction in 1891 to H. Focke of Hoffschlaeger & Company. By 1902 it was owned by J.P. Mendonça.

HONOLULU CHINATOWN

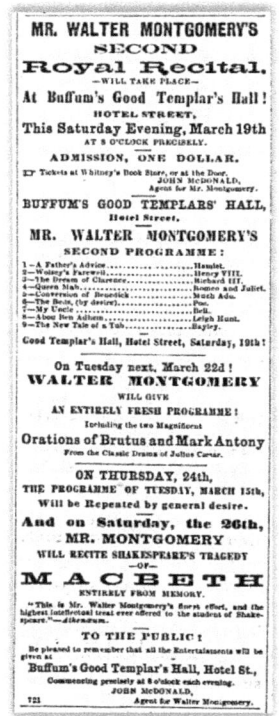

Walter Montgomery

Born in Long Island, NY, in 1827, and living in England, Walter Montgomery was a Shakespearean actor who was the first touring performer to play at Buffum's Hall in late March 1870. He toured America and Australia and married Laleah Burpee Bigelow upon his return to England. Two days later he shot himself.

Madame Cora

A renowned magicienne, Madame Cora de Lamond was the first female magician to tour Australia, New Zealand, and Hawaii. She performed legerdemain (slight-of-hand) Troublewit (paper-folding), mesmerism (hypnotism) and levitation, and would often give prizes to members of the audience, everything from silver tea sets to pickled vegetables.

One of her tricks consisted of a tableau called "The Couch of Angels" where she reclined in mid-air suspended only by her arm resting on a pole. In one performance at Buffum's she magically produced an engraved silver wreath which she presented to Queen Emma, who graciously accepted it and wore it in her hair.

Madame Cora played Buffum Hall in 1871 and 1884, and also toured China, Japan and India. Her real name was Ursula Bush, and she was once accused of murdering a young female vocalist in her troupe. She died in South Africa in 1902.

Madame Carandini

Marie Carandini was born in England in 1826 and married Jerome Carandini, the tenth marquis of Sarzano whose revolutionary activities got him exiled from Italy in 1835. They moved to Australia where she studied and sang opera at Sydney's Royal Victoria Theatre.

She was a popular performer at Buffum's Hall and played there many times in 1870, including a grand farewell concert on November 23 where every visitor received a free "carte de visite" from Madame Carandini herself.

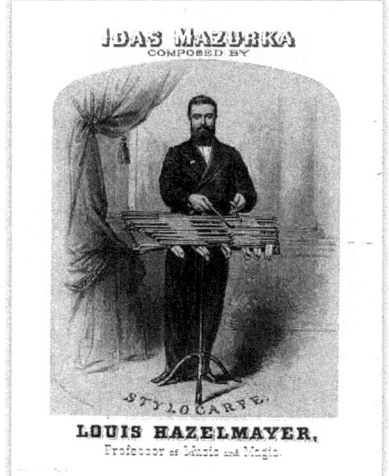

Professor Louis Hazelmayer

Called a "prestidigitator of unparalleled inventiveness", Louis Hazelmayer was born in Austria in 1838 and was performing magic shows for Austrian society by age 18. He studied chemistry, physics, drawing, and music, and invented a new musical instrument he called the Stylocarfe (similar to a xylophone) described by the *Sydney Morning Herald* as "constructed of wood and India rubber, and sounding like a dulcimer."

In 1868 he performed at the White House for President Andrew Johnson, and in October of 1871 he performed a series of shows at Buffum's Hall. The Hawaiian royal family attended at least 15 of his performances.

After Honolulu, "The Prince of Prestidigitators" went on an extended tour throughout New Zealand and Australia and South Africa before making it back to Vienna in 1876 where he "purchased a luxury villa in a fashionable district". He toured Australia and New Zealand again, including China, Siam, Japan, Delhi, and Calcutta, where he contracted malaria and died in 1885 at the age of 46.

The building here today was likely built in 1902, the same year general merchandise company Wing Wo Lung moved in. There were two Japanese merchandise firms here by 1906. T. Murakami Shoten was here from 1913 to 1917. The Honolulu Chop Sui House was at 32 N. Hotel Street from 1922 to 1940, with the Model Grocery at 34 N. Hotel.

From 1941 to 1961 it was the Trade Winds Café owned by Jerry Zucker, advertising "The Jiveiest Jazz in Town". The police briefly closed it down for "employing juveniles, contributing to delinquency of minors and common nuisance", charging the 18 employees including two girls under 16 who "danced and sang improper songs".

It was the Show Bar in 1964, featuring rhythm and blues from Rudy Hunter and the Fabulous Tones, plus a special show by the Apollas, stars of the popular *Shindig* TV show.

36 N. Hotel was the Honolulu Hat Store in 1922, and from 1937 to 1946 it was the Cut Rate Liquor Store owned by Chock Lun. He shared the space with William Lee who published the Hawaii Chinese Journal from 1938 to 1945. Albert & Mary Wong owned Liberty Liquors in that space from 1946 to 1952, and from 1960 to 1968 it was Sheena's Barber Shop owned by Jane Shinayo Santana.

The Risque Theatre

opened here on August 14, 1969, specializing in sexually oriented adult films. It initially had a large room downstairs with a big screen and film projectors just like a normal theater, but this was torn out and replaced with coin-operated single-person viewing booths.

The walls in the front room were covered with pornographic magazines for sale and they sold sex toys at the counter. A stairway just inside the door led upstairs to the Risque II Theatre which was the first gay adult theater in downtown Honolulu. There was a cashier upstairs and lockable private rooms with flat beds and porn on TV, plus one video projection room that seated about 25 people.

The whole taboo aspect made it very exciting to some and curious for others, especially young sailors who would try to sneak upstairs without being seen since being gay was not allowed in the military.

Religious groups often protested on the sidewalk outside in a mostly vain attempt to dissuade anyone from going inside.

The Risque Theatre was here for over 20 years, with the last newspaper ad in 1993.

On February 21, 2004, a huge four-alarm fire broke out in back of the Risque Bookstore and gutted the building. It also melted the neon off the sign on the front.

It has been The Manifest bar since 2009.

HONOLULU CHINATOWN

THE SWING CLUB

35-43-49 N. Hotel
1886
Architect / Builder: "Chinese builders"

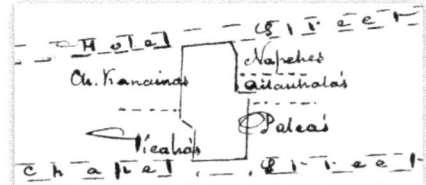

This building sits on what was once Meek Street, named after Captain John Meek who was given almost an acre of land between Hotel and Chapel (King) streets by Boki in 1820. Meek was a pilot who helped steer ships into Honolulu Harbor.

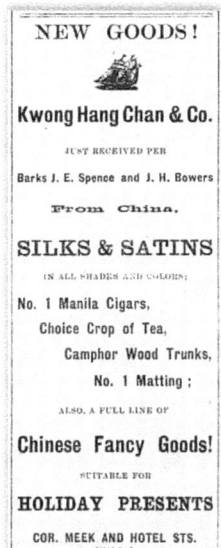

In 1884 he opened a paved asphalt street through the middle of the tract that connected Hotel and King streets. It was quickly filled with 2-story wooden shops and houses, mostly Chinese vendors of vegetables, ducks, chickens, and eggs, with a large Chinese Market at the corner on Hotel Street.

There was a Chinese employment office on Meek Street for anyone needing cooks, waiters, gardeners, laborers, or interpreters. There was also a large Chinese gambling den where one could hear the click of Chinese dominoes, "designed by rascally Chinese to rob their more-simple countrymen without a semblance of fair play".

The Kwong Hang Chan & Co. store was at the corner of Hotel and Meek streets, but it and everything else burned in the 1886 fire. Meek Street was abandoned and re-aligned with Smith's Lane, and was briefly called Konia Street until renamed Smith Street by 1900.

This building was built by "Chinese builders" in 1886 and when completed was "painted red and pencilled with white". There is a remnant of a decorative frieze in back. Kwong Hang Chan & Co. returned; they also had a store in Hong Kong.

This building was at the edge of the 1900 fire and was unaffected, but the buildings on the other three corners were completely destroyed.

There are three large stores in this building that front on Hotel Street: 35, 43 and 49 N. Hotel Street, plus a later addition (c.1906-1914) along Smith Street at the back of 49 N. Hotel Street.

35 N. Hotel

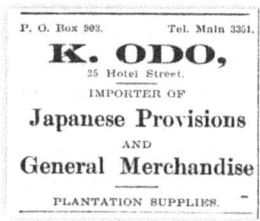

A general merchandise store was here in 1891 and 1899, and in 1901 the K. Odo store moved here from Maunakea Street after being burned out in the 1900 fire.

At some point the name officially changed to Odo Shoten and it was owned by T. Odo and A. Odo, presumably sons of K. Odo. The store was here until 1925.

The space was remodeled in 1931 by contractor K. Asakawa for the Taisho Printing Company, formerly at Nuʻuanu and Beretania streets, who were here for 10 years.

In 1942 it became the Victory Ltd café owned by Lee Po Hoon, which quickly turned into the Victory Amusement Center. There were literally dozens of places like this in Chinatown and particularly on Hotel Street to cater to the thousands of sailors and servicemen who came into town looking for entertainment.

These amusement centers typically featured a wide range of games of skill and of chance, billiard tables, barber shops, cafés, soda fountains, and sometimes shooting galleries, all attended to by attractive female hostesses.

Many also featured photo booths where a sailor could pay to have his picture taken with a hula girl. These were hugely popular souvenir items, and sometimes got a little carried away. At Victory Amusement in 1944, "hula poser" Mrs. Isabella Guzman Torres and the photographer (likely her husband) were arrested for "posing in an indecent manner" and fined $50. It had attracted 50 sailors so it must have been pretty good!

The T.K. Diner, owned by Roger K. Kaneshiro and Wallace K. Takara was here in 1946, and a year later it included the Manila Tattoo Shop, the Scoop Fountain owned by Madelaine Fo, and Johnnie's Photo owned by Johnnie Di Sopa and George Kavacevich.

In 1948 the upstairs was renovated and turned into Sweet's Ballroom, owned by Johnnie and Theresa Di Sopa. It had a huge neon sign out front and was a taxi dance hall where sailors could buy dances with female hostesses.

At that same time, the downstairs became Kilroy's Amusement, owned by Ralph Di Sopa and Angelo C. Vicari, two former merchant marine buddies who had been fined for gambling in 1944.

The back of Kilroy's suffered a fire in 1953, which might have helped them decide what to do next – they added a new concrete addition out back and applied for one of the new cabaret licenses from the Liquor Commission.

On November 11, 1954, despite 38 protests, the Honolulu Liquor Commission approved a license for the Swing Club at 35 N. Hotel, submitted by owners Janet Vicari and Althea Di Sopa.

Establishments with a cabaret license had to serve food, provide at least a 3-piece orchestra for dancing, provide "professional" entertainment, and could serve liquor until 3am. The first two applicants were Don the Beachcomber's and the Swing Club.

The Swing Club opened in January 1955 and billed itself as "The only place where the happenings are always happening".

The first house band was Frankie Kamaunu and his Swingsters, later Jimmy Williams and the Ding Dongs, and then Bobby Lester and his band.

In 1956 they opened the Swing Club Roof Garden with "gorgeous gals, comedy, dancing, entertainment and food".

Some of the musicians who played at the Swing Club: Anita Tucker, Kim Hamilton, Baby Davis, Juanita Brown, Ella Correa, Tamara Hayes, Anna Louise, Gloria Jean, Iona Wade, Laurita Alexander, Barbara Tucker, Ruby Lane, Cardella De Milo, Cene Roye, Debby Andrews, Bobbie Lester, Rock & Roll Riley, and Jackie Mayfield. It is an urban legend that Louis Armstrong, Duke Ellington, Ella Fitzgerald, and Sarah Vaughn might have also played at the Swing Club.

The downstairs initially hosted the guest musicians and house band for dancing, while the upstairs took on a more burlesque atmosphere.

By 1960 the roof garden was advertising a "Western Room" featuring Tex Boyd and his Valley Swingers, and also a unique "Merry-go-Round Bar" on the patio.

In the mid 1960's they used the upstairs for Anna's Ballroom, but it only lasted for 2 years.

In 1965, the Swing Club was the "Home of the Twist", and by 1966 they featured Go-Go girls in cages.

One of the more unusual acts in 1968 was Little Johnny Shaw, "36 in. Tall 'n Full of Soul, the James Brown of the Dwarf Set".

In 1970, the house band, Joe Banana and the Soul Checks changed their name to Joe Banana and the Mod Squad.

But everything changed drastically in 1971. The Swing Club became an X-rated live sex nightclub with X-rated movies upstairs in what they called the Esquire Theatre. It lasted for twenty years and often showed films starring the live performers in the Swing Club below.

In 1971, a doorman and a customer were both shot by someone who was having a fight with one of the strippers.

June 19, 1971 was a particularly busy night – two performers were arrested for live sex on stage, and then 3 hours later there was a shootout with a bank robber. One of the arrested performers was 26-year-old John Holmes (aka Johnny Wadd), on the verge of becoming a legendary porn star who made nearly 600 adult films.

1980 was a bad year too – John Di Sopa, the manager of the Swing Club, was almost kidnapped in the parking lot at 4:15 am, and later that year the skipper of *Windward Passage*, the winner of the Pan Am Clipper Cup yacht race, was shot in a pool game. The following year saw a big knife fight between two women.

In 1989 it became Swing Video, the largest adult video store in Honolulu, and also the site of a big drug bust in 1997 for cocaine and meth.

It was Mr. C's Club in 2003, and only lasted 6 months in 2004 as Kaspy's which featured Hawaiian slack key guitar.

In 2005, Dave Stewart, owner of Indigo Restaurant on Nuʻuanu, opened Bar 35.

Gelareh Khoie's thirtyninehotel multi-media gallery was upstairs from 2004 to 2014 in the space that was once Sweet's Ballroom and the Esquire Theatre.

Tchin Tchin! wine bar opened upstairs in 2017, by the same owners of Lucky Belly and Livestock Tavern. The name is a toast that translates to "Please-Please!".

43 N. Hotel

There was a general merchandise store here in 1891 and in 1899. From 1901 to 1917 it was the store of the Hop Hing Company specializing in imported merchandise and liquor. They had previously been at the corner of Nuʻuanu & Beretania but were burned out in the 1900 fire. One of their shipments of Chinese liquor in large 9-gallon earthenware jugs so confused the local customs agents they had to send one to the US Treasury officials in New York to help determine the proper duty (or so they said).

From 1919 to 1921 it was the Hamamura Shoten, also known as Hama's Grocery, owned by Kyoichi Hamamura.

The Independent Grill opened here in 1923, followed by Sai Fu Chop Sui from 1926 to 1929. L. Ah Leong celebrated his 71st birthday here in 1928 with 300 guests and long strings of firecrackers.

From 1932 to 1939 it was the downtown location of the P.Y. Chong's famous Waikiki restaurant, Lau Yee Chai.

It was the Lau Heong Chai Chop Sui restaurant from 1940 to 1946.

The Anchor Bar opened here in 1946, owned and managed by Ho King Yee, with partners Sam Lee, Chong Chang, and Richard W. C. Chow.

They obtained a cabaret license in 1955 and it became the Anchor Club, featuring country and hillbilly music at first, but by the 1970's they were sporting topless dancers like other nearby clubs.

Ironically, owner Richard Wah Chong Chow was 1984 Father of the Year and was president of the Chinese Chamber of Commerce and the United Chinese Society.

Nextdoor Cinema Lounge & Concert Hall opened here in 2005, featuring a wide variety of music, "from jazz to hip hop to electronic dance music, heavy metal, and everything in between".

49 N. Hotel

The first business here at the corner was Kwong Hang Chan & Company who moved here in December of 1886 from their previous location at Nuʻuanu and Queen streets. They were here until 1892, and the corner was still a general merchandise store in 1906. By 1914 the building had been expanded along Smith Street.

From 1934 to 1942 it was G. Wong Sun & Company who were wholesale and retail grocers. It was the Smith Fountain in 1942, and the Palace Grill in 1946.

In 1949 it became Johnny Welch's Porthole and they hired architect Solomon F. Kenn and contractor Richard Sugahara to do $35,000 in alterations in 1950. The club was initially known for "loud and rowdy, hoedown music and beer" and applied for a cabaret license in 1955 but was turned down. Ten years later they were still billing themselves as "The Home of Western & Hill-Billy Entertainment".

From 1965 to 1981 it was Tammy's Lounge. One of the owners, Wallace Furukawa, was well-known to the police gambling squad, and he barely survived a car-bombing by members of a local crime syndicate in 1970.

By 1972 Tammy's Lounge was "a known hangout for prostitutes and pimps". They tried to bring in a snake dancer but it was not allowed since snakes of any kind are forbidden in Hawaii.

In 1974 the city forced them to put up a special partition so the topless go-go dancers were not visible from the street.

In 1985 it became the Sunshine Lounge, and it was the Silver Fox Lounge from 1988 to 1993. It was called Amy's Place from 1998 to 2007, at which time it suffered a bad fire with $60,000 damage to building.

The building was restored in 2014 and the new tenant was the very respectable Livestock Tavern opened by Dusty Grable and Jesse Cruz, the owners of Lucky Belly across the street.

42 N. HOTEL

40-42 N. Hotel
1892 / 1980 remodel
Architect / Builder: unknown

There was a 2-stsory building built here in 1892, but it became a 1-story building after the front façade collapsed in 1980.

In 1899 it housed the Lin Sing Kee plumber and tinsmith shop, and the Hop Hing & Company general merchandise store.

From 1910 to 1932 it housed some major revolutionary activity – it was the office of the Chee Yow Shin Bo, known as the Liberty News Chinese newspaper, with offices of the Oahu Kuomintang on the second floor.

Originally the Tan San Sun Bo Long Kee (The Hawaiian Chinese News), Dr. Sun Yat-sen changed the name in 1908 to Chee Yow Shin Bo (The Liberty News). When Dr. Sun visited Honolulu between March and May of 1910, he often came to work in this office.

It was later a dry goods store, the Island Café, the Ace Portrait Studio, the Island Fountain, Nicky's Café, and the fancy INTO furniture boutique. It became the Downbeat Lounge in 2013.

The shop in the middle was the Tengu-do Jewelry Store, the United Bazaar, Hollywood Revue amusement arcade (off-limits to servicemen), the Singapore Bar, and Funville (which was often raided for pornography). In 1976 it became the Paris Theatre featuring adult films like *Teacher's & Cream*. In 2005 it became the Indochine Café.

The left side has housed a barber supply store and the Tin Wo Cong On jewelry store, plus an Egyptian phrenologist and palmist in 1928 who "reads your head like an open book", also the home of gypsy fortune tellers in the 1960's.

The building was gutted in an arson fire in 1969 and remodeled without the second floor but with a steel truss holding up the old second floor wall and parapet. This dramatically collapsed in 1980, showering the street with bricks. The building was heavily remodeled after that and only has a few original interior walls left.

The first known building on this site was George Clark's dry goods, boots and shoe store from 1851 to 1870.

50 N. HOTEL

50 N. Hotel
1897, 1901, 1980 remodel
Architect / Builder: Lee Wai

The 1886 fire started here. At the time, Smith's Lane was just a narrow little pathway located on the far side of present-day Smith Street, and there was a huge 2-story 35' x 60' wooden Chinese restaurant where the street is today. From the official report to His Majesty the King:

> "The Chinese examined state as their belief that a gambling game or lottery, in which a large number of tickets were used, was in progress. A dispute arose, and the tickets were seized by one of those present and thrust into a fire, which was burning in the room. A scuffle then ensued, during which the fire was scattered over the floor, and in a moment the room was in a blaze. Some twenty or more Chinamen were seen running out from the upper story when the fire broke out."

After the fire, Smith Street was expanded and extended to King Street.

In 1891, an enterprising Japanese man erected a pagoda-style tent on the vacant lot and held a big wrestling tournament. "There was wrestling in seven different languages, and it was not confined to any special style; they gave you a little of Greco-Roman, then a large chunk out of the Marquis of Queensbury, a trifle of catch as catch can and a bit of London prize ring rules."

This was originally a 1-story building built in 1897 and it housed a drug store on the corner and doctor's office on the left. On November 2, 1901, Lee Wai took out a building permit to add a second story.

It has hosted a variety of other businesses over the years, including a gift shop, stamp store, jewelry store, photography studio, shoe repair, tattoo, and perhaps the world's smallest tailor shop that was run by Mr. and Mrs. Placido Camello and was only 7' x 15'.

From 1935 to 1958 it housed the Aloha Barber Shop, owned by Bernardo Hintulan who was also a musician at Ft. Shafter.

The 2-story building was gutted by an arson fire in 1969, and the second-floor wall collapsed in 1980. The building was extensively remodeled afterwards. Lucky Belly restaurant opened here in 2012.

1913 MENDONÇA BULIDING

51-55 N. Hotel, 1042 Smith
1913
Architect / Builder: Harry L. Kerr / George M. Yamada

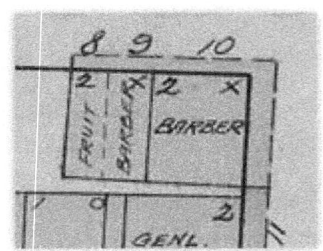
1891

Sometimes called the Mini Mendonça Building, this building was designed by Harry L. Kerr and built by George M. Yamada in 1913. The lot had been empty after the 1900 fire until J.P. Mendonça finally managed to buy up the partial interests of the various owners.

Before the fire it was the site of a 2-story wooden building housing a barber shop on the corner, another barber shop next door, and a fruit store that replaced an earlier 2-story wooden drug store that burned in the 1886 fire.

In 1888, John W. Akana had an employment office here for contracting Chinese labor.

The concrete building here today has a footprint of only 980 square feet and according to the March 22, 1913, building permit announcement it cost $6,700.

For 32 years it was the home of Sing Kee Jewelry, from 1939 to 1971, at which time it turned into the Mini Theatre and later the Bijou Theatre showing pornographic films. There were also numerous gambling raids upstairs in the 1970's.

The building was restored by Mouse Builders in 1981 and the upstairs became the office of two of the leading lights of Chinatown historic preservation – architects Spencer Leineweber and Glenn Mason.

By the mid 1990's this area was overrun with drug dealers and users, "the worst corner in Chinatown", and the building was taken in a drug forfeiture.

The building exterior was restored again in 2021.

JOSEPH P. MENDONÇA BUILDING

54-74 N. Hotel, 1112-1116 Smith, 1113 Maunakea
1901, restored 1977
Architect / Builder: Oliver Traphagen / Hawaiian Engineering & Construction Company

This is the largest historical building in Chinatown, covering almost 15,000 square feet. It was the first building restored by Bob Gerell and Pete Smith in 1978 with assistance from architect James K. Tsugawa.

Their confidence and $400,000 investment sparked a much-needed wave of historic preservation throughout Chinatown that demonstrated the economic value of preservation. *"You couldn't reproduce that architecture for two times what I am paying, if you had to build this all over at today's costs."* (Bob Gerell). He was laughed at when he bought the building in 1976, but it started a movement that ultimately saved Chinatown.

Working with architect Robert Fox they returned everything as closely as possible to the 1901 look and leased the 24,000 square feet of commercial space to a variety of tenants, many of whom were in the building previously.

The 1906 Dakin Fire Insurance Map shows a barber, jeweler, butcher, Wing Sing Wo Company, a couple of vegetable stores, dry goods, and fruit and flower stores.

Architect Oliver Traphagen prepared three different designs for contractors to bid on, with the Hawaiian Engineering & Construction Company winning the bid on April 12, 1901, to build Design No. 1 for $48,044.

The architectural style could be considered Portuguese / Mediterranean Renaissance Revival, with its unique painted window accents and decorative parapet name block on the stucco-covered brick building.

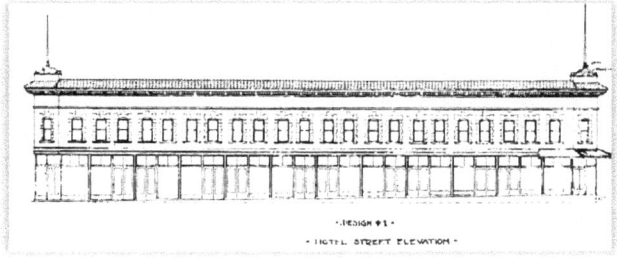

HONOLULU CHINATOWN

Not even open one year yet, the Mendonça Building experienced its first gambling raid on June 18, 1902 – the largest one to date in the history of the Honolulu Police Department, with 96 Chinese arrested in an upstairs room at 11:30 am on the Maunakea side.

Knowing they were being watched by the gambler's lookouts, Deputy High Sheriff Chillingworth and his men stayed calm in the street while Detective David Kaapa led a posse of Native Hawaiians who used a ladder and crowbars to break through a window and four barricaded doors. Inside they found five tables for pai gow, fan tan and other gambling games. The four dealers managed to escape through a trap door in the roof with two tins and two sacks of money.

After a period of relative quiet, or willful avoidance by the authorities, the raids on the upstairs gambling hall resumed in earnest in the 1960's:

- 1961 – 10 arrested in a dominoes raid
- 1962 – 25 arrested for gambling in a barricaded upstairs room
- 1963 – 18 arrested for gambling, room barricaded
- 1964 – 19 arrested for gambling, barricaded (for Ah Chin Lum it was his 15th arrest since 1961)
- 1968 – 37 arrested in a gambling raid by 22 vice officers
- 1970 – 18 arrested by 12 police using a sledgehammer on the downstairs and upstairs doors
- 1971 – 12 arrested for gambling
- 1979 – 11 arrested for on the second floor for playing paikau ("played with dice and dominoes")

Before the 1900 fire there were five 2-story wooden buildings on this site, with several butchers, doctors, barbers, restaurants, general merchandise stores, and a cake bakery. The photograph on the left shows a fancy second-floor gallery on the mauka/waikiki corner that was possibly an upstairs dining area for the restaurant.

1900

Before the 1886 fire, the 1885 Dakin Map shows this area to be crowded with mostly 2-story wooden buildings that were a mixture of shops and dwellings. On the mauka/waikiki corner was the tallest building in Chinatown, 3-stories high, owned by the Sun Hang Far Company, with a coffee shop on the first floor.

1899

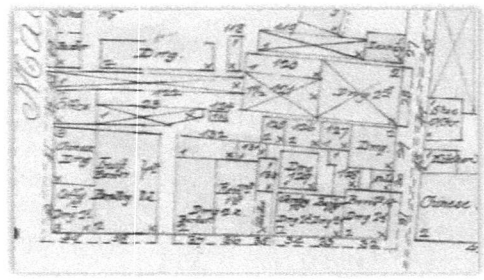

HONOLULU CHINATOWN

54 N. Hotel on the corner was the K. Samura Shoten for 30 years, from 1915 to 1944, owned by Kensuke Samura until it was taken over by the government and later liquidated as an "alien property" in World War II.

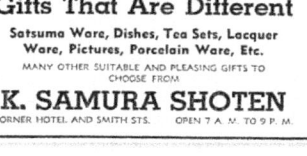

In 1949, Wilfred H. Yoshimi hired contractor T. Maeda to remodel the space into Paradise Center.

They were formerly in the Hocking Building at 14 N. King as Paradise Jewelers, and in addition to jewelry offered a modern soda fountain, lunch counter, sundries, and notions in their new Paradise Center.

Yoshimi retired in 1973 and put the business up for sale. It then briefly became Café Paradise, owned by Luke Z.H. Chang. It was Vietnam Café Pho Saigon in 2002.

56 N. Hotel was the H. Yamanaka & Co. Ltd store from 1925 to 1943. It was a variety of business after that – Ilima Gift shop, Vanda Florists, Liberty Jewelers, Ho's Kitchenette, Hotel Donuts & Pastries, and the Kamehameha Bakery.

For nearly 40 years, from 1925 to 1964, **58 N. Hotel** was the location of Bo Wo Co Ltd, jade jewelers and goldsmiths.

60 N. Hotel was the C. Nishikawa Shoten from 1926 to 1931, followed by the Damate Brothers Barber Shop in 1925.

From 1941 to 1960 it was the Lau and Company liquor store owned by Seth Lau, and it was Chang's Liquor Store from 1961 to 1978. It became the Mini Garden Noodle House in 2004.

In 1933, **62 N. Hotel** was the take home food store of famous restaurateur Lau Yee Chai. It was the Yet Char Sut Chop Sui House by 1934.

In 1936 Richard Lopal opened the Two Jacks Bar which was here for over 60 years. Redecorated in 1941, they hosted jazz nights in the 1950's. But by the 1990's it was a fairly rough place, described as "one of the crummiest bars in Chinatown". And that's saying a lot.

In 2014 it became the Grondin French Latin Kitchen restaurant.

64-68 N. Hotel was the longtime home of the Wing Sing Wo Company who were here for 66 years. It was founded by Leong Sam who was born in China in 1861 and moved to Honolulu at a young age. He founded the Po Sing Tong Company which dealt in Chinese drugs and herbs, and in 1898 also founded Wing Sing Wo as a Chinese grocery store. On March 15, 1902, he merged the two stores and moved into the Mendonça building.

After Leong Sam moved back to China in 1917, his son, Leong Han, became the owner of Wing Sing Wo. Leong Han was also the owner of the Wing Sing Fat export company in Hong Kong and Maui, plus Wing Sing Yuen (a bank) in Shekki, Chung Shan district. In 1935 he purchased the Kun Kee money exchange store in Canton (Guangdong)

The Wing Sing Wo store also acted like a Chinese post office for sending letters and money to and from a certain area of China since they had a branch store in Hachak Hee in See Dai Doo, Chung Shan district. Store bookkeepers were some of the few people who could write Chinese, and they could be hired to write impressive-sounding letters.

Wing Sing Wo had a Chinese and American grocery at 64-68 N. Hotel and a Chinese herb and drug store at 1113 Maunakea around the corner. In 1938 they hired architect Y.T. Char to build a new building next door to the Mendonça building at 1125-1127-1129 Maunakea Street to house their offices and wholesale department.

In 1968 the store suffered a bad fire in their upstairs warehouse which shared the second floor with Margaret's Muumuu Factory.

The Paradise Book Shop opened at 64 N. Hotel in 1969, specializing in pornography, and was later the Aquarius Theater 1 and 2 showing adult movies that were often seized for violating obscenity laws. The space at 68 N. Hotel became the Playboy Book Store in 1969, Lee's Liquor Store in 1978, and J's Market in 2004.

72 N. Hotel was the Honolulu Chop Suey House in 1929, and the Chee Sun Company owned by Bung Chong Lee, Young Wah Chai, and Young Bow Lin, selling general merchandise from 1923 to 1955.

It was the Southern China Trading Company from 1958 to 1969, specializing in "imported Chinese groceries and exquisite Canton ware", owned by Chew Nam Lum. It became part of the Good Times Restaurant & Lounge in 1979, and the Latulipe Restaurant and Cocktail Lounge in 1980 which specialized in Vietnamese, Korean and Chinese food. It was the Silvertown Lounge in 1981, and the C5 Nightclub from 1984 to 1987.

74 N. Hotel, at the corner of Hotel and Maunakea was a butcher shop in 1906 and was the Park Lee Hong butcher shop from at least 1919 to 1945. It was owned by Lee Hee and Donald Look Yen Yee, and the shop was famous for one of its employees, Gett Lee, who happened to win $53,600 (nearly a million dollars in today's money) in the Irish Sweepstakes in 1936.

Lee had been working there as a butcher making $60 a month for the past 12 years, but when "Bachelor Prince" came in third place and he had the winning ticket, Lee had to quit working at the shop due to all the publicity and numerous "long lost friends" appearing out of nowhere.

Parke's Gift Shop was in this corner from 1945 to 1947, followed by the Yee Brothers men's apparel store. It was The Western Store from 1955 to 1959, selling cowboy attire during the brief hillbilly music craze in the late 1950's. It became a butcher shop once again in 1962 when Siu's Meat Corner moved here from Maunakea and Pauahi, and in 1979 it was the Good Times Restaurant

On the Smith side of the building, **1112 Smith** was the H. Yamanaka & Co. store until they sold out in 1945. From 1949 to 1953 it was the Island Sales Company, owned by Horace M. Sakoda who worked with an exclusive buyer in New York to wholesale women and children's apparel to leading local clothing stores. It was Tim Tim Chop Suey in 1961, Dr. Lee's Lai An Tong Herb Shop in 1984, and then became the Ethiopian Love café in 2015.

In 1928, at **1114 Smith** on the end of the building, was the United Chinese News, the official newspaper of the Dr Sun Yat-sen's Kuomintang Nationalist Party. Western Builders, owned by George Tharp, was here in 1946, specializing in "Stran-Steel" homes and Quonset huts.

Upstairs at **1116 Smith** from 1961 to 1982 was the showroom and factory for dressmaker Mildred Dohi, doing business as Mildred's of Hawaii and specializing in muumuus and casual Hawaiian clothing. It was the local office of the Nature Conservancy from 1989 to 1998.

On the Maunakea side of the building, there was a barber shop and jewelry store in 1906. From 1914 to 1922, **1113 Maunakea** was the Sun Wo Jewelry Company, with access to the large hall upstairs that was used as a gambling den.

From 1927 to 1930 it was the grocery and general merchandise store of Wing Chong Tai Company managed by Leong Wah Hin. In 1946 the Wing Sing Wo Company took over the space for their Chinese herb and drugs department called Po Sing Tong. It was later the Mai Hein Market in 1982, the Dai Nam Market in 1985, and the Double Eight restaurant from 1990 to 2005. The tiny little Rosarina Pizza shop was carved out of the back of 74 N. Hotel in 1989.

Joseph Paul Mendonça

Born in the Azores Islands in 1847, Joseph P. Mendonça came to Hawaii as a galley hand on a whaling ship when he was about 17 years old, and jumped ship to stay in Hawaii.

He first worked with his uncle Jason Perry (Jacinto Pereira) and became active in the Annexation Party. He was a member of the Committee on Public Safety that overthrew the Hawaiian monarchy in 1893.

He acquired lots of land, particularly in Chinatown, and in 1893 he and C. Bolte created the Kaneohe Ranch and became very successful ranchers. He tired of the ranch in 1899 and concentrated on his holdings in Chinatown which needed much extra attention after the destruction of the 1900 fire.

His new buildings typically had red window frames or red brick surrounds, and he owned as many as 10 buildings in Chinatown. Mendonça died in 1927 and his estate continued to hold the buildings for many years afterwards.

ARAUJO BUILDING

61-75 Hotel
1907, rebuilt 1953, renovated 2000
Architect / Builder: unknown, AM Partners (2000) / K. Nagata (1953)

The building today looks a little like the original building that was built here in 1907, but almost none of it is original. What you see today is a 2000 reconstruction to undo a 1953 modernization that left only a few interior walls of the original 1907 building. The latest renovation was designed by the architectural firm AM Partners who also had offices in Los Angeles, Hong Kong, and Shanghai.

In 1952, Adelaide Franca Araujo and sons Roy & Elmer announced a "new building which will utilize only a small outer part of the existing structure, will extend from 61 to 75 on N. Hotel St." K. Nagata was hired as the contractor for the $85,000 project that included providing for a third floor later. There were five stores downstairs and nine offices upstairs, and it looked like this:

Mrs. Araujo was the widow of Albert A. Araujo, the Portuguese consul-general of Hawaii. Mr. Araujo was born in 1878 in Funchal, the capital of the island of Madeira (about 600 miles southwest of Lisbon). He was brought to Hawaii in 1891 at age 12 by his uncle, Joseph P. Mendonça, and grew up on the Mendonça cattle ranch in Waialua.

61 N. Hotel housed a barber shop from 1907 to 1914 and was the home of the Tensho-do Jewelry store for nearly 40 years, from 1915 to 1953. It was owned by Shizuka Makishima from Yamaguchi, Japan, and he closed it out when his lease expired right before the remodel. He then went on a 2-month buying trip to Japan and opened a gift shop on Fort Street with his brother Kenji.

From 1955 to 1962-it was D's Massage Studio, at one point deemed off-limits to members of the military.

The All-Saints Counseling Service was here in 1967, and in 1971 it was the Black Cultural Center for African-Americans.

By 1977 it was the Palace Bath House which was raided for prostitution. When it was the Original Bath House in 1988, someone threw a flaming Christmas tree out of a second story window late one night that landed on top of a passing police car. In 1989 it was the Life Foundation's Rubber Room – a source for condoms and bleach for drug users.

65 N. Hotel was used for storage in 1907 and 1914, and from 1920 to 1952 was the Mayeda Hat Store.

69 N. Hotel had a macaroni factory on the first and second floor in 1907 and 1914. By 1923 it was M. Fujiki Tailor Shop, followed by The Sun Tailor Company until 1930.

In 1934 Minekichi Oshima opened the Honolulu Liquor Store, later known as the Cut Rate Liquor Co. Ltd.

It was the offices of Hee Hau's United Investment Company real estate and insurance business from 1937 to 1950, and also the offices of Hung Wai Ching selling real estate. After the 1953 remodel, it was the Great Shanghai Restaurant.

71 N. Hotel was the Kamo Toy Shop in 1924, and the store of watchmaker W.C. Luke in 1929.

From 1936 to 1953 it was Fashion Timepiece, managed by J. L. Lum, a faculty member at the Hoo Cho Chinese School.

In 1955 it was Star-Line Hawaii, raided for gambling in 1960.

It was the Shamrock Bar from 1964 to 1975, and Cathy's Lounge from 1978 to 1993.

75 N. Hotel

Tinsmiths and plumbers Won Loui & Company were here by February of 1907. From 1919 to 1925 it was Pacific Mercantile, and from 1933 to 1952 it was a barber shop, M.S. Wong's Dragon Barber Service, followed by Dorothy's Barber Shop.

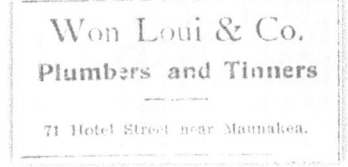

In 1995 this building and the portion of the Mendonça building at 1040 Smith Street were seized from Taipei Properties by US Marshals in a drug forfeiture and were subsequently bought by the city and remodeled in 2000 as part of the new Chinatown police station.

CHINATOWN POLICE STATION

79-83 N. Hotel
2000
Architect / Builder: AM Partners

By the mid 1990's this area of Chinatown was ground zero for most of Honolulu's illicit drug trade and all the other unsavory activities that are typically associated with it.

There was already a police station at the corner of Nu'uanu and Hotel, but after the Mendonça and Araujo buildings were seized by US Marshals in a drug forfeiture in 1995, the city decided to build a larger station and locate it right in the middle of the highest crime area in Chinatown as part of their Chinatown Community Services Center Project.

It was designed to house 114 police officers and to be "compatible with the historic character of Chinatown". It was dedicated with a big block party on May 19, 2000, that featured the Honolulu Fire Department's 5-member musical group Firehouse, the Hawaiian group Homestead Style, the rock band Blindsight, the Royal Hawaiian Band Glee Club, Chinese lion dancers and cultural performances, plus food booths by Indigo, Havana Cabana, and Murphy's Bar and Grill.

Daniel Siu Chong Liu was the fourth and longest serving chief in the Honolulu Police Department. He was chief for over 20 years, from 1948 until his retirement in 1969.

Liu was the first Chinese chief, and he improved salaries and training, redesigned the police badge, changed the uniforms to navy blue, established the chaplaincy corps, canine corps, and the Police Activities League. He was voted the "State's Most Admired Man" in 1965.

The building previously on the site was a 2-story brick building built by Su Wai in 1901 for the Wing Chong Lung gift store and saloon that was here until 1931. It matched the larger Su Wai bulding along Maunakea Street. In bad shape by the 1970's and scheduled for demolition, the building was destroyed by a fire in 1973 that appeared to have started near a gypsy stall on the first floor. The land was then used for a parking lot for the next 27 years.

SIU BUILDING

102 N. Hotel, 1106 Maunakea
1926
Architect / Builder: E.W Ellis / Saiki & Davenport

The Siu Building was designed by E.W. Ellis and constructed by Saiki and Davenport for owner Siu Kit. It is made of concrete, steel and hollow tile, and the building permit on September 22, 1926, valued it at $21,500.

Siu Kit was a native of Nam Mun village in China and came to Hawaii in 1895. In 1931 he was the manager of the Yee On and Sun Yee On butcher shops and grocery stores, and a member of the Lung Doo Benevolent Society and the Honolulu Chinese Chamber of Commerce. In 1941 he sold this property to Henry Awa Wong and H.A. Truslow for $19,400. The Wong Kong Har Tong Society bought the building in 1982 and renovated it in 1985.

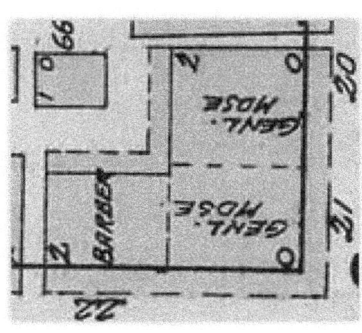

In 1885 there was a tailor shop and dwelling on the site.

After the 1886 fire a 2-story wooden building housed two stores and a barber shop.

In 1902 the Yee Yee Tong Society built a 3-story wooden building with a restaurant and a clubhouse on the top floor.

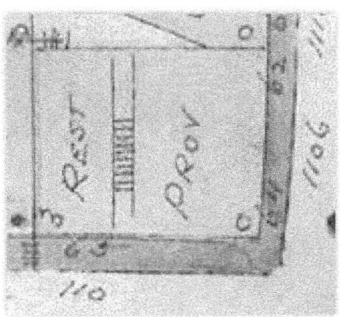

1891   1906

E.W. Ellis was the sole agent for Doane Trucks and later became inspector of construction at the Naval Air Station. An architect and construction engineer, in 1925 he designed a 1-story concrete and tile sausage factory for CQ Yee Hop and the 2-story Pang Sing Choy building on Beretania Street near River. In 1927 he was the designer for a 58' x 62' store and hotel worth $43,000 for Chun Chin at Fort and New Era Lane, and in 1928 he designed a new Dearborn Chemical Company warehouse. He was also the chairman of Pacific Club building committee for their remodel in 1939.

The Wong Kong Har Tong Society was founded in 1902 by Wong Chow, Wong Leong, Wong How, Wong Min Hoong, Wong Bat Ting (Wong Lam) and Wong Wing, all with the same family name of Wong (Huang) and coming from Zhongshan, in Guangdong province, China.

The purpose was to provide fellowship among fellow Wongs, while serving the Chinese and Hawaii communities with charitable works. They initially called the group Kong Har Gee Loo, roughly translated as "a meeting place for the Wongs of Kong Har (Jiang Xia)."

The Colusa Building, Yee Yee Tong Building, and Siu Building (1973)

YEE YEE TONG BUILDING

110-112 N. Hotel
1957, 1994 renovation
Architect / Builder: Paul D. Jones / unknown

Designed by local architect Paul D. Jones for the Yee Yee Tong Society in 1957, this building replaced a 3-story wooden building built between 1901 and 1906, plus part of the adjacent Colusa Building on the left.

Service Grill, owned by Hu York Hon, was on this site in 1934, and later the City 2nd Hand Book Store. It was The Post Card Shop in 1945 and an amusement center in 1948.

In 1950 it was the Chinese American Curio Store owned by Sing Jen Tau Chee, master musician of the traditional bowed Chinese 2-string fiddle called "yee foo" in Cantonese and "erhu" in Mandarin.

The Yee Yee Tong Society bought the old building and demolished it in 1957 to build the first modern new building in Chinatown since World War II.

For nearly twenty years, from 1957 to 1976, this was the site of Sad Sam's Bar, formerly at 186 N. Hotel. From 1976 to 1983 it was Lorraine's Lounge.

In 1994 it was purchased and renovated by the Consuelo Zobel Alger Foundation working with Architects Hawaii Ltd and Construction Associates. The remodel won top honors in the 10th Annual Building Industry Association of Hawaii awards.

The Consuelo Zobel Alger Foundation was created in 1988 to improve the quality of life of abused, neglected, and exploited children, women and families in the Philippines and Hawaii. Consuelo was married to James Dyce Alger, a 3-star American general. Her ownership shares of the family business, Ayala Corporation, the oldest and largest company in the Philippines, provided the foundation with over $100 million dollars.

WO FAT RESTAURANT

111 N. Hotel
1938
Architect / Builder: Yuk Tong Char / W.S. Ching

This building is the cultural and literal center of Chinatown, at the corner of Hotel and Maunakea streets.

And no, it's not named for the primary villain in the *Hawaii 5-0* TV series – the TV name comes from this restaurant, which translates to "Peace and Prosperity".

Famous for its Chinese-style architecture and commanding presence at the corner of Hotel and Maunakea, the Wo Fat Chop Sui House was one of the premier Chinese restaurants in Honolulu for over 100 years.

Wo Fat

According to company lore, the Wo Fat restaurant began in Chinatown in 1881. The 1891 Dakin Fire Insurance Map shows a restaurant and coffee house in a 2-story wooden building on Hotel Street just ewa of Maunakea, which could date to as early as 1886 when Hotel Street was extended from Maunakea to River Street.

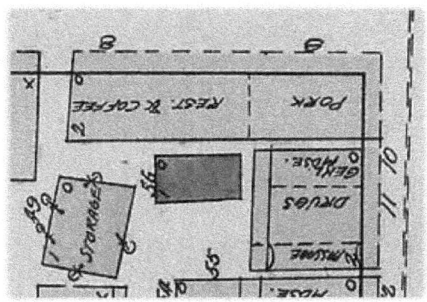

The first newspaper mention of Wo Fat's "Chinese lunch room" in this location is on December 16, 1896.

On February 1, 1897, Wat Ging and seven other Chinese formed the baking, restaurant, and candy business "Wo Fat and Nee Chong".

This building was burned in the 1900 fire, and they moved to the ewa end of a new 2-story wooden building in 1906.

In addition to being manager of the restaurant, Wat Ging was also involved in agricultural partnerships in Pauoa and the Hop Sing real estate company.

There was a huge riot outside the restaurant on April 6, 1906, with 8 or 9 police protecting the building from being demolished by hundreds of angry Chinese who were accusing Wo Fat (Wat Ging) of misappropriating $7,000 sent from China to aid victims of the 1900 fire. The restaurant was boycotted, but Wo Fat said "Chinaman stay away but policeman come and eat plenty." Everything must have eventually been sorted out as Wo Fat quickly became one of the most popular Chinese restaurants in Honolulu.

From the July 22, 1915, Honolulu Advertiser article "Chinatown Has Become Center of Night Life":

> *The famous establishments of Wo Fat and Yee Yi Chin are now a blaze of multi-colored lights and the erstwhile cramped dining rooms have been enlarged and elaborately decorated, until today they are among the brightest spots in the town's night life. The narrow staircases have given place to spacious affairs set right in the center of the building, and the lanais are resplendent with colored glass windows and verdant with potted plants."

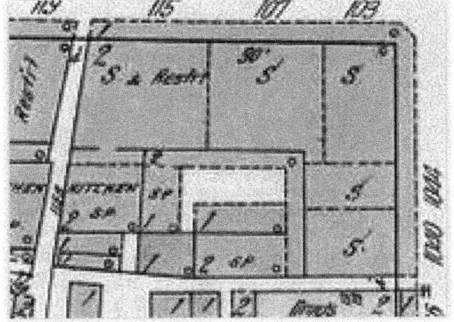

There were tenements behind the building accessed via "Wo Fat Alley" that were a hive of bootlegging and moonshining activity throughout the 1920's with one raid netting 157 quarts of beer.

The restaurant was completely remodeled in 1931, adding new private booths and now claiming to be the "Oldest Chop Sui House in Town". They remodeled again in 1933 after Prohibition ended, with work done by contractor T. Takeuchi, and then again in 1935.

After the new Lum Yip Kee building went up next door in 1936, Wo Fat announced in 1937 that they would also be demolishing their old wooden building for a new 3-story concrete structure that would occupy the whole corner.

They closed the restaurant on September 30, 1937 and took out a building permit for $43,400 for the new building.

Lee Tim, president and manager of Wo Fat Company Ltd hired architect Y.T. Char to create something in the Chinese style with a rooftop pavilion and pagoda. The restaurant was on the second floor with a third-floor roof garden, plus a liquor store and bar on the ground level along with the Kwong Tong Chong and Kwong Wah Chong grocery and pork markets. Opening day to much fanfare was March 10, 1938.

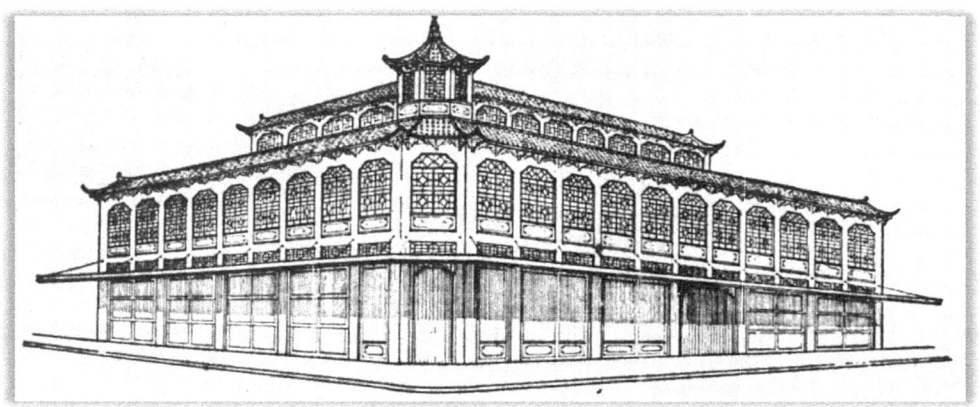

An Imposing Building

IN OLD LETTERS: The name plate—Wo Fat—written by calligraphist Wong Pung Chin. The firm is over 57 years old and for more than half a century this handsomely designed name plate has designated the business.

The interior woodwork was done by the Robert Fujino's Modern Carpenter Shop and the bar counter and back bar were by Charles Bandle of the von Hamm Young Company. The elaborate painting on the walls, beams and ceiling was by Tadao Takeuchi in the colors of a building from Nanjing, learned from consulting with the Chinese art records at the Honolulu Academy of Arts.

The restaurant could seat up to 1,000 people at once with the octagonal Dragon Room in the distinctive corner Pagoda reserved for private parties.

Many rich and famous have dined here over the years including Frank Sinatra and Jackie Kennedy plus TV producer Leonard Freeman who created the original *Hawaii 5-0* TV series in 1968.

In 1994 owner George Dang sold a controlling interest in the restaurant to the operators of the famous Lou Wai Lou restaurant in Hangzhou just outside Shanghai. The Chinese restaurant served 2,000 people a day with a staff of 400, and the plan was to open a second location in Honolulu.

The Empress Restaurant was briefly located on the second floor before moving to the Cultural Plaza, and by the early 2000's the upstairs was a nightclub that unfortunately painted over much of the artwork with black paint.

In 2017 the building was purchased for $4M with plans to spend another $6M to build dining and retail on the first floor and to convert the upper floors into a 23-room boutique hotel, combining historic preservation with adaptive re-use.

ROAST CHICKEN CANTONESE (Hong Kong Style, 4 to 6 servings)

3-pound chicken Marinade: 1 cup tamari (or any other aged soy sauce) 1 tablespoon gin 1 tablespoon honey 1 teaspoon salt 4 cloves garlic, crushed 1/4 cup scallions, cut into 1/2-inch lengths

Rub the chicken inside and out with the marinade. Let sit for 1 hour. Roast in a 350-degree oven for 1 hour and 20 minutes. With a cleaver, halve the chicken and hack into 2-inch segments -- with bone -- for serving.

Liberty Hall

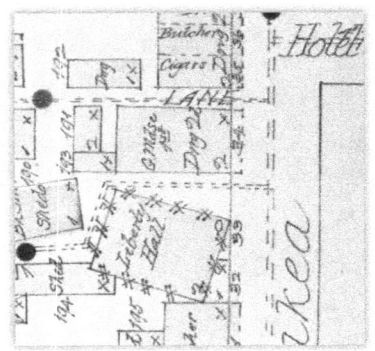

This c.1860's photograph shows the back side of Liberty Hall, located on Maunakea Street where the makai end of the Wo Fat Building is today. It opened in 1850 and was one of the most popular drinking establishments and dancing halls in Honolulu.

Kamehameha V and his cabinet were often there, dancing to mazurkas, quadrilles, reels, and lancers with fiddler and dancing master James Old accompanied by piano.

> "You asked me about the girls who danced with the boys then... they were excellent dancers and (let me whisper) they were rather good-natured."

Liberty Hall was built of coral stone and brick, 29.5' x 46' on a 46' x 96' lot, with bowling lanes added in 1856.

The proprietor, James Dawson, bought the premises at auction in 1859. He also owned several ships involved in the whaling trade – the sloop *Wave* and the schooners *Kinoole*, *Ortolan*, and *Emeline*.

Liberty Hall was closed in 1867 for "selling liquor to natives" and the building was damaged by the big earthquake in February 1871. It was briefly a temperance coffee salon & billiard room in 1871 operated by Louis Kahlbaum.

Liberty Hall in ruins after the Great Fire of 1886.

COLUSA BUILDING (SITE)

116-128 N. Hotel
(1902), 1989
Architect / Builder: William Mutch (1902), James K. Tsugawa (1989) / Mouse Builders (1989)

When the city was developing the Maunakea Marketplace in the late 1980's, they initially wanted to demolish the Colusa Building plus the adjacent Yee Yee Tong Building, but local preservationists fought back. The city then decided to sell the buildings to private developers who would be required to rehabilitate them. The city asked for sealed bids with the upset price of $300,000 for the Colusa Building and $245,000 for the adjoining Yee Yee Tong Building.

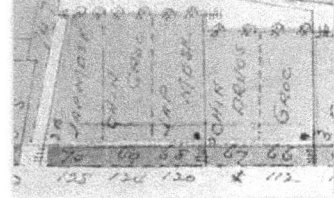

But before anyone could bid on or restore the buildings, a mattress ignited by a cigarette from a careless vagrant started a fire that destroyed the Colusa Building in 1986.

William Mutch, who also owned the Chinese Theater property in back, built the Colusa Building in 1902. By 1906 the building housed two Japanese stores, a Chinese grocery, a Chinese drug store and another grocery store.

Fujii Junichi Shoten was here from 1928 to 1949, and the Sunnyside Café from 1950 to 1965.

HONOLULU CHINATOWN

LUM YIP KEE BUILDING

119-131 N. Hotel
1937
Architect: George Hogan (Cain & Awana) / George J. Oda Contracting Company

Believe it or not, a business in this building was the inspiration for a National Book Award winner voted one of the best novels of the 20th century, and the book was subsequently made into a movie that received 13 Academy Award nominations and won 8 Oscars, and was also turned into a musical at the Shaftesbury Theatre in London.

The building was designed by George V. Hogan with the local architectural firm of Louis Cain & Toe Y. Awana for Chinese businessman Lum Yip Kee. Initially intended to be a 2-story building costing $42,000, during construction a third story was added for an additional $7,000.

It replaced a large 2-story wooden building with 6 stores built after the 1900 fire that housed a variety of businesses including: Yee Yi Chan, Eastern Chop, See Loy, Lee Chew & Co., Choy Yuen Company, Lee Yok store, Up-to-Date tattooing, and a barber shop caught selling opium on the side.

In 1891 there was a barber shop and laundry on the site, with a second barber shop added by 1899. The building burned in the 1900 fire.

The site was vacant in 1885, but in the 1860's there was a large 2-story grass house further back used as a Mormon church. A child playing with matches on the upper floor accidently set it on fire in 1868, completely burning off the thatched roof. Fortunately, there were twenty or thirty buckets of water kept on standby in case of fire and these helped put it out. No one was hurt but a large quantity of Mormon Bibles stored in the building were ruined by the water.

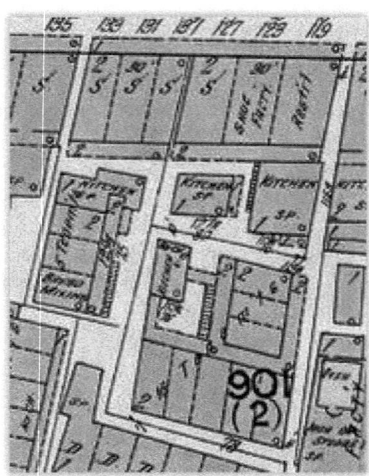

Mollie's Café was a longtime tenant of the new building at 119 N. Hotel from 1943 to 1981. It was owned by Robert T. Lee who named it after his best waitress, Mollie Williams. There was also a taxi dance hall called Danceland upstairs for many years, providing up to 50 dancing partners to the music of live bands like Dizzie's Jitter Jivers. They also sponsored Wayne Powell's All Star Jam Session every Sunday night with servicemen invited to bring their instruments and join in. Club 121 was here in 1945.

But by far and away the most famous tenants were Dorothy A. MacCready and Ruth M. Davis who operated the New Senator Hotel (121 N. Hotel) from 1937 to 1944. It was the largest brothel in Chinatown and employed 15 girls. Sailors would often be lined up around the block for the chance to spend $3 for 3 minutes. The women were mostly imported from the mainland, and they supported the war effort by investing heavily in war bonds.

The New Senator Hotel was a favorite haunt of author James Jones who wrote the best-selling 1951 novel *From Here to Eternity* based on his experiences here. The book was made into an Academy Award-winning film in 1953 starring Burt Lancaster, Montgomery Clift, Deborah Kerr, Frank Sinatra, Donna Reed, and Ernest Borgnine. There were also two television adaptations and a West End London musical.

In the book and in the movie, the New Senator is renamed the New Congress – a simple name change, or maybe something really clever that made it past the censors!

HONOLULU CHINATOWN

CHINESE THEATRE (SITE)

130 N. Hotel
Architect / Builder: unknown

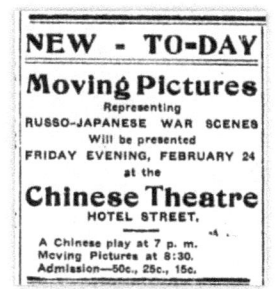

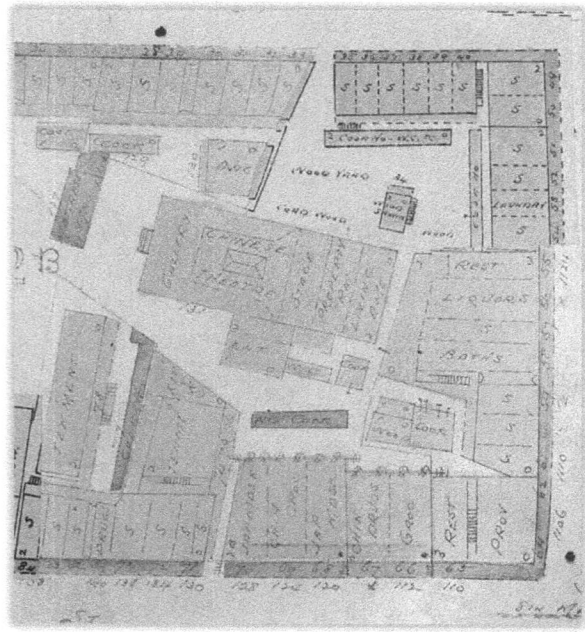

1906 Dakin Fire Insurance Map

In 1903 this alleyway led to a large Chinese Theater located in the middle of the block behind all the buildings. The land was leased to a group of Chinese merchants by William Mutch in 1902, and the theater opened for Chinese New Year in 1903.

There were entrances to the theater from each of the surrounding streets, with this one on Hotel Street being the main entrance.

The theater was the scene of a wide variety of entertainments and public meetings. On December 13, 1903, hundreds of Chinese packed into the theater to hear Dr. Sun Yat-sen make a public speech about the need to overthrow the Manchu Regime in China.

In 1904 it was the scene of a "Monster Naval Boxing Carnival" for Admiral Glass's fleet – 10 rounds, Marquis of Queensbury rules.

The theater showed moving pictures representing scenes from the Russo-Japanese War in 1905.

CHINESE MERCHANTS TO TELL CHINESE DRAMA IN ENGLISH

Players Will Do Their Acts in Their Own Language But Well Known Interpreters Will Tell It Over Again.

A number of the leading Chinese merchants of the city are the sponsors of what will be perhaps the most novel entertainment ever given in Honolulu. The plan is to give a Chinese drama of the old classic school, the new Chinese theatre on Hotel street being hired for the purpose, and interpreters being stationed on the stage to render the speeches of the actors into English as they are delivered. The play selected is called "The Double Marriage and Reconciliation," and it will be given on Wednesday evening, March 18. The proceeds are to go to the Anglo-Chinese academy, an institution that is maintained by the Chinese merchants of the city. The academy is on River street, near the St. Louis College, and has now very nearly 100 students.

On the evening of the proposed entertainment the theatre will be gorgeously decorated, after the Chinese fashion, and a band—not a Chinese band—will be on hand. The arrangements for the entertainment are in the hands of a committee composed of Wong Kwai, F. Ah Hung, L. Ahlo and Poon Kwai Leung. The following well known Chinese will be on the stage to act as interpreters: Lin Shen Chow, Chang Chaw, Chang Kim, Joseph Goo Kim, W. Kwai Tong, Charles Chong and others.

It is the desire of the Chinese merchants to have a general turnout of their Caucasian as well as of their Mongolian friends, and an invitation will be sent to the Janet Waldorf company as a whole to witness the performance, which will be the work of the best Chinese thespians in the city.

Besides the play, there will be some juggling by three Chinese youths who are said to be very clever at the business, and Wagner music will be played between the acts. Programs printed in English will be distributed, so that the audience can readily follow the play.

Tickets for this novel entertainment will be on sale within a few days.

Honolulu Advertiser, March 12, 1903

In 1926 it was replaced by the 650-seat American Theater, lasting nearly 50 years until it was demolished in 1978.

MAUNAKEA MARKETPLACE

132-150 N. Hotel
1989
Architect / Builder: James K. Tsugawa / Mouse Builders

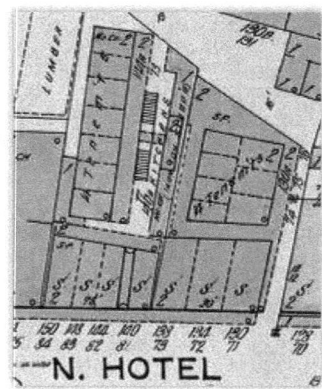

This building is part of the Maunakea Marketplace built in 1989, and is on the site of a large wooden building and tenements constructed sometime between 1902 and 1906. Between the 1886 fire and the 1900 fire there was a single 2-story wooden general merchandise store on the site. And maybe something before the 1902 fire that swept the entire block except for "the Waikiki corner".

The Sunnyside Café owned by Tomotsu Fujisaki was here from 1934 to 1949 until it moved to the Colusa Building next door. The previous building was also home to an Army and Navy Store, Diamond Head Studio and Amusements, plus a couple of employment agencies and rooming houses.

This is also the site of the last home of Charles Kaimana Dimond, Hawaiian musician and Victor and Brunswick recording artist. He was a musician and orchestra leader, teacher of steel guitar, ukulele and banjo, and a vaudeville performer on the Pantages and Orpheum circuits in the 1920's. "Kaimana" is the Hawaiian word for "diamond". Scan the QR code to hear him playing "Sleep":

KEKAULIKE COURTYARDS

145 N. Hotel
1997
Architect / Builder: Mitsunaga & Associates / Hawaiian Dredging & Construction Company

concrete building c. 1963 by C.J. Kim

In 1891 and 1899 there was a 2-story general merchandise store on the corner. After the 1900 fire, a long 2-story wooden building with 10 storefronts was built here in 1901 by the Hop Yick Company.

The City Dry Goods Company was an early tenant, followed by the Yee Wo Chan dry goods store.

From 1926 to 1947 it housed Aloha Studio, one of many places in Chinatown where servicemen could have their photograph taken with a beautiful hula girl.

> Wanted immediately: Attractive Hawaiian or part-Hawaiian girl for photo shop. Apply Aloha Studio, 135 N. Hotel, after 6 p.m.

It was Nancy's Amusement from 1954 to 1957. The police arrested the owner in 1957 for gambling after a man won $1 in a dart game. Seriously. The judge awarded a 13-month suspended sentence.

From 1964 to 1982 it was the site of The Midway Bar.

But perhaps the most famous bar on this site was Elsie's Club Polynesian from 1986 to the mid-1990's. Owned by the wife of a former State Representative and mother of a Miss Hawaii, Elsie's sponsored monthly drag queen contests with the winner crowned "Miss Puakenikeni".

The building was demolished in the mid 1990's for the Kekaulike Revitalization Project that created 75 affordable housing units.

These attractive girls help the soldiers, sailors, war-workers and others find amusement, tossing away care and cash along the streets jammed with servicemen seeking diversion.

NO. 5: BESSIE NAGAMORI

Bessie is a girl who believes in turning the tables on the usual photo concession job.

Instead of posing with service men before a camera and a painted background of surf and Diamond Head, she poses the service men and then takes their pictures.

Bessie is Miss Bessie Nagamori, 21, of 709 Winant St. She was graduated from Farrington high school in 1941 and has had several jobs since she left school.

★ ★ ★

For a while she was employed as a waitress and fountain girl in a downtown drug store. Then she went to work in a pineapple cannery.

Her girl friend was working in a photo concession at 135 N. Hotel St., and suggested Bessie join her in her work. At present she is learning photography, and although occasionally takes pictures, spends much of her time printing and developing photos.

She says she works seven hours a day and turns her salary over to her mother.

Scan the link for Larry Royston's video about Hotel Street Hula Girl photo booths:

GLADE SHOW CLUB (SITE)

152-156 N. Hotel
Architect / Builder: unknown

In 1964, Daisy Aguiar and Attilio "Tilly" Leonardi opened a cabaret called Glade Show Club here that featured live music and floor shows with female impersonators. Their advertising slogan was "Boys Will Be Girls".

It was one of nine places in Honolulu that were officially off-limits to servicemen, but of course that didn't stop them from coming in to gawk at the cross-dressers and transexuals and experience a stage show like they would never see back home.

The entertainers and the servers were all men dressed as women, as were many of the customers. It was estimated that about half of the customers were "straight" but just wanted to see the show. Even Frank Sinatra was said to have visited Glade on at least one occasion.

The master of ceremonies was Liko Johnson – 6 feet tall and 266 pounds with "pancake makeup, a knee-length muumuu, falsies, fake eyelashes, gobs of purple-black eye shadow, a woman's wig and a huge orchid over his left ear."

But by far the most famous and flamboyant entertainer at Glade was Henry Kelso Daniel, known by his stage name as Prince Hanalei. He was Honolulu's legendary male stripper and exotic fire dancer, billed as "The World's Only Male Exotic Dancer".

Prince Hanalei also performed in clubs in Reno, Las Vegas, Lake Tahoe, Tokyo, and Hong Kong. He once said Hawaii had enough kings, so he decided to be a prince.

Prince Hanalei's "twirling torchlight tush" was legendary exotica and incorporated spinning flaming butt tassels.

There is an unusual tradition of acceptance and even reverence in Hawaiian culture of someone who is "mahu" – a transgendered male or female, a third gender that bridges between the two sexes. As opposed to being discriminated against in many places in the world, in Hawaii they are often regarded as important cultural educators and practitioners who also perform chants and traditional hula.

Hotel Street in the 1960's was often clogged with cars driving up and down with curious onlookers wanting to gawk at, take pictures, and sometimes harass the mahus on the street. Many of the "queens" (as they called themselves) had a birth name, a street name, and a stage name, and were required by law to wear a large red button in public that said "I Am A Boy" which often made them targets of hate crimes.

"The Glades" was a mahu-friendly club and was a safe haven for transvestites, transexuals, transgendered prostitutes and drag queens in this dangerous time. It was open until 4am in the morning, with late-night disco dancing after the floor show.

The Glade closed in 1980 and the building was purchased by the city who demolished it in 1983. The wrecking crew found an old printing press in the building with a 1941 Filipino newspaper still on the press, but it was bulldozed and hauled away before anyone could rescue it.

In 1899 there was a 2-story general merchandise store on the site that burned in the 1900 fire. Sometime after 1906 a long narrow building was erected to show "moving pictures".

Popular Clothiers was located here in 1924, and from 1929 to 1933 it was the offices for City Mill's homebuilding department.

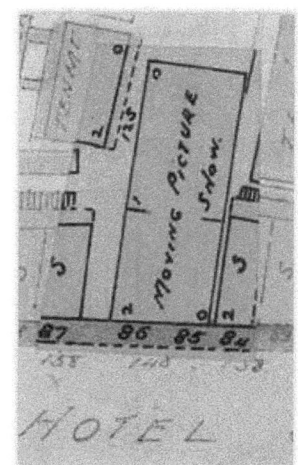

CITY MILL CO., LTD.
HOME BUILDERS — REAL ESTATE FINANCIERS
PHONE 6081   154 N. HOTEL

Pacific Brewing Company, wholesale and retail liquor dealers, where here from 1933 to 1938, and it housed Acme Brokerage in 1942.

From 1945 to 1960 it housed a variety of amusement businesses which included a photo shop, shooting gallery, games with toys and carnival merchandise, and burlesque entertainment: Honolulu Photo Shop (1945), Hotel Amusement (1947), Stateside Amusement (1947), Hotel Amusement (1948), Rex Theater (1949), Target Amusement (1956).

Plus, briefly in 1950, Eddie Cole's "El Patio – The Bottle Club" with Virginia Smith on the Hammond Organ.

HONOLULU CHINATOWN

LUNG DOO BUILDING

159 N. Hotel, 1040 Kekaulike
1965
Architect / Builder: James C.M. Young / unknown

美國夏威夷隆都從善會

This delightful little building is one of the few Chinese-looking buildings in Chinatown, especially with its large round red door and distinctive pagoda on top. It was designed by architect James C.M. Young and finished in time for the 75th anniversary of the Lung Doo Benevolent Society.

The mission of the Lung Doo Society:

> "To help one another in times of need, foster better understanding and relationships within the community, and preserve the common cultural heritage; furthermore, to reach out to the wider community through charitable contributions of time and resources."

The society was founded in 1891 by five men who wanted to provide services and support for Chinese immigrants coming from the provinces where the Lung Doo dialect is spoken. Lung Doo is a complex of 56 villages in the second district in the city of Zhongshan, located southeast of Guangzhou (Canton) and northwest of Macao, in the province of Guandong, China.

In 1895 they acquired property at Aala Lane and Kukui Street and built a clubhouse with living quarters for members who needed a place to stay. Unfortunately, the Honolulu Redevelopment Agency condemned it and everything around it for urban renewal in the early 1960's.

The Lung Doo Society was one of the founders of the Manoa Chinese Cemetery, and before World War II its members were buried there for free. Originally all male, they revised their by-laws to allow women in 1997. In 1963, Lung Doo had more than 5,000 members.

In addition to mutual assistance and protection, the society also does charitable work and supports youth education with annual scholarships to Chinese language schools as well as the University of Hawaii.

YEW CHAR BUILDING

158-162 N. Hotel
1987
Architect / Builder: Washington Char / Delco Construction

This building was constructed by Virginia Char Wong in 1987. The Owner's Certificate of Completion refers to "repairs, renovation and addition" but it is highly unlikely any of the previous c.1906 wooden building remained.

The Yew Char Travel Agency moved to this building from 1011 Maunakea in 1987, five years after Yew Char had passed away. Not wanting to sell to a stranger, the family closed the business in 2004. (See 1011 Maunakea for more information about Yew Char).

The previous wooden building had spaces for three stores, plus wooden tenements in back. Some of the businesses over the years have been The Miyako An "The Red Lantern" restaurant owned by Masaluchi Kawamoto (1924), Takahara Restaurant (1934-1944), Glory Inn Restaurant (1944-1960), The Kama Sutra Theatre featuring "first run all-male movies" (1972), Action Center Cinema (1976), and the May Flower Chinese Restaurant (1978).

Sharing the new building with Yew Char Travel were Macau Chop Suey and the Canton House Restaurant.

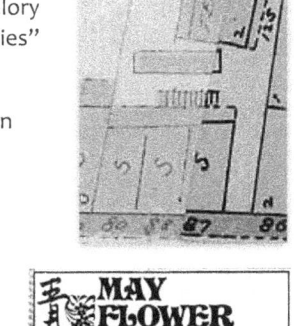

CHINATOWN MANOR

175 N. Hotel
1994
Architect / Builder: Kober Hanssen Mitchell / Hawaiian Dredging & Construction Company

As part of Mayor Frank Fasi's effort to revitalize Chinatown, the city's Department of Housing and Community development acquired several properties along Hotel and Kekaulike streets in 1991 for the Kekaulike Revitalization Project, including a large 2-story wooden building originally built on this site built in 1903 by James Armstrong.

There was a similar building on the site in 1899 that housed a doctor, barber and two general merchandise stores that burned in the big 1900 fire. The 2-story wooden replacement built in 1901 burned in the 1902 fire along with the Winston Block. The third building on the site, later bought by K.L. Wong in 1923, lasted for 91 years.

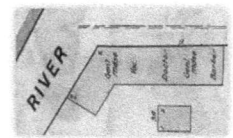

The Shiigi Drug Store was located on the corner from 1907 to 1958. The store also carried a wide variety of books including Japanese translations of Faust, Hamlet, and Emerson's essays.

Ichinojo Shiigi was from Yamaguchi prefecture and came to Hawaii around 1902. His apothecary license was the first given to any Japanese in the Hawaiian Territory.

Shiigi was a distributor for Nitto records from Osaka, and starting in 1927 he collaborated with radio station KGU to broadcast a half hour program of Japanese music, from ancient "Naga Uta" music to current popular hits.

In ancient times up to the mid 1800's this was a low-lying area adjacent to Nu'uanu Stream. According to the old land records, "Pehu's fishpond" was in the back of this property. In 1896, Kepo'olele Apau lived there – she was the oldest person in Hawaii on record at 127 years old, and had been an attendant of Kapiolani.

WINSTON HALE

158-190 N. Hotel
1965, remodeled 1981
Architect / Builder: Lemmon Freeth Haines & Jones (1965) / Town Construction (1965)

Known as Winston Hale, this building is on the site of the infamous Winston Block apartments. It was constructed in 1965 and replaced a large dilapidated 2-story wooden apartment building built by E.C. Winston in 1903. That building was the replacement of a similar building built in 1901 that burned down in a dramatic fire that ravaged the entire block on August 18, 1902.

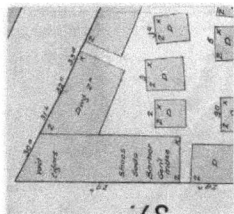

Winston's first building in 1887 was a 2-story wooden building with apartments and a barber shop plus stores that sold cigars, shoes, sodas, and general merchandise.

On the right is the only known photo of the 1901 building. Started by a cat knocking over a lantern, the ensuing fire destroyed several buildings on both sides of the street.

Police Captain J. Kanae dramatically rescued a frightened Japanese woman trapped out on a wooden awning by climbing a nearby telephone pole to reach her and then carrying her on his back down to safety.

In another rescue attempt, an elderly Chinese man rushed into the burning building to save a canary, only to realize once he reached the street that there was no bird in the cage. Several moments later, a little Chinese girl magically produced the missing bird from the folds of her blouse.

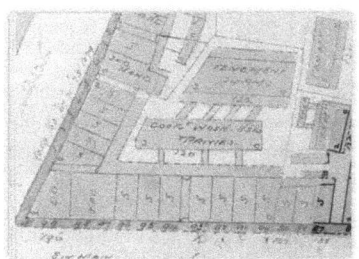

The Winston Block was rebuilt in 1903, possibly by Chinese builder Pang Chong. Rooms rented for $2 a month, and the building quickly developed a notorious reputation which by 1908 "figured largely in local criminal history" as a "focus for disorder".

> "We must take an occasional look over the Winston block. I think there is material there for a Bible class or a society for the suppression of mutual extinction through fisticuffs and hair-pulling" – Chief of Detectives Jack Kalakeila.

Residents at the Winston Block were mostly working-class Portuguese, Japanese, Puerto Rican, Hawaiian, African, Chinese, and Korean – whom the newspaper in 1910 called *"the class of people who make the night hideous at the Winston... notoriously the worst of its kind in the city from several standpoints"*.

Notable activities at the Winston included fighting, gambling, arson, drunkenness, beatings, infidelity, profanity, lewdness, brick-throwing, stabbing, murder, burglary, and Peeping Toms.

Police officer Chang Ah Ping was a frequent visitor to the Winston Block. He was better known as Chang Apana.

Legendary boxing promoter Sam Ichinose ran Sad Sam's bar at the corner of Hotel and River streets from 1941 to 1957. Known for his somber expression and incredible energy, Samuel Masuo Ichinose was known as "Mr. Boxing" for over 50 years and staged more than 425 fights in Hawaii, Tokyo, Indonesia, and Europe.

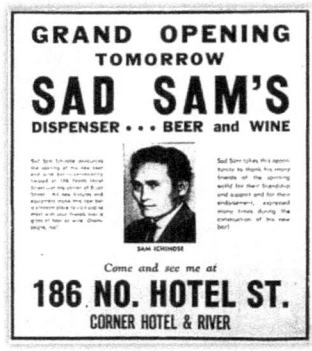

Sad Sam was a member of the Hawaii Sports Hall of Fame, the International Boxing Hall of Fame, and the World Boxing Hall of Fame.

In 1965, James Winston hired Lemmon Freeth Haines & Jones to design a replacement for the 62-year-old building to be a new affordable housing project called Winston Hale.

Since Winston did not want to follow the Honolulu Urban Renewal Plan regulations, the City bought the property in 1981 and remodeled it to the way it looks today, claiming at the time that it "was not listed on the State Registry of Historic Places nor is it of any historic or architectural value".

Established in 1963, the Mabuhay Café owned by Jean & Filomena Lumauag was here for 52 years, moving to 186 N. Hotel in 1965 and later to 1049 River Street in the same building in 1992.

Favorite dishes included Pusit Guisado, Dinaguan, Pork Sarciado, Shrimp Sari Sari, Pancit, and Shrimp Kilawen.

Chang Apana (1871-1933)
鄭阿平, 郑阿平

The person probably most familiar with all the goings-on in the Winston Block was Chinese-Hawaiian police officer and detective Chang Apana (Chang Ah Ping).

He was born in Waipio, Oahu in 1871 but spent age 3 through 10 in China until returning to Hawaii to live with his uncle. Although he never learned to read, he was fluent in speaking Cantonese, Hawaiian and Pidgin English.

He worked as a paniolo (Hawaiian cowboy) on his first job where he regularly carried a bullwhip. He then spent three years working for the Humane Society which at that time was part of the Honolulu Police Department. The society was founded by Helen Kinau Wilder, the owner of the horses he had cared for.

In 1898 he officially joined the police department and was assigned the Chinatown beat working mostly on gambling and opium cases. The diminutive detective became widely known and respected for his meticulous style and ability to solve difficult cases.

There are many stories about his various feats of daring, including an attack by a Japanese leper wielding a sickle who was resisting being sent to Kalaupapa in Molokai, being run over by a horse and buggy while chasing after contraband, and being thrown out of a second story window by drug addicts and landing on his feet. It is said he never carried a gun – he once rounded up 40 gamblers and marched them to the police station with nothing more than his bullwhip. He was also known to be a master of disguises.

in 1925, mystery novelist Earl Derr Biggers heard about Chang Apana while writing *The House Without a Key* and promptly inserted a new character into the book based on the famous Honolulu detective. The character's name? Charlie Chan.

As a counterpoint to the sinister Fu Manchu and "Yellow Peril" Asian stereotypes, Biggers' fictional detective became hugely popular and was featured in five more novels: *The Chinese Parrot* (1926), *Behind That Curtain* (1928), *The Black Camel* (1929), *Charlie Chan Carries On* (1930), and *Keeper of the Keys* (1932).

Since 1926 nearly 50 films have featured the Charlie Chan character, with the most famous portrayal being by Swedish actor Warner Oland.

A Charlie Chan comic strip debuted in 1938 and after World War II the character starred in several comic books.

Biggers met Chang Apana in person in 1928, and Chang got to meet Warner Oland when *The Black Camel* was filmed in Hawaii in 1931. Chang enjoyed the movies and was often called "Charlie Chan" and asked for autographs.

KEKAULIKE STREET

[Pronounced KAY-kow-LEE-kay]

Named for Princess Kekaulike, the sister of Queen Kapiolani, who died on January 18, 1884. It was laid out as an ungraded street after the Great Fire of 1886 and was first paved in 1912.

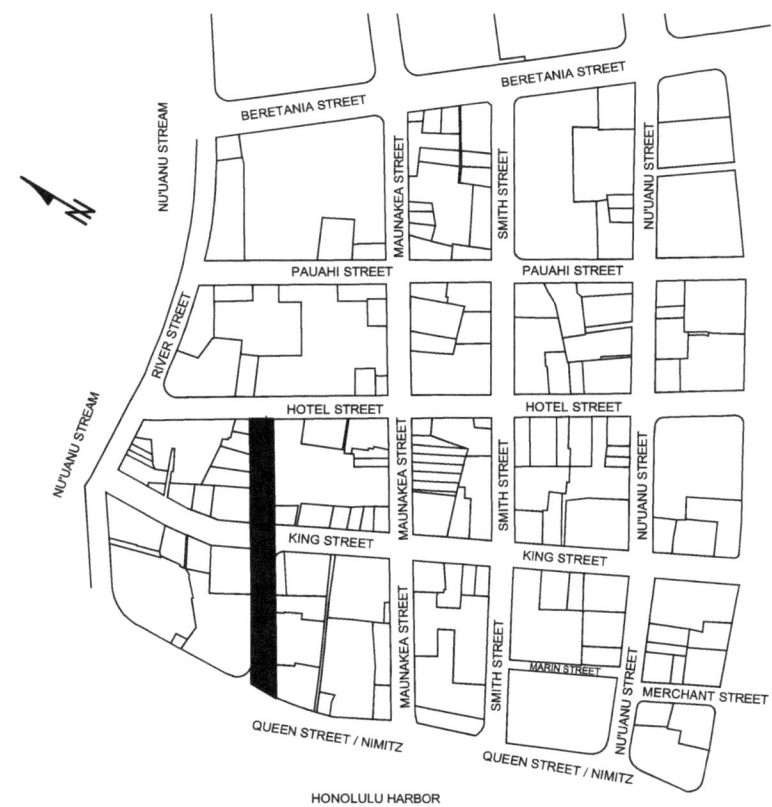

HONOLULU CHINATOWN

SPERRY FLOUR BUILDING

905 Kekaulike
1919
Architect / Builder: Emil F. Cykler? / Hawaiian Contracting Co.

This was once a very attractive Spanish Mediterranean-style building with large arches on the first floor, an Alamo-style parapet, and decorative terra cotta tiled awnings above the arched second-story windows.

It was built in 1919 for the Sperry Flour Company under the supervision of civil engineer Emil F. Cykler.

He came to Hawaii in 1915 to work for the Lord-Young engineering company, a contracting company specializing mostly in roads, utilities, and harbor work.

After J.L. Young left the firm, and then E.J. Lord, the company became the Hawaiian Contracting Company in 1918, an adjunct company of Hawaiian Dredging & Construction Company.

From 1919 to 1950 this was the Honolulu office of the Sperry Flour Company. The company was founded in 1852 and merged with General Mills in 1929. Based out of Stockton, California, Sperry was the leading West Coast milling company with mills in Tacoma, Spokane, and Portland.

In 1950 Sperry Flour moved to a new building on Sand Island and sold the property to the C.Q. Yee Hop Company.

So, what happened to this once-beautiful building?

Due to the widening of Queen Street/Nimitz Highway in 1951, one side was cut back and the rest of the building "modernized" into what you see today.

CITY MILL (SITE)

918 Kekaulike
(1899-1950)
Architect / Builder: City Mill

Currently the site of the Chinatown rail station, this is the first location for the City Mill company, incorporated on June 13, 1899. The company was created to carry on the business of "rice millers, rice merchants, planing mill, builders and contractors, lumber merchants and dealers in builders' and contractors' supplies". Wong Leong was president, C.K. Ai was vice-president and Pang Chong was foreman. All the stockholders were Chinese, although many others tried to get shares. The first two buildings built were the rice mill and the planing mill.

This Victorian house was on the ewa-mauka corner of Queen and Kekaulike and would have burned in the 1900 fire. This was also the site of the Ishizu Hotel in 1905, and a fire which gutted an adjacent grocery store.

Seven months after they were incorporated, all City Mill buildings were burned in the big 1900 fire. They did not have insurance yet, and they also had many creditors, but C.K. Ai was able to raise the capital to rebuild City Mill on the strength of his character, reputation, and ties with the community.

City Mill had the largest rice mill in Hawaii before World War II. You can see one the original coral millstones in the parking lot of the City Mill store on Nimitz Highway.

In 1929 the rice mill moved to 660 Prison Road (now Iwilei Road) and they moved their headquarters offices to Hotel Street across from Kekaulike Street. They moved their "town offices" to 138 N. King in 1933.

By the end of World War II, City Mill was one of the largest building materials suppliers in the Pacific.

When they relocated everything in Chinatown to Nimitz Highway in 1950, the road was closed for the grand opening with the governor in attendance. City Mill has eight retail stores today and nearly 500 employees.

Chung Kun Ai

CHUNG K. AI

Pronounced "Ah-ee" and known as "C.K.", the founder of City Mill came to Hawaii in 1879 with his father. At age 14 he enrolled in Bishop's School ('Iolani School) where he met and became lifelong friends with Sun Yat-sen.

His first job was partnering in a tailor shop, which he soon left to clerk with businessman James I. Dowsett who was impressed with his perseverance and work ethic. Dowsett became his mentor and it turned into a lifelong friendship. Ai even purchased Dowsett's desk, swivel chair and upright safe, and they are still at City Mill today. Every Memorial Day he visited Dowsett's grave to pay his respects.

Ai was one of the most well-known and respected businessmen in Honolulu, and he dedicated much of his time to charitable causes in China and Hawaii. At age 93 he published his memoir, *My 79 Years in Hawaii*.

VIGILANT

In 1926 City Mill purchased *Vigilant* from the E.K. Wood Lumber Company to bring in lumber from the Northwest Coast. Built in 1911 in Hoquiam, Washington, it was the largest 5-masted wooden topsail schooner in the Pacific and could carry 2 million board feet of lumber below and on deck.

She was 260 feet long with masts 130 feet tall and was the first sailing ship to have electric lights and wireless radio. Her skipper was Captain "Matt" Peasley, made famous by Peter B. Kyne's novels.

After many trips across the Pacific, *Vigilant* was sold to a Canadian firm in 1940 and renamed *City of Alberni*. It burned in 1946.

The names of the five masts: fore, main, mizzen, jigger, and spanker.

Captain Matt Peasley

Ralph Erskine "Matt" Peasley was born in Jonesport, Maine in 1866, and left school at age 14 to go to sea with the Grand Banks cod fishermen. He commanded his first ship at age 22 – a two-masted, square-rigged brig. In 1888 he rounded Cape Horn to the Northwest Coast and quickly earned a reputation for daring, including navigating the Yangtze River by himself in the middle of a typhoon.

But it was a chance meeting in 1900 with Peter Bernard Kyne, a clerk with the Dolbeer & Carson Lumber Company, that would change his life forever. Kyne was intrigued by Peasley's colorful ship master's reports, and being a writer of short stories and novels in his spare time, he took Captain Peasley's stories and created Captain Peasley the character in his popular 1915 book *Cappy Ricks, or the Subjugation of Matt Peasley*.

It is the story of many struggles between two hardheaded individualists, one a ship captain named Matt Peasley and the other being the president of the Blue Star Navigation Company, Alden P. Ricks.

The book was wildly successful and two more quickly followed. Along with serial stories in the Saturday Evening Post and Cosmopolitan magazine they made the real Captain Peasely into a celebrity. People called him "Captain Matt" on the street and many wanted their photograph taken with him.

When the large 5-masted *Vigilant* lay in the Gordon Frazer Matthews shipyard in Aberdeen, Washington, only half completed and in need of additional capital to complete, they were able to enlist Captain Peasley as the new master which instantly helped raise the money needed to complete the ship.

On the maiden voyage enroute to Sydney, Australia, the deck load of lumber shifted in a storm and the ship nearly crashed into the Great Barrier Reef. Newspaper reporters were waiting when it arrived, something that would happen time and time again at every port, eager to hear more tales of Peasley's seafaring exploits. Peasley was famous for racing other ships across the Pacific, once again ensuring a steady stream of headlines.

Peasley once said, *"Give me a ship that sails, I want no screech of a whistle nor throb of engines; the sight of straining sails fills me with a never-ending pleasure. There will never be any steamships for me."*

In 1919 the books were turned into a Broadway Play, followed by the 1921 silent film *Cappy Ricks* starring Thomas Meighan, and *The Affairs of Cappy Ricks* starring Walter Brennan in 1937. *The Return of Cappy Ricks* was the first film shown when the new King Theater opened on King Street on December 14, 1935.

Ed Van Syckle, reporter for the Aberdeen Daily World, traveled with Captain Peasley as an ordinary sailor onboard *Vigilant* for the 31-day trip from Aberdeen to Honolulu in 1927. He described Captain Peasley as weighing 190 pounds, with clear, blue eyes, and a walrus mustache that framed a quick smile. *"After a while, he began living the role that Kyne had created for him—talking with phrases from the books, and taking his morning constitutional, strutting back and forth across the poop, a cigar stuck in his mouth."*

When asked if Captain Peasley was really larger than life, Van Syckle said, "In later years, I think he worked it up a bit, but it wasn't conceit. It was just part of being 'Matt Peasley'."

SERVICE COLD STORAGE BUILDING

919 Kekaulike
1924
Architect / Builder: Herman R. Stettin / unknown

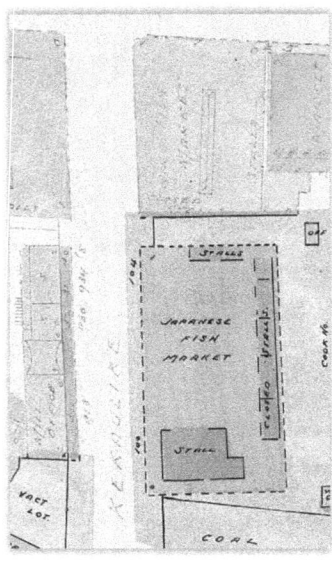

Built by the C.M. Cooke Estate in 1924, this building was designed by local architect Herman R. Stettin. In addition to Service Cold Storage, it also housed the Armour, Tai Hing, and Charles Akana companies.

The existing Service Cold Storage retail store was incorporated into the building and a refrigeration plant was built in the back. The Vice President and Manager was Richard C. Ching, formerly with C.Q. Yee Hop.

It was built on the site of the Japanese Fish Market which had turned into the City Market by 1914. It was briefly a skating rink in 1906.

Prior to 1900 this side of the street was lined with a series of 2-story wooden dwellings built after the 1886 fire. The entire waikiki side of Kekaulike Street was deliberately burned by the Board of Public Health on January 4, 1900.

Before

After

Believe it or not, there was a small church behind these buildings built in 1885 or 1886, identified on the photograph as "Kaumakapili Chapel". It was spared on January 4, only to burn down 16 days later on January 20.

Here are some of the other buildings built before 1891 that were in the interior of the block, behind what is now the Service Cold Storage Building. These all burned in the January 20, 1900, fire.

928 KEKAULIKE

928 Kekaulike
1953
Architect / Builder: unknown

This plain concrete building was built in 1953 on the site of a long wooden building built after the 1900 fire that served as the offices for the City Mill Company.

In 1923 the Wo Chong company here sold turkeys, chicken, gees, Muscovy duck, and suckling pigs.

The Oahu Poultry Company was here in 1936, claiming to be "the largest poultry store in Hawaii".

In 1956 Kam Hung Lee and Sau Tim Lee announced the See Hing Café at 928 Kekaulike.

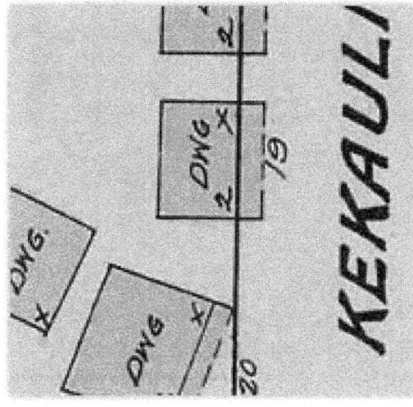

1891

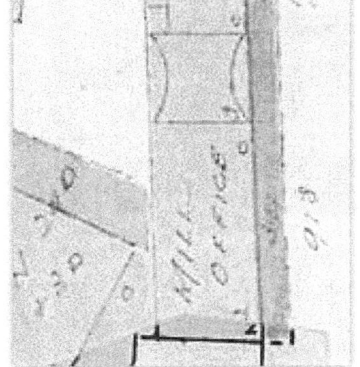

1906

HOLAU MARKET

942 Kekaulike
1936
Architect / Builder: Hego Fuchino / M.K. Goto (Aloha Building Company)

Designed by Hego Fuchino and built in 1936 by Mankichi Goto's Aloha Building Company for Captain Frank & Mary Ellen Loncke, this building was purchased by the Honolulu Authority for Rapid Transportation (HART) to be restored/rehabilitated as part of the Chinatown rail station.

Fuchino and Goto were both detained at the Santa Fe Internment Camp during World War II, along with Daizo Sumida and Yasutaro Soga (editor of the *Nippu Jiji*).

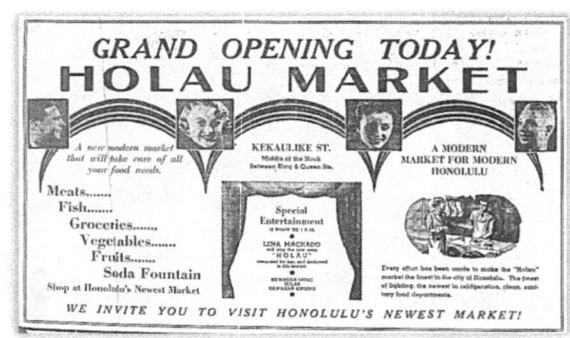

Holau Market opened on July 30, 1936, celebrated with hula and a special musical performance by Lena Machado – "Hawaii's Songbird" – who composed a new song especially for the market titled "Holau".

Scan the QR code to hear Ms. Machado singing the song:

Captain Frank J. Loncke & Mary Ellen Holau Freudenberg Leslie Loncke

Frank J. Loncke was born in Maaseik, Arrondissement Maaseik, Limburg, Belgium, and was a retired captain with the Inter-Island Steam Navigation Company. For twenty years he was the skipper of the steamship *Mauna Kea* and its much larger replacement *Haleakala*.

Haleakala was built in Pennsylvania in 1924, and Locke sailed it from Philadelphia to Hawaii through the Panama Canal. The ship was 360' long, 1500 tons cargo capacity, and had D. Howard Hitchcock oil paintings in the public room. It was not a small ship – almost half the size of the *Titanic*.

Captain Loncke made over 1,000 trips between Oahu and the Big Island during his career, which at one point included diving from the bridge into the ocean in an attempt to save a drowning crew member.

SS Maunakea

SS Haleakala

The Cook Plaque

In 1914 he married Mary Ellen Holau Freudenberg Leslie who had divorced Sam Leslie in 1906. She was the owner of a 12" x 24" copper plate left near the site of Captain Cook's death on October 17, 1837, by HMS *Imogene* that had been given to her by her former father-in-law. The plaque was originally nailed to a coconut tree stump at Kawaalao but was found by Fred L. Leslie on the beach at Napoopoo being used by a Hawaiian fisherman to patch a canoe.

Both Great Britain and the Territory of Hawaii tried for years to obtain the plaque, considering it a national treasure, but without success.

She gave it to her son-in law, Benjamin Vickers, but after he suddenly dropped dead of a fainting spell it somehow ended up with her stepson Alex Leslie. He finally agreed to give it to the Bishop Museum in 1964 after the will of Captain Loncke was probated in Hilo.

Unfortunately, Mary Ellen did not live to see the success of the market, passing away only two months after it opened. Since he had ostensibly opened the business for his wife, Captain Loncke sold it in 1937 to the M. Ichiki Group, making it their 11th store in Oahu and Maui.

After Masaji Ichiki passed away at the age of only 55, his wife, Tetsuyo, briefly continued the business, but after a year sold it to Tatsuo Goto.

The last newspaper mention of the Holau Market is in 1984.

Masaji Ichiki was born in Japan and after high school went to Maui to join his family who were sugar plantation workers. After eight years working in the Pioneer Mill Company's fields and plantation store, he opened his own store in Lāhainā in 1925.

By 1931 he had five stores on Maui and in 1935 he expanded into Oahu. His wife, Tetsuyo, was from Kaua'i and she was a co-owner of the business and took over after his early death in 1951.

Tatsuo Goto took over the Holau Market in 1952. Born in Paauilo, Hawaii, he was 12 years old when he started working for the Jamakua Sugar Plantation. He moved to Oahu in 1939 and became a fish cutter for M. Otani Fish Company and later started his own business delivering fresh fish to neighborhoods. Realizing the demand for fishcakes led to founding Red and White Foods Inc., one of the island largest fishcake manufacturers. It was sold to Kibun Foods in 1993.

Lena Kaulumau Wai'ale'ale Machado was a Native Hawaiian singer, composer and ukulele player famous for using an unusual Hawaiian vocal technique known as "ha'i" (transitioning back and forth from normal voice and falsetto), plus the use of subtle hidden meanings, "kaona", in her songwriting.

A chance encounter with a manager at KGU radio who heard her sing led to regular on-air performances, her own radio program, and a nearly fifty-year association with the Royal Hawaiian Band.

She toured extensively on the US mainland and recorded several record albums.

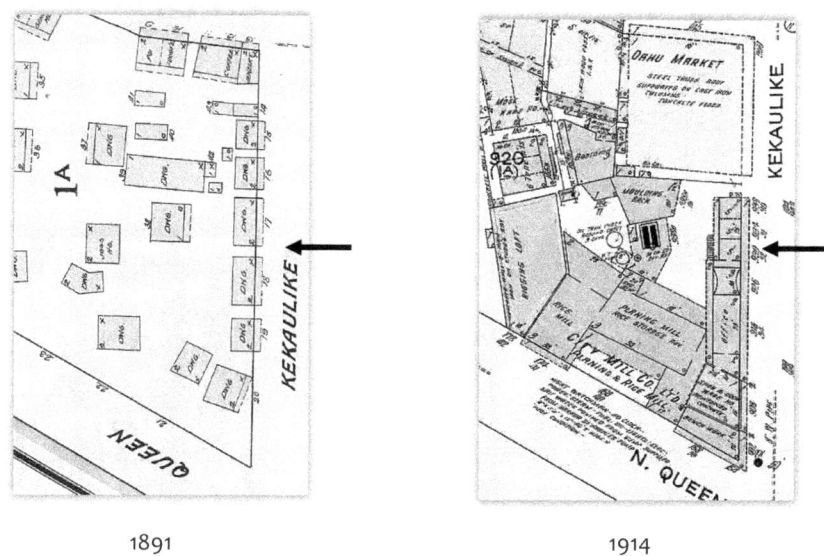

1891   1914

Probably built shortly after the 1886 fire, these 2-story wooden dwelling houses were on the site until the entire block was burned in the big 1900 fire.

From 1906 to 1936, there were several 2-story wooden stores here along with the main office for City Mill at 918 Kekaulike, with the large main yard and plant located behind it.

1011-1015 KEKAULIKE (SITE)

1011-1015 Kekaulike
c.1901-1906
Architect / Builder: (unknown)

The building here today is part of the city's 1997 Kekaulike Courtyards project. The 1906 Dakin Fire Insurance Map shows a 2-story brick building with two storefronts that would have been built sometime between 1901 and 1906.

It housed a restaurant on the right side that was the Roseland Café from 1934 to 1943, owned by Hatsuhira Miyamoto. Waitresses working there made a monthly salary of $25.70.

In 1933 the Roseland Dance Hall was upstairs, becoming the Venice 5-Penny Ballroom in 1934.

There was a bust here in 1936 with 14 arrested for playing "7-11". The police confiscated one pair of dice and 75 cents in cash.

By 1942 the upstairs was the Filipino Hotel, with furnished rooms.

From 1946 to 1950 the entire downstairs was Kekaulike Poi Bowl owned by Awai Pang, Gary W.L. Lee, Edward P.K. Wong, and Lum Hoo Henry Lee. They also had a location on South King Street opposite the Honolulu Stadium.

The building was demolished in 1952 for a city parking lot.

CITY VILLA APARTMENTS

1022 Kekaulike
1964, 1994 remodel
Architect / Builder: unknown, George Woo (1994) / DLR Construction (1994)

The City Villa Apartments were built in 1964 as a dormitory for single men, with rooms renting for $50 per month.

It replaced the previous 2-story wooden building that was condemned by the city and subsequently demolished after a fire that had one fatality. Because of this, the city initiated a drive to condemn unsafe tenements throughout the downtown area.

Originally in the Mid-Century Modern style, it was remodeled in 1994 to be more compliant with the Chinatown Design Guidelines.

The site was previously home to the City Café, who moved to 1035 Kapiolani in 1958. The owner, Wong In Properties, initially planned to build a 2.5-story building with restaurant and bar on this site in 1959, and even drew up plans with Town Construction as the lowest bidder.

In 1994 they hired George Woo to design the alterations required by the Kekaulike Rehabilitation Project, and they were constructed by DLR Construction.

YING LEONG LOOK FUNN BUILDING

1026-1030 Kekaulike
1961, 1994 remodel
Architect / Builder: unknown, James C.M. Young (1994)

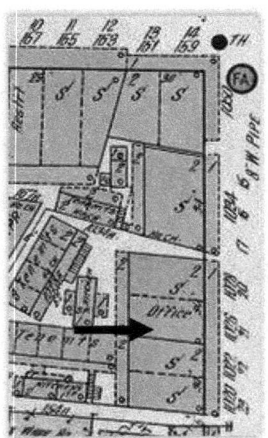

The first building on this site was a 2-story wooden building with space for 4 stores, built shortly after the 1900 fire, covering the area of this building and the adjacent City Villa site.

From 1932 to 1959 it housed the Kekaulike Café owned by Giichi Matsuda. Kimura Florist was a longtime tenant here from 1953 to 1989, in both the old and new buildings.

In 1959 the old wooden building was condemned by the city and the owner voluntarily demolished it in 1960 and replaced it with a concrete block building in 1961.

The Kamehameha Grill moved into the new building from next door and was here from 1961 to 1975. They were famous throughout the city for their sweetbread buns.

In 1994 the façade was remodeled by architect James C.M. Young per the Chinatown Design Guidelines.

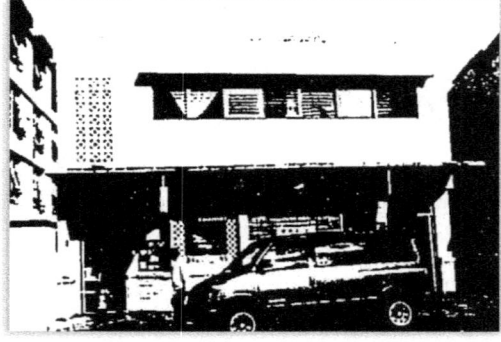

SAM CHEW LAU BUILDING

1034-1038 Kekaulike
1963, 1994 remodel
Architect / Builder: unknown, James C.M. Young (1994)

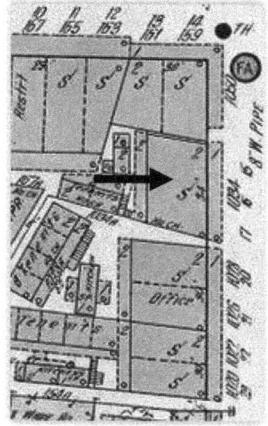

The first-known building on this site was a 1-story house in 1891, followed by a larger 2-story wooden building in 1899. Sometime around 1906 a 2-story wooden building with space for three stores was built here.

In the 1930's it housed L. Asing, tailor, and then Tong On, tailor, and in the 1940's, it housed the EDS V Barber Shop, the Uno tattoo Shop, the Kekauike Lei Shop, and the Roy & Phillip Barber Shop owned by Roy Quiamno and Phillip Songcuan.

The Kamehameha Grill, owned by Richard Shigeichi Asato and Shigeru Asato, was here from 1938 to 1961 when it moved next door to 1028 Kekaulike. They were famous for their sweetbread buns and at one point also advertised Buck's Bake Shop specializing in Portuguese Sweet Bread.

In 1963, the old wooden building was demolished and the present building completed. The Roosevelt Café moved here in 1963 from 274 N. King Street, becoming the Roosevelt Cocktail Lounge, owned by Harry H. Segawa. It became a succession of nightclubs in the 1980s – Rusty's Den in 1980, Irvin's II in 1983, and Club YC III in 1986.

The façade was demolished and remodeled in 1994 by architect James C.M. Young per the Chinatown Design Guidelines.

KING STREET

First established in 1837, this was the main road out of town headed towards Ewa Beach. By 1848 it was called Church Street or Chapel Street due to the Seamen's Bethel Church at the corner on Bethel Street, and it was also known as Main Street or Broadway. It officially became King Street in 1850 and was first paved in 1912.

In 1906, Robert K. Bonine, working for Thomas A. Edison, Inc., mounted a 16mm moving picture camera on the front of a streetcar going down King Street. Now part of the George Kleine Collection in the Library of Congress, you can view the video here: https://youtu.be/ICsli_sKmMM

The scenes in Chinatown start about one minute into the film.

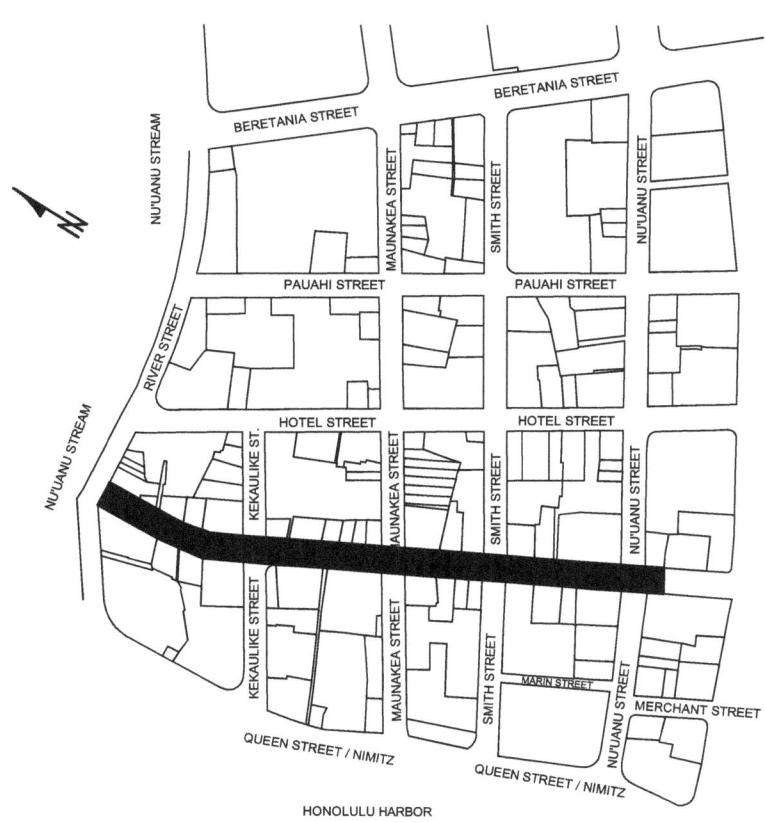

ROBINSON BUILDING / 1 N. KING

1-23 N. King, 936 Nu'uanu
1863/1864
Architect / Builder: Theodore C. Heuck / Samuel Johnson

This is the oldest building in Chinatown, and the 2nd oldest commercial building in Honolulu. The cornerstone was laid on September 26, 1863, by building owner James Robinson and architect Theodore Heuck, and the building was completed in January 1864. This is almost 20 years before Iolani Palace was constructed.

There is a lot of history at this corner, so we'll start at the beginning and work our way up to the present day.

King Kamehameha gave the land to Richard Kilday, who later sold it to James Fleming, who by 1826 was running a "groggery" here. Fleming sold it to Captain Samuel J. Dowsett c.1828 who renamed it The Ship and Whale.

In 1831, James Robinson bought it from Dowsett for $725, probably about the time Kuakini banned liquor sales. The official ruling called for seizure of property for a first offense, with a second offense resulting in having the property torn down. This lasted two years and was pretty much ignored – there was too much money to be made from liquor sales for the owners and for the licensing government.

By the mid 1830's, Englishman Joe Booth renamed it The Blonde. The original "Blonde" was opened by Oahu Governor Boki in 1827 next door on Nu'uanu Street. It was renamed Boki House after Boki disappeared in the South Pacific looking for sandalwood, and The Ship and Whale was then renamed to The Blonde.

It was named for the HMS *Blonde* which brought back the bodies of Kamehameha II (Liholiho) and Queen Kamamalu in 1825 after they died of measles in England.

THE "BLONDE."
JOSEPH BOOTH, Proprietor and keeper of the above named House, would notify strangers and the public generally, that the "good cheer" he has ever endeavored to accommodate them with will be amply provided for the future. Superior Wines, Spirituous and Malt Liquors, excellent cigars and an accomplished barkeeper, he hopes will insure him a continuance of that patronage he has ever endeavored to deserve.
The usual evening amusements will be continued as heretofore, and all are invited to participate in them. Gambling, quarreling and fighting are absolutely prohibited.   my22 1y.

Booth proudly flew the Union Jack flag outside his pub and in 1847 the premises were described as having a stone first floor and wooden second floor, and it was one of thirteen licensed grog shops allowed to sell beer and liquor by the glass.

By 1855 Booth had moved on to the National Hotel and The Blonde was advertised for lease.

> TO LET.—That well known, old established house, The Blonde Restaurant, with all its fixtures, will be leased on the most liberal terms. From its superior business locality, the above House is well worthy attention. Apply to
> 33-tf   JOSEPH BOOTH.

A Chinese merchant named Achuck had a "hawking license" for a store presumably next to The Blonde on the Nuʻuanu side. Was it the old Boki House? Probably.

On August 9, 1860, Mr. Allen, carpenter, moved the Achuck & Company store to the National Hotel property further up Nuʻuanu Street. It was a large 30' x 35' wooden building of "heavy N.W. lumber" that filled the whole street. Several awnings and veranda roofs along Nuʻuanu Street had to be removed so the building could pass.

This left the corner unoccupied, so The Blonde would have disappeared sometime between 1855 and 1860.

Achuck sold off everything in 1863 and moved to San Francisco, but he would be back by 1866 in partnership with Chun Afong on this same corner.

In 1863, James Robinson and Robert Lawrence decided to build a large 56' x 72' coral building with 8' cellar on the site of the former Blonde pub and Achuck store. In August of that year, German-born architect Theodore C. Heuck started lobbying for the second floor of this building to be used as a public hall, publishing a lengthy prospectus in the *Polynesian* and *Pacific Commercial Advertiser* newspapers. Its stated purpose was to "serve as a Concert Hall, for delivering lectures and orations, for public meetings, expositions and for many other instructive entertainments, as also for large and small balls and social parties". The lease was to be $500 a year for five years, and Heuck raised that sum through public subscription.

The cornerstone of the building was laid on September 26, 1863, by James Robinson and Theodore Heuck. It contained a time capsule with the likenesses of Their Majesties the King and Queen, the family and friends of the proprietors, and the children and grandchildren of Mr. Robinson. It also included several coins, an 1863 Hawaiian calendar, a list of the subscribers to the Public Hall, and the history of how James Robinson came to Hawaii.

> CORNER STONE.—The corner stone of the new edifice on the corner of King and Nuuanu streets was laid at 3, P. M., on Saturday last, in the presence of a large concourse. The stone was laid by James Robinson, Esq., the owner of the building, assisted by T. C. Heuck, Esq., the architect, and appropriate addresses made. The building will be completed about the first of January next. The upper story will be fitted up for a public hall, about the size of, or a little larger than, the Supreme Court room.

The contractor was Samuel Johnson, who had come to Hawaii in 1849 from Liverpool and worked on the old Royal Hawaiian Hotel, the 1857 Oahu Prison, and some of the original Queen's Hospital buildings.

> "It is an ornament to the city of Honolulu, a source of just pride to its owners, a credit to its architect, and a subject of mutual congratulation to all who can appreciate the liberalizing and refining influences to which an institution like the Honolulu Hall may in time give origin and due development." – Pacific Commercial Advertiser, April 23, 1864.

Events and performances included St. George's Society meetings, society balls, Amateur Musical Society concerts, a lecture by Walter Leman on "The Drama", Christmas sales, German Society meetings, vocal music, tableaux, plus fancy dinners with dancing until the wee hours of the morning, some of which were attended by the future King David Kalākaua.

On April 1, 1864, Captain Thomas Mossman leased the corner storefront from Robinson and Lawrence and opened a store that specialized in crockery ware. It was called Mossman & Son and was located here for 23 years from 1864 to 1887.

Captain Thomas Mossman was born in Berwick-on-Tweed, England, in 1800, and married Mary Ann Lewis in 1831. Their son Thomas was born in Rotherhithe, London, England in 1832. Thomas Sr. had previously gone to Australia and Mary and their four children followed in 1841. They came to Hawaii in 1846 and were living at Liberty Hall on Maunakea Street in 1848.

Captain Mossman briefly went into sail-making in 1850, but switched to the bakery, grocery and sundries business in 1851 with a shop on Nuʻuanu Street. In 1855 the business became T. Mossman & Son, and after Captain Mossman died in 1878 at age 78, his son, Thomas James Mossman, carried on the business as T.J. Mossman. It went bankrupt in 1887, and Thomas Jr. died in 1894 at age 62.

T.J. Mossman's grandson, George Paele Mossman was a tireless promoter of Hawaiian culture – he was a Hawaiian language teacher, ukulele maker, and music teacher who hired "Hawaii's Songbird" Lena Machado to teach dance and song at his Bell Tone Studio. He also created the Lalani Hawaiian Village in Waikiki in 1932. George's daughter, Pualani, was the poster girl for Matson and the most photographed woman in Hawaii at the time.

Afong & Achuck

In 1866, Chun Afong partnered with Achuck and leased the storefront on the Nuʻuanu side, opening a Chinese general merchandise business known as Afong & Achuck.

From 1868 to 1874 they held the only licenses for importing opium which made them immensely wealthy. In 1870 they purchased the Kaupakuea sugar plantation near Hilo, and they were also very active in the importation of Chinese laborers.

Achuk passed away in China in 1877, and a year later the business was renamed to "C. Afong".

Shortly after midnight on January 3, 1878, the C. Afong store was gutted by a fire that apparently started in the basement. He lost everything but luckily had insurance.

After being in business on this corner for 24 years, Afong held a big clearance sale in 1890 and returned permanently to China.

Here are five photographs from April 19, 1886, the day after the big Chinatown fire. The two at the bottom were taken from the roof of the Robinson Building and show the burned-out United Chinese Society and Aswan buildings. The Robinson Building was lucky and was not damaged by the fire.

From 1891 to 1900 the building housed the IXL Auction & Commission Store owned by S.W. Lederer.

The upstairs was called the American Union Hall and it was the site of the first Republican Convention in 1894.

This photograph was taken on January 20, 1900, during the second big Chinatown fire.

The Anchor Saloon is on the left, and the crowds are watching the fire while also forming a solid line on either side of the street to make sure none of the potentially plague-infected fire refugees try to escape during their forced march to temporary quarantine facilities at Kawaiahaʻo Church.

From 1900 to 1903 the California Saloon was located on the first floor of the Robinson Building.

In 1906, Robert K. Bonine, working for Thomas A. Edison, Inc., mounted a 35mm moving picture camera on the front of a streetcar going down King Street.

Now part of the George Kleine Collection in the Library of Congress, you can view the video here:

On the right is a screenshot showing the Robinson Building, taken at about the 1:00 minute mark.

From 1910 to 1932 it was the home of the City Hardware Company owned by G.K Wo (Goo Koon Wo). In 1916 they added an auto stand next door on King Street, designed by architect Y.T. Char.

This photograph from 1920 shows the Anchor Saloon on the far left. They relocated here when their building across the street was demolished for the Hoffschlager Building.

City Hardware remodeled the first-floor exterior in 1922.

OLD FRONT

NEW FRONT

Tonight Hawaiian Hula Dance

TWO GIRLS

Everybody's going to have a good time tonight!

Bring your friends up for a chop sui dinner and see the Hula Dance.

There's to be orchestra dancing on the Narcissus Roof Garden too.

NARCISSUS CHOP SUI

KING AND NUUANU

In 1923 they hired architects Ripley Davis & Fishbourne to design a new building next door at 15-23 N. King Street.

It was the second location of the Palace of Sweets, moving here from farther down King Street. Founded in 1878, it was a bakery and one of the top restaurants in downtown Honolulu. They were famous for their 50-cent dinners and for their championship softball team in the Chinese Baseball League.

Narcissus Chop Sui opened above the hardware store in 1925, featuring hula by Miss Libby Keanini and rooftop dancing.

Grand Opening Today of the **PALACE OF SWEETS** at our new location 15-23 N. KING STREET (Near Nuuanu St.)

Bakery Specials for Today Only

We want you to become acquainted with our new bakery department and our fresh assortment of bakery goods. We are offering the following at special prices:—

WHIPPED CREAM PUFFS, doz. . . Special $1.00
MARSHMELLOW LAYER CAKE . . . Special 45c
GENUINE POUND CAKE . . . Special 25c
LARGE SIZE ASSORTED PIES . . . Special 30c

Fancy Assorted Ice Cream Cakes—75c lb. — Angel Cake—40c

| Our Buffet Department Offers a Special Chicken Dinner Come in and have a real dinner | Elegant Fixtures Attractive Marble Fountain Splendidly Appointed Dining Room for Ladies and Gentlemen MUSIC BY ALL CHINESE ORCHESTRA Afternoon and Evening PHONE 1486 | Candies Every kind of candy, mostly fresh—in bars or bulk. Much of it we make ourselves. Candy Special for Today Sweet's Stuffed Hard Candies 45c Per Bottle |

HONOLULU CHINATOWN

At 10:30 pm on the night of August 8, 1932, the City Hardware Company was destroyed by a huge fire that started in the basement and destroyed the top floor and the roof, with heavy water damage on the first floor. Damages were estimated at $20,000. One fireman had to be rescued clinging to a burning wooden beam he grabbed when the roof gave way.

Oahu Furniture Company, formerly located next to the Liberty Theater, was here from 1934 to 1976. They were founded in 1925 by Yan Hoon Leong and his brother Yau On (Harry) Leong. Mr. Lee Kui, the popular former sales manager of the City Hardware Company also worked here. Both Leongs were very active in the Honolulu Chinese community. Harry Leong was a director of Aloha Airlines and Hawaii National Bank, and was active in the See Dai Doo Society, Yin Sit Sha, Leong Soong Duck Tong, and the Chinese Chamber of Commerce.

The Palace Grill was located next door at 15-23 N. King, and the top floor became Club Avalon in 1937.

The Leong brothers purchased the Robinson Building and the adjoining Palace Grill building in 1939 and hired architect Y.T. Char and M.K. Goto's Aloha Builder company to remodel and modernize the Robinson building.

Before

After

In 1947 the Leong's remodeled 19-23 N. King to match 1 N. King. The furniture store closed in 1976 after 42 years at this location. In a coincidental harkening back to shipbuilder James Robinson, the Sign of the Crab nautical antique store was located here in 1976.

Jay Shidler took a 60-year lease on the building in 1976 with plans to create a downtown restaurant, but it became an auction house instead (another nod to a previous incarnation), and it was also the location of Broad Recording Studio on where contemporary artists like Lemuria, Aura, Phase 7, Momi Riley, and Mike Lundy recorded albums.

This is the seventh-oldest building in Honolulu, after the three Mission Houses (1821, 1831, 1841), Kawaiahaʻo Church (1842), the Cathedral Basilica of Our Lady of Peace (1843) and the Melchers Building (1854) on Merchant Street.

1894

2021

Step into the alleyway on the makai side of the building and look up – you are looking at 1864. The original parapet, window openings, and segmented pilasters are still in excellent condition nearly 160 years later.

1886

2021

In the first season of the 2004 *Lost* TV Series, this building was the location of the "Melbourne Walkabout Tours" travel agency, featuring Emmy Award-winning actor Terry O'Quinn playing John Locke. O'Quinn was in 101 episodes of *Lost*, and later played Commander Joe White in 15 episodes of the reboot of the *Hawaii 5-0* TV series.

James Robinson

Born in 1799 in Thurrock, Essex, England, James Robinson came to Hawaii via the whaling ship *Hermes* which ran aground and wrecked in the leeward Hawaiian islands in 1822 on its way to Japan. He spent four months building a small schooner from the wreckage that he named *Deliverance*, and after a voyage of 10 weeks he was able to reach Honolulu.

A ship carpenter by trade, he and shipmate Robert Lawrence sold *Deliverance* for $2,000 and started the James Robinson & Co. ship repair business. With the assistance of Kamehameha II and John Young, they established their shipyard beside Pākākā Point in 1827 in the shadow of the fort. They were later joined by Robert W. Holt who had come to Hawaii from Boston. They could repair two ships at a time, and in 1840 were the only ship chandlers and carpenters in the Pacific.

> "Honest, industrious, economical, temperate, and intelligent, they are living illustrations of what these virtues can secure to men. ... Their yard is situated in the most convenient part of the harbor, has a stone butment and where two vessels of six hundred tons burthen can be berthed, hove out, and undergo repairs at one and the same time. There is fourteen feet of water along side of the butment. The proprietors generally keep on hand all kinds of material for repairing vessels. Also those things requisite for heaving out, such as blocks, falls, etc. On the establishment are fourteen excellent workmen, among whom are Ship Carpenters, Caulkers and Gravers, Ship Joiners, Block-makers, Spar-makers, Boatbuilders, etc."

In 1824 the British ship *Alderman Wood*, owned by Sir Matthew Wood (former Lord Mayor of London), wrecked off the coast of Molokai and was salvaged by Robinson. The captain gave him the figurehead and he installed it on the pulley beam of the warehouse where it greeted sailors and customers for 87 years. The grand ball celebrating the restoration of the Hawaiian Kingdom in 1843 by Admiral Thomas was held in this warehouse.

Robinson married Rebecca Kaikilani Prever in 1843 and they had 3 sons and 6 daughters. They were one of the wealthiest and most prominent families in Honolulu. Their daughter Victoria became Victoria Ward (her "Old Plantation" house was where the Blaisdell Center is today), their son Mark was Minister of Foreign Affairs in Queen Liliʻuokalani's cabinet, and daughter Mary married Thomas Foster (the founder of the Inter-Island Steam Navigation Company, better known today as Hawaiian Airlines).

It was said that he was wealthy enough to loan money to the Hawaiian government in the 1850's. The business lasted until the death of Robert Lawrence in 1868, and James Robinson died in 1876 at the age of 76.

Theodore C. Heuck

Born in Hamburg, Germany in 1830, Theodore Heuck was trained as an architect and came to Hawaii in 1850. He worked as a commission agent with Herman Von Holt until King Kamehameha IV asked him to design the first Queens Hospital building in 1860.

Heuck designed the Robinson Building and the Royal Mausoleum in 1863, and the ʻIolani Barracks in 1870. He was the German and Danish Consul, member of the legislature and the Privy Council, and Director of Public Works. He returned to Germany in 1874 and died there in 1877 at age 47.

Chun Afong 陳芳

Known simply as Afong, he was Hawaii's first Chinese millionaire. Born in 1825 as Chun Fong in Wong Mau Cha (黃茅斜村), Xiangshan, the present day Meixi Village, Qianshan, Zhuhai, Guangdong, China, and he came to Hawaii in 1849 to work in his uncle's store. He quickly became fluent in speaking English and Hawaiian.

Realizing the importance of gaining support for the Chinese business community, he organized a grand ball in honor of the wedding of King Kamehameha IV and Emma Rooke that was attended by the top levels of Honolulu society.

In 1865 he partnered with his friend Qing Ming Qwai (known as Achuck) in a store that sold imported Oriental novelties and silks. By 1870 it was listed as one of the top 8 business firms in Honolulu. He eventually built a huge fortune by investing in retail, sugar plantations at Kaupakea and Pepeekeo, and importing Chinese labor. He also owned the schooner *Haleakala* which sailed between Oahu and Hilo. His business empire eventually extended all the way to Macao and Hong Kong.

From 1868 to 1874 he had a monopoly on the government license to import opium into Hawaii, making him incredibly wealthy. He was said to have personally taken wheelbarrows full of gold from his office in the Robinson Building to Charles Bishop's bank at Merchant and Ka'ahumanu streets.

In 1870 he built a large 2-story house at the mauka/waikiki corner of Nu'uanu & School streets that was said to be "one of the handsomest homesteads on the island". When he became the Chinese Commercial Agent to the Qing Dynasty in 1880, he hosted a huge party at his house that included a ceremonial raising of the triangular Chinese flag.

Afong also had a seaside villa in Waikiki on three acres that is now the Fort DeRussy Military Reservation.

Known for his honesty and integrity as well as his business acumen, he did many things to support the community including opening his office to a rival firm who had been burned out in the 1886 Chinatown fire.

After his eldest son died in 1889 he sold off his businesses in Hawaii and sailed back to China in 1890. He died in his palatial home in Meixi village in 1906 at the age of 81. The Meixi Memorial Archways were built in his honor by the Guangxu Emperor, he was made a "mandarin" of the first rank, and was awarded four tablets inscribed: *Generous, Charitable, Selfless* and *Kindhearted*. The house and gravesite were ransacked during the Cultural Revolution but are now a museum and tourist attraction.

Afong had three sons with his Chinese wife, one of whom graduated from Yale University. With his Hawaiian-British wife, Julia Fayerweather Afong, he had sixteen children. One of the sons was later governor of Guangdong.

Jack London, the famous American novelist, published a short story in 1910 inspired by the life of Afong called "Chun Ah Chun".

In 1961, Eaton Magoon Jr. wrote the Broadway musical "13 Daughters" starring Don Ameche. It was short-lived but was nominated for two Tony Awards and caricatured by Al Hirshfeld.

In 1997, Bob Dye, who was married to one of Afong's descendants, wrote the meticulously researched and highly praised book *Merchant Prince of the Sandalwood Mountains: Afong and the Chinese in Hawai'i*.

HOCKING BUILDING / 2 N. KING

2 N. King
1914
Architect / Builder: Ripley & Davis / Hawaiian Ballasting Company

Sketch by Ripley & Davis

The Hocking Building was built in 1914 by the man who created Primo Beer – Alfred Hocking. Originally from Cornwall, England, he was the longtime president of the Honolulu Brewing and Malting Company.

The prominent local architectural firm of Ripley & Davis designed the building which was constructed by Hawaiian Ballasting for $42,000 in 1914. It was built in two phases – the first section along King Street, followed immediately by the corner section.

It replaced two buildings previously on this site: a 1-story brick building that had housed the C.R. Collins' harness shop and T.B. Murray carriage works on King Street, and the corner of the 2-story brick Aseu Building along Nuʻuanu Street. Both were built by a Mr. C. Kavanagh immediately after the 1886 fire.

The remainder of the Aseu Building is still on Nuʻuanu Street, only the corner that housed the Merchants Exchange Saloon was chopped off for the new building.

In 1916 Hocking hired Ripley & Davis and Spalding Construction to adapt the building into the home of the Chinese-American Bank. It was incorporated May 10, 1916, with officers Tong Fong (partner in Sing Chong & Co.), Ching Lum (Lum Yip Kee), C.K. Ai (City Mill), Lau Tong and Ching Shai. The interior was finished with marble and dark woodwork. In 1935 the bank was reorganized as the American Security Bank. It became the First Interstate Bank of Hawaii in 1985 and merged into First Hawaiian Bank in 1992.

The upper floors became Hotel Hocking in 1950 with rooms by the day ($2.50), week ($9), and month ($35) catering to servicemen and visitors. It had a pretty checkered history of sketchy tenants, shootings, robberies, murder, prostitution, and numerous arson fires. The hotel was last mentioned in the newspapers in 1979.

In 2004 the building was the filming location for an episode of the *Lost* TV series. The bank downstairs was used in season 1 as the bank that Kate (played by Evangeline Lilly) robbed to get her toy plane.

Alfred Hocking

"If Hawaii had a Samuel Adams, it would've been Alfred Hocking." – Paul Kan

Hocking was born in Cornwall, England, in 1852 and emigrated first to the US mainland, then to Maui c.1876 where he got a job with H.P. Baldwin. In 1885 he purchased over 8,000 acres of land at Makawao and started his own lumber mill.

He worked his way up from Commissioner of Fences, member of the Road Board and Deputy Sheriff, to senator from Maui in 1894. He was very proud of voting in favor of annexation in 1897.

In 1896 he married May Renner, and they spent several months in 1897 traveling to Paris, Lyon, Marseille, Monte Carlo, Genoa, Naples, Rome, Venice, and Switzerland. They also attended the Diamond Jubilee of Queen Victoria in England. But tragedy struck the next year when his wife died in childbirth. She was only 30 years old.

In 1898 he teamed up with H.P. Baldwin and W.F. Pogue to start a sugar plantation on 4,000 acres at Nahiku in Maui, and work began in earnest clearing the land, building the mill and laborers quarters, but it proved unsuccessful for a variety of reasons and they closed it down in 1901. Investors were offered $0.40 on the dollar.

In November 1898 he filed articles of incorporation for the Honolulu Brewing and Malting Company as president and treasurer, along with E. Coit Hobron, Louis Schweitzer, F.L. Dortch, and M. Schweitzer. The brewery license was granted in January 1899. They removed 7 wooden cottages and one store to make room for their large brick brewery building on Queen Street that today is on the National Register of Historic Places. It had a capacity of 100 barrels a day, and the first beer was poured in 1901. They named it "Primo Beer".

Hocking bought the "White Swan" property at King & Nuʻuanu in 1900 for future investment, and in 1902 he married Mrs. Harriet S. Hoffman from San Francisco. He bought the 1-story brick building on King Street in 1907.

In 1906, he traveled to Shanghai, Hankow and Hong Kong to see about opening "the first brewery in the Orient". The company selected Hong Kong and opened the Oriental Brewing Company, making "Prima" beer with the same tagline "The Beer That's Brewed to Suit the Climate".

He spent two years in Hong Kong supervising the startup of the brewery which included $75,000 for buildings and $101,000 for machinery.

When Hocking died on July 21, 1936, he left an estate worth $268,000 (over $5 million today). The Hocking Building at King & Nuʻuanu was valued at $165,000. Hocking's stone house, at 1302 Nehoa Street, designed by C. W. Dickey and built in 1904 is on the National Register of Historic Places and is considered to be the most classic example of the Queen Anne style on Oahu.

According to the Rockwood and Barrere Map published by the Bishop Museum in 1957, the earliest identifiable activity at this corner was a "Loku site". Adjacent to the two ulu maika fields, it would have consisted of a thatched building for indoor games and amusements like kilu (a gourd game), puhenehene (a hide-and-seek game with a small stone), chanting and dancing.

Kaupena, wife of Manuia, a survivor of Boki's ill-fated sandalwood expedition, ran a grog shop here called the "Sign of the Ann" in 1829. She sold it in 1830 to Alexander "Little" Smith who sold it to Stephen Reynolds in 1831.

An 1843 map shows a cluster of "native thatched houses" in this area, and it was also the location of the White Swan hotel, perhaps in the same building that had been the Sign of the Ann. In 1853 John Maxey was the proprietor, and he bought it from Reynolds in 1855. In 1855 Maxey built and opened the new Royal Hawaiian Hotel on Nu'uanu Street, later known as the Royal Saloon.

1881

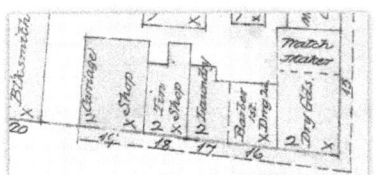

By 1851 James Whittet had a copper and sheet iron shop adjacent on King Street, and by 1880 Charles Blackburn had a carriage and wagon building business there. It was later the site of a Chinese dry goods store, but everything in this area was destroyed in 1886.

Still owned by the Reynolds family, the land was leased to Chang Yeong Sow, known as Luke Aseu. He made his money from dry goods and from recruiting Chinese plantation workers. He hired C. Kavanagh in 1886 to build a large 2-story brick building (50' x 80') that extended from the corner along Nu'uanu Street, plus the 1-story brick building next to it (with the two humps in the photo below) on King Street in 1887.

The single-story building housed T.B. Murray's Carriage shop, C.R. Collins' harness shop, a horseshoeing parlor, and Lancaster's "Horse Jewelry" store. The building was used as a fumigation station for merchandise and personal effects during the 1900 bubonic plague outbreak.

The Merchants Exchange Hotel/Saloon was on the corner for nearly 30 years, with Captain Sam Nowlein, proprietor. Over 320 people were served lunch on opening day in 1886. Nowlein was famous for owning a pet monkey, and he was also Sergeant-at-Arms of the Hawaiian Parliament and Quartermaster-General of the King's Own military company, member of the royal order of the Star of Oceania, and Captain of the Queen's Guards.

1900

A staunch Royalist, Nowlein was one of the leaders of the 1895 Wilcox Rebellion that attempted to restore Queen Lili'uokalani to the throne. He was captured, charged with treason, and initially sentenced to death. His 35-year prison sentence and $10,000 fine were suspended when he decided to become a cooperating witness.

The saloon was the scene of many heated political discussions including one "small-sized row" that came to blows between 6 Annexationists and 20 Royalists where one participant "got the contents of a spittoon" and another "got a beer mug alongside the head".

HONOLULU TRUST COMPANY

25-31 N. King St.
1923, remodeled 1928, remodeled 1999
Architect / Builder: unknown (1923), Leslie N. Gratz (1928) / Daniel L. La Fortune (1928)

On November 29, 1922, Fidelity Loan and Jewelry Company Ltd took out a building permit for this concrete store. The building cost $4,700 and was completed in early 1923. They were previously located across the street at 52 N. King Street. It was also the home of the Honolulu Typewriter Company from 1923 to 1927.

Johnson Radio & Music Company moved to 25 N. King in 1927 – they dealt in radios, phonographs, and sheet music.

Previously located next door, the Honolulu Trust Company bought the property in 1928 for $38,742 and hired architect Leslie N. Gratz to design "extensive alterations" that were built by contractor Daniel L. La Fortune for $50,000.

The Honolulu Trust Company was here for over 40 years, from 1928 to 1969.

Before 1926 it had been controlled by a group of Japanese businessmen, but by the time they moved to this building it was managed by a group of prominent Chinese businessmen including Y.M. Wee, L.Y. Aiona, G. Wong Sun, C.Q. Yee Hop, and Thomas A. Tam. The Honolulu Trust Company was acquired by Hawaii Thrift & Loan in 1969.

The building housed the La Raggs-Matazz women's clothing store in 1985.

On August 21, 1998, a homeless man set fire to architect Fritz Johnson's upstairs office to try to cover up a burglary of a downstairs shop. It caused extensive damage estimated at over $175,000.

The marble front and new windows and doors were likely added in 1999.

According to old land records, Kuihelani, Governor of Oahu in the time of Kamehameha I, was buried somewhere behind this building in 1815.

UNITED CHINESE SOCIETY BUILDING

36-42 N. King
1885, 1886, 1954 renovation
Architect / Builder: E.B. Thomas (1886), E.E. Mayhew (1887), Clifford F. Young (1954) / Calvin Ching (1954)

This was the site of a tremendous amount of heartbreak on April 18, 1886. The beautiful new 2-story brick building of the United Chinese Society built by E.B. Thomas, was dedicated on February 10 to much excitement, speechmaking, fireworks, and feasting. Two months later the building was a smoldering ruin, destroyed in the massive 1886 Chinatown fire. In all the excitement of building the new building, they had neglected to insure it, and it was a total loss.

In September 1886 they hired contractor E.E. Mayhew to rebuild the clubhouse for $6,780 which was completed by March 1887.

In 1903 The United Chinese Society built a new building at 78-82 N. King, and the Honolulu Chinese Chamber of Commerce moved to a new addition in the back of this building in 1929.

In 1953 the two organizations hired architect Clifford F. Young to remodel the building which included a new modern front with both group's names in Chinese characters. It cost $81,000 and the grand opening was November 21, 1954.

Clifford Fai Young was born in Honolulu in 1917, and earned degrees in architecture from the University of Michigan and M.I.T. He initially worked with McAuliffe & Young and Alfred Preis, and opened his own office in 1953. Young designed the United Chinese Society Building (1954), the United Church of Christ (1955), Pearl Harbor Memorial Community Church (1958), and the Kuan Yin Temple (1961). He also worked with I.M. Pei on the East-West Center at the University of Hawaii.

Young served in World War II, Korea, and Vietnam, and was a military observer at Yenan in China in 1946 where he often dined with Mao Tse-tung.

The United Chinese Society (Chun Wa Hui Quon)

美国夏威夷中華總會館

Officially incorporated under the laws of Hawaii on August 27, 1884, the mission of United Chinese Society of Hawaii is:

"To further friendly relations among the Chinese and various Chinese societies in the State of Hawaii; to promote projects of benevolence, charity, and cultural awareness; and to promote the welfare of the Chinese community."

Representing over 100 Chinese societies, clubs, and organizations, the United Chinese Society of Hawaii (UCS) moved into this building in February 1886, having met previously in Fire Station No.1 across the street.

At the grand opening in 1886, President C. Alee stated:

"Our object in forming this association is to exercise a care and supervision over such of the Chinese residents as shall connect themselves with this society; to make them acquainted with the laws and ordinances of the Hawaiian Government, particularly those laws and ordinances which concern in any way our Chinese residents; to render assistance and advice to such as may stand in need thereof, especially to sick Chinese and those in destitute condition; to prevent and settle disputes among Chinese if possible... that it may be of advantage not only to ourselves but to the non-Chinese residents of this community, and that through it you may obtain true glimpses of Chinese customs and manners."

The United Chinese Society continues its mission today, and organizes numerous cultural events throughout the year, especially for Chinese New Year.

Scenes from the Great Fire of 1886, showing the United Chinese Society Building still smoking, and then being partially demolished before rebuilding. The three men in the foreground are guarding a safe, and the burned-out Aswan Building can be seen just to the right of the United Chinese Society Building in the bottom photograph.

There is an old alleyway on the waikiki side of the building, currently gated and filled with trash, that at one time led to a house lot bought by John Robinson in 1830 from a man named Johnson. In 1842 Robinson sold it to Stephen Reynolds.

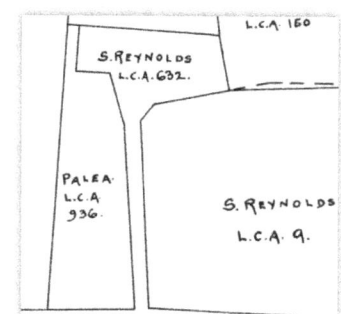

It is not known if there was a house on the lot in 1830 but it seems likely. There have been various 1- and 2-story wooden buildings built in this area over the years, but today it is an open grassed courtyard with large trees.

The United Chinese Society property is on the lot awarded to Palea by LCA 936, and LCA 9 is where the Hocking Building is today.

A challenge to the ownership of the Chinese Society property in 1887 went all the way to the Hawaii Supreme Court but was denied on the basis the plaintiffs were referencing the wrong person named Palea.

King-Smith Clothiers – Ellery & Ethel Chun

In 1930, the C. K. Chow dry goods store celebrated their 27th anniversary by moving from King and River streets to 36-38 N. King Street on the first floor of the United Chinese Society Building. Chun Kam Chow's son, Ellery, with an economics degree from Yale, joined the business during the Great Depression in 1931 to help his father.

Ellery renamed the store "King-Smith Clothiers" and, looking for ways to increase the business, hired a tailor to make some ready-made printed shirts out of colorful Japanese yukata cloth in 1933.

He patterned the shirts after the plantation workers' short-sleeved un-tucked square-bottom shirt called a palaka. He put them in the shop window and they sold quickly.

His younger sister, Ethel Chun Lum, came up with new Hawaiian designs featuring palm trees, tropical flowers, pineapples, birds, and ukuleles.

He registered the trademarks "Aloha Sportswear" and "Aloha Shirt" in 1936 and 1937 and heavily promoted the shirts on radio and in print.

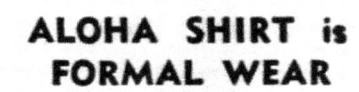

In 1947, the Hawaii Chamber of Commerce's Aloha Week encouraged workers to wear Aloha shirts all week, and in 1966 the Hawaii Fashion Guild created Aloha Friday, the forerunner of casual Friday.

Ellery Chun became a board member of the American Security Bank in 1945 and closed the King-Smith store in 1949 when he became the bank's vice president.

HAWAII NATIONAL BANK

33-49 N. King
1989
Architect / Builder: Robert Sarnoff / Bank Building & Equipment Corporation

This large concrete building was designed and built by the Bank Building & Equipment Corporation in 1989 for Hawaii National Bank. Architect Robert Sarnoff stated this 140,000-square-foot building built in the Brutalist Style "is designed to blend in with the surrounding Chinatown neighborhood". Yes, he really said that.

The building it replaced was a 10,500-square-foot Mid-Century Modern building designed by Wimberly & Cook and built by J.M. Tanaka Construction Company in 1948. It housed the Capital Investment Company Ltd, Ching Realty Company, and Wong's Drapery Shop. Tanaka Construction also built the Pali Tunnel in the late 1950's.

On September 19, 1960, the new Hawaii National Bank officially opened here with Kan Jung Luke of Loyalty Enterprises Ltd as president and chairman of the board. It was Honolulu's seventh bank and the second nationally chartered bank in Hawaii. Luke's son Warren made the first deposit to teller Jeanne Shirakawa. Musical groups from six different cultures serenaded the first customers who were also offered "lucky coins" to win new $10-$250 bank accounts. The dedication ceremony concluded with a string of over 2,000 firecrackers.

The building to the left of the 1948 building was the first furniture store of C.S. Wo & Sons, opened by a young Ching Sing Wo in 1911 at 39 N. King Street. Opened with the financial assistance of C.K. Ai of City Mill, C.S. Wo & Company is now the largest furniture dealer in Hawaii.

That 2-story brick building, 60' x 60', was built in 1888 by George Lucas as a storage facility for the Honolulu Iron Works located immediately behind. It was built on the site of the two former police Station Houses.

The police station had a jail yard and 1-story cell block in back brought from the old fort. If convicted, prisoners were "committed to the reef" in the 1857 Oahu Prison in Iwilei. This was a very noisy location between a foundry, a blacksmith shop, and King Street traffic, which often interfered with the proceedings in the courtroom upstairs.

In 1879 a new Station House was deemed "a necessity, owing to the increase of population as well as the increase of evil-doing in our midst". It was completed in March 1879 on the site of the 1855 Station House.

The Station House was the home of the Night Bell that rang every night at 9:30 pm and 10 pm, and also in case of fire. Delivered by the *Fanny Major* from San Francisco in 1857, it was said to be a "remarkably fine-toned bell".

The photograph on the left was taken shortly after noon by J.J. Williams on April 18, 1886. Little did anyone suspect that 6 hours later the building would be completely burned to the ground in the Great Fire of 1886. The loss of the old Station House bell was viewed with much sadness and even inspired a heartfelt poem by John Brash in 1886.

This 1879 map shows the location of the police station and fire department Engine House No.1. Both sites are now covered by the Hawaii National Bank Building, with Smith Street extended in 1917 along the ewa side of the engine house site.

The engine house became the home of China Engine Company No.5 in 1882, and the United Chinese Society met in the upstairs meeting hall before building their own clubhouse directly across the street in 1886.

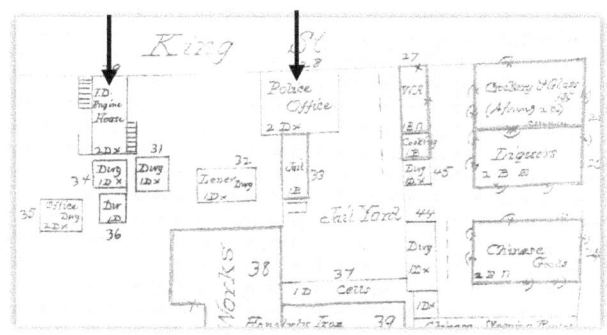

In 1851 Henry Hills opened a tailor shop here with a grass house in back, next to a bake shop with oven.

HONOLULU CHINATOWN

C.S. Wo

Ching Sing Wo was born in Hanalei, Kauaʻi, in 1889, and came to Honolulu when his father purchased the Yick Sing grocery store on Nuʻuanu Street across from the Liberty Theater. Not liking the long hours and small profit margin, he purchased the C.M. Tai hardware and sporting goods business at 39 N. North King from the Chung Mun Tai estate in 1911 when he was only 22 with financial assistance from C.K. Ai of City Mill. His brother, C.S. Nam, joined him and the company was called C.S. Wo & Bro.

The other half of the building was occupied by the Lee Toma Cigar Company, and later the Honolulu Trust Company.

In 1928 they bought the whole building and hired contractor and carpenter Masujiro Fujita to do extensive alterations.

They added furniture to the business in 1928, and when Wo's three sons joined the business in 1942 they decided to concentrate only on furniture. They remodeled the store again in 1946 and renamed the company to C.S. Wo & Sons. They went into the furniture manufacturing business in 1949 when a shipping strike cut off their shipments.

"Many people think our family name is Wo, but Wo is not a Chinese surname. My grandfather's full name was Ching Sing Wo. Ching was his surname. Sing Wo was his first name. My dad, Bob Wo Sr. was a Ching. We changed the family name to Wo in the 1950's." - Robert "Bub" Wo Jr.

A chance meeting with a Chinese furniture executive on a plane flight led to the formation of Teakwood Holdings which became one of the largest furniture manufacturers in the world, with factories in Taiwan, Singapore, Malaysia, Hong Kong and Indonesia, with more than 5,000 employees.

C. S. Wo & Sons

The company has 15 stores in Hawaii and operates as C.S. Wo Gallery, HomeWorld, SlumberWorld, the Ashley Furniture Home Store, and the more contemporary Red Knot store.

CENTRAL PACIFIC BANK

44-50 N. King, 1019-1023 Smith
1955
Architect / Builder: Ernest Hara / Town Construction Company

This building was designed by Ernest Hara and built by Town Construction Company for Central Pacific Bank in 1955. It started with the small section along Smith Street while waiting for the lease to expire on the 1-story Katsey Block previously at the corner. When the bank officially opened for business on Feb. 15, 1954, it was the first new bank in Hawaii since 1935.

It was created by nisei (second generation) veterans who had served with the highly decorated 100th Infantry Battalion, 442nd Regimental Combat Team, and Military Intelligence Service units in World War II, who saw the need to provide Japanese businesses with financial resources after the three Japanese banks in Honolulu had been seized during the war.

They were initially laughed at for wanting to start a bank, but were a young and forward-thinking group that also popularized the term "AJA" to refer to Americans of Japanese Ancestry as opposed to the traditional Japanese generational terminology of issei, nissei, etc.

The older issei (first generation) members of the community were not very supportive since they wanted to bring back the Yokohama Specie Bank. Although approached to participate, the issei demanded a controlling interest on the board and the AJA's walked out.

Instead, they spread out the ownership and sold shares to as many people as possible, starting at $105 for 3 shares with no one person able to buy more than $10,000 worth. Surprisingly, over $500,000 in shares were sold the first week and Central Pacific Bank probably has the most shareholders of any bank in Hawaii.

This Mid-Century Modern bank was a filming location for the *Lost* TV series, pretending to be a police station.

The bank is located on part of the land given to John Meek by Boki in 1820. Originally a house lot, in 1884 his son put in the private Meek Street between King and Hotel streets, and it quickly filled up with a wide variety of mostly Chinese shops in a solid row of 2-story wooden buildings. Meek Street was located slightly waikiki from where Smith Street is today – the bank building is sitting right in the middle of what was once Meek Street.

 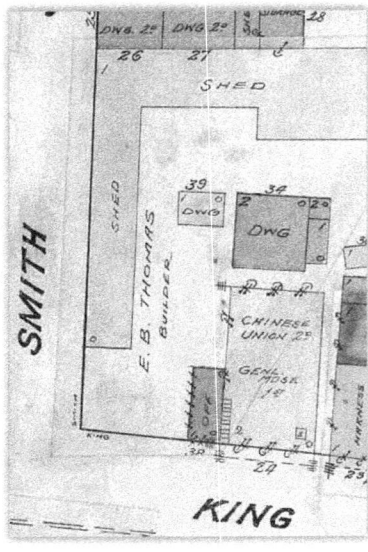

1885   1899

Everything on Meek Street was burned in the 1886 fire, and Smith Street was laid out immediately afterwards in its current location. This corner lot remained vacant through 1891 and by 1899 it was the office and yard for contractor E.B. Thomas.

In September 1900, E.B. Thomas built the 1-story glass-fronted Katsey Block at the corner. The only known image of the building is this screenshot from the 1906 Thomas Edison film of King Street.

 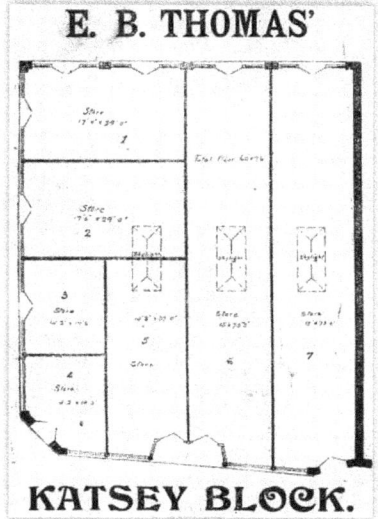

The Katsey Block was the home of the Abraham Fernandez & Son general hardware store for over fifty years from 1904 to 1955, and it also housed the Japanese provision and general merchandise store of H. Hamano.

Ernest Hara

Born in 1909, Ernest Hideo Hara was one of the first Asian architects in Hawaii. He first worked with Claude Stiehl and then C.W. Dickey before opening his own office in 1945.

Hara designed at least 43 schools, 36 apartments/hotels, and 32 commercial projects, including Robert Louis Stevenson School (1950), Central Pacific Bank (1953/55), Lee & Young Building (1957), Waikiki Grand Hotel (1962), Queen Kapiolani Hotel (1968), Waikiki Shopping Plaza (1975), Hilo Hawaiian Hotel (1976), and the new Central Pacific Bank (1981). He was a founding member of the bank and served on its board from 1954 to 1980.

MENDONÇA MAKAI / SUMITOMO BANK

72-76 N. King, 1000-1030 Smith
1901, 1919 remodel, 1930 remodel
Architect / Builder: Oliver Traphagen (1901), H.L. Kerr (1919), John Mason Young (1930) / Hawaiian Engineering & Construction Company (1901), Hawaiian Ballasting Company (1919), Tsurujiro Inouye & Sengo Tsutsumi (1930)

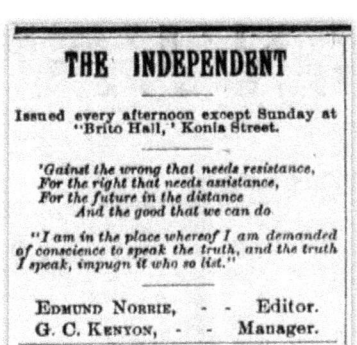

From 1895 to 1900 this was the location of The Independent newspaper, edited by Edmund Norrie from Copenhagen who was famous for his inflammatory rhetoric in the "rankest of rank royalist papers" filled with "treasonable utterances".

Norrie was an unfiltered insult-slinging staunch royalist publisher charged with criminal libel on numerous occasions, and he was sued and jailed during the 1893 overthrow.

He was unrelenting and unrepentant in his vitriol and was not afraid to call someone a "braying ass, usurper, political charlatan or black-guarding old gossiper".

After the questionably legal overthrow of the Hawaiian Monarchy, the Provisional Government passed strict libel laws and restricted freedom of speech to discourage counterrevolutions, but that didn't stop Norrie. Between 1893 and 1895 he was arrested five times and paid numerous fines.

Norrie was charged with sedition for saying every loyal citizen should "refuse to recognize a government (the Provisional Government) representing nobody, respected by nobody and despised by all". He was arrested the day after he wrote that Sanford Dole was only President of Hawaii "through treason, fraud and might", and when he and other Royalists were jailed after the three-day counter-revolution, Wallace Farrington of the *Hawaiian Gazette* said they were "enjoying a long-needed term of rest... passing their vacations in Oahu Prison".

Of *The Hawaiian Star*, Norrie wrote "a more dastardly, disgraceful and cowardly journal has probably never been published in any community." The *Evening Bulletin* called him "the little yelper".

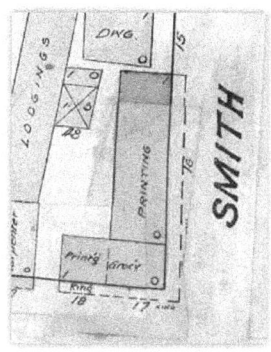

The building Norrie worked out of was a large 1-story stone building known as Brito's Hall, also called the Portuguese Hall. Owned by Caesar L. Brito, it was built in 1891. Brito also owned a grocery store at the corner and a guitar shop on Nuʻuanu just below Hotel Street.

The landowner, Antone J. Lopez, reclaimed the property in 1895 when Brito was arrested (and later acquitted) for embezzlement and adjudged bankrupt. That same year Edmund Norrie started publishing *The Independent* newspaper in the building. This was also the first location of the S. Ozaki Japanese dry and fancy goods firm.

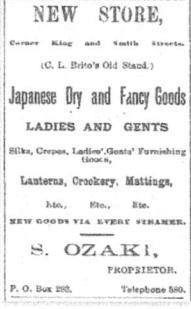

Brito's Hall was a popular meeting place for the San Antonio Society, Leilehua Social Club, International Rifle Association, Phenix Club, Mormon Church, Hawaiian Patriotic League, YMCA Mission Service, and for celebrations of Portuguese Independence Day on December 1.

In 1898, David M. Kupihea & Co., commission merchants and agents for Hawaiian produce were located here. The *Independent* newspaper was on the Smith Street side and the *Chinese News* (edited by Ho Fon) was on the King Street side.

The building was destroyed in the 1900 fire and J.P. Mendonça hired architect Oliver Traphagen in 1901 to build a massive building that covered almost the entire side of the block on Smith Street. It was built by the Hawaiian Engineering & Construction Company of "brick with stucco facing and tiled roof".

It was originally decorated the same as the other large Mendonça building on Hotel Street between Smith and Maunakea streets, with red window treatments and a similar topknot on the corner parapet as seen in this screenshot from the 1906 Thomas Edison film of King Street.

The Sumitomo Bank of Hawaii, a branch of the Japanese Sumitomo Bank, hired H.L. Kerr and Hawaiian Ballasting Company in 1919 to renovate the building for their new bank in Hawaii.

Established in Japan in 1895, the Sumitomo Bank expanded rapidly during World War I. After being shut down in World War II, they came back in 1952 and were the primary bank for several large Japanese companies like NEC and Panasonic.

In 1928 they purchased the Mendonça building for $150,000 and hired John Mason Young of Pacific Engineering along with contractors Tsurujiro Inouye and Sengo Tsutsumi to renovate the bank to the way it looks today at a cost of $80,000.

John Mason Young was born in Tennessee in 1874 and after serving in the Spanish American War he earned two masters degrees in engineering from Cornell University. In 1908 he came to Hawaii to be professor of engineering at what would become the University of Hawaii, and he also started the Pacific Engineering Company. When he retired from the university in 1940 he was the last of the original thirteen faculty members.

In addition to planning and engineering buildings on the university campus, he built Castle Hall at Punahou School, the Theo H. Davies block, the Empire Theatre, the S.M. Damon Building, and the Church of Christ Scientist on Punahou Street.

YIM QUON BUILDING

69-75 N. King
1886 / 1931 remodel
Architect / Builder: George Lucas (1886), Mark Potter (1931) / T. Nakano (1931)

Mr. Geo. Lucas has laid the foundations of a large building he has contracted to erect for Yim Quon, on King near Maunakea street. It will be of brick, two stories high, and cover a space of about 60 feet by 88 feet.

This building was built by George Lucas in 1886 for Chinese businessman Yim Quon. The original 60' x 88' building contained 3 stores (69-75-83 N. King) and looked very different from the way it looks now. It was started four months after the disastrous 1886 fire.

On the left is the earliest known view of the Yim Quon Building, from the 1906 Thomas Edison movie filmed with a camera mounted on a streetcar going down King Street.

The building faced King Street with no windows or façade on the waikiki side since Smith Street did not extend makai from King Street until 1917.

The low-relief arches over the windows are not original but date to 1931 when the windows and matching façade and parapet were added to the Smith Street side.

Liberty Bank bought the building in 1929, planning on turning it into their new office. They hired architect Mark Potter in 1931 and "spent approximately $10,000 on the improvement of its future banking site at the makai-ewa corner of King and Smith Sts. The two-story building on the premises was completely renovated". Cost was $10,000.

The remodel was completed in November of 1931. It removed a painted advertising sign on the Smith Street side of a large fat man that the Outdoor Circle had "objected to so strenuously".

Yim Quon

Born in Canton (Guangdong), China in 1847, Yim Quon moved to Hawaii in 1872 and became a naturalized citizen in 1890. He was involved in rice growing, labor contracting, wholesale and retail merchandising, plus real estate. He was president of the United Chinese Society and was instrumental in creating a relief fund and distributing food for Chinese impacted by the 1900 fire and quarantine.

Mark Potter

Born in London, England, in 1895 and raised in New Zealand, Mark Potter was brought to Hawaii in 1914 with his parents. Perhaps inspired by his father who was a draftsman for Emory and Webb, he became an architect known for romantic Arts & Crafts houses and cottages in the "regional Hawaiian Style". His most famous design was "Kilohana", the 16,000 square foot plantation house for Gaylord Wilcox, owner of the Grove Farm Plantation in Kaua'i. Potter also designed the Chemistry Building (Bilger Hall) and Castle Memorial Hall at the University of Hawaii. He was reportedly a direct descendent of English architect and astronomer Sir Christopher Wren.

69 N. King

The large Kwong Lee Yuen & Company was located in the corner store, in business since 1882 on Maunakea Street as wholesalers of Chinese merchandise. Their manager and several employees were busted for opium in 1897. In 1899 they offered to sell 5,000 bags of No. 1 Hawaiian rice every year for five years.

It was briefly Lipton's Auction Room in 1936 and in 1937 it became the home of the Canton Jewelry Company for the next 15 years, owned by Fong Choy, Wong Chip Tong, and Ching Lin Sing, who moved the business from across the street at 95 N. King.

Finance Factors, owned by Hiram L. Fong (Speaker of the Territorial House of Representatives for 7 terms and US Senator), was here from 1952 to 1957 until they built a new 7-story $600,000 building at King & Alakea streets.

 From 1961 to 1971 this was the main office of Hawaii Thrift & Loan, an affiliate of Honolulu Trust Company founded in 1952 as Honolulu Credit and Finance Ltd who moved here from 31 N. King Street. Their 11 branches were bought by First Hawaiian Bank in 1975.

75 N. King

Wing On Wo & Company moved into 75 N. King in February 1887. They specialized in imported XXX Manila cigars and where here until at least 1899.

From 1901 to 1922 it was the Wing On Tai Company, managed by Yim Quon.

The 717th branch store of the Nu-Enamel Company, owned by Wah-Chan Thom, was here from 1934 to 1953, at which time they morphed into King's Sporting Goods. They were here 55 years until closing in 1989.

LUM YIP KEE BUILDING

78-82 N. King
1968
Architect / Builder: Ross Jensen (Haver Nunn & Jensen) / Town Construction Company

This Lum Yip Kee Building (one of three in Chinatown) was built in 1968 and replaced the 1903 United Chinese Society building designed by H.L. Kerr and built after the 1900 fire.

From 1906 to 1927, storage for the Quong Chong Lung Company liquor store located at the mauka/waikiki corner of King and Maunakea was on the left side of the 1903 building and the Quong Chong Lung Candy Factory was located on the right side until the mid 1930's.

The Sun Chung Kwock Bo newspaper was also located in the 1903 United Chinese Society Building.

It is said that Sun Yat-sen organized meetings of the secret Tung Meng Hui Hawaii Chapter in the basement of the Quong Chong Lung building where they plotted the eventual successful overthrow of the Chinese government.

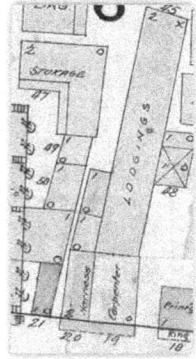

Previously on this site in 1885 was a 2-story wooden dry goods store that would have burned in 1886.

This was replaced by a couple of metal buildings housing a blacksmith shop (1891) and harness shop (1899) on the left, and the Kwong Sing & Co. carpenter shop on the right.

There was also a long 2-story wooden apartment block that extended out back, most likely for Chinese workers.

YUEN CHONG BUILDING

83 N. King
1886, 1938 remodel
Architect / Builder: George Lucas (1886), Y.T. Char (1938) / Ching Pui (1938)

1909

This building is actually the ewa 1/3 of the Yim Quon Building built in 1886. For 85 years, from 1886 to 1971, it housed the Yuen Chong Store which claimed it was the "oldest Chinese firm in Hawaii". Yuen Chong was founded by Lee Chong in 1885, and the name translates to "continued prosperity".

The building was not damaged during the 1900 fire, but several security guards from the Honolulu Iron Works in back were bribed with gin to break into the store which was subsequently ransacked and looted.

The two stores on the left side of the Yim Quon building were remodeled by Liberty Bank in 1931 to how it looks today. Yuen Chong spent $30,000 in 1938 to add a 3-story building in back and remodel the front "featuring Chinese architecture". It was designed by Y. T. Char and constructed by Ching Pui (who built the Chun Hoon Market in 1939 where the Afong house once stood at Nuʻuanu and School streets).

The walking tours of Chinatown begun by the Chinese Chamber of Commerce in 1955 started at the Yuen Chen store from 1963 to 1969.

From 1971 to 1983 this was the Goodwill Industries offices, workshop, and store, moving here from 1128 Nuʻuanu.

When the non-profit Pacific Gateway Center began renovations in 2008 to convert the building into a space for their entrepreneurship programs they uncovered several Hawaiian artifacts, including a fishing lure and two ancient ulu maika bowling stones, one made of basalt and the other of coral.

The Pig & The Lady Restaurant, serving Vietnamese Fusion food, is one of the PGC incubation projects and it opened here in 2013.

LIBERTY BANK

93-99 N. King
1952
Architect / Builder: Vladimir Ossipoff / Walker-Moody Construction

This building was designed by Vladimir Ossipoff, one of Hawaii's most famous architects, and built by Walker Moody Construction on the site of the 2-story brick Quong Sam Kee Building built by George W. Lincoln in 1886.

Liberty Bank was organized by 16 prominent Chinese businessmen who filed the charter application on February 2, 1922, with Lum Yip Kee as the first president.

Quong Sam Kee & Company renewed their lease of the land from Joseph Paiko for $155 per month and then subleased to Liberty Bank for $275 per month for 15 years. Architect Herbert Cohen designed alterations to the 1886 building.

In 1931 the bank remodeled 69 N. King at the other end of the block in anticipation of moving there but decided instead to stay and build a new building at this corner in 1952.

On December 16, 1950, they took out a building permit for $275,000 for a building of "modern design, incorporating traces of a Chinese motif".

Opening day in the new building was February 18, 1953.

Liberty Bank was bought by Bank of America in 1993 and was sold to American Savings Bank in 1997.

The first structure we know of on this site was Captain Nathan Winship's "grass house with sills" built in 1813 by Kuihelani and enclosed with a stick fence. Winship was a close friend of Don Francisco de Paula Marín (Manini) and was captain of the American merchant ship *Albatross*. He left the house to his daughter Kepane Montgomery who was married to merchant Isaac Montgomery. A young Herman Melville briefly lived with them in 1843.

Isaac Montgomery built a substantial stone house here c.1845. He was burglarized in 1846 with the thief taking $10,600 in silver and $6,200 in gold – that is about $600,000 in today's money – the reward offered was $1,500 (nearly $50,000 today). He sold the building to Ulrich Alting in 1849, and it was briefly the store of A. Helbing in 1853.

C.T. Averberg & Company, owned by Carl Theodor Averberg and J.H. Lafrenz, moved here in 1854. The building was described as 2-story coral with a store and 2 storerooms downstairs and 3 rooms on the second floor.

Averberg sold dry goods, clothing, hardware, fancy articles and jewelry, and advertised *"custom made gents' shirts, of assorted sized – a superior article. Gents' French calf-skin lace up shoes, Oxford ties, white horse hair skirts, superior black, colored, changeable and check silks; heavy brocade silk, ribbons, dress patterns, &c. &c."*

From 1855 to 1856 it was the store of G. Buhle & Company, owned by the brother-in-law of German architect Theodore C. Heuck.

This was also first store of German baker and confectioner Frederick Horn in 1862. He was born in 1819 in Dresden, Saxony. Horn studied confectionary and fruit preserving and worked in Hull and Manchester in England, and in Sydney, Australia, and was with Swain's in San Francisco. He came to Honolulu in 1862 and opened his business here at King and Maunakea streets. He was the first to preserve and sell Hawaiian fruits for export.

Horn employed large numbers of Native Hawaiians to gather and prepare guavas, strawberries, oranges, citrons, limes, pineapples, and bananas, and was known for his genial manners and kindly conduct. He started with a large 60-gallon kettle boiling fruit night and day, using 10,000 pounds of sugar a week. In 1862 he sent 12,000 pounds of jams and preserves to San Francisco via the *Comet* and 25,000 pounds on board the *Yankee*.

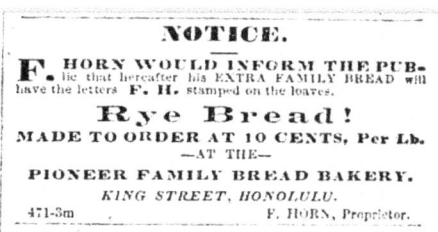

JUST RECEIVED!
NEW & FANCY GOODS!!
From Hamburg Direct!!!

THE Undersigned would respectfully intimate to the Ladies and Gentlemen of Honolulu, and the Public generally, that in addition to his well assorted STOCK, he has just received, from Hamburg direct,

AN EXTENSIVE ASSORTMENT OF
DRY & FANCY GOODS!

And which he now offers for Sale, at his Store in Honolulu, (within a few doors of the *Maine Hotel*, and formerly occupied by Mr. I. MONTGOMERY) at prices which cannot fail to suit purchasers.

The Subscriber would particularly direct the attention of Purchasers to a few of the articles lately received, viz. :

LADIES' Embroidered Dresses,
" Ready made morning gowns,
" Superior silk scarfs.
" Kid gloves and artificial flowers,
" Fancy work tables and work boxes.

A VARIETY OF

Splendid black, blue, white and other colored Silks, red and black silk velvets, linen and silk handkerchiefs, black crape, thread lace, sewing silks, bleached and unbleached calico, fancy prints and ginghams, diaper toweling, figured woolen and cotton table covers.

READY MADE CLOTHING.

Gentlemen will please observe that the Subscriber has also on sale a choice lot of superior clothing, consisting of—Superfine frock and dress cloth coats, vests, pantaloons, first quality linen shirts, flannel shirting, boots, shoes, &c.

SUNDRIES.

Among sundry other articles, too numerous to mention, on sale at the Store of the Undersigned, will be found a quantity of dried apples, several cases eau de cologne, a neat and beautiful mantle piece clock, a large assortment of black, green and white paints, crockeryware, fancy-wood portable writing desks, patent iron wool screwing machines, bake pans, wire dish covers, riding whips, accordeons, French's prepared Cocoa in ¼lb packages, together with 100,000

SUPERIOR HAVANA CIGARS.

—ALSO—

Several casks of the BEST LONDON PORTER, ALE, and SHERRY CORDIAL, in bottles.

jan4–34–tf   ULRICH ALTING.

By 1875 the bakery was owned by Quan Long & Company, then Wing Chong Tai & Co. (1875- 1878), Yim Quon (1886), and Quong Ying Wo (1886). The 1885 Dakin Map shows several 1- and 2-story buildings on the site, including a grocery, fruit shop and the large bakery complex with the 2-story stone building. All were burned in the 1886 fire.

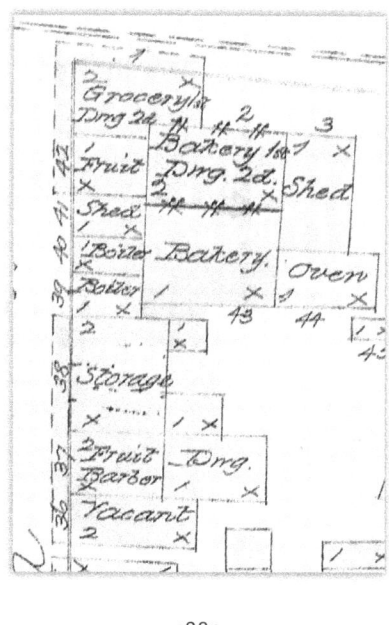

1885

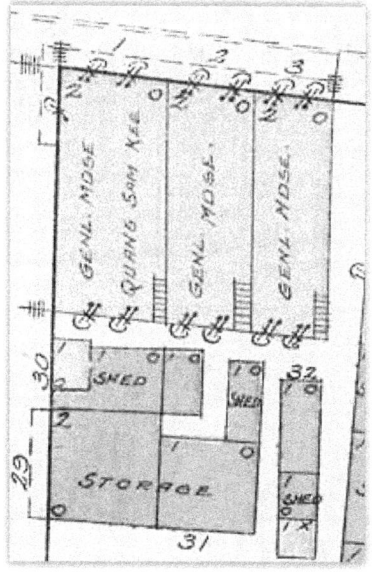

1891

Four months after the fire, on August 24, 1886, Quong Sam Kee & Company advertised for bids for a new 2-story brick building housing 3 stores. George W. Lincoln was the low bidder and he subcontracted the brick work to E.B. Thomas.

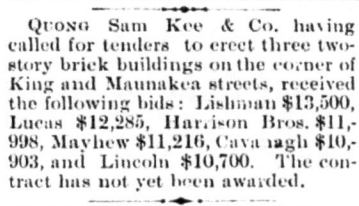

Quong Sam Kee & Company first appears in the 1879 newspaper, picking up 389 packages of merchandise delivered by *Discovery* from San Francisco.

They were here from 1886 to 1922. It was owned by Chu Gem with several Chinese partners. They also had stores at Kohala, Paauilo, Paauhou,, Kapaa, Kukaiau, Nawiliwili.

The building was at the edge of the 1900 fire and was relatively unscathed.

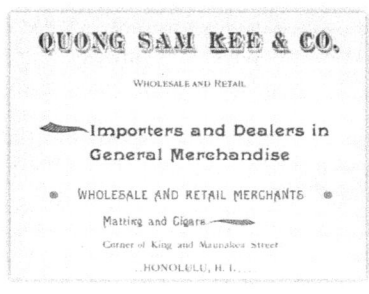

The photo on the left is a stretched screenshot from the 1906 Edison film of King Street.

The store in the middle at 95 N. King Street was Wing Mow Chan, owned by Young Bow (the widow of Mow Keong of the Wing Wo Chan Company) along with Young Chee. Founded in 1891 they were commission merchants, importers, and dealers in all kinds of provisions and general merchandise.

The American Brokerage Company moved here by 1909. It was incorporated in 1904 by Theo F. Lansing, W.M. Minton, Charles Girdler and A. Barnes, and was originally at 26 N. King Street.

It was briefly the Federal Loan Office in 1916, and the Honolulu Picture Shop in 1920 selling Island view photos and volcano scenes, and doing Kodak finishing

Canton Jewelry Co. was here from 1930 to 1936, and it was the Monroe Radio Corporation in 1937 and 1938.

On the waikiki end of the building, there was a lot of chop suey served over the years at 93 N. King. It was a general merchandise store in 1891 and 1899 and was part of the American Brokerage Company offices from 1909 to 1910.

In 1915 it became the Honolulu Chinese Chop Suey House, followed by the Orient Chop Sui Co. Ltd from 1922 to 1934, the New Orient Chop Sui Co. from 1935 to 1943, and New Asia Chop Suey from 1944 to 1950.

Vladimir Ossipoff

Born in 1907 in Vladivostok, Russia, Vladimir Nicholas Ossipoff grew up in Tokyo and came to Hawaii in 1932 shortly after graduating from the University of California at Berkeley. He initially worked with Charles W. Dickey and founded his own firm in 1936.

He was Hawaii's foremost Modernist architect, mixing Modernism with Asian and Hawaiian Territorial elements. Many of his houses and buildings incorporated large informal indoor/outdoor living spaces through open walls and multiple lanais.

His buildings include the University of Hawaii Administration Building (1949), Hawaiian Life Insurance Building (1951), the Liljestrand house (1952), Liberty Bank (1952), The Pacific Club (1959), IBM Building (1962), and the Outrigger Canoe Club (1963). Described as both "charming and cantankerous", he waged a "War on Ugliness" against Hawaiian architecture that was neither regional nor climate-friendly.

Sixty-six boxes of Vladimir Ossipoff's drawings and papers were bequeathed to Hamilton Library at the University of Hawaii at Manoa.

Y. ANIN BLOCK (KING ST.)

108-120 N. King
1901
Architect / Builder: H.L. Kerr

This is the King Street end of the 1901 Y. Anin Block designed by H.L. Kerr. At the time it was built it was the second largest building in Chinatown, almost as large as the Mendonça Building on Hotel Street. The corner was demolished in 1956, leaving this section with 6 storefronts along King Street and a similar section along Maunakea Street.

This building should probably be called the L. Ah Leong Building, and yes, there already is an L. Ah Leong Building at 136-138 N. King Street, but this building is where the L. Ah Leong grocery store was located for nearly 40 years, and where the Chinese millionaire was arrested innumerable times for a wide variety of offences.

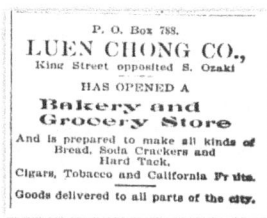

Lau Faat Leong, aka L. Ah Leong, initially leased the middle section of this block from Y. Anin on May 1, 1901. The two stores on the left first housed the Won Tai Company doing house painting and decorating, and the Luen Chong grocery store which was at the corner from 1901 to 1923.

In 1909 the Honolulu Cracker Company was located on the right side of the building.

They expanded into ice cream, candy and general baking and confectionary in 1915, and opened the Palace of Sweets across the street at the ewa/makai corner of King and Maunakea.

Honolulu Cracker Company was here from 1909 to 1932, and in addition to pies and cakes they also roasted Thanksgiving turkeys and ducks. When they went bankrupt in 1932 they were bought by L. Ah Leong.

He renamed it the New Honolulu Cracker Company and it was managed by one of his wives, Ho Ah Keau. It became the Hawaii Cracker Company in 1937 and was the second store of the Home Bakery Company from 1942 to 1950. The space later housed George's Delicatessen, the Sampaguita Restaurant, the Dalagang Bukio Restaurant, and the Busan Korean Restaurant

But the real star of the show for this building is L. Ah Leong. Called a "Merchant Prince" by some, "unrepentant scofflaw" would probably be a much more accurate description.

Lau Ah Leong

Born in Chung Yuen village, Ka Yin district, China, in 1856, Lau Faat Leong came to Hawaii at age 20 to be a cook for Lau Kong Yin Ahuna and later established a small grocery with Ahuna in North Kohala. When it failed three years later, he moved to Honolulu and clerked in the L. Ahlo store on Nuʻuanu Street before opening a small store at the corner of Punchbowl and Queen streets in Kakaako.

He opened a grocery and general merchandise store in the new Y. Anin building at King and Maunakea streets in 1901 which lasted until 1941. It was the largest Chinese grocery in Honolulu and he initially lived on the premises and personally ran the store. He invested in real estate, stocks, bonds and other assets and became very wealthy. He was president of the King Market and founder of the Lung Kong Koon society and was a director of the Chinese American Bank.

He was arrested on numerous occasions for blocking the sidewalk on King Street with stacks of merchandise which sometimes allowed only a single file of pedestrians to pass, and which on at least one occasion forced pedestrians out into the street. In 1909 he was arrested for selling on a Sunday, and also for selling opium.

He was constantly in trouble with the food inspectors who once caught him sifting weevils out of the flour and then re-bagging the flour for sale. A reporter for the Honolulu Advertiser saw sacks of flour piled "man-high" on the sidewalk whose *"lower tiers were very convenient for the mangy dogs that infest that part of town, and many availed themselves of the opportunity. People buying flour from L. Ah Leong may have the assurance that it is well seasoned."*

In 1907 he was accused of keeping a harem in Kalihi, and the 1921 court case about his Chinese-style wife, Fung Shee (aka Fung Dai Kim), versus his American-style wife, Ho Shee (aka Ho Ah Keau), went all the way to the US Supreme Court. He had 13 children with Fung Dai-Kam who sued for divorce on grounds of infidelity.

In 1933, after 30+ years of leasing, L. Ah Leong purchased the entire 15,000-square-foot parcel from the Francis M. Hatch Trust who had owned it since at least 1848. This also included the entire Y. Anin building along Maunakea Street except for the corner which by then was under separate ownership.

In 1934 he applied for a beer license for 112-120 N. King Street only 10 days before he died at age 78.

In 2002, his great-granddaughter, Pam Chun, wrote an award-winning novel based on the fictionalized life of L. Ah Leong titled *The Money Dragon*.

After the L. Ah Leong store closed in 1941, the adjoining American Dry Goods store expanded into the space.

C.Q. YEE HOP PLAZA

101-115 N. King
1965
Architect / Builder: Peter Hsi / Town Construction

This International Style building with strong Asian influence was built in 1965 by Town Construction for the C.Q. Yee Hop Company and was designed by architect Peter Hsi. This was the first building in Hawaii with structural steel and curtain wall construction, and the decorative columns were originally made with white marble chips under the red and yellow dragons and were designed to match the Yee Hop Market at Kekaulike and King Streets.

C.Q. Yee Hop

Chun Quon came to Hawaii in 1886 at age 19 from Gong Bui Village, Guangdong Province, China. He opened the Yee Hop Meat Market in 1887 and partnered with Lum Hop in 1888. There was another store with the same name so they added his initials and it became C.Q. Yee Hop.

He spoke fluent Hawaiian, some English, plus several Chinese languages and his market and grocery business grew to become one of the largest in Honolulu, serving the general public, stores, markets, restaurants, schools, steamships, and military.

After Prohibition he bought the old Primo Brewery on Queen Street and started the American Brewing Company. "Royal" beer had the Hawaiian coat of arms on the label. The company also expanded into real estate. He wrote his autobiography at age 81.

Peter Hsi was born in Shanghai, China, and started as a civil engineer but changed to architecture with degrees from Rensselaer Polytechnic Institute and the University of Michigan. After working 9 years in Detroit, he came to Honolulu in 1962 and opened his own office. He designed and developed the Magellan Condominium, the C.Q. Yee Hop Plaza, the Franklin Towers in Salt Lake, and the Gold Bond Building on Ala Moana Boulevard. Hsi was the first architect to use tilt-wall construction in Hawaii.

Charles W. Vincent

The first building that we know of on this site was the house and shop of "house carpenter and joiner" Charles W. Vincent. He acquired a narrow lot with 96' frontage on Maunakea Street and 18' frontage on King Street in 1843.

1854

2021

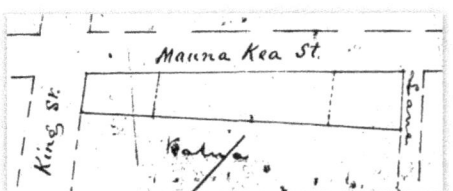

In addition to being a contractor and carpenter, Vincent was also a dealer in lumber, hardware, paint and builder's supplies. His lumberyard was located across King Street on Maunakea and at one time stocked as much as 140,000 feet of Astoria pine timber, plus a huge stock of windows, sashes, doors, nuts, bolts, etc.

He employed a sizable workforce and was the premier builder in town in the 1840's and 1850's in stone, brick, adobe, wood, or thatch. He built the Robert Wyllie house and the Sailors' Home and was also known for several house-moving projects. In 1847 he took out an ad for 4,000 coral stones, perhaps for the construction of nearby Liberty Hall.

Vincent founded Honolulu's first theater, The Thespian, across the street in 1847, and married a Hawaiian woman named Mauli in 1848.

In 1849 he teamed up with his neighbor across the street, Isaac Montgomery, in the Puuloa Salt Works.

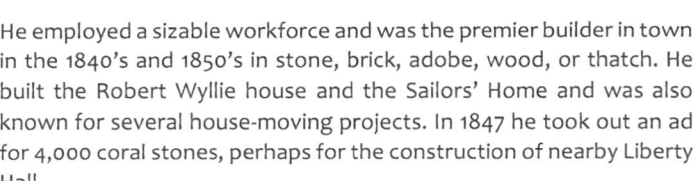

For the 1854 Fourth of July parade, he displayed a small mahogany center table that was an heirloom from his grandparents, upon which George Washington and the Marquis de Lafayette had often taken tea together in 1778.

The last newspaper reference to C.W. Vincent in Honolulu is in 1864 where he is listed as a "foreign juror". The *Pacific Commercial Advertiser* on September 9, 1865, reported: *"By the Polynesian, particulars of the death of C.W. Vincent, Esq., were received. It appears that he was murdered at Guaymas"*. Why was he in Mexico? No one knows.

This photograph was taken during the 1886 fire, looking mauka on Maunakea Street toward King Street, showing the smoldering ruins of the C.W. Vincent buildings.

A new frame building with Chinese stores was built here in January 1886, only to be burned in the April 1886 fire.

Built after the 1886 fire, these buildings were on the Maunakea Street side in January 1900:

And continuing around the block, the buildings along King Street:

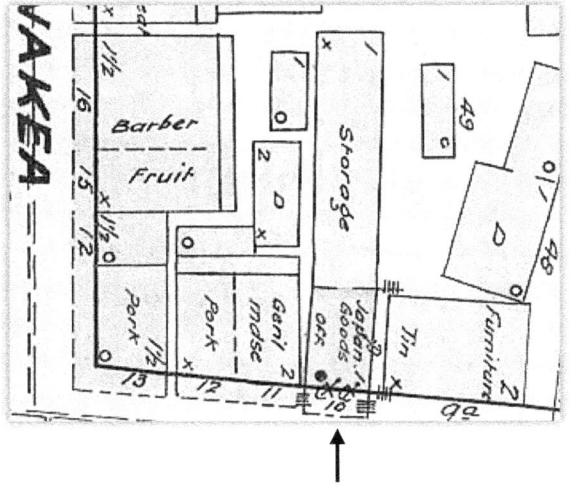

In 1900 there was one brick building here amongst the 2-story wooden buildings, owned by John F. Colburn.

Four days after the big fire on April 18, 1886, he was back in business with a temporary wooden building from which he sold hay and grain.

By July, E.B. Thomas was constructing a new building for Colburn – it was the only brick building past Maunakea Street, and lasted for almost 14 years until it burned in the 1900 fire.

HONOLULU CHINATOWN

John F. Colburn

John Frances Colburn was born in Honolulu in 1859. His father was one of the first auctioneers in Hawaii and his mother was the daughter of Captain Joseph Maughan, the first pilot and harbormaster of the Port of Honolulu. That made him part Hawaiian on his mother's side and a grandson of Don Francisco de Paula Marín.

After graduating from Oahu College at Punahou he worked for Lewers & Cooke for 13 years and later went into the grain and feed business.

He was Queen Liliʻuokalani's Minister of the Interior before the overthrow of the monarchy and was the manager and treasurer of the Kapiolani Estate. He was "intensely nationalistic and for years hoisted the Hawaiian flag to the exclusion of all others over the Kapiolani building."

In an extraordinary historical coincidence – the front door of the 1965 C.Q. Yee Hop Plaza building is in *exactly the same location* as the front door of John F. Colburn's 1886 brick hay and feed store.

Colburn leased the land from Afong in 1886 for 20 years, assigning the lease to Akana in 1897, who then assigned it to C. Achi's Hawaii Land Company in 1899.

After the 1900 fire, the Hawaii Land Company hired Yee Sing Tai to build a 1-story brick building with 5 stores at the corner in December 1901. H.L. Kerr was perhaps the architect.

The only known image of the building is this screenshot from the 1906 Thomas Edison film of King Street that was shot with a streetcar-mounted camera.

At the corner was the Progress Saloon, owned by ebullient Irishman **Thomas McTighe**. He was a "dispenser of fluid exaltation" and ran the Progress Saloon on the corner from 1902 to 1911.

Originally from Kenmare in County Kerry, Ireland, he came to Honolulu in the 1880's and initially worked for hospitality firm MacFarlane & Co.

McTighe was the self-proclaimed "Irish Consul" to Hawaii and his bartender, Terry Keven from County Tipperary, was known as "the Secretary to the Consul".

St. Patrick's Day was cause for much celebration and he imported shamrocks "fresh from the ould sod" for his loyal customers along with pins with Irish flags and the Gaelic greeting "Cead Mille Failte" which means "ten thousand welcomes".

McTighe also opened the Royal Restaurant next door in 1904. It was open all night and had electric pushbuttons to call waiters. The building later housed the Palace of Sweets, and Market Music – "The Home of Hawaiian Music" – from 1929 to 1949.

On August 2, 1901, **Sanshichi Ozaki** took out a building permit for a 2-story brick building on King Street adjacent to the 1-story Progress Saloon building. Previously located at "Brito's old stand" at King and Smith streets and then the new Waverly Block at Hotel and Bethel streets, S. Ozaki specialized in wholesale and retail general merchandise, hardware, kitchen utensils, and crockery, most of which was imported from Japan.

S. Ozaki moved into their new building in April 1902 and were here until 1926 when they moved across the street to the corner of the large Y. Anin Block.

The building later housed the United Chinese Trust Company from 1926 to 1933, Shida Dry Goods store from 1933 to 1943, and Market Music was here from 1948 to 1958.

C.Q. YEE HOP MARKET

119-133 N. King
1906, 1951 remodel
Architect / Builder: Pang Chong? (1906), Law & Wilson (1951) / Calvin Ching (1951)

When this building was under construction in August 1905 it attracted quite a crowd. It has a deep stone foundation down to coral rock that was put in by Japanese workers, and the brick superstructure was built with Chinese workers, but what captured "the idle crowd's" attention was the unusual sight of one white bricklayer working amongst the Chinese.

It was built as the offices and market for the C.Q. Yee Hop Company. In 1951 they hired Law & Wilson to remodel the building with a more modern front that was built by contractor Calvin Ching for $175,000. The remodeled building was originally painted chartreuse on the outside with varying shades of green on the interior.

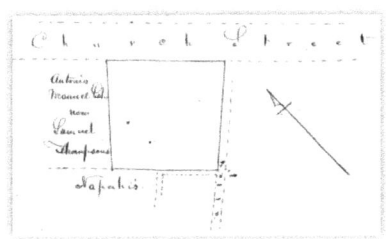

In the early 1800's, **Louis Gravier** was given this tract of land by Keikeoewa as payment for a suit of sails made for the schooner *Young Thaddeus*.

One of the witnesses at the Land Court hearings in 1846 "heard Keaniani say that Keikeoewa begged a part of the yard of him for Mr. Gravier, to discharge a debt which Keikeoewa owed him for making sails. Keaniani replied to Keikeoewa that he had no place for him, except a grave yard. Keikeoewa said, what's the harm of that? Dead bodies can be dug up, and the place was transferred to him."

According to Governor Kekuanaoa's testimony in the Land Court hearings it was indeed a graveyard, but he heard from a servant that Keikeoewa was not happy about this, blaming Kīnaʻu: "She said to him, you have been giving land to Mr. Gravier – he replied, a mere building spot. She said, what an old blunder-head you are! Is it your business to be giving away the King's land? He replied, I have not given it away, I paid it for making a suit of sails for our vessels, so that we don't have any money to pay."

According to John Ii, many of the Hawaiian chiefs – Hoopilikane, Kaikioewa, Kuahini, Kalaimoku, Poki, Naihe, Kapiolani and Namahana – met in Gravier's house when making the constitution of laws in 1827.

In addition to being a sailmaker, Gravier was the Prefect of Police and Superintendent of Public Houses in 1844, and had owned a grog house on Nuʻuanu Street in the early 1830's as well as Liberty Hall in 1844. His Hawaiian wife, Hana LiiLii, remarried after Gravier shot himself in 1849, and his heirs owned the property until 1904.

Doctors S.P. Ford and H.L. Bullions leased the property in 1855 for a City Hospital catering to seamen and shipmasters.

By 1856 it was known as the Western Hotel, owned by John Reed, but was put up for lease when he died in 1858.

1885 Dakin Fire Insurance Map

At some point the Gravier/Western Hotel was remodeled beyond recognition into cheap housing for Native Hawaiians. The old building was rediscovered in early 1886 when it was being demolished for new construction.

The brand-new 1886 building burned in the 1886 fire and was replaced by the 2-story wooden building on the left, housing a laundry and furniture store in 1891, and then a blacksmith and tailor shop in 1899. It was burned with the rest of Block 5 by the Board of Health on January 4, 1900.

The ancient alleyway beside the building was known as Gravier Lane and was a public right-of-way until 1963.

HOP SING BUILDING

124-134 N. King
1900
Architect / Builder: Lee Wai

This might be the first brick building built in Chinatown after the 1900 fire. The Lee Wai Company obtained a building permit on September 25, 1900, just two months after the Board of Health allowed construction to resume in the burned district, for a "2-story brick building, mauka side of King St., between Maunakea and Kekaulike Sts., 73x50". The new building would have been completed by the end of the year and contained 4 stores.

Lee Wai was one of 10 Chinese partners in the Hop Sing Company, formed on March 23, 1901, "for the purchasing, improving and subletting of leaseholds in Honolulu".

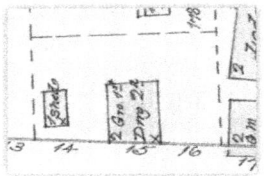

In 1885 there was only a small 2-story grocery here with living quarters above in the middle of a large open lot. It burned in the 1886 fire.

In the photograph on the right, taken on January 20, 1900, firemen are spraying water in a futile attempt to save the building of the Honolulu Chinese Times newspaper which was previously on this site.

YEE HOP MARKET

135 N. King, 943 Kekaulike
1966
Architect / Builder: Peter Hsi / Town Construction

Designed by local Chinese architect Peter Hsi and built by Town Construction in 1966, the Yee Hop Market has 12,000 square feet of air-conditioned space under one roof. It has stalls for 37 fish, meat, and vegetable dealers, each with their own refrigerated display counter and cold storage locker space. Peter Hsi had previously designed the C.Q. Yee Hop Plaza building (1965) at N. King and Maunakea streets, and he said he hoped the C.Q. Yee Hop building in between would someday be remodeled in a matching style, but so far that has not happened.

The opening date, October 1, 1966, was personally selected by Mrs. C.Q. Yee Hop after Chinese temple priests consulted Chinese moon calendars for the most auspicious day to launch a new venture.

It is built on the site of the 1906 King Market built by Pang Chong who was also the president of the King Market Company. A popular gathering spot for many years, at 5:00 am on Monday, October 19, 1964, the termite-ridden roof of the old market collapsed just as vendors were beginning to set up for the day. Luckily, no one was seriously hurt.

Before the January 4, 1900 Board of Health burning of Block 5, this large 2-story wooden building was on the site. It was built after the 1886 fire and housed C. Ahana, watchmaker and jeweler, and merchant tailor Tim Kee.

L. AH LEONG BUILDING

136-138 N. King
1909
Architect / Builder: Risuke Miyata

Welcome to Saigon! For the 2017 movie *Kong: Skull Island* the intersection of N. King and Kekaulike streets was dressed up to be a stand-in for the Vietnamese city in 1973. Local photographer Ryan Kawailani Ozawa captured these photos of the set as it was being prepared for filming:

In actuality, the building was built in 1909 for Honolulu Chinese millionaire Lau Fat Leong, known as L. Ah Leong.

And although Ah Leong's name is prominently displayed on the building's parapet, there is no indication he ever occupied the building. The L. Ah Leong store was a few doors up the street at 110-120 N. King in the Y. Anin Building for nearly 40 years from 1901 to 1941.

Ah Leong bought this lot on February 24, 1908, from Annie K. Hart, E.H. Hart, and James R. Love for $5,250. At the time it had a 1-story building that is barely visible in the 1906 Edison film of King Street, likely built by Wa See in 1901. From the Husted's City Directory it looks like L. Ah Leong briefly had a store in the earlier building.

BUILDING PERMITS.
Week Ending Sept. 11.
Miyata, R. & Co., King and Kekaulike, store building; $4450. Sept. 7.

Risuke Miyata took out a building permit for this building in September 1909. His first building permit was in 1903, and by 1907 he was regularly advertising construction services where he partnered with Zenkichi Sugihara.

In 1915 Miyata teamed up with I. Kodama in the Poi Factory & Merchandise Store but he died later that year. Sugihara continued on as the Z. Sugihara Company.

136 N. King has housed a wide variety of businesses over the years, including a restaurant, the City Mill Retail Store, the Friendly Shoe Store, and the New China Emporium.

In 1947, the American Drug Company opened two adjacent stores – American Stores and National Photo Supply. American Stores was "a new variety store offering fountain service, household remedies and sundries, toiletries, housewares, garden supplies, infants' supplies, candies, tobacco, newsstand service, etc." National Photo Supply provided cameras, projectors, darkroom supplies, books, and 24-hour film developing.

By the 1950's it was Plaisance's Gifts & Antiques, then the Nova Company appliance store, and the Silver Dollar Health Bar in 1962 that was busted for using $1 orangeade as a blind for playing bingo.

138 N. King has been a grocery, hardware store, plumbing supplies, the Home Variety Store, the City Mill store, as well as the American Stores. It was the City Inn from 1962 to 1981.

The 2-story wooden building on the site in 1899/1900 would have been built sometime between 1886 and 1891. It housed a general merchandise store, coffee shop, and barber, and was burned in the 1900 fire. The building next door housed the Honolulu Chinese Times newspaper.

For more information about L. Ah Leong, see the write-up for the Y. Anin Block (King Street) at 102-120 King Street.

SHUN LUNG BUILDING

142 N. King
1901
Architect / Builder: H.L. Kerr

This unassuming little building was designed in 1901 by local architect Harry L. Kerr. On March 21, 1901, he took out a building permit for this 1-story building plus a 1-story building at the corner of Nuʻuanu and Pauahi streets.

The first business here was Shun Lung & Co., importers of a variety of grocery and food items. They were managed first by L. Tin Hoon and later by Li Kum Tock and Li Sai Hin who purchased the business in 1903.

Lee Todd opened the Mutual Produce Co. at this location in 1918 as a cooperative market to sell goods and produce to stockholders at actual cost plus overhead expenses. Raymond Ranch Beef was one of their signature products. In 1924 the R. Odo Shoten grocery store bought out the S. Hata Shoten Grocery and was here until 1931.

Market Music was here from 1958 to 1969. They moved here from 101 N. King Street and concentrated on selling home appliances.

From 1976 to 1994 this was the Arita Store, moving here from previous locations farther out on King Street. It was owned by Zchiro and Kanoe Nakamura, originally from Hiroshima, Japan. They were big promoters of a garlic extract called "Kyolic", reputed to ensure good health and long life.

According to the Arita Store ads:

- Elder's health = pride of family
- Husband's health = security of family
- Wife's health = happiness of family
- Children's health = hope of family

OAHU MARKET

145 N. King
1904
Architect / Builder: Yong Tock

The Oahu Market was built in 1904 by Anin Young (Y. Anin) and is the last remaining open market building in Honolulu. Built of iron with a corrugated-metal roof, it initially had 56 stalls leased to independent vendors. Opening day was Saturday, July 2.

A portrait of Y. Anin proudly hangs in the market today.

From 1848 to 1878, this was the site of the Maine Hotel, "a popular dram shop" in a large 2-story building approximately 30' x 40' in size and made of coral with a veranda front and back. It had three rooms and hall on each floor, and was built by Samuel Thompson, known as "Long Thompson". He was a retailer of wines and sprit in 1844 and obtained a license to sell "spiritous liquors by the glass" in 1846.

After the license was closed due to selling liquor to Native Hawaiians, Dr. John S. McGrew converted the building into the U.S. Marine Hospital in 1869.

In 1870 it became Templar Hall for the Ultima Thule and Queen Emma lodges whose 200 members met upstairs for meetings which advocated lives of temperance. The Pacific Commercial Advertiser noted:

> There would seem to be a kind of poetical justice in this, that where formerly for so many years men assembled to carouse and drink whiskey there now will meet a band of sworn enemies to all that can intoxicate."

Based on information from 1810, the Rockwood Map shows this area was called Kapuʻukolo and was filled with grass houses.

The 1879 Dakin Fire Insurance Map shows the Maine Hotel at the bottom, across the street from the large coral-block house built by Nehemia Hoʻoliliamanu in 1846/47.

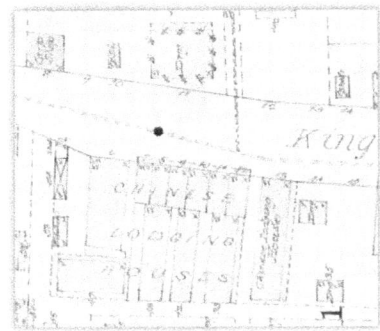

By 1885 there is a massive block of wooden 2-story Chinese Lodging Houses shown on the site. A year later they would all be burned in the 1886 fire.

At the time of the 1885 Dakin Fire Insurance map there was no Kekaulike Street yet.

Kekaulike Street side (1900)

King Street side (1900)

These large 2-story wooden buildings were built immediately after the 1886 fire along Kekaulike and at the corner with King Street. Damaged in a later fire in 1889, they housed a jewelry store and a coffee store with residences above.

The adjacent building on King Street housed a furniture store and poi store.

The entire block burned in the fire of January 20, 1900.

King Street side (1900)

TANAKA BROTHERS BUILDING

146-154 N. King
1902
Architect / Builder: unknown

This building with three stores was built in 1902 and was the longtime home of Tanaka Bros. Hardware Company who were at this location for over fifty-one years beginning in 1902.

Ryoichi Tanaka, the last surviving brother was a very active former president of the Honolulu Japanese Merchants Association.

Other businesses at this location included:

146 N. King – Tong Wo Cheong Co. (1905), groceries and general merchandise, owned by H.A. Heen.

150 N. King – Wing Sang Co. (1904), also had an office in San Francisco, but the business was seized by customs in 1904 for smuggling foodstuffs.

154 N. King – Honolulu Trading Co. (1905-1916), owned by M.H. Weinberg, Swiss Jewelry Co. (1917-1918), King Hardware (1963-1965).

This was the site of a huge 2-story stone house, approximately 40' x 30', built in 1847 and owned by Nehemia Hoʻoliliamanu. It was constructed of coral stone blocks and had 13 rooms with a cook-house, cellar, pantry, well and store-room also on the property. He was a tax collector and a favorite of the king.

Without a doubt it was the most commanding structure at this far end of Honolulu, and the bridge over Nuʻuanu Stream at King Street was known for many years as the Hoʻoliliamanu Bridge. Maybe he built the bridge too?

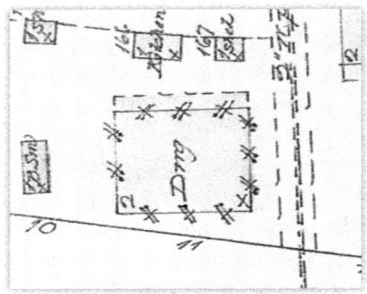

1885 Dakin Fire Insurance Map　　　　　　　　　　　　*c.1870*

The house was very likely built by Jeremiah Thomas Martin (c.1797-1860), the father of Elizabeth Aliʻi Kapeka Kalikoʻokalani Martin (aka Elikapeka Kapinao) who was married to Nehemia Hoʻoliliamanu's son Thomas. Martin had married into the royal family of Kaʻu and was known throughout Hawaii for his stonework, perhaps learned in his native Antigua. He built the Mokuaikaua stone church in Kailua-Kona (1837), the royal stone home of King Kuakini called Huliheʻe Palace (1838), as well as stone houses for Naihe and Kapiolani in Kuapehu, Kaawaloa. He was said to have been a great favorite of King Kuakini and Queen Kapiolani, and was even courted by Princess Ruth.

In the 1850's the building became the home of Thomas and Elizabeth Thrum. She ran a boarding house here until 1858 when they put it up for sale or lease when they became the managers of the Sailors' Home on Merchant Street. Their son, Thomas G. Thrum, founded the informative "Hawaiian Annual" that was published from 1875 until 1974.

On July 15, 1859 the house became the first Queen's Hospital – temporary quarters with 18 beds until they moved to their permanent location on Punchbowl Street in 1860. They maintained a dispensary here until 1862. The Hawaiians called it "Hale Maʻi o ka Wahine Aliʻi".

But by 1884 this is how a newspaper article described the building:

"Its time worn front is squeezed in between ill-fitting additions run up on either side; its quaint porch filled with Chinese inscriptions and gaudy ornaments. Where the mystic horseshoe once guarded the front door, uncouth characters red and gold warn away evil influences – perhaps. The old hall is but little changed, the doors on either side still retaining their ancient color and numbering; but every room has had a partition run across it; and in each little subdivision is crowded with the narrow sleeping platforms (one can scarcely call them "beds") where the Pake takes his rest behind the dense mosquito curtain they so much affect. Upstairs new corridors have been built, off which other rooms open, and one large room is set apart as a prayer room or Joss Temple. Up and down the dingy stairs, along the corridors, and in and out the rooms rooms move an ever changing crowd of boarders."

The house is barely visible in a photograph taken in the aftermath of the 1886 fire – the walls are still standing but the roof is gone. No trace of the house appears on the 1891 Dakin Fire Insurance Map.

ARROW HARDWARE BUILDING

158-174 N. King
1905
Architect / Builder: Lee Fai

This building housing six stores was built in 1905 by Lee Fai. He was from Nam Jon village, Chungshan district in China, and in the 1920's was assistant treasurer of the United Chinese News and manager of the Honolulu Cracker Company. Some of the businesses that have been in this building are:

158 N. King – Lam Toi Kee, honey dealer (1925), Arita Drug (1937), King Hardware (1952-1960).

162 N. King – Takahara Restaurant (1943). In 1977 it was Allen Akina's "Honolulu T.H." clothing store and fashion workshop with living quarters above. It was featured in a big half-page newspaper story that also mentioned his black part-Persian cat named Emery who was famous for having a gold stud in his left ear. But by 2010 there was a large gambling room upstairs with police seizing over a dozen illegal video gambling machines.

164 N. King – From 1933 to 1966 this was the home of Arrow Hardware owned by Wilfred C. Chang. The store had a sign in the window advertising "Sporting Goods – Guns – Munitions". Chang was the secretary of the Chinese Gun Club and he often organized shooting tournaments and sponsored medals and trophies.

168 N. King – On Chan Dry Goods (1918), Market Sporting Goods (1924-1931).

170 N. King – On Chan Dry Goods (1918), Honolulu Dry Goods (1932), Modern Clothing Co. (1933), Royal Clothiers (1940), Chong Yuen Men's Furnishings (1955), United Chinese News, Kuo Min Tang Society (1961). In 1995 there was a big gambling raid for playing pepito (a card game similar to poker).

174 N. King – Poo Chong Dry Goods (1921), Oimatsu Shoten (1933), M.C. Lum grocery store (1939).

LEE LET BUILDING (SITE)

(155-157) 161-163 N. King
(1906) / 1966
Architect / Builder: unknown / Hawaiian Ballasting Company (1906)

This concrete market was built in 1966 on the site of the 2-story Lee Let building built by the Hawaiian Ballasting Company in 1906. From 1906 to 1919 the Lee Let building housed the Wah Ying Chong dry goods store owned by Lee Let.

In 1922 it became the Asano Chuya Bank Ltd., one of three Japanese banks in Honolulu, with a head office in Tokyo and branches in Yokohama, Kyoto, Osaka, Kobe, Wakayama, Hiroshima, Fukuoka, Okayama, Kumamoto, and Yanai.

The J.M. Osumi photography studio and the first home of the Japanese Society of Hawaii were upstairs.

The bank changed its name to Pacific Bank in 1925 and they remained here until 1941 when closed and liquidated by the federal treasury after the attack on Pearl Harbor.

From 1942 to 1966 it was Uptown Jewelers owned by Eugene and Dan Ichinose, who later moved to 126 N. King in 1966.

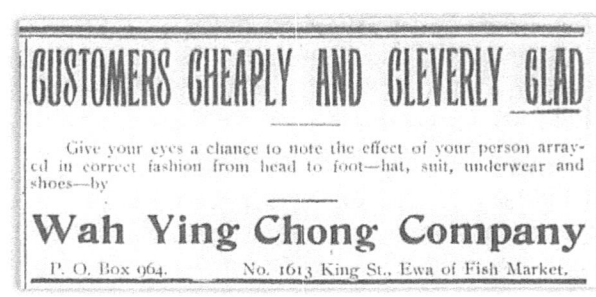

The building was demolished in early 1966 due to structural failures that created large cracks in the brick façade.

The building previously on the site was built between 1891 and 1899. It housed a fruit store and a tailor, and would have burned in the 1900 fire.

Before the 1886 fire this site contained the kitchen and a storage shed that served the massive block of Chinese lodging houses on the adjacent lot where the Oahu Market sits today.

Screenshot from 1906 Edison film

Lee Let was one of Honolulu's most prominent Chinese merchants, born in Canton, China in 1871. He moved to Hawaii in 1887 as a young man to manage the Yuen Chong store owned by his family. His father was Lee Hing Poi, the man who furnished all of the contract Chinese laborers for the Canadian Pacific Railroad. Lee Let was president of the Pacific Immigration Company, organized to supply plantations with Chinese laborers.

In addition to large real estate holdings, Lee Let owned a wholesale dry goods and wholesale grocery store, the Yuen Chong Company, and the Wah Ying Chong Company. He had branch stores in San Francisco, New York, Shanghai, Hong Kong and Sydney. He also owned a large plantation in Pahala that was managed by his brother.

He was said to be very charitable and of a "kindly and cheerful disposition". He was also quite the gambler who was often in trouble with the authorities. He may or may not have tried to bribe the Chief of Detectives to provide protection for his hui of gamblers for $1,400 per week.

E.C. WINSTON BLOCK

165-169 N. King
1901
Architect / Builder: unknown

By June of 1901 this large stone building was being constructed by capitalist E.C. Winston to replace the previous 2-story wooden building housing a harness shop and general merchandise store that burned in the 1900 fire. Before the 1886 fire there was a small 2-story wooden house here that backed up to the harbor.

The new fireproof building built in 1901 initially housed Lewis & Co., sole agents for Apenta – "the best natural Hungarian aperient water" from the Uj Hunyadi Springs near Budapest. A small wineglassful taken every morning before breakfast was said to be "one of the greatest aids to health and therefore beauty".

On the right side there was a Chinese medicine shop with names of medicines on the sign that were mostly for brain and stomach, but also for mosquito repellent.

Y. Suga Shoten, selling Japanese Provisions and dry goods might have been here in October 1901.

From 1923 to 1955 it was the M. Kawahara Shoten, a store run by Masao Kawahara that moved here from Maunakea Street.

It also briefly housed the Honolulu Hat Company in 1925.

From 1959 to 1984 it was Omochaya, a family-owned store with Japanese gifts and merchandise that moved here from its previous location on Hotel Street near River Street. The business started out in 1928 as a toy store ("Omochaya" means toy shop in Japanese), but after a few years was selling dishes, lamps, tea sets and housewares in addition to toys.

There are many ancient lanes, alleyways and pathways throughout Chinatown dating back to the Great Māhele of 1848 and before.

In 1907 the lane in the photograph was the subject of a Supreme Court case brought by Annie Woolsey against E.C. Winston and Lee Let, the owners of the buildings on either side.

It was her contention that the width of this prescriptive private right-of-way used since olden times had been illegally encroached upon and reduced from 4.5 feet to 2.2 feet in places, rendering it an essentially useless "chicken walk".

There were buildings in the interior of the block that had been occupied by Native Hawaiians for many years, and testimony was produced showing that funerals were conducted in back and that coffins needed to be carried by pallbearers on either side through the narrow path.

The Supreme Court upheld the right, but didn't change the width.

E.C. Winston

Emmet Claiborne Winston was born in Richmond, Virginia in 1848. At the age of 15 he drove four mules across the Great Plains in a wagon train of 40 wagons. Arriving penniless at Marysville, California, he walked 42 miles to Sacramento to find employment.

After several years of odd jobs and ranch work, he was inspired to sail aboard the ocean-going schooner *Anne Sophia* for many years after reading Charles Dana's *Two Years Before the Mast.* He sailed on trips to Mexico and the Bering Sea.

At age 26 he joined the American Sewing Machine Company in San Francisco as a salesman and adjuster, and in 1877 they sent him as their agent to Hawaii. Realizing an opportunity to supply California hogs to the Hawaiian market, he formed the Hawaiian Pork Packing Company with several prominent local businessmen. In 1890 he founded the first steam laundry in Honolulu, and he was also the president of the Honolulu Pineapple Company.

Other business ventures included operating a general merchandise store in Wailuku, Maui, founding the Hawaiian Tuna Packing Company, president of the Honolulu Fishing Company, owner of the Seattle Building Company, as well as having extensive real estate holdings including two large buildings in Chinatown on King Street and Hotel Street.

Winston was a member of the lower house of the Territorial government and a member of the council of state. He served on the Board of Health for 10 years, including one term as president. He was also a member of the Sharpshooters during the overthrow of the Hawaiian monarchy in 1893.

ARMSTRONG BUILDING

175-185 N. King
1905
Architect / Builder: William Mutch

After replacing his large wooden building block on Hotel Street burned in the 1902 Winston Block fire, businessman James Armstrong teamed up with Senator L.L. McCandless to build a "business block of Moiliili stone" on the corner of King Street and River Street. It was designed and built by William Mutch, with the foundation laid in September 1905.

Armstrong and McCandless had a falling out in 1922, with McCandless taking over the King Street property and Armstrong retaining the Hotel Street property. The building was renovated by Design Partners Inc. in 1982.

William Mutch was born in Scotland in 1845 and was Superintendent of Buildings for the Bishop Estate. He designed the new wing to the Bishop Museum, and he was also the head carpenter at Kamehameha Schools. He built the Moana Hotel, the Colusa Building, and the Alexander Young Hotel which at that time was the largest construction project ever undertaken in Hawaii.

He was the first foreign-born resident naturalized as an American citizen in the Territory of Hawaii.

This site was originally part of the Honolulu Harbor and Nuʻuanu Stream mudflats. It was filled in by 1891 and the first building was a large 2-story mixture of stores below and residences above, including a coffee shop, paint shop, candy store, tin store, wheelwright, and a general merchandise store.

The building did not survive the 1900 fire.

One very famous resident briefly lived on the second floor over the Wing Hong Yuen store at 177 N. King Street. Between March and May of 1910, **Dr. Sun Yat-sen** stayed here since Ching Chow, the owner of the store was a close friend and a member of the Hawaii Chapter of Dr. Yat-sen's political party, the Tung Meng Hui.

This party was the successor to the secret revolutionary group that overthrew the Manchu dynasty in China. But it was a dangerous party to be a member of – thirty members were publicly executed at one time in Kaifeng, China in 1914. The Kuomintang Party ("Nationalist Party") was a direct descendent of the Tung Men Hui.

Without a doubt, the most enterprising and entertaining store owner in this building was **Koichiro Miyamoto**, better known all over the world as Musashiya the Shirtmaker, perhaps the creator of the Aloha shirt.

It all started with several unanswered orders for cloth from England, Koichiro's very broken English, and one very clever local advertising man.

Chotaro Miyamoto came to Hawaii in 1885 from the province of Musashi in Japan near present day Tokyo and opened a dry goods store with some tailoring called Musashi-ya ("ya" means place).

When Chotaro passed away in 1915, eldest son Koichiro came from Japan to take over the business at age 19. When he didn't hear back about an order of English broadcloth during World War I, Koichiro simply resubmitted the same order again and again. After the war, a huge shipment showed up at the Honolulu docks consisting of five years' worth of orders all at once.

Desperately needing to move this huge amount of cloth, Koichiro reached out to local seamstresses to make the cloth into shirts. But when they didn't sell right away someone suggested he reach out to the Charles R. Frazier Company to help him advertise in the newspaper. Copywriter George Mellen was given the assignment.

The first ads, starting in May 1920, mostly just said "shirts made to order". But it was In December 1920 that Mellen created the more personable alter ego "Musa-shiya the Shirtmaker".

Mellen was fascinated with Miyamoto's colorful English, known as "pidgin" in Hawaii. In May 1921 he started writing the advertising copy supposedly verbatim from Miyamoto. The hilarious ads created a sensation and were enormously popular around the world.

They published a 32-page book in 1923, *How Musa-shiya the Shirtmaker Broke into Print*, "assisted by George Mellen" which sold by the thousands for many years.

By the early 1930's customers included Mary Pickford, Al Jolson, Nelson Eddy, Jeanette MacDonald, Dolores Del Rio, Douglas Fairbanks, Janet Gaynor, Alan Ladd, Loretta Young, Richard Dix, Ronald Colman, and Shirley Temple.

In 1934 Miyamoto moved his shirtmaking shop to 121 S. King Street and later to 2164 Kalākaua Avenue. Koichiro, who always used an abacus to calculate prices, retired at age 73 in 1968. The Musashiya store moved to the Ala Moana Center in 1966 and closed in 2000 after over 100 years in business.

The Musashiya store specialty was silk shirts, robes, pajamas, and kimonos. The story is told that one day in 1933 a customer asked if he could make an open-neck shirt from cotton Japanese yukata cloth – thus creating one of, if not the first Aloha shirts, known outside Hawaii as Hawaiian shirts.

This the first ever ad for an "Aloha shirt", in the Honolulu Advertiser on Friday, June 6, 1935.

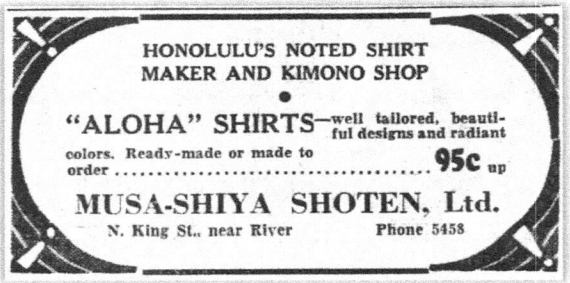

By 1936 both Ellery Chun at 36 N. King Street and Musa-Shiya were both advertising Aloha shirts. In 1937, Ellery Chun trademarked the term "Aloha Shirt" although he originally called his shirts "Hawaiian Shirts".

In an effort to promote locally made clothes, the Hawaii Fashion Guild and Aloha Week committees came up with a promotion in the summer of 1965 known as "Aloha Friday" where tropical print clothing could be worn to work. It was hugely popular and by 1967 applied to every Friday in the year.

George Mellen was born in Boston in 1875, but his parents moved to California in 1876 and he grew up on his father's ranch as a ranch hand and cowboy.

He had a natural talent for drawing but was unable to find work in commercial art and instead became a telegrapher and manager with Western Union for twelve years.

At age 32 he started working as a freelance writer and artist and moved to Hawaii in 1918. He was managing editor of the Hilo Daily Tribune before joining the Charles R. Frazier firm in Honolulu in March 1920.

In addition to his famous Musa-Shiya ads, Mellen was also known for his extensive research and writings to preserve ancient Hawaiian legends and historical places, especially the ancient and deserted village of Kaupo, Oahu, which he was instrumental in getting reserved as a 90-acre public park.

CHING LUM BLOCK

178-188 N. King
1904
Architect / Builder: Oahu Lumber and Building Company (probably)

Parapet name still visible in the 1960's

In 1848 this land at the corner was owned by a Native Hawaiian named Kawaaauwila, who sold it in 1869 to a wealthy Frenchman, Andre Alexander Corniot, who was married to a Hawaiian woman with the lovely name of Kapalehea.

Later in life Corniot contracted leprosy and spent his final days at Kalaupapa on Molokai. The newspapers at the time specifically mention a wrought iron fence "of pretty design" was made by Mr. A. Gaouen and sent to be placed around Corniot's grave when he died in 1893. In Corniot's will he gave $5,000 to endow five hospital beds at Queens Hospital, and $32,000 to the orphans at the Hospice du Havre in France.

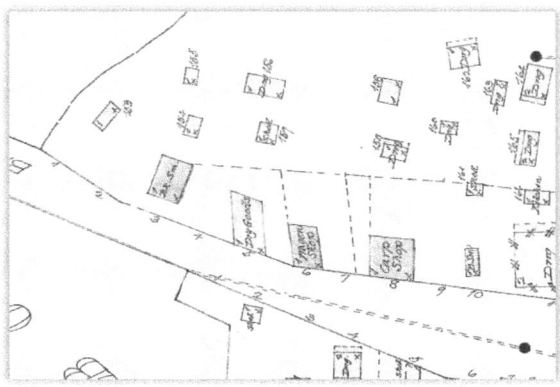

1885 Dakin Fire Insurance Map

In November 1903, the Corniot estate leased the land (6,568 square feet) to Ching Lum for 30 years at $65 per month. The estate later sold a portion of the King/River property at auction to L.L. McCandless in 1915, and the building was purchased by the Chang family in 1939.

The building was condemned by the city in 1981, but the owner spent $400,000 to renovate it in 1982.

Ching Lum (also known as Ching Cho Fai) was superintendent of the Oahu Lumber and Building Company and opened his own contracting and real estate business after the 1900 fire. He was also one of the lessees of the infamous "Iwilei Stockade", leasing the land from John Ena and then subleasing it to T. Masuda who ran the lucrative prostitution business with as many as 250 women, mostly Japanese.

When Ching Lum died in 1929 in Hong Kong "where he had gone some time ago in order to live out his days in peace and plenty among the sights and sounds of his native land" he left behind an estate worth $250,000 which was contested by two of his wives. His "Number One Wife" Ching Cheng Shee lived in Shekki, Heungshan, China and his second wife, Ching Yee Shee, lived in Honolulu. Ching Shee claimed they were married in Macao in 1902 without knowledge of any previous wife and had twelve children. She filed suit for herself and their five minor children and was granted $250 per month from the estate in spite of recently filing an annulment on grounds of deception shortly before he died.

Ching Lum

For many years the store of Chun Kam "C.K." Chow was located here. It was founded in 1903 "to carry on the business of Merchant Tailors, General Merchants and Dealers in Dry Goods and General Merchandise" under the firm name of C.K. Chow and Company. Six of the partners were from Hawaii and two were from Hong Kong.

The construction of the building is very unusual, with ashlar basalt blocks set in red mortar on the first floor, plaster covered brick on the upper floor, and rubble lava stone walls at the back and sides.

It was very likely built by the Oahu Lumber and Building Company, owned by Lee Chu and located just across Nuʻuanu Stream.

MAUNAKEA STREET

Originally laid out in 1837, some of the early 1848 land records call it Alanui "Kahawai". The name "Mauna Kea" is Hawaiian for "White Mountain", presumably named after the largest mountain in Hawaii (on the Big Island).

It was first paved in 1912 and was extended mauka of Beretania in 1970.

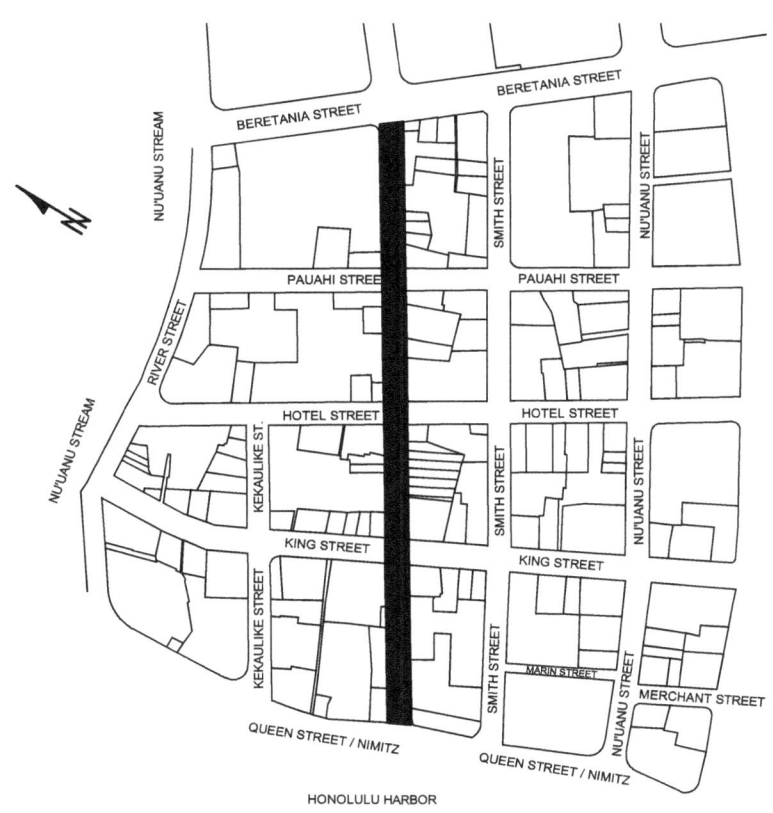

M. KAWAHARA BUILDING

900-910 Maunakea
1902, 1911-1912
Architect / Builder: Lucas Brothers (1902), Solomon K. Fukumura (1912)/ I. Izui (1912)

Hawaii Times / Nippu Jiji

Composed of two buildings built at different times, the building on the left is a 2-story brick building built in 1902 by the Lucas Brothers, probably for John F. Colburn to replace his brick building on King Street that was lost in the 1900 fire.

In 1905, A.S. Montgomery ran a recycling business here for iron, brass, copper, lead, old machinery, bottles, and even rags with a large yard out back.

The building on the right with the four upstairs windows was built for $6,000 in 1911. The building permit notice states it was built of "Hawaiian lava" which is readily visible on the back side. In 1912 Masao Kawahara hired architect Solomon K. Fukumura and builder I. Izui to remodel the building on the left.

The previous building on the corner from 1885 to the 1900 fire was at the very end of Queen Street and Maunakea Street. The hanging sign reads "C. Eon", the store of a most unfortunate Chinese merchant who was burned out of this store in 1900, burned out of his next store on Kukui Street in 1902, and then again in his store by the Railway wharf in 1904.

In 1891 and 1899 the adjoining two buildings housed a restaurant, a tailor, and a laundry with residences on the second floor.

These earlier buildings were not affected by the 1886 fire so it is very possible they could have been constructed many years before what is shown on the 1885 Dakin Fire Insurance Map. Unfortunately, they were burned in 1900 fire.

In 1985 the building was renovated by Eagle Construction and it became Robyn Buntin's Chinatown Gallery of Oriental Art for the next eight years.

It was foreclosed on by the US Government in 2002 for illegal casino gambling operations.

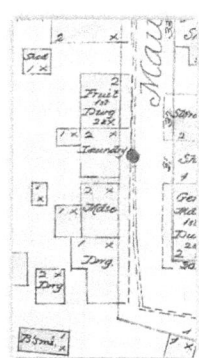

Masao Kawahara

… came to Honolulu in 1894 from Hiroshima as part of the great wave of Japanese immigration. But instead of becoming a laborer in the fields he ended up working in Queen Liliʻuokalani's household and later in the household of prominent local attorney J. Alfred Magoon.

Although of limited education, he more than made up for it with "health, energy, and honesty, and his determination to make his own way in the world".

In 1900 he built a kitchen and warehouse behind Kawaiahaʻo Church, and in 1904 he bought out a store in Honouliuli that included all merchandise plus 2 horses, 2 wagons and a harness. By 1909 he had a wholesale business on King Street, was a shareholder of the *Nippu Jiji*, and was very active in the Zokyu Kisei Kai (Higher Wage Association), the plantation labor association that organized the 1909 strike for equal wages for Japanese workers.

Kawahara was President of the Honolulu Nippon-Jin Shonin Doshi Kai (Honolulu Japanese Merchants Association) which was created to aid the Japanese victims of the 1900 fire. Over 7,000 people were left homeless after that fire, half of whom were Japanese. The association helped individuals find housing, obtain food and clothing and other supplies, and also assisted with filing claims with the government. There were 37 charter members, all leading Japanese businessmen. The organization became the Japanese Chamber of Commerce in 1916.

He became a food wholesaler and was the local distributor for Aji-No-Moto, a wheat-based powder seasoning also advertised as a meat substitute. Essentially monosodium glutamate (MSG), it was invented in Japan in 1908 by Dr. Kikunae Ikeda and it is now a $10B company with 35,000 employees.

Kawahara was also on the board of directors of T. Sumida & Company, the Pacific Bank, the Japanese Rice Mill Company, and the Japanese Sake Brewing Company.

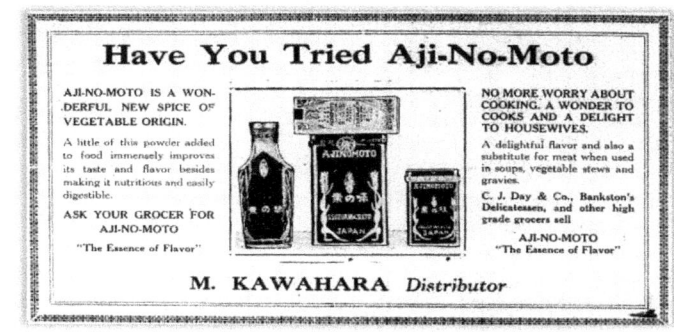

He relocated his office to his retail business, Kawahara Shoten, at 165 N. King Street in 1923.

J.H. SCHNACK BUILDING

922-942 Maunakea
1916
Architect / Builder: Emory & Webb / unknown

The J.H. Schnack Building cost $14,600 in 1916 and was designed by Walter Emory and Marshall Webb, the same architects who designed the Hawaii Theater in 1922. It is built of reinforced concrete and has seven stores on the first floor and 18 apartments on the second floor. It was rehabilitated in 1986 by Mouse Builders.

John Henry Schnack was a real estate dealer and financial collector born in 1853 at Lohbarbeck in Schleswig-Holstein when it was part of Denmark. Apprenticed as a merchant in Hamburg, he left immediately after the Franco-Prussian War and spent time in Paris, London, New York, Havana, New Orleans, and San Francisco, eventually landing in Honolulu in 1882.

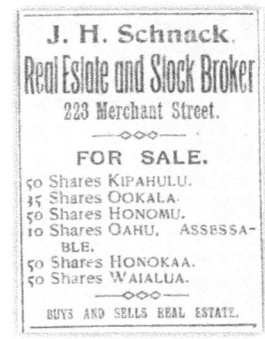

Schnack started out as a bookkeeper for the Metropolitan Meat Market and later owned the Germania Market on Fort Street. In 1896 he entered the real estate business and developed several properties in Chinatown. He was also a world traveler fluent in English, German, French, Dutch, and Spanish.

Originally from North Dakota and Pennsylvania respectively, **Walter L. Emory and Marshall J. Webb** both came to Hawaii independently in the early 1900's. Emory was the Assistant Superintendent of Construction on the Alexander Young Hotel, and after meeting up with Marshall Webb they opened an architectural practice together in 1909. In addition to the J.H. Schnack Building, they were the architects for the Hawaii Theatre, the Blaisdell Hotel, Union Trust Building, Castle Hall Dormitory, Cooke Art Building, and buildings at St. Louis College.

Here is what the building looked like brand new in 1916:

Over the years it has housed a variety of tenants, including Baron's Gymnasium, Hawaii Vulcanizing, Fountain Supply Company, The Sample Store, Kwong Chong Lung, S. Koyama Shoten, Iwakami & Co., China Import Company, Kwong Wah Chong, The Ilima Shop, The Ambler Furnished Rooms, American Veterans Committee, Harry I. Choy Realty, Hobby Center, AAAloha Antiques, and Bushido Antiques.

In 1961, Galerie Lamoi was in the basement of the Nicholas Char law office. His wife, Lam Oi from Hong Kong, was an abstract painter who had exhibited at Galerie d'Orsay in Paris and the Leppich Gallery in Cologne. The opening show included works by Lam Oi, Wong Bung Hung, Chang Woo Chong, and Tchang Ta Ts'ien (known as the best tiger painter in China). The gallery also showcased a 15-foot scroll painted by Wang Hui (1632-1720).

In the 1980's it housed the Precious Ink Chamber Gallery and featured Chinese brush paintings by a variety of artists.

Before the 1900 fire, the wooden buildings (c.1886-1891) on the site were used for housing, storage and selling fruits and vegetables.

Captain Joseph Maughan, Honolulu Harbor Master in the early 1800's, had an adobe house built here in 1834.

C.Q. YEE HOP COLD STORAGE & DORMITORY

948 Maunakea
1919
Architect / Builder: unknown

This lava rock building was part of the large C.Q. Yee Hop operation on this block and was constructed in 1919 as an icehouse and dormitory for $11,987.

They needed an icehouse since a lot of their meat products were shipped in from the mainland either chilled or frozen during the 5 to 7 days enroute.

The second floor was a dormitory for approximately twenty single men employees whose families were still back in China. A separate building housed a dining room.

The third floor was rented out to a German they called "Baron" who ran a gymnasium used by many of the employees.

In 1927 they hired engineer E.W. Ellis to convert the bottom floor into a large cold storage facility with 16 cooling rooms, with 40,000 square feet for butter, fish, poultry, fresh fruit, and vegetables.

In 1995 the C.Q. Yee Hop company wanted to demolish this building for more parking spaces, claiming it was unusable and subject to vandalism and vagrancy. It was spared since the State Historic Preservation Division and the Historic Hawaii Foundation objected, as did the city Department of Land Utilization.

This alleyway dates back to ancient times and has been here for at least 200 years.

HAWAIIAN MERCANTILE BUILDING

950-954 Maunakea
1917
Architect / Builder: unknown

This rather nondescript building might take the prize for housing the greatest variety of different businesses.

Its first known use was in 1920 as the salesroom for the Hawaiian Mercantile Company, owned by Rev. Akaiko Akana, whose specialty was poi made at their factory at Kalani and Kalihi.

It has also been:

- 1921 – Bankston's Delicatessen
- 1927 – C. Akana (produce company)
- 1934 – Maunakea Inn (owned by Mrs. Matsu Asato)
- 1945 – Filipino Public Service Bureau (owned by Roman R. Cariaga)
- 1946 – Cabras Commercial Photographer
- 1947 – Ladies wear store
- 1950 – L.S. "Sunny" Lai Real Estate and Tax Consultant
- 1955 – The Multi Investment Company (owned by Pang Kam Cheong and Mark Y. Murakami)
- 1968 – KC Realty

Rooms upstairs were rented out, and it was raided in 1948 for prostitution.

In 1995 the C.Q. Yee Hop company wanted to demolish the building but were prevented from doing so due to objections from the State Historic Preservation Division and the Historic Hawaii Foundation.

Before everything on the block was wiped out in the 1900 fire, this large 2-story wooden building stood on the site. It was constructed sometime after the 1886 fire which destroyed half the block, and before 1891, the date of the Dakin Fire Insurance Map. It contained a pork shop, meat shop, and general merchandise store.

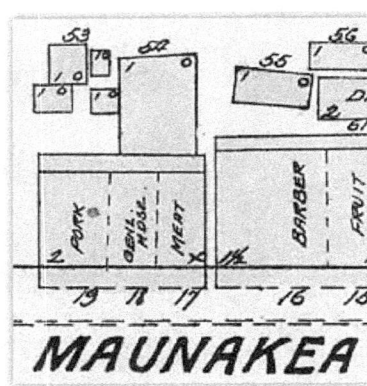

A particularly intriguing feature of the 1900 Board of Health photograph are the words written in Hawaiian on the meat shop side of the building.

HONOLULU CHINATOWN

LEE & YOUNG BUILDING

1007-1017 Maunakea, 98 N. King
1957
Architect / Builder: Ernest Hara / Century Construction

 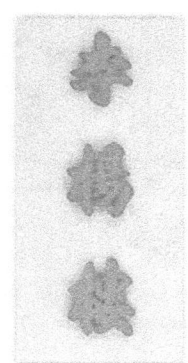

This building was designed by Ernest Hara, the architect who also designed the Central Pacific Bank at Smith and N. King streets. It was originally supposed to be "a modern building, but with definite Chinese motif", that somehow ended up just Mid-Century Modern without the Chinese.

On land leased from the Bishop Estate by Lee & Young Ltd, the building was also designed to house the new Chinatown Post Office, the first one in the United States to have "Chinatown" in the name.

It was completed in 1957 and was built by Century Construction owned by Everard Quan Sun Au. It housed 5 stores and 11 offices in addition to the post office.

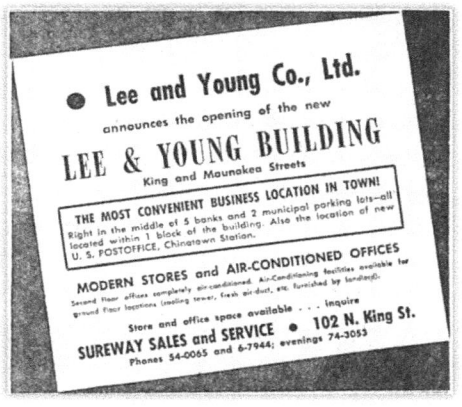

The Lee & Young corporation consisted of Y.S. Lee (president) and brothers Henry, Ah Kau, Yankee, and Munny, along with sisters Amoi Lee Chock and Lillian Chung, plus their mother, Mrs. Young Kat Oi Lee. She was the widow of Lee Leong who founded the grocery store business 25 years earlier in the previous building.

Ernest Hideo Hara was a graduate of Punahou and the University of Southern California School of Architecture and worked for Claude Stiehl and C.W. Dickey before opening his own office in 1945.

In addition to the Central Pacific Bank, Hara designed the Queen Kapiolani Hotel, The Waikiki Grand Hotel, the Hilo Hawaiian Hotel, and the Waikiki Shopping Plaza.

The first building on this site that we know of was a large 2-story wooden structure housing a pork market, barber shop, fruit stand, dry good store, Chinese stores, a corner grocery, and a large 2-story Chinese Club House in back.

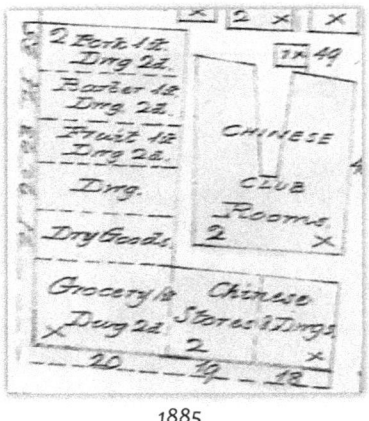
1885

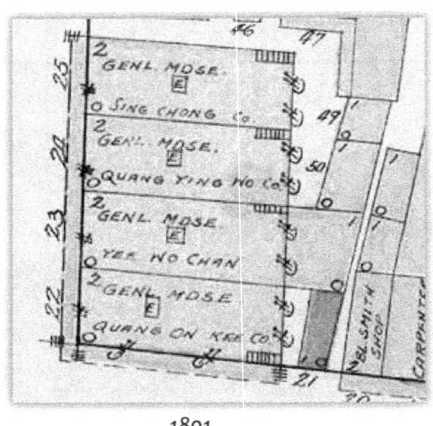
1891

After the April 1886 fire destroyed everything on this block, Sing Chong & Company hired E.B. Thomas in July 1886 to build a large 2-story brick building, 93' x 60', with iron doors and windows that was completed in September. It was one of only two brick buildings built outside the Fire Limits imposed after the 1886 fire.

This new building housed Sing Chong & Company, Quang Ying Wo, Yee Wo Chan, and Quong On Kee.

But disaster struck on January 20, 1900, during the great accidental fire that torched most of Chinatown:

> "The large brick buildings at the corner of King and Maunakea streets were no barrier, and all within the firm walls was soon blazing. Thousands of dollars worth of firecrackers, bombs and every sort of celebration explosives were stored in these buildings. The noise from the explosions continued for nearly an hour. When these began the firemen and people in the vicinity beat a hasty retreat, as it was known that many cases of kerosene were stored in the neighborhood, and fears were entertained that lives might be lost."

The 1900 fire also burned over 500 bags of rice in the Sing Chong warehouse. Four safes were in the fire for 36 hours, one of the 5-ton safes opened easily with all contents in perfect condition, two others were later opened with a crowbar, but the contents in the fourth safe were burned black and damaged by water.

c.1890

This was one of the first substantial buildings to go up after the 1900 fire, with Joseph A. Fink getting a building permit for "2-story brick stores, mauka Maunakea and King streets" on January 18, 1901. Sing Chong and the other businesses were able to move in by May 16, 1901.

Before the 1900 fire, **1001 Maunakea (98 N. King)** was the store of Quong On Kee & Company.

After the fire, it housed the wholesale merchandise store of Kwong Chong Lung from 1901 to 1931. It was owned **by Young Kwong-Tat**, who was born in Buck Toy, Leong Doo, Chung Shan District, China. He came to Hawaii in 1883 and started the Wing Chong Lung Company in 1896 and Kwong Chong Lung Company in 1901.

Young was an important supporter of Sun Yat-sen, was a member of the Chung Hua Keming Jun, and the chairman of the secret society known as the Tung Meng Hui that worked to overthrow the Chinese government. This store is where the Tung Meng Hui held their meetings. They later became the Kuomintang (Chinese Nationalist Party) and Mr. Young was also chairman of that group.

The store was gutted by a fire in 1926 but they reopened within a few weeks.

From 1931 to 1941 this was the Lee & Young grocery store specializing in nationally advertised brand goods and owned by Lee Leong (also known as Lee Sing Kung). Lee Leong was born in Honolulu and was president of the Chung-shan school and director of the United Chinese News. He also organized the Chong-Wah Import & Export Company headquartered in Hong Kong.

In 1941 the family got out of the grocery business and went into real estate, and the corner became New Orient Chop Suey (1935) and the Mayfair Restaurant from 1941 to 1955.

With the catchphrase "See the World Before You Leave It" this was the home of Yew Char Travel for nearly 30 years, from 1958 to 1987 when they moved to 160 N. Hotel Street.

Yew Char was born in 1893 in Kohala, Hawaii, the son of Chinese contract sugar plantation laborers. He worked in canefields and pineapple canneries, sold newspapers and shined shoes, eventually earning enough to attend the Modern School of Photography in Chicago in 1915.

He and his brother ran City Photo studio on Hotel Street from 1916 to 1925, and he opened The Tiffany Photo Studio in 1927.

He was the first person of 100% Chinese ancestry to be elected to the Territorial Legislature, serving from 1927 to 1945.

In 1933 he organized his first tour – a trip to the Chicago World's Fair. Char's Tour & Travel Service became Hawaii's first commercial travel agency, taking thousands of people on tours of Asia, Europe, and the Mainland, including one tour in 1937 on board the *SS President Hoover* that was bombed by a Chinese plane near Shanghai.

The business expanded to 1011 Maunakea in 1958 on their 25th anniversary and featured three trips as prizes. He was still traveling up to the time of his death in 1982 at the age of 89, after which local flags were flown at half-staff.

1007 Maunakea was the longtime location of the Yee Wo Chan Company. They were established in 1879 and were located here from 1886 to 1944.

After the 1900 fire their insurance company refused to pay damages, claiming they were caused by "civil commotion" but the Hawaii Supreme Court eventually ruled in Yee Wo Chan's favor.

It was the location of Sureway Sales & Service from 1947 to 1960, at which time they moved across the street to a new building they built that replaced the corner of the 1901 Y. Anin Block.

1011 Maunakea was the store of Quong Ying Wo from 1886 to 1899 according to the Dakin Fire Insurance maps which also indicated it was being used to store Chinese goods in 1906.

It was the Quong Sam Kee drugstore in 1928, Café Long John in 1944, and the Roseland Café from 1945 to 1956 owned by Hatsuhira Miyamoto. In 1958 Yew Char Travel also took over this space adjacent to their main office on the corner.

1017 Maunakea was the location of Sing Chong & Co., one of the largest importers of groceries from Hong Kong who were here from 1886 to 1929. They even owned two schooners, *Kawailani* and *Moluola*.

This was no little Chinese shop – in 1880 the *Ho Chung* Chinese steamer brough 320 tons of general merchandise consigned to the Sing Chong & Co., and in 1884 the bark *Catalina* transported $9,000 in gold shipped by Sing Chong & Co. They were the biggest dealers in rice in Hawaii for half a century.

The first mention of Sing Chong is in the 1874 newspapers, and in 1878 they were located at the corner of Beretania & Nuʻuanu streets. From 1879 until the 1886 fire they were at Buffum's Hall on Hotel Street, and in July 1886 they hired E.B. Thomas to build them a new 2-story brick building at the corner of Maunakea and King streets that housed four stores.

This was the office of the United Chinese News from 1931 to 1951 and also the headquarters for the Kuomintang in Hawaii Chinese society. It was the Blaisdell for Mayor campaign Chinatown storefront in 1956, after which it became the Chinatown Post Office in the new building from 1956 to 1975.

It became Lin's Lei Shop in 1986.

KWAI CHAN TRUST BUILDING

1010 Maunakea, 102 N. King
1956, 1995 remodel
Architect / Builder: Century Construction (1956), Allied Builders System (1995)

2021

1966

1901

This was once the proud corner of the massive Y. Anin Building which covered a quarter of the block along King Street and Maunakea Street. It was the second largest building in Chinatown and was designed by architect H.L. Kerr and built in 1901. The building had 16 stores with basements below and storerooms above and a frontage of 133 feet on King Street and 183 feet on Maunakea Street.

At some point early on it lost its topknot parapet, then the entire corner was replaced in 1956 with a finned Mid-Century Modern building, and then that building was remodeled in 1995 in a sad attempt to mimic the original and meet the requirements of the Chinatown Design Guidelines. It is the sixth building that we know of on this site.

The design of the original 1901 building is unusual in that it more closely resembles the architectural style of the buildings built after the 1886 fire, especially the look of the ornamental brickwork.

For 30 years, from 1926 to 1956, this was the home of S. Ozaki Hardware who moved here from across the street at 109 N. King Street.

Complete line of
PERFECTION STOVES and PARTS
S. OZAKI HARDWARE
102 N. King St.   Phone 5167

On July 8, 1956, Sureway Sales took out a building permit for $40,000 and gave Century Construction 10 days to demolish the old building and then replace it with a modern 2-story building with large concrete fins on the second story.

As part of the Kekaulike Courtyards project in 1995, the Kwai Chan Trust hired Allied Builders to remodel the façade to supposedly be more compatible with the surrounding historical architecture.

The earliest photograph of buildings formerly on this corner dates to about 1890, shortly after the 1886 fire. In 1891 and 1899 there was a 2-story wooden building that housed two barber shops, a Chinese medicine store, a butcher shop, and a fruit store (see photo). This building was a victim of the 1900 fire.

R. Coady & Company was located at this corner in 1850. Owned by Richard Coady, they were ship's chandlers and commission agents.

In 1855 this was the site of the American House Hotel owned by J.A. Burdick. The American House was managed by Mr. Kirchhoff in 1866 when the officers of the bark Swallow along with a group of American Ministers "stayed at the American House, and on leaving said that nowhere, since they started from New York, had they found better accommodations at any hotel where they stopped, or more attentive hosts than this."

Mark Twain stopped at the American Hotel to rent a horse in 1866 and might have stayed here too.

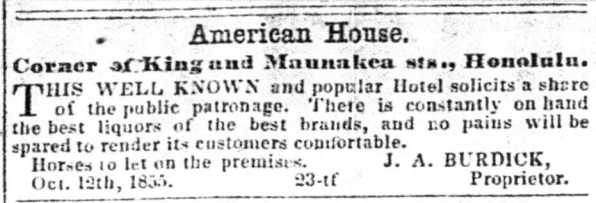

By 1885 there were two butchers and a tailor here in a 2-story wooden building that would have burned in 1886.

Sanshichi Ozaki

Originally from Kanagawa Prefecture, Ozaki was born in Shizuoka in 1864 and came to Hawaii in 1892. He was the first to sell Japanese books in Hawaii, carrying a load over both shoulders and selling *ezoshi* (picture books) for 20¢ to 30¢ and novels for 70¢ to 80¢ to Japanese immigrant workers.

In 1891 he opened the first independently owned Japanese store in Honolulu – S. Ozaki Shoten.

In 1895 he was president of the Japanese Merchants Union.

Ozaki hosted a large meeting of Japanese at his store during the plague quarantine of Chinatown in 1900. He also represented the fire victims in pursuing claims against the government – over half of the 7,000 people burned out were Japanese, and initially the government only offered to pay for 2/3 of the damages.

Young Anin

Y. Anin was born in 1853 at Buck Toy, Kwangtung (Guangdong), China. He came to Hawaii in 1872 and quickly built a large empire of business, real estate, and financial interests.

He started out vegetable farming and opened the Chin Wo dry goods store with his savings in 1879. He expanded into the rice business and was a partner in several plantations and built a number of rice mills. He was also in charge of sugar cane for a 160-acre tract in Kapalama.

Y. Anin was also general manager of Kwong Chong Lung Company and manager of Wing Chong Lung Company. His youngest son was commander-in-chief of the Chinese Air Forces in the Sun Yat-sen government.

KEKAULIKE COURTYARDS

1016-1028 Maunakea
1997
Architect / Builder: Mitsunaga & Associates / Hawaiian Dredging & Construction Company

This building is part of the city's large 1997 Kekaulike Courtyards redevelopment project that extends all the way to Kekaulike Street and fills most of the interior of the block. It is also the entrance to a multi-story municipal parking garage from Maunakea Street.

This site was originally part of the large Y. Anin Block designed by H.L. Kerr and built in 1901. But on November 11, 1964, it looked like the photograph on the right. About 4:00 in the afternoon the front wall collapsed in a shower of bricks, fortunately no one was injured.

Throughout the 1900's it housed an unbelievable number of restaurants on the first and second floor: Me Ing Low, Chong Loy Chan, Man Fong Lau Chop Suey House, Lee Quon Lum Chop Sui House, Jooklum Chop Suey, Shanghai Chop Suey, 2-Gun Mokumaia, National Steak House, Bow Sing Chop Sui, Maunakea Café, Welcome Inn, Sun Lee Chop Suey, Chin Lee's, Peltier's Hawaiiana, New Hop Inn, Hoy Sing Chop Suey, Ting Yin, Chop Suey, and Suzuran Shokudo. In the 1940's the Dragon Lair Ballroom, Club Rendezvous and Latin American dancehalls were upstairs. Tanwahchi Buddhist Temple was here in the 1950's.

Before the 1900 fire the wooden buildings here housed two tailor shops and a general merchandise store in 1891 and 1899, and a tailor shop, barber shop and fruit shop in 1885. All were destroyed in the 1886 and 1900 fires.

Back in the 1840's this was the site of the large lumber yard for local builder Charles W. Vincent. In 1847 he advertised 140,000 feet of pine timber, 6x6 square timbers, 20,000 feet of pine boards, 3,000 feet of koa lumber, 40,000 shingles, 20 kegs of wrought iron spikes and nails, plus assorted locks, hinges, latches, bolts, sashes, blinds, etc.

CHEE WO TONG BUILDING

1021-1037 Maunakea
1901
Architect / Builder: Su Wai

About ten weeks after he started the building on the corner of Hotel and Maunakea, Su Wai took out a building permit on August 2, 1901, for "2-story brick stores, 1033 Maunakea" built to match in the exact same style.

The most notable thing about this building is that the Chee Wo Tong Chinese medicine store was here for *over 100 years* at **1033 Maunakea Street** – the longest tenancy in all of Chinatown.

Chee Wo Tong & Company started in October 1900, with Tang Chu Lung and 8 partners on Beretania Street. They were here by 1904 when Tan Chu Lung became the sole owner.

Later owner Norman F.C. Tang was born in Kwong Tung, Hoi Ping, Wu Leung District, Yan Hing Lee Village, China, in 1917 and came to Hawaii in 1928 when he was 11 years old. In addition to running the shop, he was also an actor in the original *Hawaii 5-0* and *Magnum P.I.* TV shows.

The Chee Wo Tong store was reportedly a favorite of New York fashion designer Geoffrey Beene.

1023 Maunakea was the Wui Chun Tong Drug Company, perhaps as early as 1902 and until the mid-1920's. It was owned by William H. Crawford, called "Che-fa Willie" by the *Honolulu Advertiser*. He was also arrested for a fan-tan gambling game upstairs in 1919. Goo Kim was the company treasurer, and he passed away here in 1924 at the age of 66.

From 1938 to 1943 the Kwong Wah Chong Hop Kee Company was located here, specializing in merchandise and pork. The owner, 64-year-old Ching You Tong, was arrested for selling opium over the counter in 1938.

In rapid succession it was the Golden Dragon Café (1944), Eddie's Café (1945), Maunakea Grill (1946) and the Tan Kong Company market (1948).

For the next twenty years it housed the Tai Yen Trading Company selling retail and wholesale Chinese merchandise, and they were also one of the top five sellers of fireworks.

It was the Wong-N-Wong restaurant from 1983 to 1997, the Glowing Dragon Seafood Restaurant from 2001 to 2004, and Chin's Chinatown Restaurant from 2009 to 2011. It is now the Tea Hut & Chinese Art Gifts store.

1027 Maunakea was a dry goods store in 1906. From 1934 to 1943 it was Quong Sam Kee & Co., billing itself as "Honolulu's Oldest Chinese Drug Store", formerly at 99 N. King Street for 36 years.

It was briefly the Maunakea Gift Center, and then Frank's Closet in 1946, which Francis Siu apparently started with merchandise stolen from the submarine base ship's service store.

It was Tim's Party House in 1953, a BYOB club owned by T.S. Tom.

From 1956 to 1961 it was Paul Williams' Honolulu Barber School with 12 chairs and "no waiting".

Kuong Chong Yuein opened here in 1962, specializing in candies, cakes, roast duck, and chicken.

From 1979 to 2007 it was a pastry shop and candy store with a similar name, Shung Chong Yuein.

In 2009, Mei and Wesley Fang, relatives of the Ng family that owned Shung Chong Yuein, opened Sing Cheong Yuan Chinese Bakery, a local favorite for moon cakes.

1029 Manuakea was the Tin Wo jewelry store from 1905 to 1917 and a variety of businesses after that including the Leong Yick Company, the Lau & Company liquor store, the China Chop Sui restaurant, and the Mun Chung Chinese restaurant.

For twenty years, from 1961 to 1980, it was the China Emporium, importers of Chinese merchandise.

It was briefly two Vietnamese restaurants in the 1980's – Nam Cuisine and the Pho Mai restaurant.

By 1997 it was the Nam Fong store, famous for roast duck.

1037 Maunakea was the longtime home of the Lin Fong Company, a restaurant and confectionary famous for moon cakes and wholesale manapua sales for nearly 70 years, from 1925 to 1994.

The space has been occupied by the Bo Wah Trading Co. since 2002.

1041 Maunakea housed a small Chinese market downstairs. The upstairs was raided for gambling in 1919.

It was the Seung Fat Company grocery and Chinese merchandise store from 1928 to 1937. In 1931, 10 people were arrested here for shooting craps.

One of the longer tenants was the M.T. Lau Chow Market, specializing in meat. They were here for over 25 years, from 1940 to 1966.

From 1982 to 2008 it was the Hawaii Martial Arts Supply store which also included the Hi-Kong Jewelry store.

It became the Chinatown Express Restaurant in 2009, and in 2014 the Zwick Academy of Fine Art was located upstairs. In recent years it has been the Bread House Bakery.

Y. ANIN BLOCK (MAUNAKEA)

1034-1036 Maunakea
1901, renovated 1991
Architect / Builder: H.L. Kerr

This is one of two remaining pieces of the large Y. Anin Building that wrapped around a quarter of the block along King Street and Maunakea Street from 1901 until the mid-1950's. The corner at King Street was replaced in 1956, and a large section along Maunakea collapsed in 1964.

Yin Nin Tong Kiam Kee was one of the first stores here, opening in 1905. It has also housed Sun Pun Heong Chop Suey in the 1930's and 1940's, Mun Tin Market, and Koon Yik Siu's butcher shop which added a roast pig oven in the 1950's. It has also been the Palomares Photo Studio (upstairs) and the Wing Lung Chinese Store in the 1950's and 1960's.

Cindy's Lei Shoppe opened here in 1961 and is one of the oldest lei stands in Hawaii, for four generations. Their most unusual customer was a fossilized Tyrannosaurus Rex at the Bishop Museum.

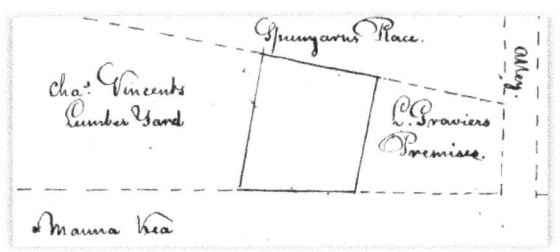

In the late 1840's this was the site of the house of Dr. Richard Ford from England. French blacksmith John Jason previously lived here in 1844, and in 1847 the property included a bake-house, oven and wooden building occupied as a baker's shop by John Bowden.

In 1854 it was the site of Daniel Janner's Restaurant Republic, serving "meals at all hours, and with the best the market affords".

The "L. Gravier Premises" on the map was also known as Liberty Hall. Everything here burned in the 1886 fire.

MAUNAKEA MARKETPLACE

1108-1110 Maunakea
1990
Architect / Builder: James K. Tsugawa / Mouse Builders

This building looks old but isn't – it was constructed in 1990 as part of the Maunakea Marketplace development and was designed by architect James K. Tsugawa to mimic the older historical building façades per the Chinatown Design Guidelines.

There was a 1-story house and a tailor shop here in 1885 which burned in 1886. It was replaced by a 2-story wooden building with a tailor shop and dwellings which burned in 1900. A large 2-story wooden building housing 7 stores was here by 1906 – it burned in 1926 along with four other buildings.

In 1949, P.S. Lum hired Interisland Contracting to construct a new fireproof concrete and concrete block building on this site. This building was demolished in the 1980's by the city for the Maunakea Marketplace.

Some of the businesses here have included Municipal Market (1921), Municipal Dairy Association (1923), Cosmopolitan Flying Club (1930), homebuilder Takeo Yoshikawa (1932-1938), Betty's Photography Studio (1945), Roseland Café (1945), Tan Wah Photo (1947). There was a Mah Jongg gambling bust here in 1949.

From 1950 to 1985 it was Honolulu's most famous late-night Chinese restaurant – Tin Tin Char Sut, later known as Tin Tin Chop Suey. It had 10 booths and 8 tables and was started by Chinese actor Kam Mun Goo. It had quite a varied late-night clientele, but sometimes the drunk sailors would harass the female impersonators and there would be fights. Moomoo's pool hall, next door, had a sign that said: *"Female Impersonators Not Allowed, Servicemen Off Limit"*.

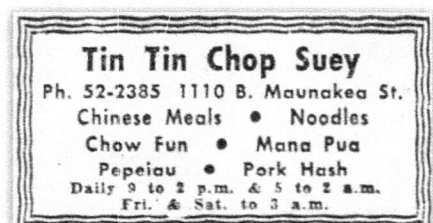

Honolulu Gypsy King, Tennis George, and his fortune-telling family operated upstairs in the 1950's.

The second floor also had two taxi dancehalls: the Orchid Ballroom and Palace Ballroom. For 50 cents a single man could buy a dance and enjoy a few minutes of social contact with music provided by a live band. Taxi dance halls were enormously popular after World War II with at least 8 in Honolulu. The average age of the dance hostesses was 22 years and a study in 1936 found that out of about 300 girls, *"40 are Portuguese, 31 are Filipino, 28 are pure Hawaiian, 27 are Hawaiian-Chinese, 24 are Japanese, 15 are Korean and 12 are pure Chinese. The older dancers are of the Caucasian races… and they are old hands at the game"*.

MAUNAKEA MARKETPLACE

1112-1120 Maunakea
1990
Architect / Builder: James K. Tsugawa / Mouse Builders

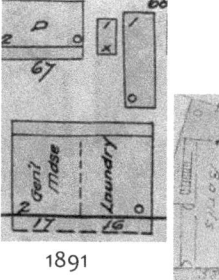
1891

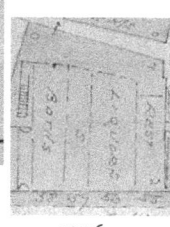
1906

1914

From 1891 to 1899 there was a 2-story frame laundry and general merchandise store here that burned in the 1900 fire.

By 1906 there was a new 2-story wooden building with a restaurant, liquor store and bath house, burned in the big 1926 fire that consumed the ewa-waikiki corner of the block.

After that fire, Loo Chu built a service station and taxi stand here in 1931, and in the 1940's this was the site of a juke box repair shop and pool room. In 1945 this was the site of Kaleo's Poi Bowl restaurant featuring hula dancers.

In 1948, Mr. P.S. Lum hired C.W. Winstedt to build a 2-story concrete and concrete block restaurant and dance hall called Chinatown Grill. Royal Danceland was upstairs, owned by Froilan B. Villalba and Dolores Rhoda Aea.

In 1963, Jack Cione, operator of the Forbidden City club in Waikiki, changed the Chinatown Grill into The French Quarters featuring burlesque-type entertainment with female strippers and a four-piece band. Shows were continuous from 8:30 pm to 3 am, seven nights a week, no cover charge but there was a two-drink minimum.

It briefly became "Country Quarters" in 1966, managed by rodeo performer and Western singer Jerry Hopkins. Later that same year it reverted back to burlesque featuring the dancing of "Tini Bubbles" and "Sinful Miss Coco Barr".

For being the 20,000th patron of Chinatown Burlesk, seaman Gary Heiss of the USS *Eversole* was awarded a night on the town with exotic dancer Mai Ling.

In 1968, the second floor became the Busy "B" Theatre and later the Rex II Theatre showing adult films with many arrests on charges of pornography. After being purchased by the city for the Maunakea project, there was much concern about the city being the landlord of a pornographic business, but there was nothing they could do about until the building was demolished in the 1980's for the city-sponsored development of the Maunakea Marketplace.

Architect **James K. Tsugawa** graduated from Hilo High School and received his degree in architecture from the University of Oregon. He spent five years in California before opening his own office in Honolulu in 1965.

WING SING WO BUILDING

1125-1127-1129 Maunakea
1937
Architect / Builder: Y.T. Char / W.S. Ching

1938

This building was designed by local Chinese architect Y.T. Char and built in late 1937 at a cost of $28,700 by W. S. Ching for the offices of the Wing Sing Wo Company. They were a kamaaina Chinese firm started in 1898 by Leong Sam and other partners on Aala Street near Beretania, specializing in Chinese groceries.

In 1902 they merged with Po Sing Tong, a firm that sold Chinese drugs and herbs. Their retail department which sold Chinese and American groceries was at 64-68 N. Hotel in the large Mendonça Building, the drug department selling Chinese drugs and herbs was at 1113 Maunakea Street, and the wholesale department was located at 1125 Maunakea Street.

It replaced a 2-story wood frame building built c.1906 that housed two stores and a laundry. Before the 1900 fire, between 1891 and 1899, there was 2-story wooden building on the site with a barber, a tailor, and a restaurant.

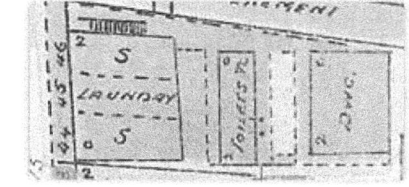

S.Y. Lum, Hawaii's largest importer and exporter of jade jewelry was here from 1955 to 2006. It was owned by Yat Sau Lum who was from Kwangtung (Guangdong), China.

From 1952 to 1970 it housed the Mun Tin Market, managed by Ah Gett Lee who had over 30 years' experience in roasting and cooking Chinese dishes. They moved here from 1036 Maunakea Street.

LUM YIP KEE BUILDING

1130-1136 Maunakea
1926
Architect / Builder: Herbert Cohen Cayton / Saiki & Davenport

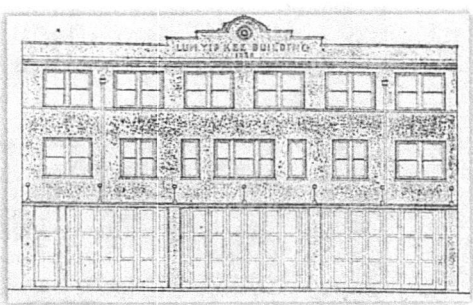

Architect's sketch

This is the hottest site in Chinatown – it has been subjected to at least 6 fires that we know of: 1886, 1900, 1902, 1926, 1957, and 1972.

The 2-story general merchandise store, barber shop and dwelling house that was on the site in 1885 was destroyed in the 1886 fire. This was replaced by a similar 2-story wooden building that burned in the 1900 fire. If there was a new building here in 1902 it would have been the victim of the August 18, 1902, fire that destroyed all but one building on the entire block. A large 2-story wooden building with 12 shops followed c.1906.

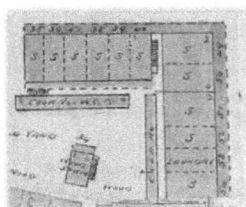

At 2:00am on May 8, 1926, a fire started in Yee Nam Kee's butcher shop at the corner of Pauahi and Maunakea that burned 10 stores at the corner of the block and caused about $75,000 in damages, leaving 40 families homeless.

The Yoshihiro family with four small children were awakened and saved by the family dog moments before their ceiling collapsed. An elderly Chinese man, Tom Min Nan, was unsure where to go to avoid the flames until a young boy pushed him out a second-story window where he luckily landed on a pile of merchandise in the street.

Young Sik Kim, a 78-year-old paralyzed stroke victim, died in a mysterious fire in his apartment here in 1957. A 1995 pseudo-science book claimed it was a case of spontaneous human combustion, but the man was a heavy smoker with a history of setting small fires.

In 1972 a faulty kerosene stove caused a fire that gutted a third-floor apartment.

The building here today was designed by Herbert Cohen Cayton and built by Saiki & Davenport for Chinese businessman Lum Yip Kee in 1926. It replaced his grocery store that was burned in the 1926 fire. It cost $25,000 and had space downstairs for 3 stores, 10 offices upstairs and 10 rooms on the third floor.

Instead of having a basement, the building had trap doors between the first and second floors for moving goods back and forth. From 1949 to 1961 it housed the offices of Lum Yip Kee Ltd.

It also housed a business in the 1930's and 1940's known as the Pacific Rooms, owned by Frances Norman and Hazel Russell, with Ruth Ashby later replacing Ms. Russell. On October 27, 1938, the police raided the Pacific Rooms and arrested the 63-year-old madam and 6 women between 22 and 25 years of age, charging them with prostitution.

In 1945 there were ads for the Maunakea Hotel having overnight rooms for servicemen – one wonders if they came furnished with any of the residents of the Pacific Rooms? Perhaps, since there were later prostitution busts at the same address. The Pacific Rooms partnership dissolved in 1944 when most of the other brothels in Chinatown officially shut down. Undoubtedly some carried on unofficially, but by then the years of police regulation of this illegal activity had ended.

Seven Women Nabbed By Police Vice Squad

The police vice squad raided the Pacific rooms, 1130 Maunakea St., at 6 Wednesday evening, arresting seven women on charges of resorting to a house of prostitution.

All the women forfeited $25 bail apiece today in district court. Their names are:

May Walker, 63; Josephine Armstrong, 23; Toni Delano, 23; Irene Conners, 25; Louise Raleigh, 23; Jackie Meyers, 23, and June Miller, 22.

The raid was staged by Capt. Tatsumi Matsumoto of the vice squad, assisted by Officers Richard Miller and John Stanley.

The son of famous detective Chang Apana lived here in 1968. He was "the only steeplejack in Hawaii". When he was younger his strict policeman father caught him gambling and put him in jail for two weeks.

In 1981 the city purchased the building since the owners were unwilling to subject the property to the requirements of the Urban Renewal Plan. It was then sold in 1984 to developer and preservationist Bob Gerell for $300,000. He subsequently spent an additional $450,000 in renovations designed by local architect Spencer Leineweber.

Lum Yip Kee was known as the "Taro King". Born in Koon Fai, Hongshan district, Kwantung province of China in 1866, he came to Hawaii in 1884 when he was 18 years old and worked as a taro planter for 3 years. He returned to China in 1887 to marry and worked for two years in Saigon.

He came back to Hawaii in 1893 and operated a taro plantation where the University of Hawaii is today. He founded the Oahu Poi Factory in 1905, the Honolulu Poi Factory in 1913, and the See Wo Poi Factory in 1915 which was the largest in the territory.

Lum also organized the Wing Duck Chong company and managed the Lung Doo Wai rice company that at one time controlled 700 acres in Waikiki. He was an organizer and director of the Chinese-American Bank, and in 1922 was one of the founders and president of Liberty Bank. He built three buildings in Chinatown that bear the name Lum Yip Kee.

Herbert Cohen Cayton graduated from the University of Chicago in 1902 and went to work as an architect for the U.S. Treasury Department. In 1908 he married a woman from Honolulu and relocated to Hawaii as the supervising architect for the Hilo Federal Building.

He designed the 1926 Lum Yip Kee Building, the King Theater, the Furneux Building in Hilo, the Edgewater Apartments in Waikiki, the Community Church in Ewa Beach, the King Theater, and the U.S. Immigration Station with C.W. Dickey.

PANG LUM MOW / ALOHA HOTEL (SITE)
1133 Maunakea

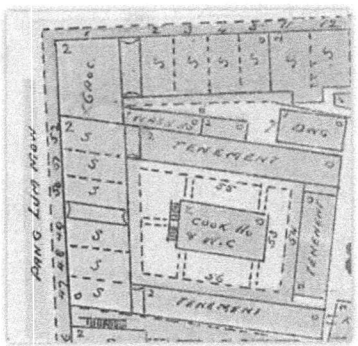

This might look like an ordinary parking lot, but in 1976 it was the scene of a dramatic standoff with the Honolulu Police involving several hundred people who were trying to prevent the forced eviction of residents of a rundown tenement known as the Aloha Hotel that was scheduled for demolition.

The 1970's were heady times full of righteous indignation and grassroots activism, and few groups were more prominent and more effective than the People Against Chinatown Evictions (PACE).

The building was originally built in 1907 by Pang Lum Mow as part of a large tenement complex at the corner of Maunakea and Pauahi streets (see also 1147 Maunakea Street). Over the years it housed a variety of small restaurants, tea shops, cleaners, and general merchandise stores. During the 1940's the second floor was known as the Modern Rooms, one of many brothels in this area of Chinatown catering to sailors and the military.

By 1976 the building was in pretty sad shape, housing the Lee Wing Yuen Trading Company on the first floor and mostly elderly Filipino men upstairs. The conflict started with the city's urban renewal efforts to remove blighted buildings, including this one, and how to deal with the subsequent displacement of cheap and affordable housing. The protesters ignored the court orders, locked arms, and held off the police until they were assured the city would immediately provide the displaced residents with low-cost housing in Chinatown.

In 1885 this was the site of the American House, a hotel run by Z.S. Squires who obviously did not care one bit for the immigrant Chinese, calling them "the planter's Mongolion pets".

The American House burned in the 1886 fire and was replaced by the large 2-story wooden building in this photograph that was built by Pang Lum Mow. It was deliberately burned by the Board of Health on January 1, 1900.

SUMIDA BUILDING

1138-1140 Maunakea
1927
Architect / Builder: Solomon F. Kenn / Saiki & Davenport

c.1889

Formerly the site of the 1889 China Engine Company fire station, Daizo Sumida purchased the land from William Mutch in 1926 for $40,000 and erected this building designed by architect Solomon F. Kenn. It was built by Richard Davenport and Masataro Saiki for a construction cost of $54,000.

The date on the parapet commemorates the day they got the building permit, December 13, 1926.

The buildings previously on this site and on the adjoining Lum Yip Kee Building site were burned in a fire on May 8, 1926. It started at the corner butcher shop owned by Yee Nam Kee.

The fire ignited "great quantities of fireworks" stored in a back room and scorched awnings on buildings across the street. Meat hanging in the butcher shop ice box was thoroughly cooked.

The new 1927 building housed the offices and warehouse of T. Sumida & Company. Founded in 1904, they were initially in the imported liquor wholesale business but branched out to groceries, canned goods, flour, and rice during Prohibition.

By 1927 they had 20 people in this office and 5 on other islands, as well as a fleet of delivery trucks.

The grand opening was attended by "every flower in Honolulu" complete with abundant floral gifts from both Oriental and Occidental businesses plus a temporary shrine.

China Engine Company No.5

As early as July 1851, the Chinese Engine Company, along with the officers and men of the British ships *Portland* and *Swift*, helped stop a fire that threatened the businesses of D.N Flitner (watchmaker), Dr. T.C.B. Rooke, and Victor Chancerel & Medaille (Hotel De France).

Officially organized in 1879 with 60 members, in 1881 they first moved into the former location of Engine Company No.1 on King Street. From 1882 to 1886 the United Chinese Society met there until building their own clubhouse.

The Interior Department was so impressed with the efforts of Chinese Engine Company No.5 that they appropriated the money for a new brick engine house on Maunakea Street.

A NEW ENGINE HOUSE.

The following tenders were received yesterday at the Interior Department for the erection of an engine house for China Engine Company No. 5, on Maunakea street:

Walker & Redwood	$9,763
Edward Hingley	9,525
Peter High	8,975
Geo. W. Lincoln	8,900
Sam. Mahoe	8,630
E. B. Thomas	8,581
J. J. Carden	8,185
Geo. Lucas	7,650
Fred. Harrison	7,398

The tenders also contained figures for foundation and excavation. The tender of Fred. Harrison was accepted, his price for foundation per cubic yard being $8 and for excavation 20 cents.

On April 13, 1889, the cornerstone was laid for the new "fireproof brick" engine house accompanied with much feasting and speeches plus music by the Royal Hawaiian Band.

It was built by Fred Harrison and was the first brick fire house in Honolulu. It was 55' x 65', two stories high, with a cupola and 13-inch-thick walls. The grand opening was November 28, 1889, featuring the return and housing of their fire engine with much feasting and toasting with "the fireman king" himself, King Kalākaua.

In the 1889 Fire Department parade the 45 members marched in two lines, "dressed in brilliant ultramarine blue blouses with dark hats and trousers", with 2 horses pulling their engine and 1 horse pulling their hose reel.

Ten years later the building was engulfed and destroyed in the 1900 fire, as were the houses of Engine Company No. 1 on King Street and Engine Company No.4 on Nuʻuanu Street.

While clearing the rubble in December 1900, 14' below the pile of ruined bricks and mortar they found the tin box time capsule that had been placed in the cornerstone in 1889. It was still intact with all of its contents, including banners, coins, and documents.

This photograph shows the aftermath of the devastating 1900 fire, with the only things left standing being the charred ruins of: Kaumakapili Church, Chinese Engine Company #5 (in the center), a small brick storehouse, and the 1886 Sing Chong building at King and Maunakea streets.

Daizo Sumida

Born in the village of Niho in Hiroshima prefecture in 1887, Daizo Sumida came to Hawaii in 1904 at age 16 to help his brother Tajiro in the liquor business. Their first location was a 1-story wooden building on Maunakea where they were wholesale liquor distributors and sole agents for Homaretai sake.

In 1908 they opened the Honolulu Japanese Sake Brewing Company in response to the high price of imported sake. By 1914 they were making 300,000 gallons a year and in 1920 he was the most successful Japanese businessman in Hawaii.

Daizo took over the business when Tajiro returned to Japan ahead of Prohibition and he continued the general merchandise and grocery import business while converting the sake brewery into an ice-making business.

In 1927, T. Sumida & Company built a 3-story office and warehouse at Maunakea and Pauahi streets. It was the first Japanese business to have a third floor with an elevator.

After the repeal of Prohibition in 1933 Sumida restarted the sake brewing, producing Daikoku Masamune, Takara Masamune, and Takara Musume sake.

Sumida was considered a "king-maker" in the Japanese community and was president of the Honolulu Japanese Chamber of Commerce. He was also instrumental in raising funds for the Japanese Hospital (Kuakini Hospital).

After the Japanese attack on Pearl Harbor on December 7, 1941, Sumida was arrested since he was considered an influential business and community leader. One of over 2,000 Japanese internees, he was first held at Sand Island and was later sent to an internment camp near Santa Fe, New Mexico. He was not allowed to return to Hawaii until December 1945.

Sumida spent much of the post-war period working to rebuild the Honolulu Japanese community and to build good will with the many other ethnic groups in Hawaii. For his years of community service he was awarded the Order of the Sacred Treasure (Gold and Silver Rays) by Emperor Hirohito. In addition to being president of T. Sumida & Co. Ltd he was also VP and Managing Director of Pacific Bank.

Honolulu Sake Brewery

Incorporated in 1908 to deal in "sake, shoyu, soy, and miso, to manufacture and deal in ice, to manufacture 'soft' drinks, to establish bonded warehouses, and cold storage and refrigerated warehouses and to deal in refrigerating plants", the Honolulu Sake Brewery was in business for 84 years, closing in 1992.

There were about 60,000 Japanese living in Hawaii in the early 1900's, many of whom could not afford the cost of their imported national beverage.

Hawaii's warm climate made sake brewing difficult, but Tajiro Sumida developed an innovative refrigeration process so they could make affordable local sake.

Their first brew was named Takarajima – "Treasure Island".

PANG LUM MOW BUILDING (SITE)

1147 Maunakea
(1907), 1988
Architect / Builder: unknown (1907), James K. Tsugawa (1988) / Mouse Builders (1988)

c.1929

After the 1886 fire, a large 2-story wooden building was built on this corner. There was a general merchandise store there in 1891 and a coffee shop in 1899. On January 1, 1900, the Board of Health torched the building, the second plague burning to take place in Chinatown.

January 1, 1900

In 1907, Pang Lum Mow built a large replacement 2-story wooden building with stores and tenements that extended along Maunakea and Pauahi streets with a grocery store on the corner. From 1947 to 1956 it was known as Siu's Meat Corner.

The corner portion of the building was gone by 1976 and Chinatown Associates built this modern 1-story building in 1988.

Pang Lum Mow was a well-loved businessman "with a ready smile and twinkling eyes". He was born in China in 1859, immigrated to Hawaii in 1876, and became a US citizen in 1890. He supported schools in China and Hawaii and was known for his generosity to benevolent causes.

HAWAII HOCHI / Y. ANIN BUILDING

1149-1153 Maunakea, 74-86 N. Pauahi
c.1912, 1948 remodel
Architect / Builder: unknown (1912), Harry Kaonohi Stewart Jr. & Phillip K.H. Lee (1948) / C.W. WInstedt (1948)

Over 150 years ago this was the "World's End" – a hotel from about 1839 to at least 1859. And probably very aptly named since it was at the far northwestern edge of the city of Honolulu, overlooking Nuʻuanu Stream. The land was originally purchased in 1833 by Edward Brown from the King's Cook, a man named "Bill the Baker", and sold to Henry S. Swinton (Sheriff and Customs Officer) who "built upon and improved it" sometime after 1839.

Shortly after the 1886 fire a new 2-story building housed a barber shop with the Sing Kee Coffee Saloon on the corner that also sold cigars, tobacco, and groceries. The building was burned along with rest of the block on January 16, 1900, by the Board of Health.

The land was vacant for several years after the fire and this large 3-story concrete building was most likely constructed in 1912 after the land ownership was sorted out in the courts.

From 1912 to 1922 it was the main plant and offices for the *Hawaii Hochi Sha*, a six-day-a-week Japanese-language newspaper founded in 1912 by Frederick Kinzaburo Makino. He had recently served a 10-month prison sentence for his role in the 1909 plantation labor strike.

Due to the other local papers' poor coverage of issues relevant to the Japanese community, Makino's paper purportedly presented a "non-party and independent" perspective. After the bombing of Pearl Harbor by Japan, the newspaper was renamed the Hawaii Herald but reverted to its former name in 1952. In the 1990's the *Hawaii Hochi* had a circulation of 9,000.

During World War II a business on the second floor of this building was known as the Service Hotel, one of the largest brothels in this part of Chinatown. The madam was Darlene Foster and she had 12 women working here.

In 1948 the Y. Anin Ltd. Company moved their offices here and hired the team of engineer Phillip K.H. Lee, architect Harry Kaonohi Stewart Jr., and contractor C.W. Winstedt to do an extensive $95,000 renovation and reconstruction. The tiling at the top was added at that time to "give a touch of the Orient to the roof line".

Between 1952 and 1962 the Roosevelt Hotel was on the third floor, and from 1962 to 1982 it was called Roosevelt Hale which provided unfurnished rooms for single men for $35 and up per month.

On Wednesday, October 21, 1970, at about 1:30 pm there was a gangland killing right in front of the building on Maunakea Street. Francis Burke, one of the top lieutenants for reputed crime syndicate boss Alema "The Man" Leota, was walking along the street with two companions when a gunman fired five or six shots at Burke and then quickly made his escape. The 38-year-old Burke collapsed dead in the rain-soaked gutter and the newspapers ran a photo of the body on the front page.

Witnesses were uncooperative, and George "Fat George" Arashiro and Paul Kea Lono were tried and acquitted. In the words of the prosecutor:

> "You do the best you can with what you get... The prosecutor does not make the evidence and the prosecutor does not have the power to compel witnesses to testify. If the public doesn't care if a man is gunned down in broad daylight on the streets of Honolulu, then the public is getting the judgment it deserves."

In 1980, two Chinese benevolent societies, the See Yup Society and the Yee Yee Tong, bought the building for $350,000 and spent $200,000 on renovations. Both societies have a long history in Honolulu of providing social and cultural services. They were originally founded by plantation workers to help and support each other while also providing entertainment and places for social gatherings.

See Yup was incorporated in Honolulu in 1897 as a meeting place for Chinese immigrants from the four districts of Toi Sun, Sun Hui, Hoi Pang, and Ing Pang. When their clubhouse was purchased by the city in 1957 for redevelopment they moved in with the Yee Yee Tong in the Siu Building on Hotel Street.

For this location, commercial tenants were on the first floor, with the second and third floors occupied by the Yee Yee Tong, See Yup, Chinese Community Service Association, the Ching Wan Musical Group, and the Kwong Chau Society.

T. SUMIDA BUILDING

1152 Maunakea
1909/1916
Architect / Builder: K. Tashing

Tajiro Sumida

This bluestone building was the T. Sumida Liquor Store owned by Tajiro Sumida. It was initially built in 1909 as a 1-story building, the second story was added in 1916.

From 1934 to 1964 it was the Riverside Grill, owned by the colorful K.C. (Kam Chong) Wong.

In the mid 1930's, Mrs. Delia Williams operated a brothel upstairs called the Lark Rooms.

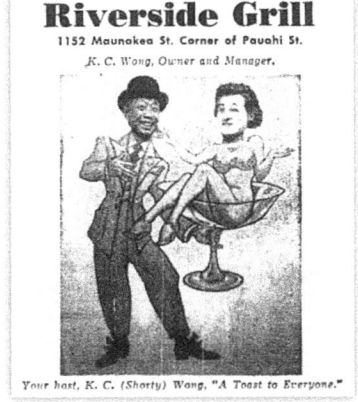

The Minatoya Shokudo (Shokudo = dining hall) opened in 1964 and by 1970 was known as the Minatoya Cocktail Lounge, billing itself as "the oldest Japanese Restaurant/Bar in Honolulu".

The upstairs was a notorious gambling spot for over 50 years, often raided by police with search warrants and crowbars and arresting large numbers of people for dice games, pai kau, mah jongg, and pepito.

Local underworld figure Francis Burke was sitting in the Minatoya Bar moments before being gunned down across the street on October 21, 1970.

One of the biggest raids was in 1996 when they caught 60 people enjoying a full-blown Vegas-style casino with felt-lined tables, dealers, chips, high stakes, pai kau, blackjack and baccarat. The gambling room was open 24 hours a day with security doormen and two electronic doors watched by TV cameras. It was reportedly the most successful gambling operation in all of Chinatown.

In 1981 the building was forcibly purchased by the City and resold to a sympathetic buyer after the previous owners refused to renovate the building per the terms of the Urban Renewal Plan.

But the gambling upstairs continued, and the building was seized by the Federal government in 2004.

Before the 1900 fire there was a restaurant on the corner in a 2-story wooden building that also housed a shoe store in 1891 and a barber in 1899.

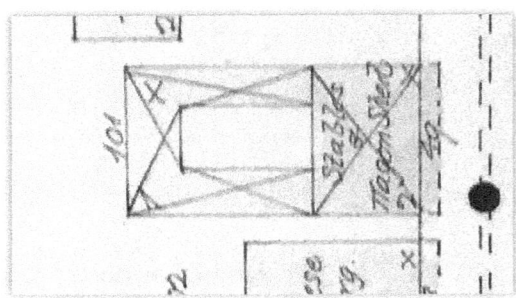

In 1885 there was a large wagon shed and stables on this same corner that burned in the 1886 fire. (Pauahi Street did not exist until after the fire).

From 1891 to 1900, Choy Lee's horseshoeing and blacksmith shop was right in the middle of Pauahi Street, next to the restaurant.

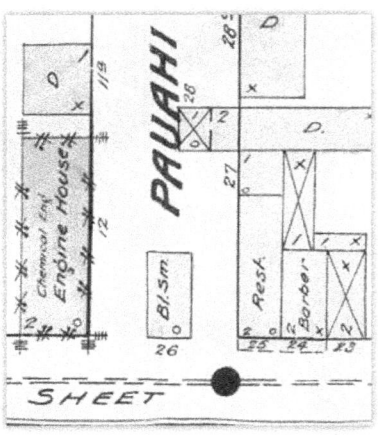

K.C. SIU BUILDING

1155-1157 Maunakea
1965
Architect / Builder: unknown

The first building on this site was a 2-story frame building with two shops with a bake house and residences in back built sometime after 1906 – before that it was an empty lot at least as far back as 1891. In 1913 the store on the right was the tailor shop of E. Shigemura, specializing in shirts, kimonos and pajamas made to order.

In 1934 it became the office of Masataro Saiki, a general contractor who did plastering and cement work and formerly with Saiki & Davenport.

It was also the home of the Yamada family and the Yoshida-ya Mochi candy store for nearly 25 years, owned by Tamano Yamada who was born in Fukuoka prefecture, Japan, in 1894.

K.C. Siu built this 2-story concrete building in 1965 for $35,000, and the first tenant was the 24-hour Jo-Jo Coffee Shop. In 1967 it was one of nine Honolulu businesses officially placed off-limits to servicemen due to the number of homosexual and mahu customers who frequented the place. The local paper interviewed the lady at the cash register but she wasn't too concerned since they spent more money than servicemen.

In 1970 it became Jo Jo Chop Suey, owned by Chinese-born Peter Quock Chui Lee who also owned the Busy "B" adult movie theater at 1122 Maunakea Street.

A variety of different restaurants have been here since, including Heong Kwong Chop Suey (1975), Good World Restaurant (1981), Fat Kee Food Center (1989), Esan Thai Cuisine (1993), and Café Oriente (1994).

ASAHI / OAHU THEATER (SITE)

1158-1168 Maunakea
(1899/1908/1927)
Architect / Builder: Hego Fujino (1927) / Saiki & Davenport (1927)

This is the site of the Asahi Theater, the first Japanese theater in Honolulu, built in 1899. Destroyed in the 1900 fire, it was rebuilt and opened on April 30, 1908, with a seating capacity of 1500.

The first performance was a stirring drama of the Russo-Japanese war presented by local Japanese actors. The theater had regular seating plus cushions on the floor in front.

It had the largest stage in Honolulu and actors could enter from the wings or behind the audience on an elevated promenade along one wall. It also featured electric spotlights and footlights.

In addition to Japanese performances it also hosted lectures, vaudeville shows, trick cyclists, boxing matches, trained monkeys, political meetings, and was a major rallying place in fomenting the plantation wage strike of 1909.

The Asahi Theater was demolished in 1927 and replaced with the Oahu Theater by three Japanese businessmen: Isamu Takano, Mataji Nagamori, and Masataro Saiki. It was designed by Hego Fuchino and built by Saiki & Davenport who also built the St. Francis Hospital, Kapalama buildings, Lum Yip Kee Building, Siu Building, Sumida Building, and Fong Building. The new theater was designed to present Oriental plays and movies as well as American plays and motion pictures.

In a brilliant stroke of marketing, the Oahu Theater staged a week of screen tests for hundreds of hopefuls, in front of real cameras and lights, conducted by motion picture director Lawrence Tareyton from Tec-Art Studios. The screen tests were shown along with the regular entertainment programs for everyone to see.

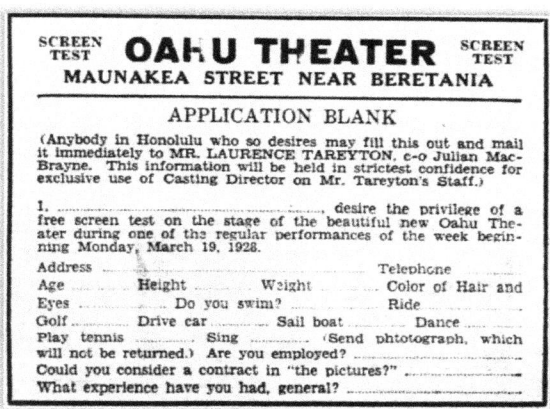

Hego Fuchino was born in Saga prefecture in Japan in 1888 and came to Honolulu to study at the University of Hawaii. He graduated with a degree in civil engineering but taught himself architecture by studying traditional Japanese design.

Fuchino was the architect for the Oahu Theater, the B.K. Yamamoto Building, the Maikiki Christian Church, Kuakini Hospital, Sodo Mission, Shinto Temple in Palama, Park Theater, Kaimuki Theater, YMBA Building and many of the Japanese shrines throughout Honolulu.

The theater was renamed the Roosevelt Theater in 1934 and was operated by Franklin Theatres and later Royal Theaters. The opening week program included "Love in Morocco", Joe E. Brown comedies, scenes of Kilauea volcano erupting, scenes of the Salinas Rodeos and a serial featuring the famous dog Rin-Tin-Tin.

In 1956 the Royal Theater chain hired nightclub owner and entertainment promoter Jack Cione to help convert the Roosevelt Theater into a full-time burlesque operation. This was his first experience in the "take-it-off" business and it taught him how profitable "forbidden entertainment" could be.

The Roosevelt Theater became an adult film theater in 1959, underwent a massive renovation in 1969, and was renamed the Rex Theater in 1970. The Rex Theater was infamous for showing X-rated movies, and occasionally had films seized that were deemed obscene by the police.

In 1976 the city bought the Rex Theater in preparation for the upcoming urban renewal Pauahi Project. This led to a huge discussion as to whether it should remain open until the renewal project was started, and if so, concerns about whether the city should be the landlord of a pornographic movie house. It was finally demolished in 1985.

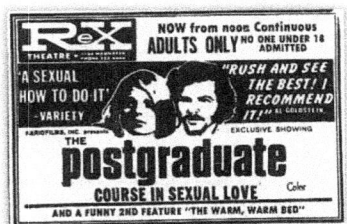

Before the entire block burned on January 20, 1900, these buildings were on the site. They housed a general merchandise store, the Ping Chan Coffee Saloon, a meat market and residences.

There was a dry goods store and a general merchandise store here along Maunakea Street in 1885, with a handful of houses and dwellings in back. None survived the 1886 fire.

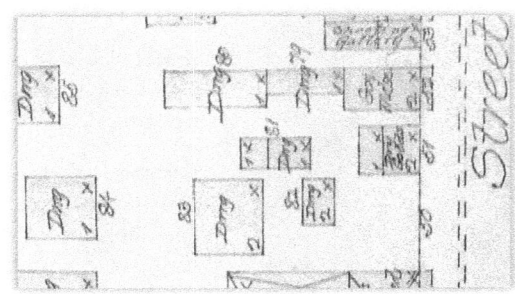

TSUNG TSIN ASSOCIATION BUILDING

1159 Maunakea
1916
Architect / Builder: unknown

This building was built as the headquarters for the newly organized Chinese Chamber of Commerce – opening day was February 2, 1916. The initial membership consisted of 150 prominent merchants and businesses. Chu Gem, manager of the Quong Sam Kee store, was the first president.

The downstairs has been a variety of different businesses over the years: Pang Sing & Co. (1918), Hawaiian Supply Company wholesale groceries (1920), Western Pacific Fruit Co. (1924), Ho Ti Yuen Co. wholesale and retail merchandise (1930), Mew-Tong's Barber Parlor (1933), Mew Tong Inn restaurant (1944), Fook Look Sau Chop Sui (1952), Gum Yu Chop Suey (1960), Johnny's Café and Blackies Café (1961), MLM Soul Food (1972), and F.C. Chee's Chinese Acupuncture clinic.

On Feb. 22, 1927, it became the new clubhouse for the Tsung Tsin Association in celebration of their 16th anniversary. Formerly known as Nyin Fo Fui Kon, they are a benevolent society founded in 1921 by Young Kin Leong for Chinese people speaking the Hakka dialect. The opening was attended by over 700 people and included feasting, large floral displays, and thousands of firecrackers. The society has been at this location for 95 years.

Before the 1900 fire there was a 2-story frame building on the site housing a tailor shop in 1891 and a general merchandise store in 1899.

LOO CHOW BUILDING

1161 Maunakea
1968
Architect / Builder: unknown / Town Construction

1900

This 4-story concrete apartment building was built by Town Construction in 1968 for Fabian and Katherine Chow. It replaced a small 2-story wooden building built in c.1906 that housed a saloon on the first floor.

The saloon was later known as the Kamehameha Saloon and when it closed in 1918 they auctioned off 9 large bevel glass mirrors, the 14-foot oak top counter and back bar, and 2 pool tables.

From 1918 to 1923 it was the Kamehameha Auction Rooms, selling everything from clothing to household goods to furniture to bales of hay.

It was Loo Chu's Liquor store from 1934 to 1958. During this time, 22 people were arrested for playing pai kau on the second floor in 1955.

Loo Chu sold the business in 1958 and it became Loo Chow Liquor.

Before the 1900 fire there was a 2-story wooden general merchandise store on the site that would have been built sometime after the 1886 fire. It was burned on January 16, 1900, by the Board of Health along with everything else on Block 9.

K.C. WONG BUILDING
1165-1169 Maunakea
1952
Architect / Builder: unknown

This concrete building was built in 1952 by Kam Chong Wong, the owner of the Riverside Grill at 1152 Maunakea from 1934 to 1964. It replaced a 2-story wooden building built in 1901 by San Tong that was home to the Honolulu Carriage Co. that also included 1-story residences in the back.

Before the Block 9 fire on January 16, 1900, this large 2-story wooden building was on the site housing a barber shop, two fruit shops, and a shop selling ice cream and cold drinks. It had replaced a building that was at the extreme northern end of the 1886 fire.

1168-1172 MAUNAKEA (SITE)

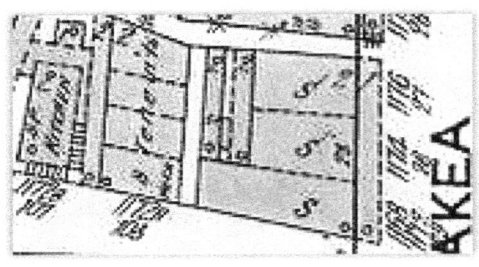 

Built sometime after 1906, there was a 2-story wooden building here with three shops below and residences above plus tenement apartments in back.

In the 1920's it was the office for Ching Sang real estate and later a succession of restaurants: It Café (1939), Hop Lee Inn (1952-1959), Koon Fong Chop Suey (1960), Hong Kong Chop Suey (1961).

The Hong Kong Chop Suey restaurant was gutted by fire in 1961, with *Star-Bulletin* photographer Terry Luke famously capturing the anguish of owner Kwock Kwai Wong.

A new store-building was constructed here by Century Construction in 1962 for owner Tim Choy Lee. From 1965 to 1982 it housed Café Dalisay specializing in Filipino foods.

There was a lot of moonshining going on in the tenements out back, with many police raids for the possession of okolehao (Hawaiian moonshine), an alcoholic beverage distilled from the ti root. The name translates to "iron butt" and comes from sailing ships' iron pots that were converted into stills.

All of the buildings on the site were demolished in the 1980's for the Urban Renewal Pauahi Project and were replaced with the current Hale Lahui parking garage.

Before the 1900 fire there was a small 1-story laundry here in 1891, a 2-story wooden coffee shop in 1899, and this photograph taken in January 1900 shows a barber pole out front.

1171-1187 MAUNAKEA (SITE)
(c.1906-1973)

Although it is a parking lot today, there have been several buildings on this site including a general merchandise store, several restaurants, and a doctor's office between 1891 and 1899.

This lot was unaffected by the 1886 fire, so these buildings could have been built before that date.

After the entire block was burned on January 12, 1900, by the Board of Health, a large 2-story wooden building was built here sometime around 1906 with an open passageway in the middle that led to large 2-story tenements in back with separate cook house and toilets.

After a bad fire damaged the second floor in 1972 the building was condemned in 1973 and demolished.

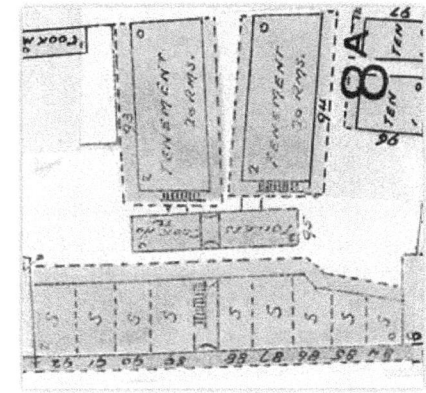

TOM'S GRILL (SITE)
1178-1180 Maunakea

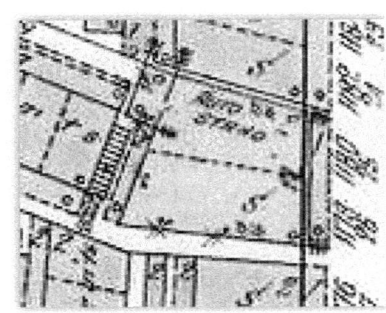

Now the Hale Lahui Parking Garage, there was previously a 2-story brick building on the site built in 1914 which replaced a c.1900 2-story wooden building owned by Chun Kim Sut that burned on September 30, 1913 when Chun Kit Sen threw a lit kerosene lantern out of a rear window. Saichi Arita had operated a Japanese bath house on the first floor and he subsequently leased the Fishel property at 79 Beretania Street. The brick building here housed the Takamori Shoten from 1929 to 1934, the Canton Inn in 1937, and Wong's Chop Suey in 1938.

The most notable business was Tom's Grill, located here from 1940 to 1982, moving from 138 N. King at Kekaulike where it first opened in 1932.

Tom's was owned by Tom Tai Leong (T.L. Tom) who also owned a restaurant in Manila. Tom's Grill advertised itself as "The Home of Hawaiian Foods."

It was also a bar and over the years saw more than its share of gambling, shootings, stabbings, and killings. There was an unsolved gangland-style killing here in 1967 and in 1968 one woman and 37 men were arrested in a barricaded gambling den upstairs.

In the latter days most of the customers were retired and Tom's was a combination meeting place, social club, senior citizens home, and small loan company. Great-grandmother Minnie Tom was the last owner, stringing leis when not tending bar. She closed it in 1982 after 42 years in business. The building was purchased by the city to be included as part of the Pauahi Redevelopment Project but suffered a devastating fire in 1983, with the burned-out shell being demolished in 1984.

A coffee shop and barber were on the site in 1891, and a meat market in 1899. The building in the photograph was built after the 1886 fire and burned in the 1900 fire.

MAUNAKEA HALE (SITE)

1182–1190 Maunakea
(1962)
Architect / Builder: unknown

Now the site of the parking structure for Hale Lahui built in 1987, this was the location of Maunakea Hale, a public housing project built in 1962. It provided "rooms for single Filipino men" for $39.50 per month.

From about 1906 to 1962 there was a 2-story wooden building here that at various times housed a Japanese hotel, drug store and several small restaurants, plus a large gambling den on the second floor. The city ordered the owner to demolish the dilapidated buildings in 1962.

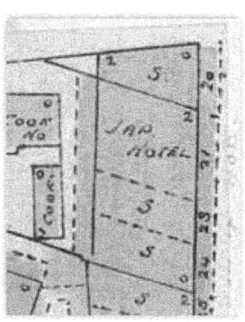

On the left, these buildings were on the site in 1900 and were built after the 1886 fire. A furniture store was on the right and a dwelling on the left. It did not survive the 1900 fire.

There was a building called the Eureka House on this site that was deliberately demolished by order from King Kalākaua during the 1886 fire in a successful attempt to halt the spread of the fire. Known as the Eureka Temperance House, it had a new shooting gallery in 1882.

The Eureka House in the photograph below was built after 1886 and was on Maunakea Street on the high bank of the old Nuʻuanu Stream adjacent to Smith's Bridge. Ironically, a Norwegian named Gustave Abramsen ran a speakeasy in the back, selling whiskey, gin, beer and "saki". A police raid netted seven drunken sailors in 1895.

Today this building would be sitting in the middle of Beretania Street. It was destroyed in the 1900 fire.

HONOLULU CHINATOWN

NUʻUANU STREET

In Hawaiian "Nuʻuanu" means "cool cliff", and this street was first opened in 1838 as the main road leading inland from the harbor, then to the Nuʻuanu Valley, and eventually reaching all the way to The Pali.

Sailors in the 1840's called it "Fid Street" due to the number of saloons found along its length. "Fid" was a slang word for a bottle of liquor.

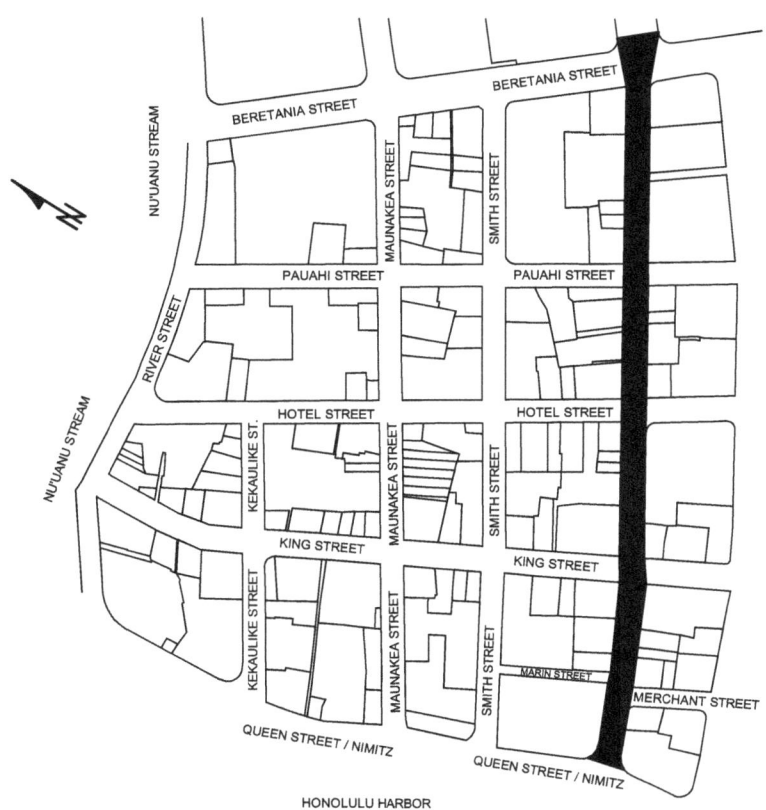

There were once two large buildings along the waterfront near the foot of Nuʻuanu Street on what would later become Queen Street / Nimitz Highway.

In 1848, a large 3-story coral stone Custom House, 40' x 60', was built by Hawaiian laborers on a coral point at the waterfront on the site of Keliʻimaikai's house, located in what would now be the middle of the Waikiki-bound lanes of Nimitz Highway in front of Pier 13.

It was a landmark for 56 years until demolished for the widening of Queen Street in July 1904.

Also at the foot of Nuʻuanu Street, on the site of an ice house constructed by C.H. Lewers in 1858, A. Frank Cooke (son of Castle & Cooke founder A.S. Cooke) built a large 3-story coral warehouse on the waterfront in 1882 with a sail loft on the 3rd floor. The photograph below was taken in 1890 from a sailing ship, looking up Nuʻuanu Street. The Cooke Warehouse is on the left, with the Brenig Block beside it on the right. The warehouse was the home of the California Feed Company when it was demolished in the Queen Street widening of 1904, and the site straddles what is now both lanes of Nimitz Highway.

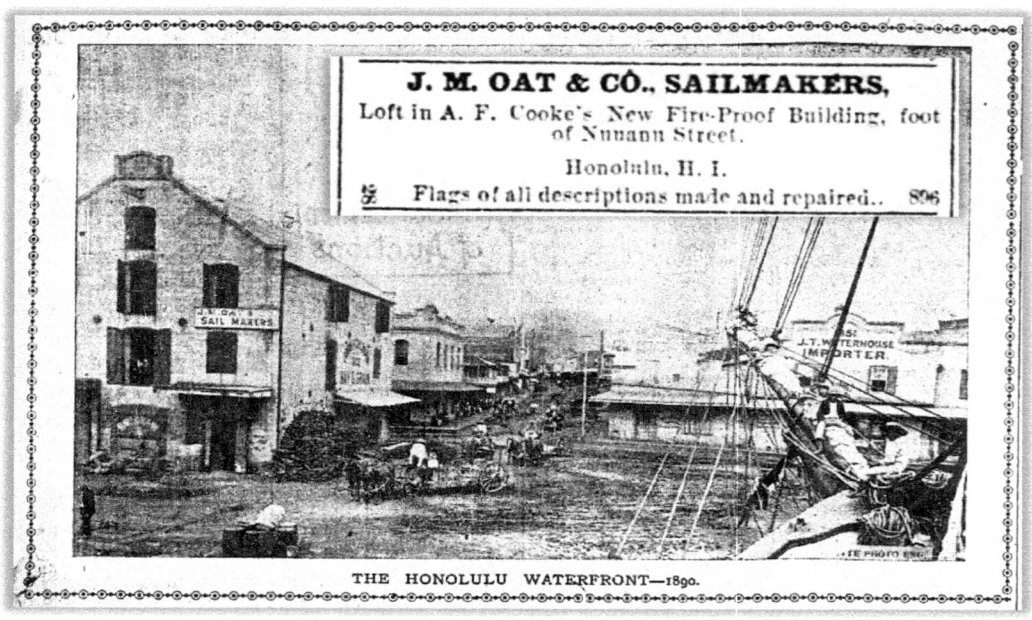

NUʻUANU COURT (QUEEN'S COURT)

801 Nuʻuanu, 800 Bethel
1994
Architect / Builder: James M. Severson (Lacayo Architects) / M.A. Mortenson Company

This 44,000 square foot condominium office space was built in 1994 on the site of the police station parking lot and the City and County Tax Office. It was developed by Harbor Court Developers, a joint partnership between Mike McCormack and Dick Bradley, with financial partners C. Itoh and Mitsui Trust and Banking Company of Japan.

Completed at the tail-end of the big 1990's Japanese investment boom and bust, Nuʻuanu Court (also known as Queen's Court) sat vacant for 9 years until bought in 2003 by Richard Emery of Hawaii First Inc. and Richard Weiser.

It was the site of George W. Punchard's 1-story coral store built in 1847. From 1858 to 1882 it was a coffee shop called The Old Corner, owned by Henry J. Nolte who came to Hawaii in 1852 from Hamburg, Germany. Famous for dispensing "the Arabian stimulant" they also carried a wide variety of American and European newspapers and Cuban cigars. In 1881 it was renovated into a full-service restaurant.

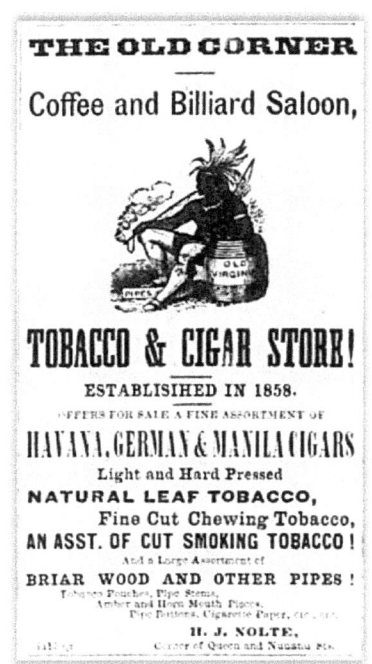

> COFFEE SALOONS.—These popular resorts for supplying the wants of the inner man, have become great institutions in this, our city of Honolulu. They have, in a great measure, supplanted the Bar Rooms of former days, and minister to the same tendencies of human nature to congregate together. As a morning resort, the establishment of Messrs. Kruger & Nolte, on the corner of Nuuanu and Queen streets, appears to be the best patronized. Here, from 5 to 8 o'clock, A. M., may be gathered, by the eager listener, the gossip of the business portion of the town, or the patient waiter will be able to meet with any one whom he is desirous of falling in with, of those who pursue avocations which require them to be up betimes. Although not so well filled as in the matutinal hours, the current of droppers in continues vigorous during the remainder of the day and evening, and the tables are well covered with the latest European and American illustrated papers, among which, as diamonds among gems of lesser value, can always be found files of the *Commercial Advertiser* and *Polynesian*, in loving proximity, tempting the person of elegant leisure, to linger a little longer over his cup of coffee, bottle of Dashaway Beer, slice of California Cheese and a bit of ham, or whatever else, with which he is regaling the inner man. Success to these gentlemen, who have, we are glad to know, acquired a competency in administering to the wants of poor bachelors, who cannot marry, and must, perchance, go somewhere to eat.

After Nolte moved to Fort Street to open the Beaver Saloon in 1882, The Old Corner was run by the Hart Brothers and later by Hop Lee. By 1905 it was known as the "The Old Corner Saloon" run by William Lishman and Charles T. Day, but the Liquor Board refused to renew the license in 1910, saying "the place has long had an unsavory reputation".

From 1916 to 1943 it was the Wo Hop Hing Kee store owned by Fong Hing and Fong Kui Lam, providing sailors outfits and cold drinks.

Fong Hing came to Hawaii in 1895 from Canton (Guangzhou), China, and eventually opened the first Chinese steam laundry in Hawaii. He also owned the Honolulu Chop Sui House, Bow Wo Jewelry, the New York Shoe Store, Tai Loy Jewelry, and the Kai Kau Real Estate Company.

Badly damaged by termites inside, the building was demolished for a police parking lot in 1948.

802-830 NU'UANU (SITE)

A parking lot today, there has been a lot of activity on this block, starting with the homesites of Kamehameha advisor Isaac Davis and Oahu governor Kuihelani.

King Kamehameha I was quick to embrace Western ideas and technology, especially if it helped him conquer the various Hawaiian Islands. Two of his most-trusted advisors were Englishman John Young who lived on the Big Island, and Welshman Isaac Davis who lived here on Nu'uanu Street. Like others in the area, his house would have been made of pili grass.

Born in Wales about 1758, Davis was the sole survivor of a Hawaiian attack on the American schooner *Fair American* in 1790. He became a close advisor to Kamehameha I and later married one of the king's relatives.

When King Kaumuali'i of Kaua'i came to Hawaii to negotiate the peace agreement with Kamehameha in 1810, a group of chiefs conspired to kill him with poison. Warned by Davis, he managed to escape back to Kaua'I, but it is believed that same poison was then used to kill Davis.

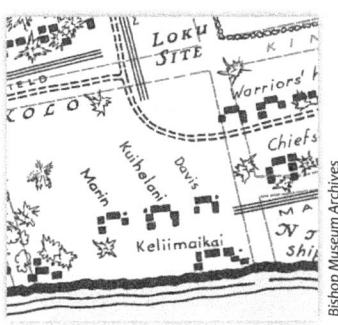

This area was called Kapapoko, and Kuihelani lived next to Isaac Davis in a house named after his father, Ka'aloa. He also built a boat shed here.

On the waterfront was the house of Kalanimālokuloku-i-Kepo'okalani Keli'imaika'i, a High Chief and brother of Kamehameha I who was known as "The Good Chief".

This area quickly developed into the busy commercial waterfront for Honolulu Harbor with Nu'uanu Street as the main thoroughfare leading up into the town of Honolulu. Josiah Marshall and Dixey Wildes, traders from Boston, obtained a large portion of Kuihelani's land and they expanded it further in 1823 to include the entire block. In 1819 their agent, Captain William Babcock, erected a 2-story frame prefabricated building brought by the company ship *Paragon* that featured the first wallpaper in the islands. The house was also known as the American Consulate.

In 1825, Marshall and Wildes built the first wharf consisting of the hulk of the *Eliza Ann*, and they built the first stone quay a year later. Due to the decline of the sandalwood trade they left the islands in 1832.

In 1833 this was the location of Ladd & Co. founded by William Ladd, Peter Brinsmade, and William Hooper, who built a 2-story coral building facing the harbor.

Ladd & Co. built the first commercial sugar plantation at Koloa on Kaua'i in 1835. But they overextended themselves in a questionable land scheme and when investors in Europe pulled out they folded in 1844.

Drawing by Paul Emmert, 1854

The building later housed the wholesale liquor business of H. Robinson & Co. on the first floor, and the second floor housed the general commission and auction firm of Rice & Co., owned by William B. Rice and A.P. Everett with John F. Colburn Sr. as their auctioneer. When the building was demolished in 1875 the blocks of coral were used in an attempt to pave Ka'ahumanu Street.

In 1853, Ed Burgess' Coffee Shop opened at the corner of Nu'uanu and Queen (Nimitz) streets and was reportedly "the pioneer refreshment saloon of its kind in Honolulu". According to historian Warren Goodale it was bought by Heinrich Julius Nolte and G. Wilhelm when the owner retired. Nolte moved across Nu'uanu Street in 1858 and called his new place "The Old Corner".

Charles Brenig built a 2-story brick building at the corner of Nu'uanu and Queen (Nimitz) streets known as the Brenig Block in 1883. Originally from Germany, Brenig tried to make wine in Manoa in 1858, had a bakery on Maunakea in 1859, and by 1868 had a men's clothing store at Nu'uanu and Marin streets.

From 1901 to 1907 the building housed the Red Front Store owned by Morris Rosenberg who dealt in sailors' clothes. The Seamens' Institute met in the hall upstairs.

In 1914 it was the grocery store of the Territorial Marketing Division run by A.T. Longley.

From 1945 to 1949 the Café Pagoda was located in the Brenig Block, featuring live music from members of the highly decorated 442nd regiment of American-born soldiers of Japanese ancestry.

In 1840, Eliab and Hiram Grimes established the E. & H. Grimes general mercantile store at the corner of Marin and Nu'uanu streets. Known as "Old Grimes", Eliab's Hawaiian brother-in-law, Manuahi, was a salesman known for giving a little extra to women and other Hawaiians and his name became a catchphrase throughout Hawaii for a free "extra".

Grimes built a large 2-story stone warehouse in back of his shop in 1846/47 and sold the business to French merchant John J. Caranave in 1847.

The building was destroyed in a huge fire on December 29, 1860, that started in the wooden 1854 steam flour mill (shown here in the 1854 Paul Emmert drawing) and destroyed 14 buildings.

The Caranave property was bought by the Honolulu Iron Works in 1864 and they later expanded to cover most of the block.

In the middle of the block a 2-story wooden building that housed the Honolulu Restaurant dated to at least 1847 and was originally the store of J.J. Caranave who dealt in assorted goods plus wines and spirits. It was later occupied by ship chandlers Mitchell & Fales, the John G. Lewis general merchandise store, and the Honolulu Restaurant.

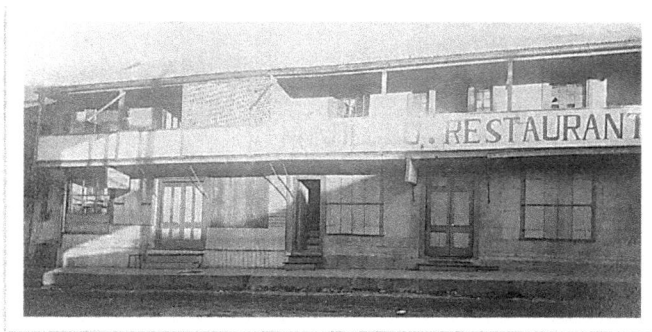

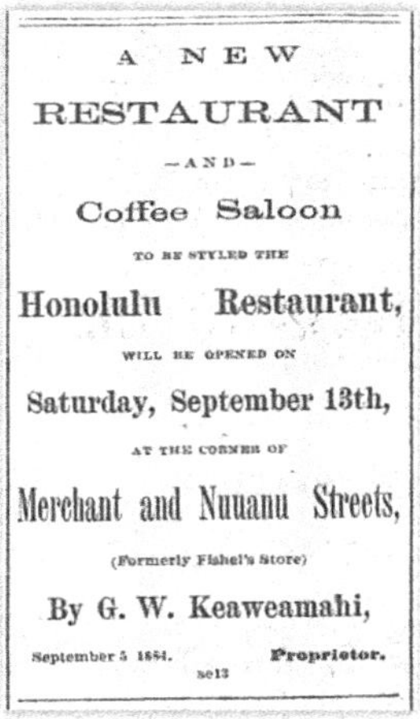

A NEW
RESTAURANT
—AND—
Coffee Saloon
TO BE STYLED THE
Honolulu Restaurant,
WILL BE OPENED ON
Saturday, September 13th,
AT THE CORNER OF
Merchant and Nuuanu Streets,
(Formerly Fishel's Store)
By G. W. Keaweamahi,
September 5 1884. Proprietor.
se13

These buildings were burned by the Board of Health on January 6, 1900, since Leong Yet from the Honolulu Restaurant had died from plague at the Chinese hospital's pest house. At the time of the fire, there were three Chinese restaurants, two Japanese barber shops and a Japanese ice cream saloon in the buildings.

In the photographs, Marin Street is on the right and the Brenig Block is on the far left.

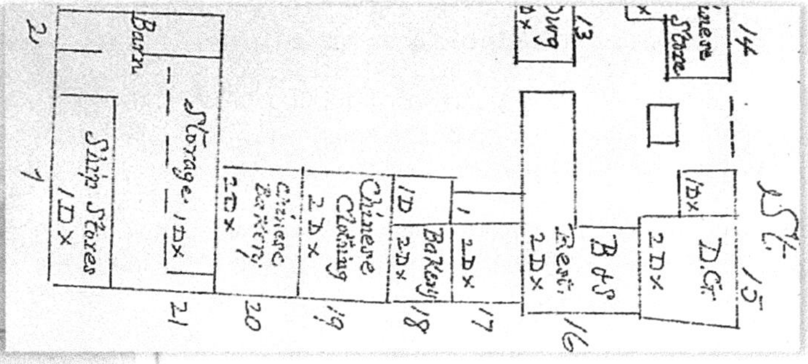

1879

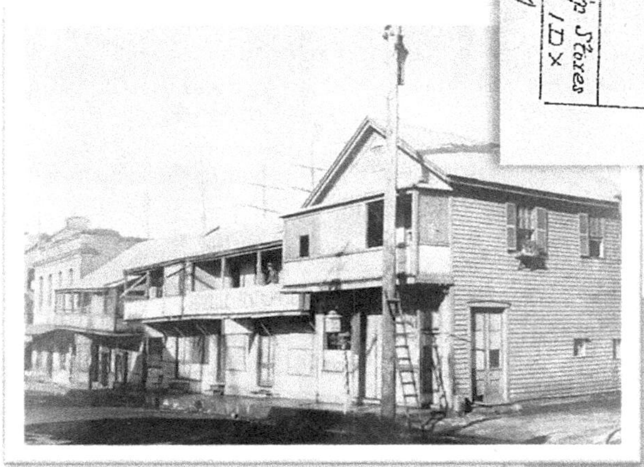

January, 1900

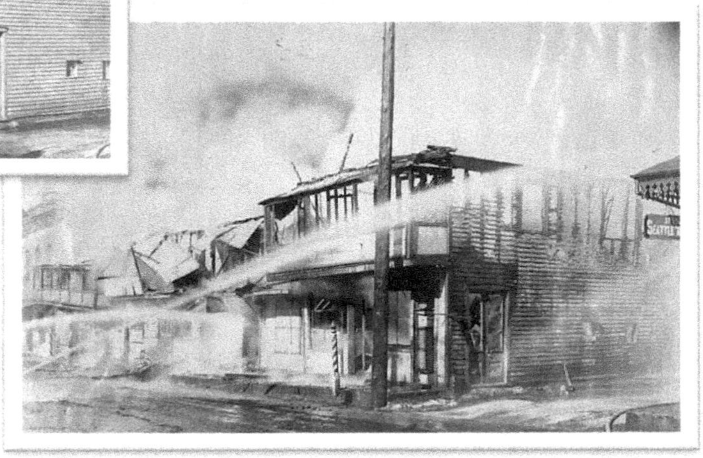

January 6, 1900

OAHU HOTEL (SITE)

821-829 Nuʻuanu

Now the picturesque backside of the Spanish-Mediterranean-style 1931 Police Station, this was King Kamehameha's ulu maika playing field in 1810 and the site of the Oahu Hotel from 1826 to 1832. The hotel had a bowling alley, a 20'-25' wharf, a well with a pump, and a separate boarding house that was popular with ship masters and businessmen. The "sleeping house" was 18'-20' long and 14'-15' wide and was located farther back and close to the water on what would later become the site of a large native Hawaiian market.

For the 4th of July in 1827 a party of about fifty including the King, Kaʻahumanu, Boki, Hoapili, Keikiowa, Kauluohe, Kauanohi, and Kīnaʻu, along with the American and Catholic missionaries and other important foreign residents met at the hotel with the American Consulate, John C. Jones, for a "splendid dinner" and "many toasts".

The Oahu Hotel was originally owned by Amos Knight and George Manini, and was purchased by Stephen Reynolds in 1830. When it closed in 1832 some of the furnishings went to the Warren Hotel and the yard was used by George Pelly for lumber storage.

The Wren's Nest restaurant was on the corner in a 2-story brick building in 1864, and by 1879 it had become a Chinese coffee shop.

From 1896 to 1918 it was the Royal Annex owned by W.C. Peacock. A more posh version of the Royal Saloon across the street, it was known for serving oysters, crabs, frog legs, and lobsters.

The Royal Annex also displayed a supposedly original 16th century Corregio painting acquired by Walter Peacock for $7,250 ($240,000 today) from London. It featured "a satyr at the side of a nude woman being watched over by a cupid".

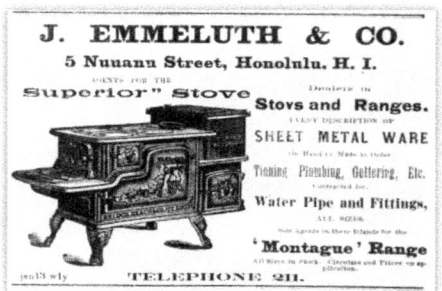

Next to the restaurant was a 2-story stone store building that was the plumbing and tinsmith business of G. English & Company.

In 1883 it became the J. Emmeluth & Co. store specializing in stoves, ranges, and plumbing supplies. They built a new 3-story building on King Street in 1897 that featured the first electric elevator in Hawaii.

ROYAL SALOON

901 Nuʻuanu, 2 Merchant
1890
Architect / Builder: Isaac A. Palmer? / Walker & Redward

According to Paul Rockwood's and Dorothy Barrere's map "Honolulu in 1810" the houses of Hawaiian chiefs were once on this corner and along Merchant Street.

Stephen Reynolds, prominent merchant and chronicler, had a store near this corner in 1829 made of grass. He replaced it sometime in the 1830's with a 2-story coral building shown in the 1854 Paul Emmert painting (on the right) that was torn down in 1855.

The first drinking establishment on this corner was the 2-story wooden Royal Hawaiian Hotel built by John Maxey. Opening day was July 2, 1855, and it featured live music three nights a week "for the lovers of music and good fellowship".

Maxey was also proprietor of the White Swan Hotel on the mauka/ewa corner of King and Nuʻuanu streets and had purchased the land on this corner from Stephen Reynolds with the understanding he would be able to build a saloon. But the construction of the Sailors' Home that same year on the waikiki/makai corner of the "Bethel Block" led to much rancorous debate about whether spirits being sold a few doors away would "thwart its usefulness".

By 1856 it was simply known as the Royal Hotel, with the Varieties Theater upstairs featuring "Tragedies, Comedies, Farces, Singing, Dancing, Burlesque Operas, Ballads, Violin Solos, &c."

(A completely different business called the Hawaiian Hotel opened downtown in 1872, becoming the Royal Hawaiian Hotel in 1880).

 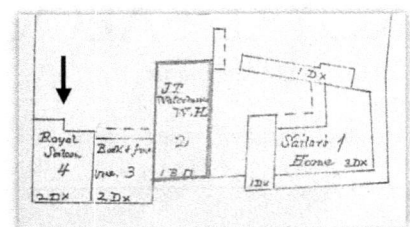

By 1883 the building at Nuʻuanu and Merchant streets was called the Royal Hotel Saloon, or just the Royal Saloon, managed by E.H.F. Wolter.

THE NEW ROYAL SALOON.

The new Royal Saloon building nearing completion is a beauty. It occupies the site of the old building at the corner of Nuuanu and Merchant streets. The structure is of one story and is built of brick. The street facings are relieved and ornamented by nine stuccoed pilasters. Skew backs, for the imparting of correct arches above the tops of the doors and windows, project from these. Commencing with the top of the verandah is the cornice, composed of series of stop blocks of beautiful architectural design surmounted by a stucco railing of semi-mullions against a background of brickwork. This railing is crowned with a fitting cap of stucco. The summits of the pilasters are appropriately topped with ornamental heads. The corner of the building on Nuuanu and Merchant streets is splayed sufficiently to allow of large double doors. There are double doors also in the front and on the Merchant street side. The windows are large and tastefully arched. The verandah extends along the street facings covering the stone pavement in width.

The interior is graced with wainscoting and finish of Eastlake style. The saloon room has dimensions of 37 by 35 feet. In the rear of this is a store-room 21 feet by 22 feet. Separated from this by a partition are a hall room 16 feet by 22 feet and two card rooms taking up the balance of the building. The contract for the construction of the building is in the hands of Walker & Redward. It will probably be ready for occupancy the last of this week.

By the late 1880's saloonkeeper and liquor dealer Walter Chamberlain Peacock, originally from Lancaster, England, had bought the Royal Saloon, and on November 7, 1889, W.C. Peacock & Company announced they would be erecting a new building on the site due to the upcoming widening of Merchant Street. Contractors Thomas Walker and Fred Redward paid $100 on November 14 at auction to remove the old 2-story wooden building.

In addition to a wholesale liquor business Peacock also owned at least two other saloons in town, the Pacific and the Cosmopolitan, both further up Nuʻuanu Street.

The new 1-story brick building was built by Walker & Redward for $6,127, and the new Royal Saloon opened on March 25, 1890.

The design is classic Eastlake Victorian with cast iron decorations and stucco pilasters, balustrades, and cornices, and shares many similar design elements with the 1888 Perry Block at the corner of Nuʻuanu and Hotel Streets and the 1891/1892 T.R. Foster Building across the street. Isaac A. Palmer was most likely the architect of all three.

Peacock bottled his own liquors in clear and amber bottles that are still very collectible today. He sold three grades of gin, but his nephew who once worked filling bottles said all three came from the same barrel!

Peacock built a large mansion in Waikiki, but recognizing the need for high quality visitor accommodations in Honolulu he moved his house off the beach and hired noted architect Oliver Traphagen to design a luxurious old Colonial-style hotel called "The Moana Hotel."

The building of the Moana Hotel marked the beginning of the tourism industry in Hawaii. It opened in 1901 with 75 rooms, billiard room, saloon (of course), main parlor, reception area and library. The hotel was beautifully restored in 1989 and is affectionately known as "The First Lady of Waikiki."

The Royal Saloon closed during prohibition and the building later housed a print shop, real estate office, stockbrokers, a warehouse, and a furniture store, with George's Diner on the Merchant Street side from 1950 to 1970.

In 1969, Alan C. Beall and William R. Lahmann Jr. proposed developing a Hawaiian version of San Francisco's Ghirardelli Square to be called Merchant Square. The plan was to recreate the romantic gaslight Old World charm of the late 1800's and called for the restoration of up to 12 buildings on Merchant Street.

Tom and Gipsy Norton, along with Mary Louise Walker, restored the empty Royal Saloon building in 1971 and turned it into the Royal Spaghetti House featuring old-time 1890's melodramas on Monday nights.

In 1973 it was purchased by Lin Comito who wanted to use the original Royal Saloon name, but the liquor commission refused because of the word "saloon". It became the Golden Guinea instead.

The building was purchased in 1976 by Richard Gusman and Duncan MacNaughton who hired architect Spencer Leineweber to convert it into Matteo's Royal Tavern. They also bought and restored the Wing Wo Tai Building for the Nu'uanu Underground restaurant, and the adjacent J.T. Waterhouse building for Jamieson's Irish Coffee House.

San Francisco native Don Murphy opened the popular Murphy's Bar and Grill at the corner in 1987. The Murphy's St. Patrick's Day block party has been a major downtown event for over 34 years.

During the filming of the *Lost* TV series the street in front of Murphy's and O'Toole's was used to film a snowy scene supposedly taking place in Boston. A local ice company provided the snow, which lasted about five minutes, but that was enough to get the shot.

T.R. FOSTER BUILDING

902-904 Nuʻuanu
1891/1892
Architect / Builder: Palmer & Richardson? / E.B. Thomas

Begun in 1891 and completed in 1892, the Inter-Island Steam Navigation Company built this ornate cast-iron and brick building and named it after its recently deceased founder, Thomas R. Foster.

Captain Foster was a Canadian shipbuilder who moved to Honolulu in 1857 and originally worked for John Robinson, marrying Robinson's daughter, Mary, four years later in 1861.

In 1883 he incorporated the Inter-Island Steam Navigation Company, providing service to Kauaʻi and the Kona and Kaʻu ports on the Big Island. By 1904 they had seven ships in their fleet, and they acquired their major competitor, Wilder Steamship Company, in 1905.

Adapting with the times, the Inter-Island Steam Navigation Company created a subsidiary called Inter-Island Airways in 1929 with service to Hilo via two Sikorsky 8-passenger amphibious airplanes. In 1941 the company was renamed Hawaiian Airlines and it is now one of the world's top-performing airline companies.

But the Inter-Island Steam Navigation Company never officed here. From 1892 until Prohibition in 1918 it was leased to wholesale liquor dealers Lovejoy & Company owned by David H. Lewis and John D. Holt. The company also owned the Anchor Saloon at the corner of Nuʻuanu and King streets.

The Christian Gertz shoe store was also located here in 1893, and the upstairs included a hall where groups like the Theosophical Society and the Young Hawaiians' Institute held their meetings.

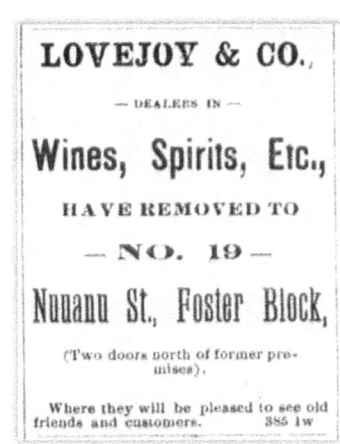

As early as 1851, this was the site of Pierre Michel's French Store. A dealer in general merchandise, he closed up shop on November 15, 1857.

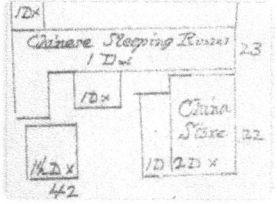 

There was a 2-story wooden Chinese store here in 1879, it was the T. Graham barber shop in 1885, and in 1891 it housed Ah Kung's cigar and grocery store with Chinese sleeping/ gaming quarters on the second floor. Described in 1891 as a "rickety old building, dry as tinder", it burned down on April 10, 1891 and was replaced by the large 2-story brick T.R. Foster Building begun in September and completed in March 1892.

Built by E.B. Thomas, it was described as "a highly ornamental building and a credit to the architects".

The architects were most likely Palmer & Richardson. Isaac Palmer designed the Perry Block (1888), and he is also the likely architect for the Royal Saloon (1890) across the street.

All three buildings are in the classic Eastlake Victorian architectural style and contain many similar decorative motifs inspired by Eastlake furniture.

A BRICK building will replace the wooden one lately burned at Nuuanu and Marine streets. It will be named the "Foster Block."

MR. E. B. Thomas, the contractor for the Foster building to be erected on Nuuanu street, to-day awarded the contract for the cast iron front of the same to the Union Iron Works Co. of this city, the tenders from both foundries being very close.

After Lovejoy & Company, the building housed the Durant-Irvine plumbing and A/C company from 1930 to 1948, and later National Photo Supply, Custom Tours and Travel Service, and Dentists Supply Company.

The building was restored by contractors Stone Enterprises in 1970 for Alfie Lenz who opened Alfie's Pub downstairs. It was the first restaurant in this area as part of the proposed Merchant Square redevelopment plan for Nuʻuanu and Merchant streets. Alfie's later became William Tell, Red Baron, and Sam's Place.

In 1976 Ron Dougherty opened O'Tooles Irish Pub & Restaurant which was here for 44 years. It was a favorite shooting location for the rebooted *Hawaii 5-0* TV series (2010-2020) as well as the *Lost* TV series (2005-2006).

IRWIN BLOCK (NIPPU JIJI BUILDING)

910-922-928 Nuʻuanu
1897
Architect / Builder: Ripley & Dickey / John Ouderkirk

The New Irwin Block.

The contract to erect the new Irwin block on Nuuanu street between Queen and King streets has been awarded to J. Ouderkirk and work will be begun at once.

Mr. Irwin intends to put a handsome two-story building with stone front and another ornament will be added to the numerous handsome structures of the city.

The building now on the premises is a landmark in Honolulu. It is over 60 years old and for a number of years was occupied by Chulan & Co. from whom W. G. Irwin purchased it.

The old adobe building looks as solid as ever and shows the excellent mortar derived in former days by the burning of coral. The main building is surrounded bo a number of dilapidated wooden shanties formerly used by the employees of the Chinese firm and others.

In the great fire in 1886 the buildings of the Ewa side of Nuuanu street, makai of King street were saved and the wall of the old Station House still stands with its broken glass bottles on the top.

The new building will be used for stores and offices.

Initially called the Irwin Block, this building was designed by Clinton B. Ripley and Charles W. Dickey and built by John Ouderkirk for wealthy businessman William G. Irwin. Although Archibald Sinclair and Thomas Walker were the lowest bidders, they were unable to meet the bonding requirements. The stonework was done by Japanese stonecutters.

The building is native basalt in the Richardsonian Romanesque style and was completed in early 1897 at a cost of $19,325.

The dates on the parapet were added later and commemorate the founding of the *Yamato Shinbun / Nippu Jiji* newspaper in 1895 and when they bought the building in 1923. The building is also known as the Hawaii Times Building.

One of the first tenants was the Kwong Yuen Hing Company who later moved to the ground floor and yard of United Chinese Society around the corner on 36-38 N. King Street in 1903.

From at least 1906 to 1923 it was the store of Y. Takakuwa & Company, wholesale dealers in Japanese provisions, groceries, and general merchandise, owned by Yoichi Takakuwa. In 1919 they took over the schooner *Nichigo Maru* when the captain skipped town without paying the crew.

In 1923 the building was bought by the NIppu Jiji Company for $65,000, with a formal opening on Monday, December 3, 1923. Roughly translated, "Nippu Jiji" = "Japan Current Events". They were here for 63 years until closing in 1985.

Architect Norman Lacayo and his wife Pam bought the building in 1981, saying it was "the biggest antique they've ever collected". They restored it in 1985, adding a new office, penthouse, and condos onto the back which won an AIA design award.

The first building on this site that we know of was the house of Queen Kaʻahumanu. It had two rooms on the ground floor used for receptions or housing retainers, and there were two private rooms upstairs that opened onto a balcony, plus it also had a large garret (attic room).

But this wasn't the house's original location – it was a prefabricated Western-style frame house that had come from Boston and was first erected at Pākākā (also called "The Point") beside the fort and where the State of Hawaii Department of Transportation Harbors Division building (formerly the Matson Building) sits today. The house was painted and wall-papered and was one of six foreign-style buildings in Honolulu in 1824.

It was built by Captain Andrew Henry Blanchard, master of the 85-foot bark *Thaddeus*, the ship that brought the first missionaries to Hawaii from Boston in 1819. Upon completion he sold it to Kaʻahumanu for "a considerable price". This is also the house where Lord Byron and his party stayed in 1825.

In May 1827, Oahu Governor Boki put the building on rollers and moved it with block and tackle to this location on the ewa side of Nuʻuanu Street where it became his store, hotel and grog shop called The Blonde. It was named for the HMS *Blonde* which brought back the bodies of Kamehameha II (Liholiho) and Queen Kamamalu in 1825. After Boki disappeared in the South Pacific looking for sandalwood in 1829 it became known as Boki House.

From 1834 to 1846 this was also the site of the legendary traders known as the Hudson's Bay Company.

In 1863, Governor Mataio Kekūanāoʻa hired native workmen to build a large 57' x 83' fireproof 2-story coral building with 11' ceilings that was occupied by Chung Hoon & Company. By 1879 the site also included several 1-story "Chinese sleeping rooms".

CHUNG HOON & CO.,
Commission Merchants and general agents—Agents for the Paukaa and Amauulu Sugar Plantations—Importers of teas and other Chinese and foreign goods and wholesale dealers in Hawaiian produce at the new Stone Store, Nuuanu Street, below King.   359-1y

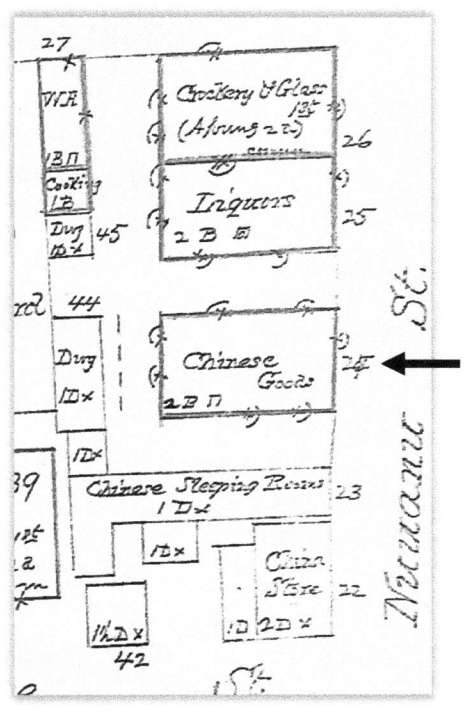

1879

1885

The *Nippu Jiji* (日布時事)

Established in 1895 by Shintaro Anno and initially called the *Yamato*, the *Nippu Jiji* was the first newspaper in Hawaii to print in both Japanese-and English languages.

The first editions were semi-weekly and printed on a lithograph machine. Yasutaro Keiho Soga took over in 1905 and renamed it *Nippu Jiji*, expanding it to a 12-page daily paper printed on a professional rotary press.

Initially written for Japanese plantation workers, the paper was known for supporting the sugarcane worker strikes in 1909 and 1920. Soga was imprisoned for 10 months in 1909, accused of conspiracy to incite violence during the strike.

They also fought against the governmental attempts to restrict Japanese language schools and education programs.

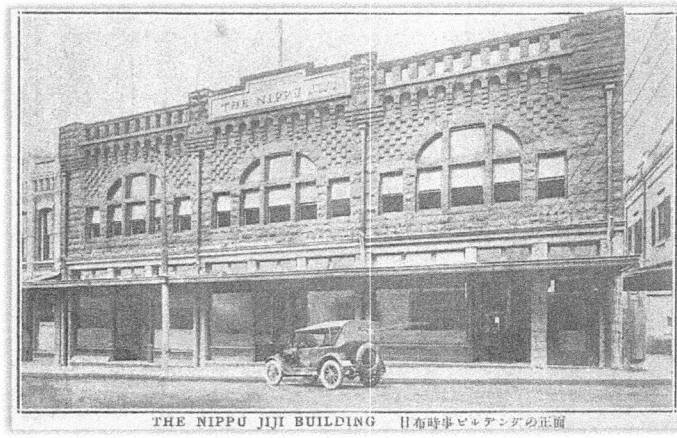

THE NIPPU JIJI BUILDING　日布時事ビルデングの正面

With Japanese rapidly becoming the largest ethnic group in Hawaii, the paper introduced an English language section in 1919 in order to "promote better understanding between the Japanese and the Americans".

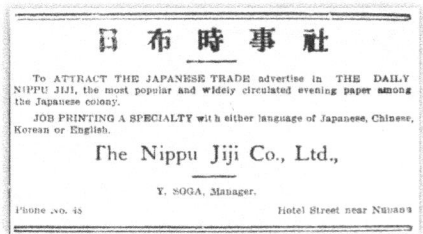

Five days after the attack on Pearl Harbor on December 7, 1941, the military government shut down the *Nippu Jiji* and Yasutaro Soga was arrested and sent to internment camps in New Mexico. But when the military realized they needed to be able to communicate with the Japanese-speaking population of the islands they reopened the newspaper under heavy surveillance and censorship with articles being checked by FBI and Army linguists before publishing.

Due to widespread anti-Japanese sentiment, as well as an attempt to assimilate and Americanize, the government also changed the name of the paper to *The Hawaii Times* on November 2, 1942.

The last newspaper was printed in 1985 and many items from its collection of photos and documents are available online in the Hoji Shinbun Digital Collection of Stanford University's Hoover Institution Library.

Yasutaro Soga 相賀安太郎 渓芳

Born in Tokyo in 1873, Yasutaro Keiho Soga was educated in pharmacy and law before coming to Hawaii in 1896 at age 23. He first worked at plantation stores in Waianae, Waipahu, and Moloka'i, and became assistant editor of the *Hawaii Shinpo* newspaper in 1899. In 1905 he became the editor of the *Yamato Shimbun* and was responsible for improving and renaming it the *Nippu Jiji*.

Considered a "man of gentle demeanor but sturdy conviction", he became very influential in the Japanese community and worked tirelessly for justice and understanding between the American and Japanese communities.

He was one of the leaders of the 1909 Plantation Strike and was arrested as a "dangerous and disorderly person", released, and then re-arrested for conspiring to obstruct the operation of five sugar plantations "by intimidating and threatening violence against, and by instigating and inciting others". He was convicted and sentenced to 10 months in jail.

He was an avid tanka poet (using only 31-syllables) writing as Keiho, and he published a book about his travels in Manchuria in 1934 titled *Nichiman o Nozoku* (*A Glimpse into Japan and Manchuria*).

He was arrested at age 68 on the night of December 7, 1941, and in August 1942 he was part of the Fifth Transfer Group sent to the Angel Island Detention Facility in California. He was then transferred to the Lordsburg Internment Camp in New Mexico, and from June 1943 to October 1945 he was held at the Santa Fe Internment Camp. He returned to Honolulu in November 1945 with 450 other internees on the troopship *Yarmouth*.

In 1948 he published a memoir of his internment titled *Tessaku Seikatsu* (Life behind Barbed Wire) that was not published in English until 2008.

After the passage of the Immigration Act of 1952 he became a naturalized citizen, and in 1953 he published his autobiography *Gojunen no Hawaii Kaiko* (Fifty Years of Hawaii Memories).

William G. Irwin

…was born in England in 1843 and came to Hawaii as a small child with his family who were headed to the California Gold Rush. After working as a bookkeeper for various firms he later partnered with California capitalist Claus Spreckels to form W.G. Irwin and Company and quickly became a wealthy financier, sugar company president, and member of the Kalākaua and Lili'uokalani Privy Councils.

In 1885 Irwin and Spreckels opened the second bank in Honolulu known as Claus Spreckels and Company. It became the Bank of Honolulu in 1910 when Irwin moved to San Francisco.

When Irwin died in 1914 at 71 years of age his net worth was estimated to be over $10M ($273M in 2021 dollars).

Nippu Jiji special issue, July 26, 1910
Commemorating Governor John Mott-Smith's pardon and early release of the imprisoned Japanese strike leaders.

WING WO TAI BUILDING

923-927 Nuʻuanu
1917
Architect / Builder: Emory & Webb / Kanichi Nomura

The Wing Wo Tai Company was a powerful Chinese export business founded in Hong Kong in 1845. They were originally located at 941 Nuʻuanu, Street next to the Anchor Saloon, but had to move when the new Hoffschlaeger building took over a large portion of the makai/waikiki corner at King and Nuʻuanu Streets in 1917.

The 40' x 87' building was designed by Walter Emory and Marshall Webb and built of Hawaiian stone covered with cement plaster by K. Nomura for $13,575. Wing Wo Tai moved into the new building in October 1917. The dates on the parapet reflect the year they came to Hawaii and the year they got the building permit to start this building.

Walter L. Emory and Marshall H. Webb also designed the Hawaii Theatre, the Blaisdell Hotel, the Advertiser Publishing Company Building, the James Campbell Building, the Honpa Hongwanji Temple, the Masonic Temple, Love's Bakery, the Hawaiian Electric Building and the Palama Theatre.

On December 11, 1899, You Chong, a 22-year-old bookkeeper with Wing Wo Tai was the first person in Honolulu diagnosed with the bubonic plague which had been devastating other major cities around the Pacific Rim. The next day, You Chong and 4 others died of the dreaded disease. This sparked a massive chain of events that led to fencing off and quarantining the entire Chinatown area, numerous controlled burns and fumigations of infected properties, and the resultant accidental 1900 Chinatown fire.

Wing Wo Tai was here for 38 years, from 1917 to 1955. The Office Appliance Company was here from 1955 to 1975.

The building was restored in 1977 by Hawaii/Western Construction for Wing Wo Tai Associates led by Richard W. Gushman II of Gushman & MacNaughton. From 1978 to 1985 it was Deli's of Hawaii, Merchant Square Oyster Bar and Seafood Restaurant, and Zachary's restaurants.

The Hawaii Society of the American Institute of Architects (AIA) were briefly upstairs in the mid 1980's. In 2000 the building was purchased by The Nature Conservancy for their local headquarters.

WING WO TAI / WING WO CHAN (SITE)

931-/ 941 Nuʻuanu
(1886)
Architect / Builder: George W. Lincoln with E.B. Thomas, George Lucas

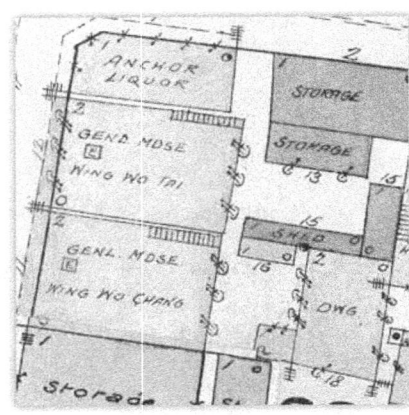

1899

There are no known photographs of the two buildings that were on this site next to the Anchor Saloon, so we will have to rely on the descriptions posted in *The Daily Bulletin* on August 6, 1886, when they were being rebuilt after the 1886 fire.

On the right side was the Wing Wo Chan building, built by George Lucas's Honolulu Planing Mills and described as "really an ornament to the business quarter". It was built for Widemann and Spencer and leased to Wing Wo Chan & Company to replace their building burned in the 1886 fire.

> "Of two stories, 40 feet front and 60 feet deep, it has a basement 7 feet deep, the first floor's ceiling is 14 feet high, and the second's, 12 feet. The first story has an ornamented iron front, the second a front of pressed brick. Four turned columns, 10 in. x 10 in., supported on oak bolsters, from a center bearing for the second floor, which is reached by an ample staircase fitted with bannisters having a rail of nor'west pine and octagon-based newel. There is a hand hoist, with safety rachet, from the basement to the upper flat. The walls of the building are 17 inches thick throughout, with ventilating shafts inserted in them, terminating above a fire wall of three feet. There is an ample supply of light, the windows being 3 ft. 2 in. x 4 feet, one light sashes, and six windows in the second story front alone. The cellar is a very fine one, having ten openings with iron shutters, with the height and ventilating arrangement above-mentioned, making it dry and keeping it free from stale odors. The counter in the store on the ground floor is the handiwork of Chinese artisans, the chief peculiarity of which is fancy and elaborate carving on the front, the top being of solid koa."

Behind the building was a 2-story 30' x 50' brick tenement for the employees, sleeping 7 to a room, with a cook house furnished with a brick oven.

> "The next to the Wing Wo Chan building is that belonging to S.M Maguin, to replace the one occupied by Wing Wo Tai & Co. at the fire. G.W. Lincoln is the contractor, E.B. Thomas doing the brickwork for him. This building has a solid front, covered with white cement. It is the same ground size as the adjoining structure, but a trifle lower in height, and is a substantial structure. With their corrugated iron roofs and fire walls, these buildings ought to resist a pretty lively siege of fire."

Both buildings were demolished 30 years later in 1916 along with the Anchor Saloon for the new Hoffschlaeger Building. This new building, completed in 1918, was subsequently demolished 44 years later in 1962 for the Bishop Insurance Building (now known as One South King) designed by Lemmon Freeth Haines & Jones.

ANCHOR SALOON (SITE)

945 Nuʻuanu, 1-3 S. King
(1886)
Architect / Builder: E.B. Thomas

The site of a Native Hawaiian market in the 1840's, from 1883 to 1916 this was the location of the Anchor Saloon initially owned by Capt. Enos M. Nordberg, the former master of the American barkentine *Eureka*.

But he went bankrupt in 1884, the building was destroyed in the great fire of April 1886, and that same year his wife divorced him on grounds of "extreme cruelty and habitual drunkenness" (she remarried the next day). He went back to sea in 1888 on the barkentine *George C. Perkins* taking 700 tons of sugar to San Francisco and that's the last we hear of him.

After the 1886 fire, the Lovejoy liquor company hired E.B. Thomas to build a new 1-story brick Anchor Saloon.

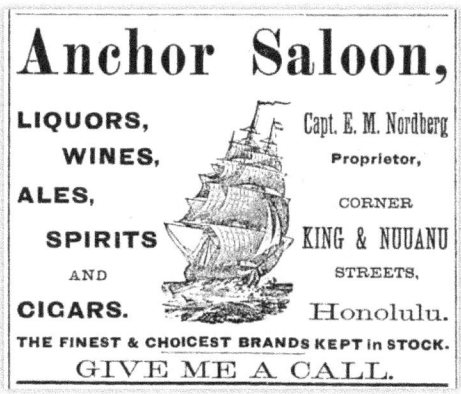

Due to being demolished and replaced by the 2-story Hoffschlaeger Building designed by Ripley and Davis, the Anchor Saloon relocated across the street to the Robinson Building in 1916. Completed in 1918 the Hoffschlaeger Building was demolished in 1962 and replaced by the Bishop Insurance Building (now known as One South King) designed by Lemmon Freeth Haines & Jones and built by Tani Construction in 1964.

HONOLULU CHINATOWN

FLORES BUILDING (PACIFIC SALOON)

1001-1013 Nuʻuanu, 2-6 S. King
1887
Architect/Builder: E.B. Thomas

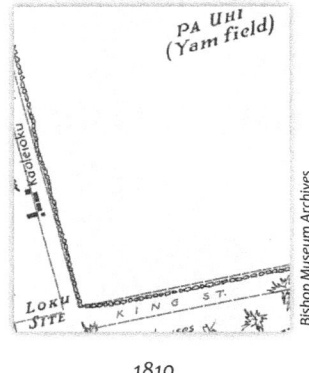
1810

1881

1903

Once upon a time, c.1810, this was the corner of a huge 30-acre yam field that was used to provide provisions for ships in harbor. It extended to Beretania and Alakea streets and was enclosed by a stone wall.

By the 1830's Joel Deadman and Alex Smith, and later James Vowles (known as "Yankee Jem" but he was actually from Bristol, England) ran a grog shop here. Vowles lost the license for "noisy and disorderly conduct, assault, battery, and drunkenness".

In 1846 James Austin & William Bacle opened a general merchandise store near the corner, later selling to Charles P. Turner who opened the Honolulu Restaurant featuring oysters and lobsters. The 1881 photograph shows the Hop Yick & Company boarding house and restaurant begun in 1880 by Chung Wa, C. Apo, Young Tang, Lum Chung, Chang Oi, and C. Mee How.

By 1884 it was the Wolfe and Edwards grocers, but not for long. As the 1886 fire approached from the north a group of men worked desperately to pull down the building in an attempt to prevent the spread of the fire. The Anchor Saloon across King Street was already on fire, and when the Chinese store at the mauka-ewa corner became a mass of blazing timbers it also ignited the grocery store and forced the "axemen" to run to safety. The building next door on King Street was brick, so the fire went no further.

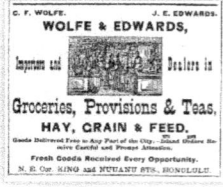

HONOLULU CHINATOWN

In January 1887, E.B. Thomas began building the brick building you see on the corner today. The first tenant downstairs was the Dew Drop Inn serving ales, wines and spirits and owned by a Hawaiian, A.K. Palekaluhi. In 1899 he was one of the pall bearers at Queen Kapiolani's funeral.

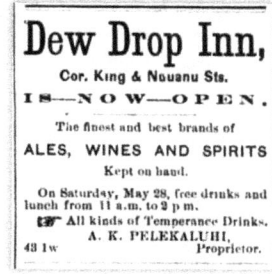

From 1889 to 1918 this was the Pacific Hotel, also called the Pacific Saloon. Major Edward H.F. Wolters, formerly with Royal Saloon, became manager in 1893. Their specialties were Knickebein and Kummel cocktails.

A German singing group, the Mannerchor Harmony Society also met weekly and practiced at the Pacific Saloon. But all was not as genteel as it may appear – there were numerous fights and squabbles at the saloon, mostly between crews of rival English and American sailing ships.

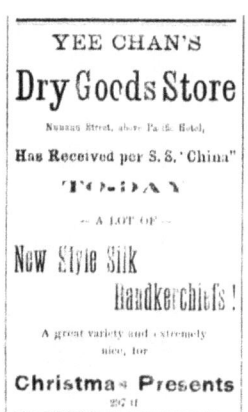

Other businesses in this building have included Yee Chan's Dry Goods Store (1891-1908), the Ayau Shoe Company (1908-1923), the Pan-Pacific Shoe Company (1930-1940), and Sing Fat & Company Dry Goods (1908-1914) owned by Loui You, Loui Lum Hop, Hee Dong, Leong Yau, Samuel Leong Alina, Yim Kong, Wong Buck, and Lee Yoke Hin.

The Hawaii Sales Company was at 1013 Nuʻuanu from 1920 until 1954, specializing in musical instruments and music players. They claimed to have "10,000 phonograph records and 2,000 Hawaiian records".

In 1964 the HIFI Loan Company specialized in providing drafts in pesos for Filipinos. HomeStreet Bank opened here in 2000.

Architect James K. Tsugawa bought the building in 1977 for $208,000 and spent $250,000 restoring it.

The Chinese Chamber of Commerce of Hawaii purchased the building for their offices in 2008, and in 2016 they renamed it the "Flores Building" in honor of Eddie and Elaine Flores for their support of the Chinese Chamber of Commerce and the Chinatown Community Development Center.

Eddie Flores Jr. grew up in Chinatown after his family emigrated from Hong Kong in 1963. His father was Filipino and his mother Chinese and they worked menial jobs while young Eddie studied business and real estate. He eventually earned enough to purchase the tiny L&L Drive Inn restaurant on Liliha Street in 1976 as a gift for his mother. He coined the term "Hawaiian Barbecue" to describe the mix of Hawaiian and Asian flavors that make up the popular "plate lunch" known as the "State Food of Hawaii".

In 1988 Flores teamed up with his friend Johnson Kam to create a very successful franchise model, and there are now over 200 L&L Hawaiian Barbecue restaurants in the US, Guam, and Japan, with 65 of them in Hawaii.

ASEU BUILDING

1006-1018 Nuʻuanu
1886
Architect / Builder: C. Kavanagh, with carpentry by Crewes & Mayhew

This building was built in 1886 by Mr. C. Kavanagh ("lately from Los Angeles") to replace a 2-story wooden Chinese store and tailor shop and 1-story c.1865 Mossman grocery store building that burned in the 1886 fire.

Most of the Aseu building is still intact but the corner with the Merchant's Exchange Saloon was demolished in 1914 for the construction of the Hocking Building.

Some of the tenants over the years have included: Ho Yen Kee & Co, Sheu Lun Merchant Tailor, San Yuen Kee crockery store (1912-1915), Wing Tai Dry Goods (1921-1927) and the Lai Cheong / New Lai Cheong fabric store (1928-1957).

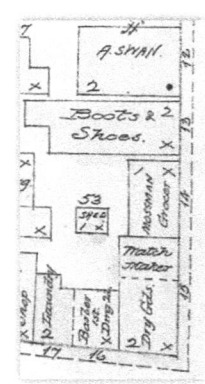

HO YEN KEE & CO.,
Tinsmiths and dealers in Crockery ware, Glassware, etc.
Water Pipes Laid and Repaired.
Plumbing Neatly Executed.
No. 41 Nuuanu St., between King and Hotel Streets,
Aseu Building.

SHEU LUN
MERCHANT TAILOR.
Suits Made to Order.
Best Linen Duck and Silk Pongee.
All Suits in the Latest Style.
1006 Nuuanu, near King, P. O. Box 947.

CROCKERY.
Sang Yuen Kee & Co. Tinwire, crockery, fancy china ware. Tin and plumbing shop. Specialty repair work.
1014 Nuuanu Street.

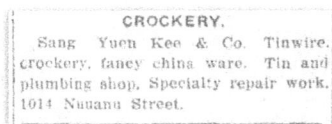

4500 DOLLS
to be
Given Away
FREE

WING TAI---Dry Goods
1014 Nuuanu Street

Lai Cheong Co.
"Home of Fancy Chinese Silks"
1014 Nuuanu St. nr. King   Phone 5680

The Kim Chow shoe store was located at 1018 Nuʻuanu for 45 years. Founded on Bethel Street in 1908, they were here from 1916 to 1961.

Kim Chow Chun was born in Doong Goon, Canton, China in 1868 and came to Hawaii in 1898. He proved too small for his first job, a steamship stoker, so he went to work for a cobbler and later opened his own shoe repair shop.

By 1961 Kim Chow's was the largest locally owned shoe store chain in Hawaii with 20 retail stores throughout the islands. His four sons, Philip, Frederic, Paul, and Anthony all entered the family business started by their father.

Here is a rare inside photograph of the Kim Chow shoe store taken in the 1920's. Kim Chow Chun is on the right.

Before Kim Chow's time, on December 23, 1896, police officers climbed over the roof of this part of the Aseu Building in order to drop in and make a surprise raid on the opium den in the Aswan Building next door.

Luke Aseu Chang

His original Chinese name was Chang Seu (Chang was the family name) but in the Cantonese tradition he was called "Ah Seu" which got shortened to Aseu. One of the founders of the Chinese Christian Church in Hawaii, he added the name "Luke" and was known as Luke Aseu, which was more often abbreviated to L. Aseu. In 1871 he married a Hawaiian woman named Moakeawe.

L. Aseu was reportedly the first person in all of China to adopt Western dress and forego wearing his hair in a queue – long and braided in back with the front of the head completely shaved.

In 1876 he opened a clothing and dry goods store at the corner of King and Nu'uanu streets that was later destroyed in the 1886 fire. That same year he was commissioned by the Hawaiian government to recruit plantation laborers in China and it appears he might even have brought in laborers from San Francisco.

But all did not go smoothly. At 11 pm on August 27, 1891, two hundred Chinese laborers surrounded Aseu's house at Makapala, Kohala, demanding he come out and be confronted about the promised contract arrangements not being properly fulfilled. The police were called, the crowd refused to disperse, shots were fired. One "Chinaman" was shot in the arm and another in the leg, others were injured by thrown rocks.

A member of "a secret society" had apparently started the rumor that Aseu was robbing them of $75 each and that $3.75 deducted from their pay each month went to Aseu's pocket and not to the Board of Immigration.

The workers had also been told that all their contracts had burned up in the recent Kohala Sugar Company fire and therefore they were free men. As is often the case with rumors, none of the allegations turned out to be true.

In 1878, L. Aseu was also the manager of the Sam Wo Chong crockery store at Nu'uanu and Chaplain streets, and he teamed up with G.C. Akina to open the Akina & Aseu store at Kaiopihi, Kohala, on the Big Island.

Aseu and Akina went into the sugar cane business at Niulii and raised rice at Pololu.

He was instrumental in obtaining pledges and subscriptions for the Chinese Church Building Fund in 1879, and in 1881 he helped raise money for a smallpox hospital just for Chinese where they could be attended to by Chinese doctors.

Aseu visited the Chicago World's Columbian Exposition in 1893 and leisurely toured the US mainland. He left Hawaii and moved to Shanghai in 1907.

NATIONAL HOTEL (SITE)

1017-1051 Nuʻuanu
(1847), 1990
Architect / Builder: unknown, Norman Lacayo (1990) / Hawaiian Dredging & Construction Company (1990)

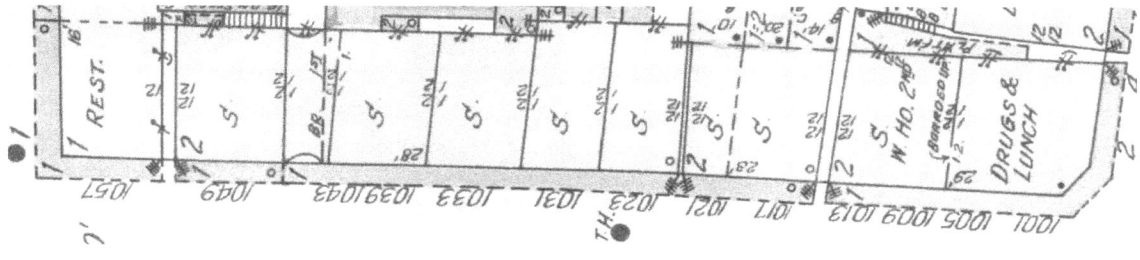

Acquired by the city in 1969, all of these buildings were mostly destroyed in a fire that started in the Waverly Block on Bethel Street on March 23, 1970 and were subsequently finished off by bulldozer for what was supposed to be a multi-level parking garage.

The land was a surface parking lot for the next twenty years until it was turned into the $23M, 27-story, 200-unit Chinatown Gateway Plaza redevelopment project designed by Norman Lacayo.

A Chinese lion dancer dug the first shovel full of dirt at the groundbreaking ceremony in 1988. Built by Hawaiian Dredging & Construction Company, it was completed in 1990.

In 1840, Joseph Booth leased the 0.25-acre Eagle Tavern tract in the middle of this block, accessed from Nuʻuanu Street, from a man named Kapihi. When Kapihi died in 1844 he willed the land to Kamehameha III who sold it to Dr. T.C.B. Rooke who the same day sold it to Joseph Booth for $200. Booth was also the owner of The Blonde hotel at the corner of King and Nuʻuanu streets.

In 1847 Booth built the 2-story coral and wood National House Hotel for the enormous sum of $10,000 and hired James F. Lewis to manage it.

Big mistake. Lewis was an American, "about 35 years of age, dark swarthy complexion, black eyes and hair, roman nose, stout, well built, and about 6 feet tall…[with] small gold ear-rings in both ears". How do we know this? From the ad posted by Joseph Booth after Lewis stole over $8,000 in gold and silver and escaped on the ship *Herny Tuke* and was never seen or heard from again, in spite of the $500 reward for his capture posted for two years.

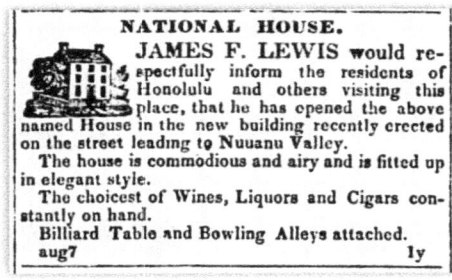

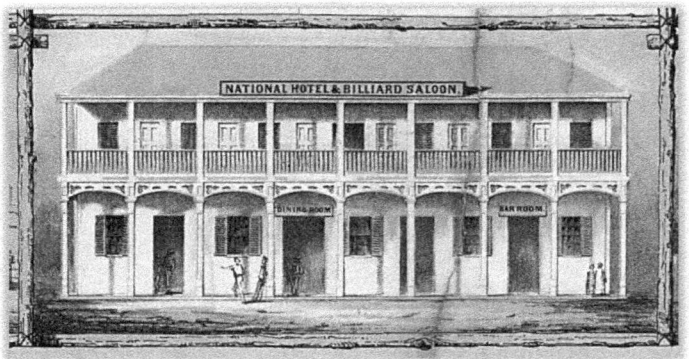

The drawing on the left is by Paul Emmert (1854), and the only known photograph is by I.W. Taber (1880), taken from the bell tower at Fire Engine Station No.2.

By 1868 it was known as the International Hotel. Its walls were badly cracked in the 1871 earthquake, and during the 1886 fire it was gutted and the veranda pulled down to prevent it catching fire. Already in poor condition, this damaged it beyond repair. But being of stone construction with a slate roof it stopped the progress of the fire and saved the buildings on Fort Street. Less than a month after the fire it was auctioned and sold for $150 to W.R. Scale who pulled it down for the materials.

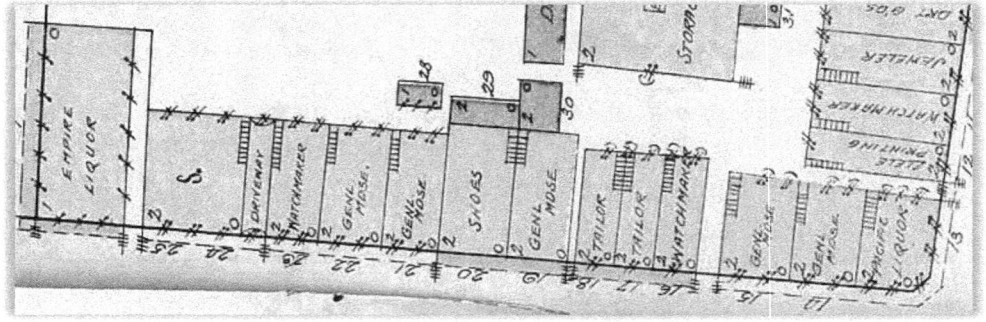

By 1891 this side of Nuʻuanu Street was lined with 2-story brick buildings. The one on the far right, the Pacific Saloon, is the only one still surviving today.

ASWAN BUILDING

1024-1026 Nu'uanu
1886
Architect / Builder: E.B. Thomas

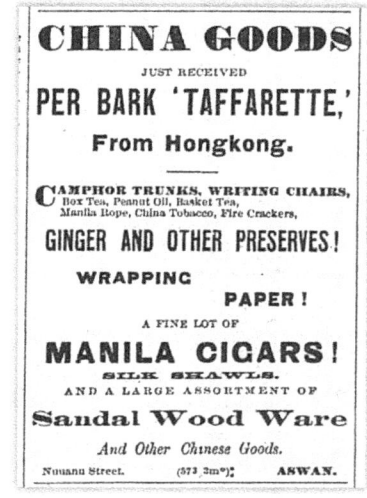

Built by E.B. Thomas in 1886 for $10,000, this building replaced a large 2-story brick building built by "the well-known architect and builder" T.J. Baker in 1878 for a Chinese businessman named Aswan. To celebrate the grand opening, Aswan decorated the upstairs room "in the highest style of Chinese art… no expense being spared" and hosted a large banquet that lasted until the wee hours of the night.

The 1878 building had been advertised as "fire-proof".

This photograph was taken from the top of the Robinson Building at King and Nu'uanu streets on April 19, 1886, looking mauka along Nu'uanu Street.

It shows the 1878 Aswan Building still smoldering from the devastating 1886 Chinatown fire. The twin spires of Kaumakapili Church can be seen in the distance, luckily unaffected by this fire.

Aswan had just received a large overseas shipment which he stored in the building. And since it was one of the few brick buildings in the area, adjacent shopkeepers had hurriedly stored many of their goods at Aswan's for safety.

But the fire overwhelmed the building, the interior was gutted, and the walls were damaged beyond repair.

Aswan's 1886 building displays extraordinary craftsmanship, a lasting tribute to the skill of 19th century brickmason E.B. Thomas. This is the finest brickwork in all of Chinatown. In 1982 architect Lew Ingelson hired contractor T. Iida to remove thick layers of old paint by hand to expose the original pressed-brick façade.

At least two other buildings had similar detailed brickwork – the Sing Chong building directly across Nuʻuanu Street and the Chinese Society Building around the corner on King Street, both built by E.B. Thomas but no longer extant.

Pressed brick is much more durable than regular brick and that accounts for its excellent state of preservation 135 years later. The newspaper at the time declared this to be "one of the finest structures in town".

Wo Chong & Co., shoemakers who had been in the previous building, were the first to move into the new building in 1886.

For 24 years from 1898 to 1922 this was the location of the Kwong Hing Chong Company. They were importers and dealers in English, American, Chinese, and Japanese dry goods, hats, shoes, trunks, mattings, baskets, and general merchandise.

For the next 25 years from 1922 to 1947 it was the Leong Chew store specializing in women's, men's, and children's clothing plus oriental goods.

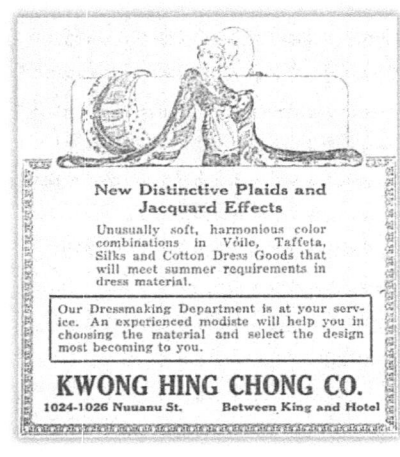

In 1953 it was split into two stores, with the Hawaii Benri-sha (1953-1960) owned by Mrs. K. Kawamura moving here after 30 years on Smith Street, and the Louis Stambler Auction Room.

Honolulu Theatrical Supply Co. was located at 1026 Nuʻuanu and the New Lai Cheong store moved here from 1014 Nuʻuanu in 1958.

In the 1980's the Metronome Music Store was at 1024 Nuʻuanu.

In 1982 this was the location of the Hawaiian Heritage Center, offering regular Chinatown Walking Tours in addition to curating Chinatown and Hawaiian history. They moved to 1128 Smith in 1986 and are now located at 1140 Smith.

In 2009, after 17 years in Kauaʻi, the Tin Can Mailman dealing in Hawaiiana moved to 1026 Nuʻuanu. The store was the site of a stakeout in 2014. In an episode of the *Hawaii 5-0* TV series, Jerry Ortega (played by Jorge Garcia), suspected a bookstore owner of counterfeiting. Coincidentally, Jorge had worked at a bookstore for six years until successfully becoming an actor. Before *Hawaii 5-0* he starred as Hurley in the *Lost* TV series, also filmed in Hawaii.

Aswan

Ho Sin Kee, better known as Aswan (Ah Swan), was born in China in 1834 and came to Hawaii in 1851, initially working as a servant for furniture dealer C.E. Williams and soon becoming the owner of a dozen coffee shops and small stores. He first appears in the 1869 newspaper buying the Ahuna Restaurant on Nu'uanu Street.

He went into the butcher business at the corner of King Street and Maunakea Street and invested in sugar and rice, acquiring leaseholds at Anahole, Kaneohe, and Laie that grew about 40 tons of rice each year.

By 1878 he had a store at King and Maunakea streets (Aswan & Aseu), the Aswan Restaurant, plus a store on the Big Island at Kailua, Kona. In 1879 he was a partner in the Kwong Yin Sing & Company and in the 1880's he owned the Laiewai Rice Plantation and had a rice mill at Waiahole, Oahu.

He had a second house in Amoy (Xiamen), China, but was never incredibly wealthy due to various business setbacks, including the wreck of a cargo ship off Molokai and the 1886 Chinatown fire. And then there was the opium use.

On December 23, 1896, police officers on the roof of the Aseu Building climbed into the second floor to catch Aswan and 11 others "with opium smoking outfits galore".

The police were back on January 11, 1897, using a sharp saw and a 15-pound hammer to bust their way in. They arrested Aswan and three others – "it is claimed that Aswan is the proprietor of an opium den largely frequented by natives and the police are very anxious to break it up."

Five days later Aswan petitioned the Board of Health for permission to use opium, claiming he was 62 years old, had been in the country 46 years, and that he was "suffering very much from various diseases, and having been addicted to the habit of opium smoking nearly all his life, found that he could not do without it."

Surprisingly, in April 1897 he was hired by the government as an expert to test the opium in a police case. But the next month he got arrested for smoking opium, again.

In September 1897, the Hawaiian government issued only 19 licenses to Chinese for opium smoking. Aswan, "the king of all smokers", was permitted to use the most – 60 grains of the drug daily.

In 1898, Li See, the 32-year-old widow of his brother and her two children (age 10 and 12) who had been living at Aswan's house put on their best clothes and overdosed on opium; only the mother survived. Still distraught over the loss of her husband 10 years previous, she didn't want to be a burden to Aswan. She said, "In the world it is much trouble. After death it is all happiness". And the children had agreed to follow their mother.

She wouldn't have been a burden for long – two months later Aswan passed away at age 64. He had 2 children from his first wife and 9 children from his Chinese second wife.

"He was always honorable in his dealings and had the respect not alone of his countrymen but of the mercantile portion of the community in general." His funeral was one of the largest seen in Honolulu and included several bands in the procession.

UYEDA BUILDING

1028-1044 Nuʻuanu
1886 (mauka section added 1891)
Architect / Builder: E.B. Thomas

We are calling this the Uyeda Building since K. Uyeda had three different clothing stores here for over 60 years.

Purchased by George Wilkinson from James Ruddock in 1843, the Telegraph "public house" once stood on this site. By 1885 there were two 2-story wooden buildings here with stores selling tin, shoes, dry goods, and jewelry.

This 2-story brick building was built after the great fire in 1886 by E.B. Thomas for Aswan. Thomas was called back in 1891 to add one more bay on the mauka end to match the rest of the building, making a total of four storefronts with the addresses 1028, 1034, 1038 and 1044 Nuʻuanu Street.

K. Uyeda, later Uyeda's Men's Store, was at **1028** Nuʻuanu for 62 years – from 1905 until they retired from the business in 1967.

Kamejiro Uyeda originally founded the K. Uyeda Hat Store on River Street and was here by 1905. In 1931 he incorporated the business and opened the Style Hat Store and the Style Dress Shop, managed by his four sons Shotaro, Francis, Alfred, and George. He was active in the Honolulu Japanese Chamber of Commerce. Kamejiro and his wife left Honolulu for Japan in 1941, right before World War II.

From 1985 to 1990 this was the location of Separate Tables restaurant which featured local artwork, part of the art and gallery renaissance that took place in Chinatown in the late 1980's.

The Chock Look & Bros. tailors were next door at **1034** Nuʻuanu from 1900 to 1918, followed by the James Chong men's furnishings store in the 1930's, the Gold Star Clothing store (1936-1947), and Loui's Sportswear (1948-1961).

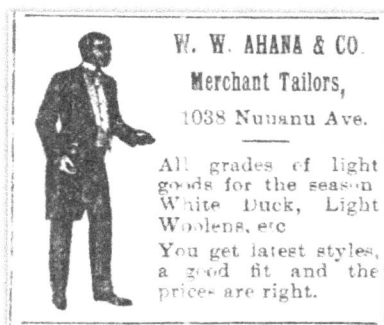

W.W. Ahana & Co, merchant tailors moved to **1038** Nuʻuanu in 1901 after being burned out in the 1900 fire further up on Nuʻuanu Street.

From 1931 to 1961 it was The Style Shoppe, later Style Dress Shop owned by K. Uyeda.

In 1964 it was remodeled and for the next eight years was Joe Gutierres' Bar. They moved here from their previous location at 1196 Nuʻuanu which was demolished for the building of the new Kokusai Theater (later known as the Empress Theater).

It became Hope's Cocktail Lounge in 1972, but there was not much hope here since there were at least two shootings on two separate occasions.

It was a succession of clubs after that: Club Shioya (1973), Club Cindy (1975), Club Yokohama (1980), Nuʻuanu Lounge (1987), and Dougy's Place (1991).

In 1998 it became Hank's Café, owned by local Samoan artist Hank Taufaasau, and it featured his Polynesian paintings along with food and live music.

There have been a lot of hats at **1044** Nuʻuanu – from 1896 to 1902 it was the hat store of T. Murata, the tailor shop of Yamatoya in 1903, and the Fuji Hat Store from 1924 to 1931.

For 36 years, from 1931 to 1967 it was the Style Hat Store, owned by K. Uyeda.

In 1972 it was briefly Peg Leg's Restaurant until the building was gutted by a huge fire.

McCandless Properties hired EDW Architects in 1978 to design the rehabilitation of 1024, 1026, 1034 and 1044 Nuʻuanu.

1044 Nuʻuanu was the location of the Designers Emporium from 1983 to 1987.

COSMOPOLITAN SALOON

1058 Nu'uanu, 11 N. Hotel
1886
Architect / Builder: George Lucas

This building was the first brick building completed after the disastrous 1886 fire. It was built "in six weeks and a day" by George Lucas of the Honolulu Planing Mills for George Freeth and Walter Peacock. They were the largest saloon owners and wholesale liquor dealers of their day, and they also owned the Royal and Pacific saloons on Nu'uanu Street.

Known as the Cosmopolitan Saloon, the interior was "wainscoted in redwood with black walnut graining, and the bar was topped with solid black walnut. All openings have swinging blinds of cedar. The building is 75 feet by 53 feet, with ceilings 13 feet high".

In the 1830's this was the site of an adobe building that was the Chinese store owned by Wong Tai-hoon. Also spelled Tyhune, Tyhoon, Tihune, Tyhoun, Tihoon, Tyhung, Taihoun or even by the Hawaiian name of Taihuna. This was the second Chinese store in Honolulu, dealing in dry goods, groceries, wines, and spirits. It also had rooms/opium dens for fellow Chinese in the back.

Like many early Chinese he married a Hawaiian woman, Wahinekapu, and obtained full title to the property in 1852 through his father-in-law, Kahanaumaikai, who had purchased it from William Wallace, a "colored man" (African-American? Caribbean?) who had occupied the premises with William Johnson Parker.

Tyhune was no mere shopkeeper – he was one of the premier Chinese businessmen of the day and had interests in sugar and shipping as well as owning other stores at Koloa, Kaua'i and at Lāhainā, Maui. There are indications he might have owned at least one commercial sailing vessel. Tyhune died in 1855 and the property was still owned by his heirs in 1960.

The Cosmopolitan Restaurant/Hotel/Saloon opened on this site in 1881 with proprietor Peter Acosta who was formerly the Chief Steward of the steamer *Likelike*. In 1882 the "Cosmopolitan Hotel Co." was founded by F.T. Lenehan, W.C. Peacock, Chung Waa, Tom Dow, Lee Chat and Apah. It was managed by M. Camacho in 1883 and then by Jun Hee. Room and board was $4.50 per week in 1884. The dinner menu included crab salad "with all the etceteras", plus "roast goose stuffed with sage and onions and served with apple sauce". Favorite beers served were Pabst Milwaukee and Buffalo Beer.

The Cosmopolitan Saloon was on this corner for 22 years from 1881 to 1903. It was renamed "The California" and operated by State Representative Henry C. Vida but was foreclosed in 1905 by the Sheriff for not paying the liquor license fee. Everything was sold at public auction including a 22-foot oak bar with mahogany top and a 19-foot oak bar with large beveled mirrors.

From 1914 to 1952 this was the New York Shoe Store owned by Choy Hoy An. He was a native of Seongchak village in South China and had come to Honolulu as a boy. His wife, Mrs. Choy Chang See, ran the business after his death in 1932. They front of the store was remodeled in 1930.

In 1952 she sold the business to James V. Kunst from Prague, Czechoslovakia who renamed it the "Ka-ma-aina Shoe Store". He retained many of the former employees, some of whom had worked in the New York Store for 25 years.

They opened a second store in the Ala Moana Mall in 1966 and closed this location in 1968.

Walter Chamberlain Peacock

... was born in Lancaster, England, and came to Hawaii via New Zealand in 1881 at age 23. He started off as a bookkeeper and then worked for wholesale liquor dealer F.T. Lenehan. Upon the death of Mr. Lenehan, he and George Freeth bought the business in 1884 and built it into the largest liquor dealership on the island, also owning the Royal, Pacific and Cosmopolitan saloons. He also bottled and packaged his own liquor and made customized bar tokens and shot glasses.

In 1893 he built a mansion for himself in Waikiki, and realizing the opportunity for Waikiki Beach tourism, he created the Moana Hotel Company and hired architect Oliver Traphagen to design the 4-story Moana Hotel in the Spanish Renaissance style that was "one of the most handsome and best appointed seaside hotels outside of the United States". To make room for the hotel he hired George Lucas to move his mansion out of the way.

It is said that Peacock personally planted the famous Banyan tree in the hotel's courtyard.

PERRY BLOCK

1101-1111 Nuʻuanu, 2-8 S. Hotel
1888
Architect / Builder: Isaac A. Palmer / E.B. Thomas

This Eastlake-style building was built for Mrs. Anna Dos Anjos (Henriques) Perry, the 49-year-old widow of Jason Perry who had been the Portuguese Consul to Hawaii for 10 years. Which could explain why the Portuguese coat-of-arms is prominently featured in the keystones of the arched windows and doorways on the first floor.

Jacinto Pereira was born in 1826 in the village of Frequezia de Pedro Mignel, near Horta, on the Ilha do Faial (Island of Fayal) in the Azores, and came to Hawaii c.1851 on a whaling ship. He went into the dry goods business and in 1868 outfitted the whaling schooner *W.H. Allen* in partnership with Manuel Paiko. When he died in 1883 at age 56, his headstone showed the Anglicized name – Jason Perry.

Anna Dos Anjos Henriques was born on the same island in 1839 and came to Hawaii in 1865. Shortly after their marriage they built a 1-story coral building with gable roof on this corner in 1867 that was 30'x40', with 14' ceilings, and had a cellar blasted out of solid coral. In 1878 they built a 2-story wooden building next door on Hotel Street.

They also owned a wooden building next door on Nuʻuanu Street that housed the Frank Cunha grocery which unfortunately caught fire in 1887 and resulted in the death of 16-year-old John Silva, a Portuguese boy living upstairs.

The 1867 coral building was untouched by the 1886 Chinatown fire, but after the tragic 1887 fire next door Mrs. Perry sold off the burnt shell and demolished her coral building to build this larger building in 1888 which covered the entire lot.

The Perry Estate's "Statement of Expenses Incurred in Connection with New Building" shows a payment to E.B. Thomas for $15,951.87 and $550 to "J.A. Palmer, for services." This is probably "I.A. Palmer" as the architect's first initial was often shown both ways in the newspaper. The Perry Block was purchased by preservation architect Robert M. Fox in 1980 and the building was restored in 1985 by K. Nagata Construction.

The first business in the corner was very likely the Yokohama Bazaar, a dry goods store run by Murata & Company that first advertised in 1893 and was there until 1900.

They were succeeded by M. Chiya & Company who also specialized in Japanese and American dry goods.

From 1906 to 1918 it housed the Makino Drug Company, and then the People's Drug Store from 1921 to 1940.

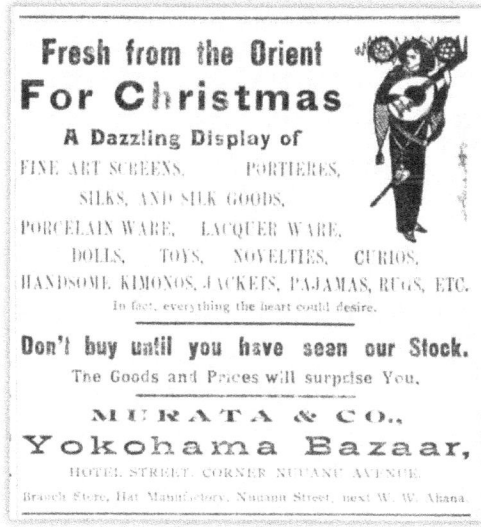

Bill Lederer's Bar was here from 1940 to 1985, including an upstairs bar called "Odd & Ends" with strippers. It was a neighborhood bar, "a hard-drinking saloon without fancy frills". Muhammad Ali would stop here when he was in town, Japanese movies were filmed here, and a 320-pound bosun's mate once rode in on a Harley-Davidson motorcycle, ordered a drink, downed it, and roared out.

Edgar William Leeteg, "the Father of American Velvet Painting", was a frequent customer who occasionally paid his bar tab with paintings. He later built an estate in Tahiti called "Villa Velour". In the 1960's his paintings sold for as much as $20,000 each. James Michener called him "the Remington of the South Seas".

In 1988, Andy Friedland of the Downtown Improvement Association and developer Bob Gerell raised $150,000 from 80 downtown businesses, with Fox Hawaii Inc. donating architectural services and Mouse Builders donating the construction work, to make it into a Police Substation. Which caused some to remark that there were now "nearly as many cops in the place as when it was a bar".

While there are many unfounded urban legends about tunnels under Chinatown, one was supposedly found here during the remodeling for the police station. No one is sure what it would have been used for, or where it went, or why.

There were two additional storefronts along the Nuʻuanu Street side. The one in the middle initially housed a shoe store and a shoe factory. From 1921 to 1933 it was the Victory Barber Shop.

For 24 years (1936-1960) it was the Hawaiian Book Exchange owned by Joe Herwig and said to be the best used-book store in town, with piles of old books that reached almost to the ceiling.

Sherwood Men's Hair Styling and the Soul Music Village store were here in 1972.

It was a video store in the 1980's and in 1989 it was the Sharps and Flats Second-Hand Music Shop, owned by local character Jack C. Young. He was an inveterate wheeler dealer, 78 years old, who sat on the sidewalk sprawled in a lounge chair wearing jade beads, solid gold American coins on every thumb and finger, and playing a ukulele upside down.

From 2004 to 2011 this space was the Louis Pohl Gallery. Pohl was an American painter who was invited to Hawaii in 1946 to establish the Honolulu Museum of Art School where he taught for 35 years.

The store on the mauka end started off as a general merchandise store and briefly housed a tailor shop in 1902 but has been a succession of restaurants ever since.

The Hop Sing Company had a restaurant here from 1904 to 1924, after that it was the Victory Café, the New Columbia Café, and briefly the Kuhio Café. It was the Royal Annex Café from 1934 to 1948, and then Pete's White Palace from 1948 to 1955, and then Esposito's Italian Restaurant in 1956.

The Goodwill Industries store was briefly here from 1959 to 1960.

For over 20 years it was the Tahiti Bar (1961-1982) owned by Harry & Priscilla Yamada. When they moved to 1128 Smith Street in 1983 it became Sheik's Tavern.

From 1994 to 2013 it housed the highly acclaimed Indigo Restaurant featuring "Eurasian" specialties prepared by proprietor-chef Glenn Chu.

Isaac A. Palmer

Born in St. Clairsville, Ohio in 1835, Isaac A. Palmer served in the Wisconsin 30th Regiment as Principal Musician in the Civil War. He moved to Seattle, Washington in 1871 and by April of 1872 was advertising as an "Architect and Builder". He designed the county courthouse and jail, several houses and commercial buildings, plus the towering 12-room 1883 Central School on Sixth Street with French mansard roof, clock tower and tall central belfry.

By 1887 he was in Honolulu and was the architect of the new Perry Block on Nuʻuanu Street. He also designed the Hoffschlaeger Building (1887), the T.H. Davies Building (1888), the Cartwright Building (1889), the Honolulu Dispensary (1889), the Cummins Building (1891), the British Club (1891), the Hawaiian Hotel veranda (1891), and the Daily Bulletin Building on Merchant Street for W.G. Irwin (1892). He designed the Peacock Block, the first brick building in Hilo, for W.C. Peacock, which was built in 1900 from plans by Oliver Traphagen instead.

In 1891 Palmer teamed up with former USS *Benecia* ship's carpenter W.W. Richardson to form Palmer & Richardson, advertising "Eastlake, Queen Anne, Renaissance, Gothic, Italian, Classic and Norman" styles of architecture in "stone, brick, iron or wood".

By 1896 Palmer was in Medford, Oregon, where he designed at least 20 downtown buildings and houses until 1908.

Based on stylistic similarities with the Perry Block (1888) and the Cartwright Building (1889), along with his stated interest in Eastlake architecture, Palmer was very likely the architect for the Royal Saloon (1890) and the T.R. Foster Building (1891). These three Chinatown buildings exhibit classic Eastlake decorative details and would be the three best surviving examples of Isaac A. Palmer's work.

MENDONÇA / ENCORE SALOON

1102-1112 Nuʻuanu, 2-20 N. Hotel
1887, restored 1979
Architect / Builder: George Lucas (1887), James K. Tsugawa (1979)

After the April 1886 Chinatown fire destroyed the 2-story wooden building on this corner (pictured on the left), Joseph Mendonça called for tenders to erect this brick building in August of that same year. George Lucas won the bid at $9,554 and had the foundation laid by November and the building enclosed by March of 1887.

With all the construction going on after the fire there was a shortage of building material until the bark *Ceylon* arrived from San Francisco in December with 253,000 bricks, half of which were for George Lucas.

The first section started was on Hotel Street, then the corner and section along Nuʻuanu were added plus an additional section on Hotel Street, resulting in 8 storefronts with rooms above. An 1888 newspaper story referred to it as the "Wo Lung Sam Sing building" since the Wo Lung & Sam Sing Company, owned by Lo Sam Sing, Won Wing, Au Hoon, and Lo Sau were one of the first occupants in 1887, running a dry goods store at the corner.

On the Hotel Street side, Wo Sing & Company ran a general merchandise store in 1887. There was a doctor's office next to them and at the ewa end was another general merchandise store.

During restoration of the building in the 1980's they reportedly found a "Shanghai compartment" between the floor and the ceiling with a trap door, the idea being that drugged/drunk sailors would be kidnapped and held here until ship captains paid to have them sent to ships bound for places like Shanghai. There is nothing in the historical record to confirm this, and the days of sail were drawing to a close by the late 1880's, but it might have been used for hiding opium or smuggling.

In 1892 the Yee Wo Chong Company was at the corner, followed by Chong Kee & Company from 1893 to 1900. It was a general merchandise store owned by Lee Soy Chong, Ho On Yin, and Tun Hing.

On January 1, 1901, Paddy F. Ryan and Charles R. Dement opened the Encore Saloon at the corner. Paddy was also the bartender, known for the catchphrase "What are you going to take?". They also owned the Depot Saloon by the train station. In 1907 Louis D. Warren bought the business and moved it diagonally across the street in 1908. Warren was a big horse racer and had previously been in business with Joseph P. Medeiros in the Waialua Wine Company.

Although only open at this location for a few relatively uneventful years, the building has become known as the Encore Saloon building due to the photograph on the left taken in 1901 or 1902, with the prominent sign proudly advertising Primo Lager Beer.

From 1931 to 1934 this was the location of the Honolulu Shoe Company, formerly located at "the white corner" across the street.

They added purple and red tiles to the front along with maroon awnings and a bright neon sign. For the grand re-opening over 30 local firms sent large floral displays.

The Honolulu Shoe Company was founded in 1919 by Young Kwong Hoy as the Honolulu Hat and Shoe Company at 1026 Nuʻuanu Street. When he retired in 1926 his son, Young Sam Wood, continued the business until closing it during the Great Depression in 1934.

But the story ends much more tragically than that. When Young Kwong Hoy retired he moved back to China, to Bucktoy village, Leong Doo, Chungshan (Zhongshan), Guangdong. In 1951, when he was over 60 years old his name appeared on the blacklist for people to be tried and tortured by Mao Zedong's new government, so he jumped into the well at this house and drowned.

On a much cheerier note, and possibly named after the 1949 Doris Day song, the Café Rendezvous owned by Gentaro Kaneshiro and Yasunobu Uyezu, and later Joe Vicari, was at the corner from 1950 to 1963.

10 N. Hotel housed the Eagle Oyster House in 1900, The America in 1901, the New York Café in 1913, and it was the Salvation Army Hall in 1915 and 1916. The police vice squad raided a bootlegging place here in 1930 that had a 17-year-old Japanese girl bartender, confiscating ten quarts of beer and a quart of okolehao.

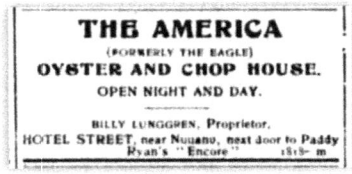

In 1930, police used a 200-pound steel ram to bust an illegal saloon in back of the N.R.A. Shooting Gallery.

From 1939 to 1949 it was Wee's Café, then Sportsman's Bar run by professional wrestler, judo expert, and sumo champion Oki Shikina. It was the Tokyo Bar in 1954.

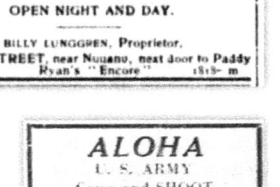

From 1971 to 1980 it was the Rendezvous Theater, open 24 hours, and often busted for both pornography and gambling.

In 2005 it was the Black Pearl Lounge, owned by female impersonator Brandy Lee.

The Honolulu Oyster House was at 16/18 N. Hotel from 1904 to 1904, then a Japanese print shop, and from 1936 to 1959 it housed the W.W. Ahana Printing Company. It was the Zig Zag Club from 1964 to 1977, then Club Oriental, and it became the Brick Fire Tavern in 2017.

20 N. Hotel was initially a Lovejoy liquor warehouse and then a Sayegusa store warehouse, the Harry Lawson White Palace tattoo parlor (1925), Nani's Portrait Studio (1943), and from 1950 to 1961 it was the fancy Goldtone Photo Studio owned by Wallace Tsuha, George Tsuho, and Seichi Kaneshiro. In the 1970's it was Mitsuko's Furo Bath & Rub Down, Diamond Cue II, and later Mel's Videocade.

On the Nu'uanu Street side at 1110 Nu'uanu there was a tailor shop in 1902 whose owner was charged with counterfeiting, the Standard Barber Shop, and from 1982 to 2001 it was the offices of the Legal Aid Society of Hawaii.

1110 Nu'uanu was the longtime home of the Look You Shoe Store, owned by Chee Look (1936-1971).

On the mauka end, at 1112 Nu'uanu, there was the Tong Wo Shoe Store (1927-1931) and the Boston Shoe Store (1931). But after that it became the Pub Café in 1934, owned by Seichi Kishimoto and later Mary Ann Boisse, Maria Kamano, Walter Foo Yuen Liu, and Mrs. Genevieve H. Liu.

It was called The Pub in 1958, and became the Cub Tavern, owned by Victor Vallies from 1963 to 1975. It was Rosie's Lounge from 1979 to 2000, and later the New Hana Hou Lounge.

PAIKO BLOCK / LAI FONG BUILDING

1118-1120 Nuʻuanu
1880
Architect / Builder: S.D. Burrows

This is the second-oldest building in Chinatown and one of the few survivors of the 1886 Chinatown fire – but only just barely. It was built in 1880 by S.D. Burrows for Portuguese immigrant Manuel Paiko, and it was one of the first substantial brick buildings in Chinatown.

Its construction was severely tested on April 18, 1886, when it became "a great burning cauldron within, the flames bursting out around the iron shutters". Firemen attempted to put out the fire in the building, but "the shutters which kept the fire in also kept the water out". These same shutters are still visible on both sides of the building today.

The good news was this brick building stopped the fire from spreading across this section of Nuʻuanu Street.

After things finally cooled off three days later, workers were able to pull out a large safe that had crashed into the basement.

A month after the fire, workmen started restoring the interior since it was one of the few buildings whose walls remained structurally sound and had not fallen.

S.D. Burrows was born in Lāhainā in 1840 and was half-Hawaiian. At age 16 a friend took him to Brockton, Massachusetts, where he spent 6 years learning carpentry and stone masonry.

He built the Emma Street mansion of Princess Ruth Keʻelikōlani (the largest and richest landowner in Hawaii), as well as the 1881 Chinese Church, and had a planing mill and lumber yard on Fort Street.

Well-loved and well-respected, he was supposed to be the superintendent for the new brick Kaumakapili Church but heart disease caused an early death in 1881 at the age of 41.

The front of the building looked very different when it was first built. This photograph was taken on July 4, 1881:

Although made of brick, the front was stuccoed and scored to look like stone blocks.

The photograph above is from 1884 and shows Manuel Paiko's house in back, with Buffum's Hall towering behind.

The building had a fancy name block on the parapet: "PAIKO BLOCK, 1880". This and the decorative cornice were undoubtedly burned off in the 1886 fire and were replaced with the arched brick parapet on the building today. George Lucas was probably the contractor since he was an old friend of Mr. Paiko and had served with him in the same fire engine company for many years.

HONOLULU CHINATOWN

The first stores to move into the new Paiko Block were the Hollister Drug Store and the Goo Kim dry goods store.

Hollister & Co. started out as Hollister & Hyland in 1863 and were the first company in Hawaii to sell soda water. They later became a full-service drug store and opened an additional store on Fort Street. The business lasted until 1955.

The wholesale division of the Hollister Company was on the left side of the building from 1880 until 1888 when they consolidated with their main store near Fort & Hotel streets.

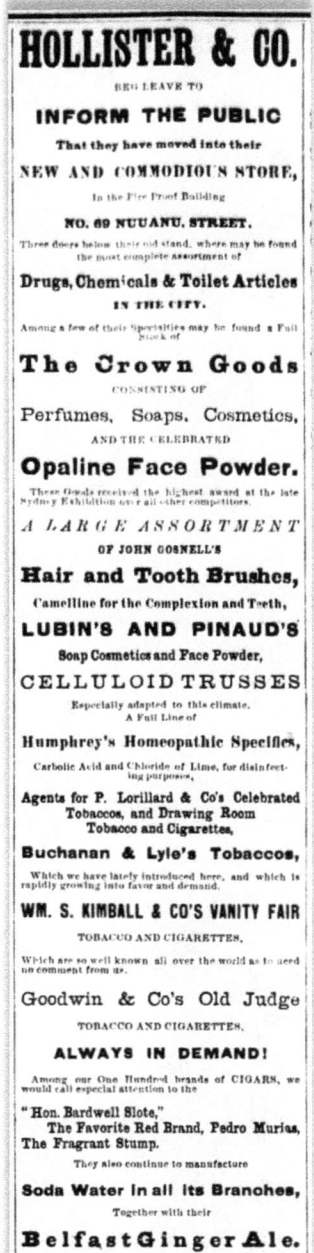

From 1899 to 1919 it was the Sayegusa Shoten Japanese Store, expanding into both sides of the building in 1915.

It was succeeded by the Yonekura Company in 1919, who moved to Fort Street in 1932. In 1933, architect Herbert Cohen Cayton remodeled the interior for the K. Iwakami Company.

The Lai Fong Department Store moved here in 1947 from their previous location at Beretania and Bethel streets. They are still here today, 75 years later, though in a much-reduced capacity.

The Goo Kim store, one of the largest Chinese stores in Honolulu, was located on the right side of the building for 25 years from 1880 to 1905, at which time everything was auctioned off in a voluntary bankruptcy.

After Sayegusa Shoten and Yonekura Company, the right side housed a series of different businesses: China Gifts (1937), the Me P.Y. Chong restaurant (1941), the Chong Wah Yuen restaurant (1941), Teragawachi Jewelry (1942), the Tor Inn Restaurant and Chop Suey (1943-1945), the Best Food Tavern (1945-1947), and the Golden Star Inn (1949).

From 1949 to 1959 it was the home of Horner's Music Supply who later relocated to Bethel Street.

From 1959 to 1964 it housed Aveco World Travel, owned by Diosdado and Caridad Avecilla, and it became the World Wide Tours & Travel Service in 1988.

Goo Kim Fui

Known as Goo Kim, he was a well-known Chinese merchant and pastor, owner of the largest Chinese dry goods store, and was one of the most influential leaders in the Hawaiian Chinese community. He was major defender of the Chinese people during the anti-Chinese sentiments in the 1880's.

He was born in Ka Yin Chau, Leen Tong Heung in the Guangdong Province of China in 1826 and came to Hawaii in 1867. He married a Hawaiian woman, Ellen Kamae, in 1872.

His fluency in English was a major factor in his business and negotiating success. He converted to Christianity in 1875 and was instrumental in creating the Chinese YMCA and the Chinese Christian Church. He became friends with Dr. Sun Yat-sen and later provided financial support for the revolution.

Goo Kim was the Chinese Consular Agent to Hawaii and from 1884 to 1889 was president of the Honolulu United Chinese Society. He helped set up the Chinese Hospital in 1897, and he also fought for the right of Chinese to obtain American citizenship. He was one of the most active leaders in re-establishing Chinatown after the 1900 fire, working to help victims and businesses re-establish themselves, often using his own money to help.

When he died in 1908 at 82 years of age, his funeral was one of the largest in years and included music by the Royal Hawaiian Band.

Lai Fong

Born the daughter of a village chief in Canton (Guangzhou), China, Lai Fong Tom Au was a "picture bride" who was chosen by the parents of her future husband, Edward Au. He had fought in the 1911 Chinese Revolutionary War with Dr. Sun Yat-sen and had previously lived in Hawaii and attended school here. They were married in 1911 and moved to Hawaii two years later.

They opened their first store in 1934, the Lai Fong Silk House at 71 S. Hotel Street. In addition to selling silk cloth she made Chinese gowns and the store sold Chinese furniture, jewelry, carved screens, and clothing.

Manuel Paiko

Originally from the island of Pico (Ilha do Pico), one of the 9 main islands of the Azores located in the Atlantic Ocean 1,000 miles off the coast of Portugal, he came to Hawaii as a whaler in the 1840's and became known as "Manuel do Pico", which was Hawaiianized into "Paiko". He was one of the first Portuguese to settle in Hawaii, arriving many years before the first group of Portuguese laborers who came in 1878.

By 1850 he had a license for "hawking and pedling" and owned the 33-ton schooner *Marianna*. Paiko owned half the ahupuaa of Kuliouou in Waimanalo and had one of the first commercial cattle ranches in Hawaii. The Dowager Queen Emma and her retinue of 150 breakfasted at Paiko's in "Kulioo" on her tour around Oahu in 1877.

In 1880 he hired S.D. Burrows to build a large brick building on Nuʻuanu for Hollister & Company and for the Goo Kim dry goods store.

Formerly active in volunteer Fire Company No. 1, he was later elderly and infirm and lived behind the building. He died in 1890, followed by his wife Domitila in 1906. Their son Joseph named his new schooner after his mother, and when he died in 1942 Paiko Beach was named for him.

MCLEAN BLOCK

1113-1123 Nuʻuanu
1903
Architect: Oliver Traphagen? / Fred Harrison

James L. McLean

There is a surprising lack of information about this impressive building in historical written accounts. At least the original parapet block name survives, identifying it as the McLean Block built in 1903.

It was built by contractor Fred Harrison for James L. McLean, the son of George C. McLean whose brick and timber buildings had been ordered to be moved back for the widening of Nuʻuanu Street in 1903.

Instead of moving, McLean built this large new block instead. Oliver Traphagen was listed as the supervising architect in the December 1903 issue of *Paradise of the Pacific*.

The European Restaurant, owned by Hop Sing (Chock Sing), in the previous building since 1893, returned to the new building in February 1904.

This building replaced three brick buildings built by James' father, George McLean.

George Christie McLean was a native of Aberdeen, Scotland, and the grandson of Sir William Sidney Smith who was famous for destroying the French fleet at Toulon in 1793.

After spending a few years in Tahiti he left for the 1849 California Gold Rush but only made it as far as Honolulu. He was said to be "always genial and cheery, his well-known face on our streets seemed to carry with it an atmosphere of hearty good will and the enjoyment of life".

He had a store on this location as early as 1856 and he built one of the brick buildings in 1875 featuring a decorative brick style known as "pointing". The third brick building was added in 1877.

That same year he bought a 30-ton tugboat in San Francisco that was brought to Honolulu by the barkentine *Discovery*. His son James later worked his way up to vice-president of the Inter-Island Steam Navigation Company, owned by James' brother-in-law, Captain W.B. Godfrey.

In 1889, James married Jennie Grieve, the daughter of Robert Grieve who was a printer and the owner of the *Hawaiian Gazette* newspaper.

When George died in 1878, his four sons took over the general store business – James L., Robert C., George T., and William H.

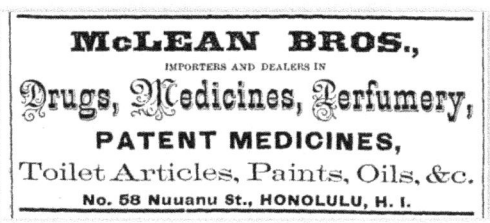

In 1900, the three businesses in the old McLean buildings were Sayegusa (dry goods), Y. Mansing (dressmaker), and Wo On (tailor).

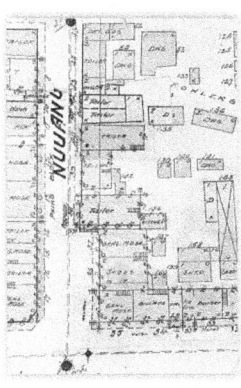

This c.1902 photo shows the old McLean buildings sticking out into the Nuʻuanu Street right-of-way.

HONOLULU CHINATOWN

LOVE'S BAKERY

1126-1128 Nuʻuanu
1917
Architect / Builder: Ripley & Davis / Hawaiian Ballasting Company

This site was the home of Love's Bakery for 79 years, from 1853 until 1932, with the current building designed by Clinton B. Ripley and Louis E. Davis and constructed by the Hawaiian Ballasting Company in 1917.

The story begins on June 19, 1851, when the American ship *Adirondack* brought Glasgow-born Robert Love and his family to Hawaii from Sydney, Australia. They were on their way to California to partake in the Gold Rush but realized there was an opportunity here for supplying provisions, especially bread, to the whaling fleets that made Hawaii their temporary home every winter.

Love was granted a license to "operate a bakery and sell its products" on July 12, 1851, less than a month after landing at Honolulu harbor. The re-baking of ships' bread was a big business, as well as providing hard sea biscuits made only of flour, salt, and water, known as Pilot or Navy bread. Love added a little shortening to the recipe to create the Saloon Pilot cracker that is still popular today.

In 1853, in the middle of the smallpox epidemic, Love purchased this piece of land with buildings from James S. Moody for $2,500 and opened his bakery across the street from J. Fox's Bakery and Grocery Store. He also opened a bakery and store by the wharf in 1854.

But tragedy soon struck – Robert's wife Margaret died in 1855 at the age of 39, and Robert died in 1858 at age 42, leaving three sons, ages 15, 18, and 22, to run the business. Two years later, fire struck the business.

In 1861, Robert Love Jr. imported machinery from San Francisco and hired George Thomas to build a new 30' x 56' brick building that included ovens and steam engine room. In addition to pilot and navy bread they also made "Jenny Lind and nut cakes, sugar, butter, water, Boston and soda crackers".

By 1867 it was called the Honolulu Steam Bakery with R. Love & Brothers as proprietors. Robert Love Jr. later became the sole owner but passed away in 1883 at the age of 48, leaving his wife Fanny (from Hobart, Tasmania) to run the business while also taking care of six children.

In 1884 the "fire fiend" struck again. At 2:40 am on August 23 the bakery and five adjoining buildings burned to the ground in spite of the valiant efforts of the volunteer fire department, including King Kalākaua himself. Estimated damages were $100,000.

Fanny immediately started to rebuild, hiring E.B. Thomas to construct a new 2-story brick building, 32' x 92', with a pressed brick front that was completed in November. The building was constructed in only six weeks.

Bishop Museum Archives

When the big fire struck Chinatown in 1886, Love's was at the far edge, and only suffered the loss of a few wooden sheds. Undoubtedly the large ovens provided quite the buffer and the bakery was open for business the next day. They were also unaffected by the 1900 fire even though an adjacent building was burned by the Board of Health on January 19, 1900. Fanny Love must have been relieved and grateful once again. She died in 1916 at the age of 73.

In 1917, the Love Biscuit & Bread Company hired Ripley & Davis to design a much larger bakery to replace their 1884 building. The new facility was one of the most modern in the United States with a capacity of 20,000 loaves of bread per day. Large plate glass windows in front allowed the public to watch the machinery in action.

They opened a new facility on Iwilei Road in 1924 and converted the former bread ovens into cake ovens, making 1,500 cakes per hour, or 24,000 cakes a day. Operations were consolidated to the Iwilei plant in 1932.

The business was sold to ITT Continental Baking Company in 1968, and in 1981 to First Baking Co., Ltd. of Japan, becoming Daiichiya-Love's Bakery. Local management bought the company in 2008 and renamed it Love's Bakery.

In its heyday, Love's Bakery produced 206 varieties of bread, 70 varieties of buns and rolls, and 14 varieties of cakes. They distributed about 400,000 loaves of bread every week, with the neighbor islands accounting for 40% of their business. The bakery closed for good in 2021, citing overwhelming modernization costs.

From 1936 to 1960 the building housed the China Gift Chest store owned by S.Y. Wong, Mrs. L.T. Yuen, T.F. Chee (manager), and Theodore Char. The storefront, entrance, and partitions were designed by architect Y.T. Char. Mr. Wong was also VP of Wing Sing Wo Company.

In 1960, Goodwill Industries of Honolulu moved their thrift store here from 1111 Nuʻuanu and also opened a workshop to provide jobs for the handicapped. Goodwill Industries of Honolulu was founded in 1959 by Rev. Euicho Chung of the First Korean Methodist Church. They moved to 83 N. King Street in 1971.

In 1988 the building was purchased by internationally acclaimed hair stylist and hair products magnate Paul Mitchell. Born in Scotland and raised near Buckingham Palace in England, Mitchell popularized the use of mousse for hair-sculpting in the 1980's and built a hair products company that in 1985 was #71 on the Inc. Magazine's list of Top 500 privately held US companies.

Mitchell moved to Hawaii in 1974 and created John Paul Mitchell Systems with John Paul DeJoria, making professional hair salon products available through salons. He bought the Dowsett estate in Lanikai, established a ginger farm on the Big Island, and funded a car that was Hawaii's entry in the World Solar Challenge in Australia.

Paul Mitchell products are sold worldwide, and there are over 100 Paul Mitchell the School locations in the US teaching cosmetology and hair design. He died of cancer in 1989 at age 53, and his Lanikai estate sold for $18M.

Having nothing whatsoever to do with the fact that the building briefly housed temporary offices for Aloha Airlines in 1960, there is an airplane on the second floor. Seriously.

The fuselage of the former Air Molokai-Tropic Airlines DC-3 "N104RP" which was commissioned in 1944 and saw action in World War II in Algeria was installed through the roof in 1988 to become the second-floor entrance lobby to graphics design firm Williamson & Associates.

It was the brainchild of local architect Carey Smoot who had parachuted out of DC3's in Vietnam and whose father had worked for Douglas Aircraft Company. One enters the "lobby" through the tail section and arrives in the office by deplaning through the main cabin door. As of 2022, the airplane is still inside the building.

PANTHEON BAR

1129 Nuʻuanu
1911
Architect / Builder: unknown

At one time proclaiming to be "the oldest bar in Honolulu", this is the third and final location of the Pantheon Bar.

Taking over the premises known as the Bartlett House, it opened as the Pantheon Hotel in 1878 with Irishman James Dodd as the proprietor at the corner of Hotel and Fort streets. It featured a large mahogany bar that had been shipped around Cape Horn at the tip of South America in 1883.

Dodd demolished the building in 1883 and built new on the same site with 50' frontage on both Hotel and Fort streets, renaming it the Pantheon Saloon. But on February 7, 1900, the whole block at Fort and Hotel including the Pantheon Saloon was deliberately burned by the Board of Health, less than a month after the death of James Dodd.

It was rebuilt close to the same site at the ewa/mauka corner and Joe T. Silva became the new proprietor. Silva came to Hawaii in 1880 from San Francisco as a photographer but ended up working in the liqour business, eventually owning the Pantheon Saloon.

In 1910 he was forced to relocate due to the construction of the new Pantheon Block. He moved the bar to this location in 1911 and was the owner and barman until 1934. During Prohibition it was the only public bar left in Honolulu, staying open as a gathering place and selling soft drinks, chewing gum and smokes.

The Pantheon Bar appeared in two episodes of the original *Hawaii 5-0* – "Dear Enemy" in Season 3, and "Draw Me a Killer" in Season 6.

These titles are very appropriate, since even as early as 1911 the bar had an unsavory reputation, "known as the ordinary hang-out of a certain tough element, consisting largely of ne'er-do-weels, prizefight hangers-on and other undesirable citizens."

Even in its latter years it was home to a motorcycle club called "Devils Breed". It's hard to believe it was originally a classy place that was frequented by King David Kalākaua!

Prizefighter Moose Taussig was later co-owner of the bar, which closed for good in 1989.

The whereabouts of the great mahogany bar are unknown.

The building previously on this site housed a tailor shop and wasburned by the Board of Health in 1900.

HONOLULU CHINATOWN

NOVELTY THEATER/CHINESE BAZAAR

1131-1139 Nu'uanu
1909
Architect / Builder: John Ouderkirk (1911 remodel), Albert Ely Ives (1938 remodel)

This building was built in 1909 as the Novelty Theater featuring motion pictures and a variety of traveling vaudeville acts, and located in front of the Princess Skating Rink. Although very popular, the theater only lasted two years until it was closed when Honolulu Amusements consolidated their theaters.

Owned by the Austin Estate, the building was remodeled in 1911 by John Ouderkirk. One of the first tenants was a watchmaker, N. Shigemura. Later tenants included Re-Tire & Supply (1915), L.J. Wong "military tailor" (1916), Y. Leong Jewelry (1923), and Sing F. Chun real estate (1926).

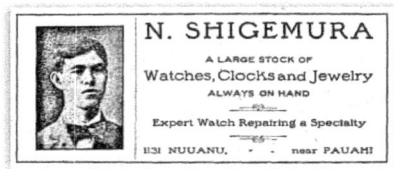

The building was remodeled and modernized by architect Albert Ely Ives in 1938 and became the home of the Chinese Bazaar store for almost 50 years.

Originally called the "New Chinese Bazaar" to distinguish it from Yee Yap's Chinese Bazaar which had recently closed at 1170 Nu'uanu, they moved here in 1938 from across the street and shortened the name to "Chinese Bazaar".

It was owned by Woo Shu Bin, better known as **S.B. Woo**, former manager of Yung Shun Lace Company at 1117 Nu'uanu. From Shantung province in China, before he came to Hawaii in 1933 he was a manufacturer and importer of laces and embroideries at Chefoo (Zhifu), Shanghai, Hong Kong, and Manila. The store specialized in silk fabrics and Chinese hope chests made of teak and camphorwood, and initially shared the building with the Moderne Gift and Novelty Shop and the National Shoe Company. After nearly 5 decades in business they closed in 1984.

In 1985 it became the Pollitt Gallery and was the site of the Sweet Dreams La Boutique in 1989.

From 1891 to 1900 there was a 2-story wooden dry goods store and tailor shop here that was burned by the Board of Health on December 31, 1899, in the first Chinatown plague fire.

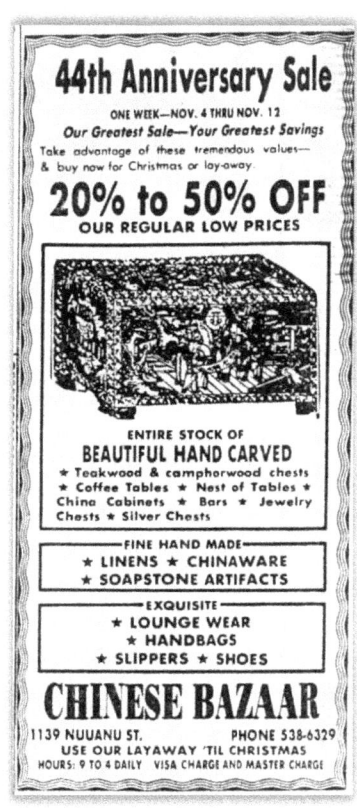

This was also the site of J. Fox's bakery and grocery from 1853 to 1858. When an old storehouse behind this building was demolished in 1875 they found a case of "Extra No.1 Havana Sixes" cigars that had been under the floorboards for at least 16 years.

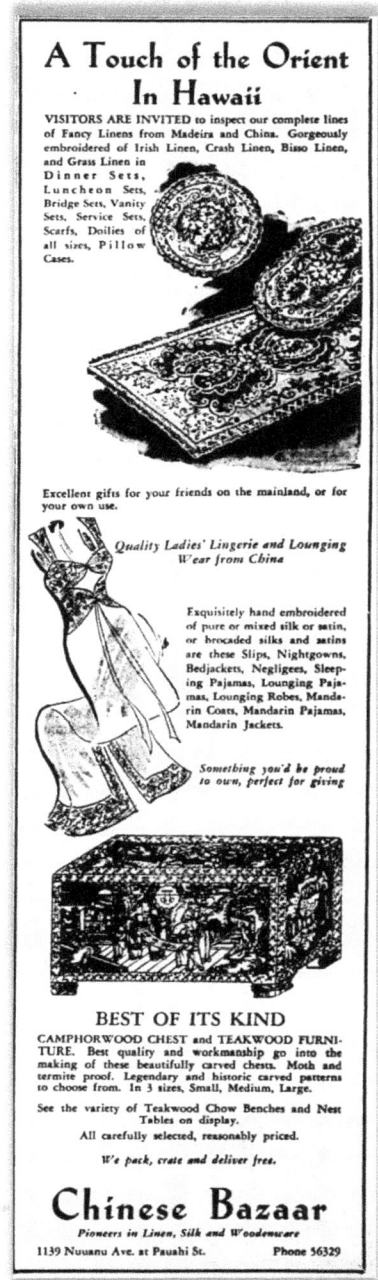

C. AHI BUILDING

1150-1154 Nu'uanu
1901, 2004 reconstruction
Architect / Builder: H.L. Kerr

In the early hours of October 9, 2001, a goodly portion of this building collapsed, spilling bricks into the street.

It was designed by H.L. Kerr and built in 1901 for C. Ahi shortly after this block was burned by the Board of Health on January 12, 1900. A hundred years later, in 2004, after much discussion the owners were convinced to reconstruct the historic building instead of demolishing it.

Much of the land around this corner had been owned by C. Ahi, including several wooden tenements in back that housed "yoshiwara women" – Japanese prostitutes. In fact, Pauahi Street had an infamous reputation and was the subject of an exposé in 1896 identifying nearly a dozen houses of "vice and immorality".

Ahi had a furniture store at the corner, and after he died in 1902 the world-famous Fong Inn antique oriental art and furniture store was here from 1903 to 1938.

These photos are of the buildings that were on the corner and along Nu'uanu Street just before they were burned by the Board of Health on January 12, 1900.

In 1894, the building on the right housed the guitar shop of Augusto Dias, one of the three Portuguese luthiers credited with the invention of the ukulele.

On the left, the corner building during the controlled burn.

Fong Inn

Yuen Kwock, also known as Fong Inn, was born in Chung Shan (Zhongshan) District, Kwantung Province, China, in 1873, and came to Hawaii in 1898. He started the Lin Wo Chan import company on Maunakea Street, but it was burned out in 1900. In 1903 he was located at 1152 Nuʻuanu, specializing in koa wood furniture.

He started importing teak furniture and was the first in Honolulu to import fine art objects from China. His customers were among Honolulu's wealthiest, including the Cookes, Judds, Dillinghams, Spaldings, and Damons, and he obtained many Asian treasures for the Honolulu Academy of Arts. He also helped Mrs. Cooke acquire the famous 13th century "Hundred Geese" scroll attributed to painter Ma Fen.

San Francisco's millionaire banker Herbert Fleishhacker once spent well over $10,000 at the House of Fong Inn:

> "Among the articles purchased from Fong Inn, numbering about 75 in all, were several authentic pieces dating back to the Sung Dynasty (960 to 1127 AD), several made during the ascendancy of the Ming Dynasty (1368 to 1644 AD), and one very rare piece from a period about 185 BC."

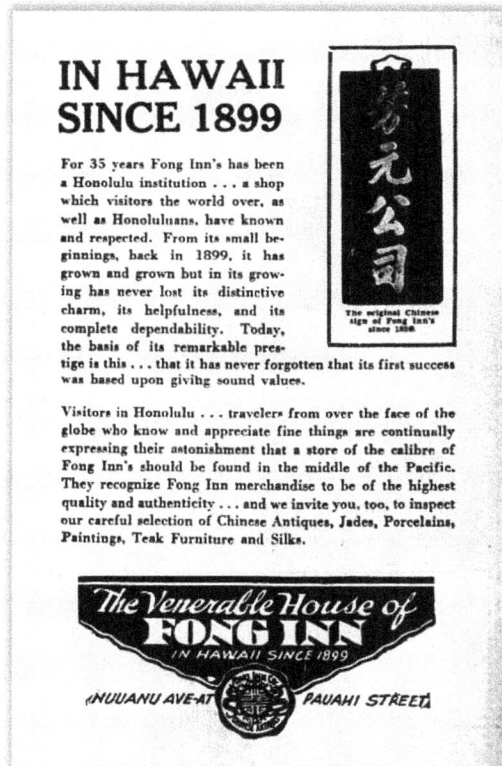

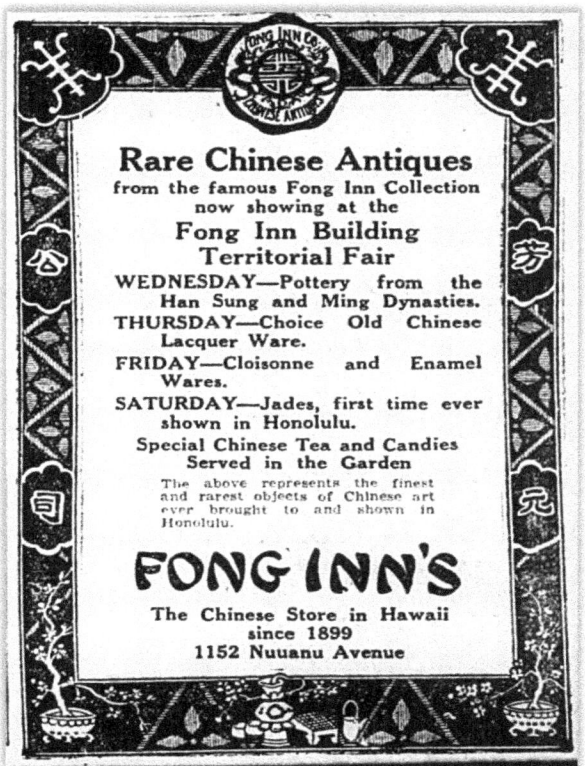

Fong Inn built a new building in Waikiki in 1938 using yellow tile similar to the roof of the Imperial Palace in Beijing. It was designed by architect Roy C. Kelley, who would go on to become the founder and CEO of Outrigger Hotels. That building was demolished in 1989 for the Kyo-Ya Restaurant.

After Fong Inn, it became Jamal's Department Store from 1939 to 1944, owned by the "world-famous linenist" Norman N. Jamal.

They changed the name to Sales Co. of Hawaii in 1946 but that didn't last long, and it became Angus Dunford Ltd, the local dealers for Montgomery Ward in 1947.

Angus Dunford became Tradewell in 1950 when they no longer represented Montgomery Ward, lasting until 1952.

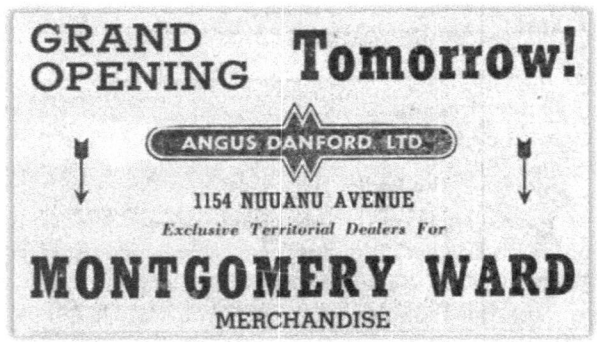

On July 31, 1953, this became the location of the Blue Note after-hours club owned by Eddie Sartain of the Brown Derby.

it was open from 1am to 6am and featured "fine food and crazy entertainment" consisting of blues and rhythm, and female impersonators.

There was a "lit up" sign inside with the words "Blue Note" in blue with a large musical note underneath that flashed on and off – in green.

Nat King Cole's brother, Eddie, performed here in 1954 with the Three Loose Nuts and a Bolt.

But the fun didn't last long – it was up for sale in 1955, subjected to federal tax liens in 1956 and 1957, all fixtures were sold off in 1958, and Eddie Sartain was busted for heroin possession in 1959.

George W. Forbish opened the Volcano Club here in 1959, and a skirmish was reported by the police as "an eruption". In 1962 it became the Four Seas Chop Suey restaurant, serving Hong Kong food with seating for 600 customers.

The next business here in 1983 was the Golden Platter restaurant serving Szechwan and Yanchow Mandarin food.

By 1988 the Health Department was proposing to convert the site into a center for mentally ill street people, but this never happened. The building sat vacant for many years until purchased by Allen Stack Jr. who was renovating it when it partially collapsed.

KIMURA BUILDING

1158-1160 Nuʻuanu
1905
Architect / Builder: Carl On Tai

Carl on Tai took out a building permit for this gray stone building in 1905, housing the S. Kimura liquor warehouse. It was built on the site of the Beehive Saloon, later known as the Louvre Saloon.

Henricus (Henry) Vierra was born in 1828 on the Island of Pico in the Portuguese Azores and came to Hawaii in 1852 on a whaling ship. From 1883 to 1895 he was the owner of the Beehive Saloon. He sold it to W.H. Wolters, formerly of the Pacific Saloon, in 1895, who reopened it as The Louvre. But when this block was burned by the Board of Health on January 12, 1900, it still had the Beehive name on the building.

S. Kimura & Co., a wholesale liquor store owned by Saiji Kimura was here until 1918. It was the Nuʻuanu Florist shop from 1922 to 1933.

It has been a variety of other businesses including the Modern Carpenter Shop (1935), The Lamp Post gift shop (1942), Paradise Amusement Center (1943), a pool hall (1952), AVECO World Travel Services (1970), and the Hawaii Association of Filipino Travel Organizers (1980).

It was also the scene of a prostitution bust in 1951, a morphine bust in 1952, and a huge immigration scam in 1982 that resulted in three people being charged with 71 counts of forging documents.

The building was restored by architect Harold Hallonquist in 1977.

MARKS BUILDING (MARKS GARAGE)

1159 Nuʻuanu
1957
Architect / Builder: Merrill Simms & Roehrig with John J. Gould / Ben Hayashi (contractor)

Marks Central Garage was the first multi-level municipal parking garage in Honolulu and the largest parking garage in Hawaii. It cost over $1M and held more than 400 cars. Mayor Blaisdell cut the opening lei and Miss Hawaii (Sandra Forsythe) rode the first car into the garage.

It was designed in Mid-Century Modern style by John J. Gould, a San Francisco architect and consulting engineer along with local architect Ken Roehrig from Merrill, Simms & Roehrig.

The land had sat vacant for many years after the 1900 fire, but by 1927 it was a parking lot and taxi stand until this garage was built. The property was owned by the McCandless Estate and named after A. Lester Marks, chairman of the estate and son-in-law of L.L. McCandless.

Alfred Lester Marks was a wealthy local politician and territorial land commissioner in the 1940s. He quit his government post over a disagreement with Governor Ingram Stainback who subsequently planned to route the new Pali Highway across land owned by Marks and his wife. This land included the multi-million-dollar historic Clarence Hyde Cooke House designed by Hardie Phillip in 1932, and access to it would be cut off by the new highway.

Marks was unsuccessful in running for governor so he subsequently initiated a seven-year court battle to fight the condemnation of the property. The government ended up buying seven acres of the 17-acre estate for the highway in 1956, including all improvements.

The deal allowed the Markses to continue to live in the mansion for free at first and then later for a mere $500 a month. Twenty years later, 83-year-old Mrs. Marks created a political storm by drastically raising some rents on other property she owned, which led to the state evicting her from the Cooke House.

Before 1900 this side of Nuʻuanu was filled with a variety of 2-story wooden buildings. On the left was the grocery store of Lee Ahlo. He was born in Chong Lok near Canton, China and came to Hawaii in 1865. After working seven years as a cook for Mr. Lewers of Lewers & Cooke, he married Lahela Kauhi Kehuokalani, reportedly a descendant of Kamehameha.

In 1873, L. Ahlo started a small grocery at the corner of Maunakea and King Streets and in 1876 moved it to the corner of Nuʻuanu and Chaplain Lane.

He owned most of the land along this side of the street, and other businesses included a watchmaker, coffee store, tailor, cigar store, photography studio, dry goods, and general merchandise stores.

"Pai kii emi loa" translates to "cheap picture taking or cheap picture developing" for the photography studio upstairs, probably owned by C. Ahi ("Ahi Hale" = "House of Ahi").

The very first plague fire in Chinatown conducted by the Board of Health occurred on this site on December 31, 1899. Hundreds gathered to watch as the infected buildings were doused with kerosene and set on fire while firemen trained water hoses on nearby buildings to contain the blaze.

This photo was taken of the crowd halfway down Pauahi Street watching the scene below on Nuʻuanu Street.

Pauahi Street would later be extended towards downtown, through the Hawaiian lettering in the photograph.

Behind all these wooden buildings along Nuʻuanu was a large coral stone building that was called an "elegant mansion" when first built in 1840 by wealthy English merchant Henry Skinner. Historian Gorham D. Gilman said it was "one of the most pretentious mansions in the town built of coral stone, handsomely joined, with wide verandas facing the beautiful Nuʻuanu Valley".

 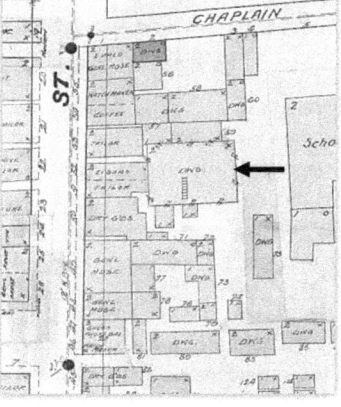

Painting by Paul Emmert, 1854   *Dakin Fire Insurance Map, 1899*

Sometime around 1848 it was purchased by Scottish doctor Robert C. Wyllie. He was the British Consul as well as the Hawaiian government's Minister of Foreign Relations for twenty years, serving under three kings: Kamehameha III, Kamehameha IV, and Kamehameha V.

Robert Crichton Wyllie was born in 1798 in the Hazelbank area of Dunlop parish in East Ayrshire, Scotland, and came to Hawaii in 1844.

As Minister of Foreign Relations he was a huge proponent of Hawaii's national independence and he worked hard to balance the threats from the various world superpowers who had their eyes on Hawaii, especially the United States of America. He negotiated treaties with Denmark, England, France, and the United States that acknowledged Hawaii's independent sovereign status.

When King Kamehameha IV, Queen Emma, and two-year-old Prince Albert visited his plantation on Hanalei Bay on the north shore of Kauaʻi, he renamed it "the Barony of the Prince" (now known as Princeville.). When Wyllie died in 1865, Kamehameha V insisted he be buried in the Royal Mausoleum.

Wyllie was instrumental in creating the Hawaii State Archives. He started collecting documents in 1847 from all the chiefs as well as the commander of the fort. Two of the oldest documents include a letter by Captain Simon Metcalf written in 1790, and a letter by Captain George Vancouver from 1792.

In 1849 Wyllie offered the former Skinner house to Captain Eden and the officers of HMS *Amphitrite* for an extended stay and it acquired the names "Eden Place" and "Eden House".

The *Amphitrite* was a British Navy warship built in Bombay in 1816, with 46 guns on two gundecks and a crew of 284. It is immortalized in the traditional folk song "The Rounding of Cape Horn" also known as "The Gallant Frigate Amphitrite".

Between 1851 and 1862, the house was the location of the French Consulate, led by French Consul Louis-Emile Perrin. He spent a lot of his time apologizing for the abortive French invasion of Honolulu in 1848 by Admiral Louis Tromelin that trashed the fort and mostly just annoyed the general public. One newspaper called it the "French Rumpus".

Between 1863 and 1867 it was the residence of Dr. Charles Fleury Bien-aimé Guillloû. He had served on the USS *Peacock*'s exploration of Antarctica in 1839, the USS *Columbus*' 1845 voyage to Canton (Guangzhou), and the USS *Constitution*'s diplomatic trip to Europe in 1849 where he treated Pope Pius IX for seasickness. He came to Hawaii in 1854 to open a private medical practice.

But by the mid 1880's 2-story wooden buildings filled the yard along the street and the building was used to house Chinese immigrants. One neighbor reported 67 Chinese people coming out of the stone house and estimated at least "150 to 200" people were being housed there.

In 1899 the first floor was being used for storage by Chinese merchant L. Ahlo, with the upper floor used as a dwelling place for "Japanese yoshiwara women" – sex workers.

The building was fumigated at the start of the bubonic plague outbreak and during the controlled burn of the adjacent wooden buildings the Board of Health made valiant attempts to protect it. But it caught fire anyway and the roof collapsed bringing down part of the walls. It was said the contents of this building were worth more than all the other structures facing on Nuʻuanu Street, especially considering the loss of many valuable barrels of sake.

Sketch of "Mr. Skinner's House" and "Dr. Rooke's" (Queen Emma Hall) by Lydia Nye, 1843.
Beretania Street is in the center and the "native church" on the right is the first Kaumakapili Church.

PEGGE HOPPER GALLERY

1162-1164 Nuʻuanu
c.1901-1906
Architect / Builder: unknown

1900

From 1990 to 2021 this was the gallery of internationally acclaimed artist Pegge Hopper. Her pastel paintings of South Seas women have been sold all over the world and several of her large paintings are installed prominently in the Honolulu International Airport.

The building was built sometime between 1901 and 1906 and was designed to accommodate two storefronts.

One of the earliest businesses here was contractor H. Mirikitani from 1912 to 1915.

For over thirty years it was the home of the Sun Lee Tai furniture factory, specializing in custom and imported koa wood furniture at this location from 1922 to 1956. The business was founded by Lum Ting Ling who was born in Canton (Guangdong), China in 1878 and came to Hawaii in 1896 at the age of 18. He opened his first store on King Street between Nuʻuanu and Smith streets in 1907.

This building has seen a lot of different small businesses over the years, including a camera shop, tailor shop, beauty shop, office appliances, auto supply, bakery, clothing store, jewelers, barber shop, and pool room.

When Pegge Hopper was remodeling the store she found a lacquered box full of immigration papers hidden above a door frame.

Before the January 12, 1900 burning of Block 10 there was a 2-story wooden building on the site that housed a furniture business.

HOLT BLOCK / BROWN DERBY (SITE)

1166-1182 Nuʻuanu
(1887-c.1970), (1901-c.1976), 1983
Architect / Builder: George Lucas (1886), unknown (1901), Leonard Takayama (1983) / Dynamic Industries Corporation (1983)

The $12M, 22-story Smith-Beretania Apartments were designed by Leonard Takayama and built by Clarence T.C. Ching's Dynamic Industries Corporation in 1983 for George A. Fan's Smith-Beretania Associates. It is on the site of the Holt Block built in 1887 by George Lucas with brickwork by the Harrison Brothers. Although the People Against Chinatown Evictions (P.A.C.E.) were very supportive of this new high-rise housing project, William A. Grant, the executive director of the Downtown Improvement Association was less than enthusiastic:

> "The architecture is undistinguished and reminiscent of the dark ages of public housing design. The building is an inappropriate addition to Chinatown and a negative factor in the area's renewal. The city should not approve a project of such poor design quality for so prominent a site."

James Robinson, Robert Lawrence, and Robert Holt purchased the land in 1841 and by 1846 it was the site of Israel Wright's paint shop. There were also 3 "well-finished" grass houses on the site. Behind the shop was a large 1-1/2 story house erected by Andrew Auld that was the homestead of the Holt family. It later became the Oregon Eating House, most likely named for the steamship or the state.

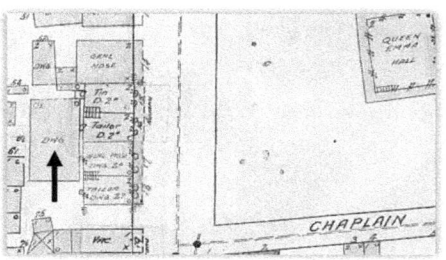

When the Holt Estate decided to trim back the old house in 1886 to make room for the new 2-story brick building they discovered it was a mortise-and-tenon timberframe structure with numbered parts that had been imported from Boston and assembled on site. Unfortunately, it did not survive the Board of Health burning of Block 10 on January 12, 1900.

The Holt Block fared better – they removed the wood flooring, closed the iron shutters tight, and fumigated it with sulfur.

Club Polynesia

From 1943 to 1965, Club Polynesia was located in the Holt Block at 1176 Nuʻuanu Street. It was initially owned by H.K. Hee and A.C. Char.

Herman Fong (Fong Ah Sum), the younger brother of Senator Hiram Fong, bought the business in 1946 and sold it in 1964 to Bill Miller and Genoa Keawe.

Open every day from 11am to 3am, it was famous for Hawaiian food and performers like Keawe, Myrtle K. Hilo, Myra English, Kealoha Kalama, and Linda Dela Cruz, and many performers often came here after gigs elsewhere.

In 1965 the IRS seized the club for non-payment of taxes and auctioned off everything. The sale included all furnishings and fixtures, including 52 tables and 125 chairs, along with the piano and three black velvet paintings.

Aunty Genoa Keawe

A legendary icon in Hawaiian music born in Kakaʻako in 1918, Genoa Leilani Adolpho Keawe-Aiko started out singing in Lāʻie as a member of the Mormon girls' choir, and first sang professionally on the Johnny Almeida radio show. She sang in the traditional Hawaiian haʻiahʻi style and was famous for her high falsetto note in the song "Alika".

Here is a recording of Aunty Genoa Keawe singing "Mauna Loa" and "Alika" along with her sons Eric Keawe, Arthur Keawe, Gary Keawe Aiko, and granddaughter Pomaika'i Keawe.

Her first recordings were on the 49th State Hawaii record label in 1946 and she eventually recorded over 20 albums and more than 150 singles. Aunty Genoa performed 3 shows a night, 6 nights a week at Club Polynesia and was also busy with radio, TV, and studio recordings while being the mother of 12 and grandmother of many more. She loved to sing – "it's not work; it's a pleasure."

She later performed every Thursday night at the Waikiki Beach Marriot Resort & Spa for 14 years. She never quit playing, and in her final days she insisted her children bring her a ukulele so she could play from her hospital bed at age 89.

Mint Saloon / Brown Derby

Before the burning of Block 10 on January 12, 1900, these buildings were immediately makai of the Holt Block and were built sometime before 1891, housing a fruit store and a butcher shop, and Kwong Chan's dressmaking shop in 1900.

After the fire a 1-story building with the decorative arched brick front was built in 1901 that housed the **Mint Saloon** for the next 19 years. It had a reading room at the front and a 40' x 50' main room with a "long highly polished bar" backed by a "large mirror and furnishings that cannot be surpassed by anything in town". There was also a beer garden in the back. And yes, although it sounds really nice, it had its fair share of fights and disturbances too.

This building became the Yee Yap oriental Furniture store from 1922 to 1932, and briefly the Oahu Furniture store before they moved to the Robinson Building at the corner of King and Nuʻuanu streets.

From 1934 to 1942 it was the **Lido Café**, but its most notable occupant was the **Brown Derby** night club from 1946 to 1955. Billing itself as the "House of Jive" where "even the squares jump 'round" it was the premier live jazz music venue in Honolulu.

Under the ownership of Eddie Sartain they had jazz jam sessions every Monday night and also broadcast brief snippets live every night on KPOA radio. Louis Armstrong played here in 1953, and Billie Holiday was booked for an entire week in 1952. Other legendary jazz singers who performed here included Carmen McRae, Dinah Washington, Helen Humes, and Anita O'Day.

In 1959, Sartain was fined $20,000 and sentenced to jail for 20 years for selling heroin – he had imported 2.3 pounds with a street value of $3-4M. The judge said that amount contained "enough death and misery and suffering to people that it could be likened to an atomic bomb". His sentence was commuted by President Lyndon Johnson in 1967. Sartain's son Jesse worked for Walter Cronkite and Frank Sinatra, and became a famous chef who founded Chefs in America and was a "master taster" at the American Tasting Institute.

In Person! DINAH WASHINGTON
Queen of the Juke Boxes nightly at the **Brown Derby**
NO COVER CHARGE
NO MINIMUM
1166 Nuuanu Ave.

EDDIE SARTAIN presents
For A Return Engagement
HELEN HUMES
FROM THE JAZZ HALL OF FAME
As only she can sing them
"LONG JOHN" the dentist
(Honolulu Dentists, don't miss this)
"BE BABA LEBA"
(From the Gal who made it famous)
"LAZZIEST GAL IN TOWN"
"MILLION DOLLAR SECRET"
(Especially to the Ladies)
and her latest releases on
"DOO-Tone"
"Woo Ga Ma Coo Ga," "All I Ask Is Your Love"

Dance To The Q. Martyn Quartet

THE BROWN DERBY
1166 Nuuanu Ave.   Phone 59335

ANNOUNCING
Eddie MANLEY
formerly of Waikiki Tavern
At His New 1947
Electric
Hammond Organ
Playing the tunes you love to hear!
Daily from 5 to 11:30 P.M.

Downtown Honolulu's luncheon and night spot.. where you'll find entertainment in fine MUSIC.. LIQUORS of your choice.. and delectable FOODS

FEATURING
- A Business-Men's Luncheon with SUGAR CURED HAM or BEEF Cold Plate
- REAL ITALIAN SPAGHETTI
- FRENCH DIP SANDWICHES
- HOME-MADE MEXICAN CHILI

LUNCHEONS SERVED—
10:30 a.m. to 8 p.m.
BAR SERVICE—
8 a.m. to 11:30 p.m., daily—12 N. to 11 p.m. Sundays

BROWN DERBY
Formerly LIDO CAFE
1170 Nuuanu Ave.
L. E. Sartain—Ex-Chief-USN

The Brown Derby Presents... LOUIS "Ol Satchmo" ARMSTRONG
appearing with his great band in Honolulu. (Only appearance in this city.)

With him are FAMOUS NAMES
- VELMA MIDDLETON (Vocalist)
- TRUMMY YOUNG (Trombone)
- BARNEY BIGARD (Clarinet)
- KENNY JOHN (Drums)
- BILLY KYLE (Piano)
- MILTON HINTON (Bass)

Cover Charge $2.50 Tax Incl.
New Year's Eve Only $5.00 Tax Incl.
Opening Today, Dec. 30
through January 9 (8 p.m.)
For Reservations Phone 5-9335
1166 Nuuanu Street   The Brown Derby

HARRY the HIPSTER
The Hottest Jazz Pianist-Comedian to hit Hawaii!
EVERY NIGHT
(No Admission Charge)
At The
BROWN DERBY
1166 Nuuanu Ave.

Eddie Sartain Presents
In Person
ANITA O'DAY
plus
- Rampart Streeters
- Anna Maria

Appearing just 3 more nights at the
BROWN DERBY
1166 Nuuanu Ave.   Phone 5-9335
no cover charge   no minimum

Terrific TOMMY NOONAN
and lovely Carol
Take a tip from Buck Buchwach
Don't miss "America's fastest rising young comic."

CARMEN McRAE
Voted "New Vocal Star of '54" by Downbeat.
Metronome named her singer of the year.
You'll listen well and remember long her unusual repertoire of songs.

The Brown Derby
1166 Nuuanu Ave. Ph. 59335

KOKUSAI THEATRE / EMPRESS THEATER

1190 Nu'uanu
1964
Architect / Builder: Merrill Roehrig Onodera & Kinder

In 1964 the large 2-story brick building built on this site by Chew Fong Chong in 1902 was demolished for the new Kokusai Japanese motion picture theatre managed by Mr. & Mrs. Muneo Kimura. It cost over $500,000, had a seating capacity of 850, and featured 70mm widescreen technology from Japan. Daiei Motion Picture Company of Tokyo helped underwrite the costs.

At the time Daiei produced about 54 movies a year including *Rashomon*, *Gate of Hell*, and the first-ever 70mm film *Shaka (Buddha)*. Masaichi Nagata, president of Daiei, and four of their most popular stars (Yasuko Nakada, Jiro Tamiya, Miwa Takada, Shiho Fujimura) attended the grand opening on December 11, 1964, performing on stage before a premiere showing of *Zatoichi Kessho Tabi (Fight, Zatoichi, Fight)*.

Hong Kong moviemaker Run Run Shaw renamed it the Empress Theater in 1973. It became an American movie house in 1986 but closed in 1988 as the last downtown movie house. It has since been converted into a church.

Merril Roehrig Onodera & Kinder also designed the Liberty Bank (1963) and the Neal S. Blaisdell Center (1964).

Views of the same corner on January 12, 1900

HONOLULU CHINATOWN

QUEEN EMMA HALL / YE LIBERTY THEATER (SITE)
Kaopuana, "Kuini Ema Holo"
(1830's-1911)
Architect / Builder: unknown

Although it might look like just another asphalt municipal parking lot, this is the site of a royal palace known to many as Queen Emma Hall, the house built by Dr. Thomas C.B. Rooke in the 1830's.

It faced the Nu'uanu Valley and sat on a 1.5-acre site called Kaopuana, which translates to "Raincloud". It was one of the largest private homes in Honolulu, roughly 50' x 50', with 5,000 square feet on two stories, and was surrounded on all sides by a wide columned veranda.

Dr. T. C. B. Rooke

Thomas Charles Byde Rooke was born in Bengeo, Hertford, England in 1806. He studied medicine at Christ's College Hospital in Hertford and graduated from the Royal College of Surgeons in 1826.

After training at St. Bartholomew's Hospital in London he set sail for the Sandwich Islands on a whaling ship in 1829. Initially landing in Lāhainā, a season later he arrived in Honolulu where he was asked to stay and practice medicine.

In 1830 he married Grace Kamaʻikuʻi Young, daughter of Kamehameha advisor John Young and widow of Keʻeaumoku (brother of Queen Regent Kaʻahumanu).

The Rookes had no children of their own, but they informally adopted the newly born child of Grace's sister, Emma, who became their *hānai* daughter in the Hawaiian tradition.

The family lived upstairs while the downstairs was used for his medical practice, dispensary, and library. He played a very active role in the education of young Emma and he instilled in her a love of learning through spending many hours in his personal library.

Dr. Rooke was the physician to King Kamehameha and was one of ten physicians in Honolulu who signed the charter for the Hawaiian Medical Society in 1856. He was the first chairman of the Board of Health and he campaigned and wrote articles in the newspaper advocating for the establishment of a hospital for Native Hawaiians.

Although he didn't live to see it happen, his daughter Emma took up the torch and later created the Queen's Hospital, known today as the prestigious Queen's Medical Center. Dr. Rooke's medical instruments were a major donation that helped get the hospital started.

From 1851 to 1855 Dr. Rooke served as a representative to the Hawaiian Kingdom legislature and was appointed to the Privy Council in 1858.

Keenly interested in science, Dr. Rooke studied meteorology and was one of the pioneers in the cultivation of coffee. He helped organize the Royal Hawaiian Agricultural Society in 1850.

He was a long-time friend of Hawaiian royalty and his adopted daughter Emma became Queen Consort when she married Alexander Liholiho (Kamehameha IV) in 1856.

A popular and beloved local doctor and scholar, Dr. Rooke passed away in 1858 at age 52 and was initially buried on the grounds of the Iolani Palace. His remains were later moved to the Royal Mausoleum where he is one of only four Europeans that have been allowed to be buried there

Emma Kalanikaumaka'amano Kaleleonālani Na'ea Rooke

Known as Queen Emma, she was born in 1836 to High Chief George Na'ea and High Chiefess Fanny Kekelaokalani Young, the daughter of King Kamehameha advisor John Young. She was a descendant of Kamehameha I's first cousin and was sometimes called Emalani.

As the *hānai* daughter of the Rookes she grew up in the big house and was educated in the Royal School established by American missionaries. She spoke both Hawaiian and English "with a perfect English accent" no doubt learned from her very British father. She was encouraged to read from Rooke's extensive library and was an accomplished singer, pianist, dancer, and equestrian.

In 1856, when she was 20 years old, she married Alexander Liholiho whom she had known since childhood. Alexander just happened to be King of Hawaii – he had become Kamehameha IV the year before – making her Queen Emma.

She was known for her humanitarian efforts and in 1859 she established Queen's Hospital to help Native Hawaiians. She also founded St. Andrew's Priory School for Girls.

Queen Victoria of England agreed to be godmother to their son in 1862 and sent a large silver christening cup, but before it arrived 4-year-old Prince Albert became sick and died. The following year King Kamehameha IV (Liholiho) suddenly died. To assuage her grief, Emma went on a long tour of Europe where she met with Queen Victoria and many other European royals and foreign dignitaries like Emperor Napoleon III.

She and Queen Victoria became good friends and wrote often, both having the shared history of lost sons and spouses.

In America she met with President Andrew Johnson and was the first queen of any country to visit the White House. She cut her trip short upon hearing of the death of her *hānai* mother, Grace Rooke.

After William Charles Lunalilo died in 1874, she decided to become a candidate for the throne in a hotly contested election against David Kalākaua in the 1874 royal election, claiming Lunalilo had wanted her to succeed him. She was pro-British and also pro-Native Hawaiian.

Although she was supported by the people, the Legislative Assembly voted to install Kalākaua as King. This caused her supporters, known as Emmaites or Queenites, to riot. Thirteen people were injured with one later dying, and both American and British troops were called in from warships in the harbor to quell the revolt.

Queen Emma retired from public life afterwards and although King Kalākaua always left a vacant chair for her she rarely attended any events, and she refused to speak to Queen Kapi'olani.

The "Old Queen" passed away in 1885, and the Queen Emma Foundation was established to provide income for the hospital. The Queen Emma Land Company currently has over $650 million in assets.

Rooke House / Queen Emma Hall

The large 2-story house was built in the middle of the block in the 1830s and had a wide veranda on all sides. One visitor remarked that it was "the most English-looking house I have seen since I left home, except Bishopscourt at Melbourne".

The first floor contained Dr. Rooke's clinic and dispensary, his library, and a large room for entertaining guests. Upstairs were the family quarters with koa wood trim, red Kashmir carpets, mahogany and dark oak furniture, and framed oil paintings.

The Rookes were known throughout Honolulu for their hospitality and the house was the scene of many fancy dinners, receptions, and parties. It was also the gathering place in 1874 for those supporting Queen Emma's claim to the throne.

In 1887 the trustees of the Queen Emma Estate fixed the house up for a Reading Room, Social Hall, and Classrooms for Hawaiians, naming the facility "Queen Emma Hall". The Hawaiian Branch of the YMCA was one of the first to rent the hall, followed by the Kindergarten Association. In 1901 the Francis Murphy Temperance Club remodeled it to have a concert hall, reading room, dining room, billiard parlor, offices, and a fancy saloon that sold no intoxicating liquors.

By 1904 the house had been turned into cheap apartments for Japanese workers and the grounds were occupied by two Japanese contractors who used it to store firewood, lumber, and other building materials.

The *Pacific Commercial Advertiser* opined:

> *There is no evidence of royalty there now. Instead there are huge piles of wood, lumber, many drays, rock ballast and in fact a varied assortment of belongings of a sort of small Japanese village. The former halls of royalty are occupied by a Japanese doctor, a Japanese boarding establishment and are the headquarters of several small Japanese enterprises. Most of the koa finishing in the interior has been removed. The whole place presents an air of a haunted house. A small coral building, once Queen Emma's cookhouse, is now used by a Japanese horseshoer.*

QUEEN EMMA'S FORMER PALACE.

The *Hawaiian Star* in 1907 described Queen Emma Hall as: "that ancient and historic frame pile set far back from the road and surrounded by rubbish".

When the Mission Houses on King Street near Kawaiahaʻo Church were being restored in 1907 there were questions as to why Queen Emma Hall was not getting the same treatment, but the Rooke heirs did nothing. Things only got worse – a Japanese gambling joint was raided at the hall in 1909, and by 1910 most of the trees had been cut down and the flower beds were buried under piles of lumber.

"The passing of the old Queen Emma palace is a thing to regret, but whatever is done with the site will be a relief from the eyesore made of it by Japanese tenants." – Hawaiian Star, 1911

Liberty Theatre

After Queen Emma Hall was demolished in 1911 it was replaced with the Ye Liberty Theatre designed by A.P. McDonald. Later called the Liberty Theatre, it had 1,600 seats, murals by Hawaiian artist Lionel Walden, and was the largest theater in Honolulu.

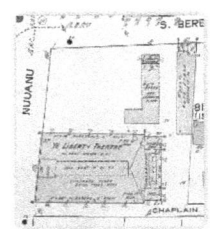

It was built of brick and concrete with a 70-ton structural steel roof that did not require any posts or columns, so every seat had a clear view. Music was provided by a large pipe organ.

Grand opening day was February 22, 1912, and initially it featured a wide variety of performances including vaudeville acts, musical comedy, operatic quartettes, moving pictures, a Portuguese violinist, and a traveling troupe of trained lions and leopards. The world-renowned contralto Dame Clara Butt performed here, and Chinese Opera mega-star Mei Lan-Fang, "China's greatest actor in 400 years" and "the idol of 500,000,000 people", created a local sensation doing 8 shows in one week in 1930 that broke all box office records in the territory.

It was part of the new Consolidated Amusement Company, now known as Consolidated Theaters. The president of Ye Liberty Theatre Company was Goo Tai Chong who also worked at First America Savings and Trust. He mysteriously disappeared one day in 1912, was accused of embezzling $50,000, and was tracked down in Yokohama by the Honolulu Chief of Detectives. He said he stole the money to invest in moving picture films, but he was also a known gambler.

Convinced by a local stock company producer that "talkies" were merely a fad, the Consolidated Amusements Company commissioned a massive $70,000 renovation in 1929 that was hailed as a "triumph of artistry". It was designed by local architect Louis Davis who was also the designer for the Princess, Pawaa, and Palama Theaters.

The New Liberty Theater had only 796 seats, no balcony, a larger stage and orchestra pit, more dressing rooms, and a Moorish design on the ceiling. The lobby featured the largest lighting fixture ever constructed in Hawaii.

But by the 1950's it was showing first-run war movies as well as films like *Creature from the Black Lagoon in 3D*. In 1965 it was leased to show Chinese movies like *Spring Blossoms*, *The Swordmates*, *Princess Iron Fan*, and *The Invisible Fist*. By the end of the 1970's it was showing Japanese erotic films like *Mesu Neko no Yorokobi (Ecstasy)* and *Akujo (Bad Girl)*.

The Liberty closed in 1986 and was demolished in 1990 along with an adjoining Chevron gas station. The site was turned into a "temporary" 97-car parking lot that is still there today, over 30 years later.

THE COMMERCIAL HOTEL (SITE)

(1846-1903)

In 1975 the 35-story twin-tower 908-unit apartments called Kukui Plaza were developed by Oceanside Properties Inc., as part of the city's Block G Kukui Redevelopment Project, designed by Daniel Mann Johnson & Mendenhall.

In the early 1840's this was the absolute edge of town – there was nothing further up Nuʻuanu Street other than a few scattered houses, many of them made of grass.

Scotsman Henry MacFarlane was on his way to California from New Zealand in 1846 on his own ship with his new bride, Eliza, but when she needed medical attention they stopped in Honolulu.

He was surprised to meet his fellow countryman Dr. Rooke and consequently they decided to stay. He briefly partnered with J.O. Carter in the Mansion House at Beretania and Garden Lane, and built the Commercial Hotel in 1847 at the distant intersection of two dirt streets called Nuʻuanu and Beretania.

Drawing by Paul Emmert, 1854

The land was originally bought by Honaunau from King Kamehameha III in 1835. He built a 2-story adobe building with veranda which he leased to MacFarlane and which his estate sold to him for $3,500 in 1854.

MacFarlane expanded and built a new section in front and the Commercial Hotel became one of the finest establishments in Honolulu, a favorite of whaling captains and visiting officers and dignitaries.

The café and dining rooms were on the first floor with sleeping rooms above plus a billiard room and a bowling alley. It opened in January 1846. There were stables adjoining where guests could obtain horses.

> "It was the custom of a quartet of whaling captains to purchase a barrel of bottles of beer, roll the barrel into the bowling alley and there roll ten pins until the question of who should pay the chit was settled."

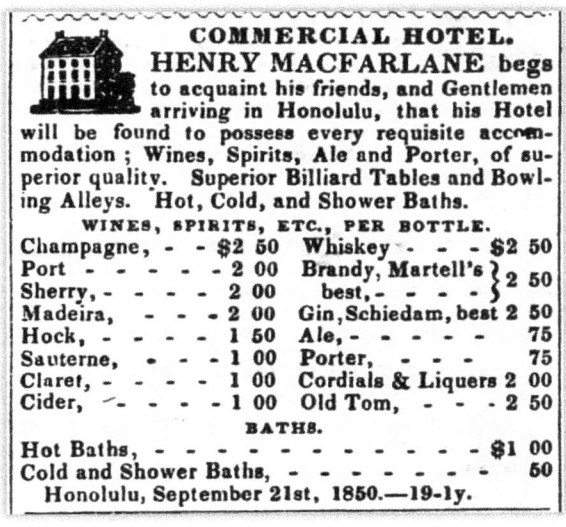

HONOLULU CHINATOWN

Macfarlane was the first to bring gas lighting to Hawaii. In 1858 he brought in a special apparatus from California and used it to light up his billiard table to everyone's great amazement. That same year he also launched several unmanned illuminated balloons, including one that was 28 feet in diameter.

The Commercial Hotel was one of the first to advertise hot and cold water for baths and showers.

The MacFarlanes had a home in Waikiki at a place called Kaluaokau where Eliza planted the large Indian banyan tree that is now surrounded by the International Marketplace.

After Henry MacFarlane passed away in 1860 the hotel was managed by James S. Lemon and was later purchased by Jim Welch in 1886 who refurbished the reading and billiard parlors and offered 12½-cent beer with hot lunches.

This is the only known photograph of the Commercial Hotel, taken in 1903 just before it was demolished.

The S.M. Iida store was built on this corner in 1912. Suisan Matsukichi Iida came to Honolulu in 1896 from Osaka and initially opened a store on Maunakea Street in 1900 selling Japanese goods and novelties. This building was built in 1912, probably by contractor George Yamada who was heavily advertising "concrete buildings" at the time.

Iida's son Koichi, who was later president of Central Pacific Bank, managed the store after his father died and he opened a branch in the new Ala Moana Mall in 1959. The old building was demolished in 1969 as part of the Kukui Redevelopment Urban Renewal Project.

The intersection at Nuʻuanu and Beretania had the first traffic light in Honolulu, installed February 19, 1936.

HONOLULU PARK PLACE

1212 Nuʻuanu
1990
Architect / Builder: Norman Lacayo / Charles Pankow Builders Ltd

This 40-story, 437-unit condominium was built by CAP Development as part of the large-scale urban redevelopment of the entire block. The Kukui Redevelopment Project had earmarked this site to be a park, but the developer threw some extra money at the city and was able to build a 40-story residential tower instead.

Called Honolulu Park Place Condominium, it was designed by Lacayo Architects and built by high-rise specialists Charles Pankow Builders Ltd.

It was the first luxury condo in Honolulu to feature extensive recreational facilities like air-conditioned squash and racquetball courts, a full-sized 2-lane bowling alley, and a 2-story fitness room with aerobic equipment, Nautilus exercise machines, men's and women's lockers, a thermal spa with travertine decking, and a 28' x 60' outdoor pool with "European water jets".

Outdoor features also included a koi pond, picnic tables, tennis court, putting green and a driving range (into nets).

As early as 1881 the Hop Hing grocery store was previously on this corner. The twin spires of the 1888 Kaumakapili Church are just a little farther down Beretania Street on the left in the photo.

On the far right is the former Engine House No.4 built on Nuʻuanu Street in 1861 for Fire Company No.4 which was composed of Native Hawaiians with William Webster as their foreman.

In 1896 the old engine house became a Japanese theater operated by a group of local musicians. The first performance was an opera that was "a combination of tragedy and comedy, with inspiring music".

Everything on this corner and the entire block was burned on January 20, 1900, when the plague fire deliberately set just behind these buildings got out of control and resulted in the disastrous 1900 Chinatown Fire.

Chinese contractor Pang Chong built this building in 1902 using bricks and mortar from the ruined Kaumakapili Church. But it was done without a permit and when the wall of a brick building he was building nearby fell down into Nuʻuanu Street it caused enough of an uproar to create the first Building Inspector office in Honolulu.

Architect Charles W. Dickey was consequently employed by the city to oversee Pang Chong's work to make sure this building was safe.

From 1902 to 1918 it was the store of S. Shiraki who sold hardware and also did house painting and wallpapering.

The building and business were purchased by B.K. Yamamoto from Mr. Shiraki (his former employer) in 1918 and it was renamed the B.K. Yamamoto Hardware Store.

In 1938 Harry Yamamoto hired local Japanese architect Hector Fuchino to design this replacement building in the Art Moderne Style, built by contractor Y. Aoki.

By 1960 the building was on the city's hit list for potential "slum clearances" and it disappears completely from the newspaper record after October 1961.

Kumanosuke "B. K." Yamamoto

A survivor of the 1906 San Francisco earthquake, Kumanosuke "Brown" K. Yamamoto was born in Yamaguchi-ken, Japan in 1880. He immigrated to San Francisco in 1902 and after two years in the Mission school he opened a furniture store on Eddy Street. Left penniless after the earthquake, friends helped him secure passage on a steamer to Hawaii in 1906.

He opened a cabinet shop on Nuʻuanu Street in 1910, and then worked for and managed the S. Shiraki store on the corner of Nuʻuanu and Beretania streets, eventually buying the business and renaming it B.K. Yamamoto Hardware.

Yamamoto was president of the Japanese Merchants Association, working his way up from director to auditor to treasurer and vice-president. He was also treasurer of the Honolulu Trust Company and was active in the Hawaii Japanese Society. He died of illness in 1932 at age 52 and his son Harry took over the family business and built the new building in 1938.

PAUAHI STREET

Hawaiian for "end of the fire" since it was close to the northern extents of the 1886 fire. Or maybe for Bernice Pauahi Bishop. Or perhaps even a reference to Pa Uhi, the giant yam field that used to be between Nuʻuanu, Beretania, Alakea, and King streets?

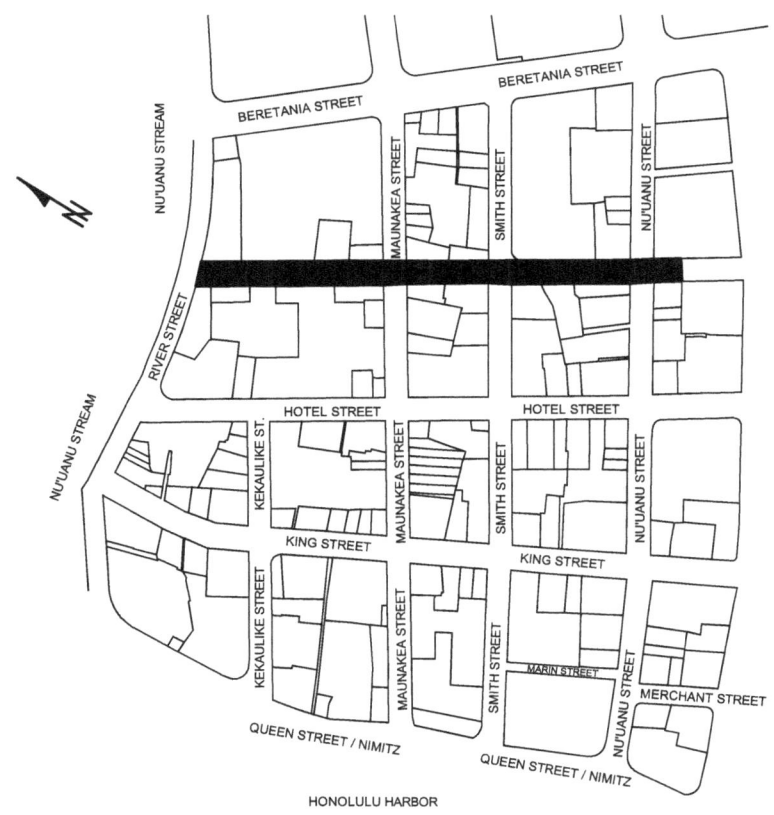

L.L. MCCANDLESS BLOCK

1 N. Pauahi
1910
Architect / Builder: H.L. Kerr / unknown

This 3-story building was designed by H.L Kerr and built in 1910 on the site of a 2-story wooden building built in 1885 that was burned by the Board of Health on January 19, 1900. That building had a tailor shop on the downstairs corner and the Chinese lettering ("Discount Pictures") indicates there was a photo studio on the second floor.

The new building was built for local developer and politician Lincoln L. McCandless and was the first concrete building in Chinatown. It was renovated in 1985 by McCandless descendent Tina Stack.

The uppers floors were originally a boarding house for single men with retail stores on the ground floor. By April of 1911 it was the office and printshop of *The Record* published by Edmund Norrie. A review of the first edition noted "here and there are characteristic 'Norrieisms', such as used to make the *Holomua* and the *Independent* unique in Honolulu journalism". Norrie was an unfiltered firebrand who had previously been sued, fined, and imprisoned during the overthrow of the monarchy.

Lincoln Loy McCandless was born in Indiana, Pennsylvania in 1859 and moved to Hawaii in 1882. He was the brother of James and John McCandless who were the first to drill artesian wells (over 600) throughout Hawaii. Lincoln was also involved in ranching and politics and was elected to the legislature in 1898 and the US Congress in 1932.

In support of his political aspirations in 1912, George Kelii composed a Hawaiian mele in "Linekona's" honor and "for the well-being of Hawaii".

"Lincoln is the Morning Star, The shining lantern, Appointed by you, O Heavenly Powers, Assisted by the Trinity…Heard across the Islands, Here is the one who will save the Lahui, The eagle will make right, The Equal Rights of the land. Let the story be told, Lincoln the Representative for the Well-Being of Hawaii.."

BILTRIGHT SHOE REPAIR

10 N. Pauahi
1952?
Architect / Builder: unknown

In 1952 this was the location of the Biltright Shoe Repair Shop owned by Roland W. Chai.

Carlos Navarrete from Mexico City came to Hawaii on a tour in 1984 and having met a friend here in the shoe repair business he returned a year later and bought the Biltright Shoe Repair business.

The building previously on the site was built sometime before 1891 and housed a fruit shop, barber, and tailor shop. It was burned by the Board of Health along with the rest of Block 10 on January 12, 1900.

WING COFFEE COMPANY

31 N. Pauahi
1917
Architect / Builder: Ripley & Davis / Hawaiian Ballasting Company

This building was built in 1917 and was originally the delivery and motor pool area for Love's Biscuit & Bread Company. In 1947 it became the new location for the Wing Hing Company offices and wholesale department for grocery and fruits, moving from their former place around the corner at 1153 Smith Street.

The Wing Hing Company was founded in 1904 by Chong Sum Wing. They imported groceries and fresh fruits from the mainland and roasted coffee from Kona. They pioneered vacuum packing for coffee.

In 1922 they officially created the Wing Coffee Company and purchased the Takakura coffee mill at Captain Cook in Kealakekua, Kona, Hawaii.

They were the first in the Hawaii coffee industry to feature Diamond Head, hula girls, surfers and volcanoes in their advertising. They were also the first to make Aloha Gift Boxes labeled "Greetings from Paradise" and "Aloha from Hawaii".

They did their coffee roasting and grinding on the second floor and produced over 20,000 sacks of coffee in 1931. They were in this location from 1947 to 1998 – over fifty years.

Chong Sum Wing was born in Guangzhou (Canton), China in 1885 and came to Hawaii in 1897 at the age of 13. His first business was running a cold drink concession at the Territorial Market on Alakea Street.

In 1903 he bought the Hong Kee Fruit Store on Nuʻuanu Street which he sold a year later to purchase the Wing Sang company with his cousin and a friend, changing the name to Wing Hing (translated as "forever prosperous").

Initially specializing in groceries and fresh fruits from the US mainland, he became known as the "King of Coffee" with agents in San Francisco, Los Angeles, Sacramento, Manila, Shanghai, and Hong Kong.

During the Great Depression he purchased the mansion of the McCandless estate and used it for many Wing Coffee events.

This 2-story dwelling built between 1886 and 1891 was previously on the site until this part of Block 11 was burned by the Board of Health on January 19, 1900.

WANG BUILDING

51-79 N. Pauahi (1134-1150 Maunakea)
1997
Architect / Builder: James K. Tsugawa / S&M Sakamoto

This building was built in 1997 for Dr. Ching I. Wang and Hai Tou Pan, and was designed by James K. Tsugawa, the architect who also designed the Maunakea Marketplace.

Shortly after the 1900 fire a large 2-story wooden tenement block was built along the entire block face of Pauahi Street with storefronts on the first floor and dwellings above.

One of the shops was raided in 1952 and 12 people were arrested for illegal mah jongg gambling.

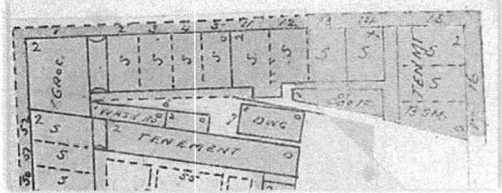

1906

Between 1920 and 1961 there was a 1-story stone building on the left side that was the Wah Yip Grocery, a watch repair shop, a barber shop, a pool hall, and an unofficial gambling joint raided for Pai Kow games.

In 1899 there was a large 2-story wooden building on the site with a soda shop on the corner and horseshoeing parlor next to it on Smith Street.

In 1891 there was a barber shop on the corner and a blacksmith shop on Pauahi Street, and in 1885 there were several small 1-story houses on this site that would have burned in the 1886 fire.

1900

CHAR HUNG SUT

62-66 N. Pauahi
1963
Architect / Builder: unknown

Founded in 1946, this is the long-time location for the most famous manapua shop in Honolulu – Char Hung Sut. Their specialty is a steamed bun filled with pork, called "char siu bao" in Chinese. The word *manapua* comes from the Hawaiaian phrase *mea 'ono pua'a* which translates to "bun delicious pork". A box of manapuas from Char Hung Sut quickly became the standard gift taken to neighbor islands when visiting business associates and family.

Founded by Bat Moi Kam Mau and Kim Tow Ho in 1946, it started out as a very popular full-service restaurant called Char Hung Sut Chop Suey.

Bat Moi Kam Mau was born in Yin Jai Boo village in Chungshan, China, and came to Hawaii when she was 15. Initially working on the family farm raising ducks and children, she worked at the Dole Cannery during World War II. She started work every day at the restaurant at 2 a.m. preparing the dim sum ingredients, and opened the restaurant before dawn every day of the week.

They temporarily closed for four months in 1963 to construct the current building, and in recent years they have only sold manapuas to-go out of the first floor "factory".

The building previously on the site was built between 1901 and 1906, was wooden, 2-stories with six shops, and housed a coppersmith, a bicycle shop, the Hawaii Carpenter Shop (1938) and two restaurants before Char Hung Sut: Shanghai Bill's Barnyard Café (1945) and Chix Tavern (1946).

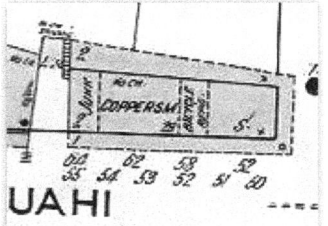

Before the 1900 fire the building on the site housed a coffin shop. It replaced a couple of 2-story houses that were burned at the edge of the 1886 fire.

PAUAHI HALE

120-128 N. Pauahi
1963 / 1981 renovation
Architect / Builder: unknown (1963), Park Associates (1981) / K. Nagata Construction (1981)

1906

Pauahi Hale was built in 1963 and advertised as "single rooms for men" for only $49.50 per month, furnished. It replaced a 2-story wooden building built between 1901 and 1906 that had 3 stores on the first floor and residences above, plus an opening leading to more tenements in back.

This building was renovated in 1981 by Park Associates and K. Nagata Construction, which is presumably when the gabled parapet was added on top. This was done to many other buildings in Chinatown about this same time in an attempt to make the newer buildings fit in better with the older ones.

Before the fire on January 20, 1900, this 2-story wooden dwelling was on the site, built between 1891 and 1899. The land was vacant in 1885 and 1891.

GUM CHEW LAU BUILDING (SITE)

137 N. Pauahi
(c.1903-1979)
Architect / Builder: unknown

This was the site of the Gum Chew Lau Noodle Factory who moved here in 1953 from 1232 Kamanuwai Lane. It was founded in 1948 by Hong Kong native Gum Chew Lau and his wife Eunice Y.O. Kong.

He had always dreamed of becoming a chef and started out as a second cook at the Waikiki Lau Yee Chai restaurant and later at the Pearl Harbor Naval Hospital. During World War II he worked as a carpenter at Hickam AFB and afterwards opened a small fountain and grocery business and restaurant until 1948.

Before opening the noodle factory Gum Chew Lau traveled to Japan, Hong Kong, Macao, New York, San Francisco, Canada, and Mexico to study other factories and meet with machine shops. By 1953 he had 9 employees and sold noodles wholesale and retail to caterers, schools, restaurants, and supermarkets.

An old man gave him a 500-year-old coin for good luck when he first opened and that coin became a featured image in his branding.

Gum Chew Lau moved across the street to 138 N. Pauahi in 1967 and this building later became the office of the powerful grassroots organization People Against Chinatown Evictions (P.A.C.E.). In spite of their protests it was demolished by the city in 1979.

At the time it was one of the last remaining wooden buildings in Chinatown that had been built immediately after the 1900 fire.

PAUAHI KUPUNA HALE

167 N. Pauahi
1986
Architect / Builder: Kajioka Okada & Partners / Dynamic Industries Corporation

This 48-unit senior housing apartment building was designed by Kajioka Okada & Partners and built in 1986 by Clarence T.C. Ching's Dynamic Industries Corporation for the Retirement Housing Foundation and the Hawaii Conference of the United Church of Christ at a cost of $27M.

It is on the site of the Asahi Service Station, and before that, the River Planing Mill built shortly after the 1900 fire.

The River Mill Company was owned by Chang Chan and sixteen Chinese partners. Their specialties were contracting, building, painting, repairing, house materials, and furniture. It was destroyed by arson on August 18, 1902 but was quickly rebuilt. They undoubtedly provided much of the materials for the rebuilding of Chinatown after the 1900 fire. In 1914 the River Mill Company won the bid for the $118,939 six-building extension of the Fort Shafter hospital by a margin of only $32.

Chang Chan advertised as an architect in 1912, perhaps the first Chinese architect in Honolulu? He left the management of the firm in 1916 to concentrate on general contracting and designing and building houses and apartments.

By 1927 the planing mill building was being used for automobile repairs and sign printing. It was demolished in 1952 for the expansion of the Asahi Service Station which provided automobile repairs here for 45 years.

Before 1900 there was a Chinese joss house (temple) here plus other wooden dwellings that were burned by the Board of Health on January 4, 1900.

PAUAHI RECREATION CENTER

171 N. Pauahi
1987
Architect / Builder: Kajioka Okada & Partners / THOHT Construction Inc.

Before 1891 this site was on the edge of the Nuʻuanu Stream that was later straightened and channelized in 1896. There were a couple of 2-story wooden dwellings here when the 1900 fire struck the area, most likely housing Chinese immigrants.

After the fire this side of the street was lined with a long wooden 2-story block of shops and tenements with the River Planing Mill located directly behind from 1901 to 1925. It was later the site of the gas station for the Asahi Service Station facility.

The current building was designed by Kajioka Okada & Partners, the architects who designed the larger Hale Pauahi project across the street, and it was built by THOHT Construction founded by Henry Fusao Horii.

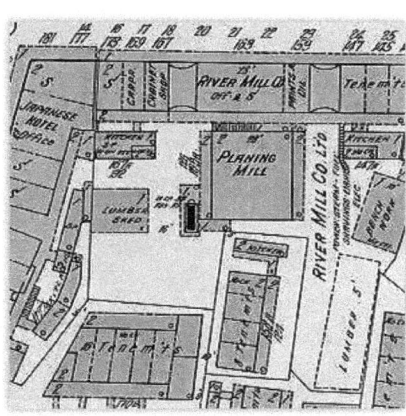

1914

RIVER STREET

Adjacent to Nuʻuanu Stream, River Street was constructed on reclaimed land after the extensive dredging and straightening of the waterway in 1896/1897.

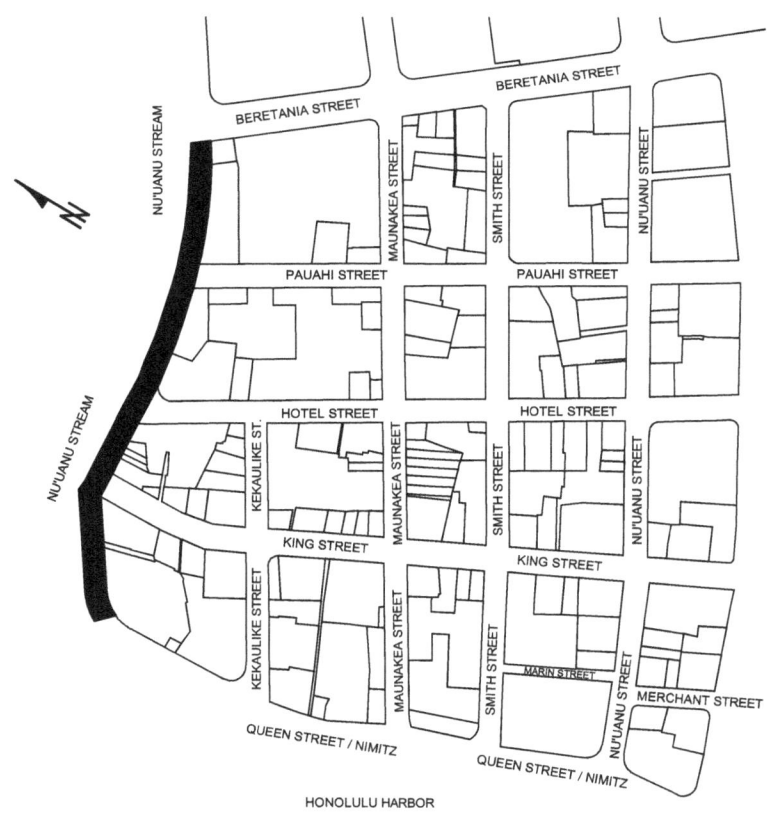

HARBOR VILLAGE APARTMENTS

901 River
1991
Architect / Builder: Stringer Tusher & Associates, Daniel Mann Johnson & Mendenhall / Hawaiian Dredging & Construction Company

This site was once a hive of boat-building activity, housing the Inter-Island Steam Navigation Company wharves and boat repair workshops along with a large boat-making shed and iron warehouse, separated from the rest of the block by a long 8' high concrete sea wall.

The land was mostly vacant before 1906 since it was low and muddy and subject to flooding at the confluence of Nuʻuanu Stream and Honolulu Harbor. When their lease expired in 1914 the Inter-Island shops moved to a larger location and the land became vacant again until a large sewer pump station was built here in 1928. The River and Queen Street Pump Station was built of reinforced concrete and had a large 40' x 50' foot pit 30' below sea level.

In 1987 the city decided to use the site for a new affordable housing project, 25 stories high with 144 studio and 1-bedroom units to cost $12M, but the project was scaled back due to opposition from neighbors and preservationists claiming the initial plan was incompatible with the Chinatown Special Design District.

The revamped plan resulted in a stepped back terrace design for a 6-story, 90-unit rental apartment tower with 9,000 square feet of 2-story commercial and a 5-level parking for 184 cars. Construction began in 1989 and the first model unit opened in May 1991.

Architect **David Stringer** was born in the charity ward of the Los Angeles County Hospital in 1933 and obtained his architectural degree at the University of Southern California. He was hired by the Kaiser organization in 1967 to design an office building and subsequently moved to Honolulu. He won many awards for projects like the Kapiolani Park Bandstand, 1100 Alakea Street, The Mauna Luan, and the restoration of the Punahou School President's House. He was also the Commissioner of Culture and the Arts for the City and County of Honolulu.

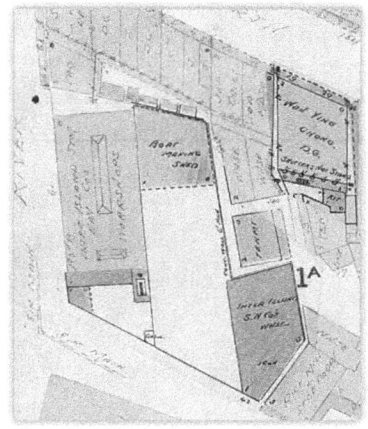

Mauka from Queen (Nimitz) Street in 1900   *1906 Dakin Fire Insurance Map*

The Inter-Island Steam Navigation Company

Headquartered in Honolulu, the Inter-Island Steam Navigation Company provided passenger and cargo service between Honolulu and the neighboring Hawaiian Islands from 1883 to 1947. It was founded by shipbuilder Thomas R. Foster who came to Hawaii from Canada in 1857, worked at the John Robinson shipyard, and married Robinson's daughter Mary in 1861.

In 1905 they bought out the Wilder Steamship Company and became the largest provider of inter-island passenger and freight service. They built the Kona Inn, designed by William Dickey, in 1928 to promote travel to the Big Island and to provide hotel accommodations for their passengers.

James A. Kennedy was president between 1902 and 1926, and due to his son's experience in flying Curtiss H-16 flyingboat aircraft in World War I, he convinced the Board of Directors to expand their business into aviation. The first fleet consisted of one Bellanca monoplane and two 8-passenger Sikorsky S-38 amphibious airplanes. In 1941, Inter-Island Airways was officially renamed "Hawaiian Airlines" and they currently carry over 10 million passengers per year.

Since air service reduced the travel time to the Big Island from 14 hours down to an hour and a half, they halted the steamship side of their operations in 1947.

The T.R. Foster Building at 902 Nuʻuanu was erected by the company in Foster's memory shortly after his death at age 54 in 1889. He had previously bought German botanist Dr. William Hillebrand's house and gardens, and his wife willed the property to the city in 1930 to be named "Foster Botanical Garden".

KOMEYA APARTMENTS

1079-1149 River / 175 N. Pauahi
1970
Architect / Builder: Ernest Hara? / Hirano Brothers

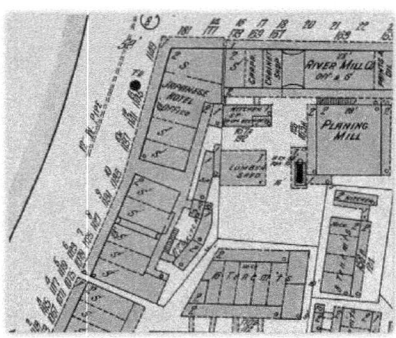

Before 1896 this location was in the middle of Nuʻuanu Stream, which was rerouted in 1896 in a massive public works project to remove mud flats and minimize flooding. By 1899 there was a general merchandise store on the corner and a long 2-story wooden dwelling building on the newly reclaimed land. Both burned in the 1900 fire.

In 1902 the big Winston Block fire burned down the brand-new Ah Seu building on the corner and immediately afterwards he built a 2-story wooden hotel here with 24 rooms and 7 stores for Miyozuchi Komeya, known as the Komeya Hotel. In 1909, the four leading Japanese hotels were the Kawasaki, the Komeya, the Yamashiro, and the Kobayashi.

From 1906 to 1925 the No. 1 Postoffice Station on River Street was located in the Komeya Hotel.

On February 26, 1968, a fire of unknown origin began at the base of the stairwell and proceeded to burn out all 24 rooms with significant damage to The Barber Shop, Yonemoto Gift Shop, Dry Goods Center, Komeya Travel Service, U. Ogata Jewelers, and Riverside Tailor Shop.

The building was replaced by the concrete Komeya Apartments in 1970 built by Hirano Brothers Ltd, one of the top 400 construction firms in the US. They usually worked with Ernest Hara, so he was very likely the architect.

Myozuchi Komeya was born in Yamaguchi, Japan, in 1867 and arrived in Hawaii in 1888, spending time in Maui and the Big Island before coming to Honolulu and opening a store on Smith Street. He opened his first hotel in 1896 which burned in 1900. In 1909 he was instrumental in helping set up The Japanese Bank at the Mendonça Building at Smith and Hotel streets and was one of its first managers.

He was also a member of the Japanese Hotel Keepers' Association and one of the directors of the Honolulu Sake Brewery Company. His grandson James was assistant manager of the Halekulani Hotel, and he later managed the Ilima Hotel, the Waikiki Resort Hotel, Aloha Surf Hotel, and Waiakea Village in Hilo.

The Komeya Hotel (1902-1968)

(The Japanese characters, right to left: "Kome-Ya Ryo-Kan" – Komeya Inn for travelers)

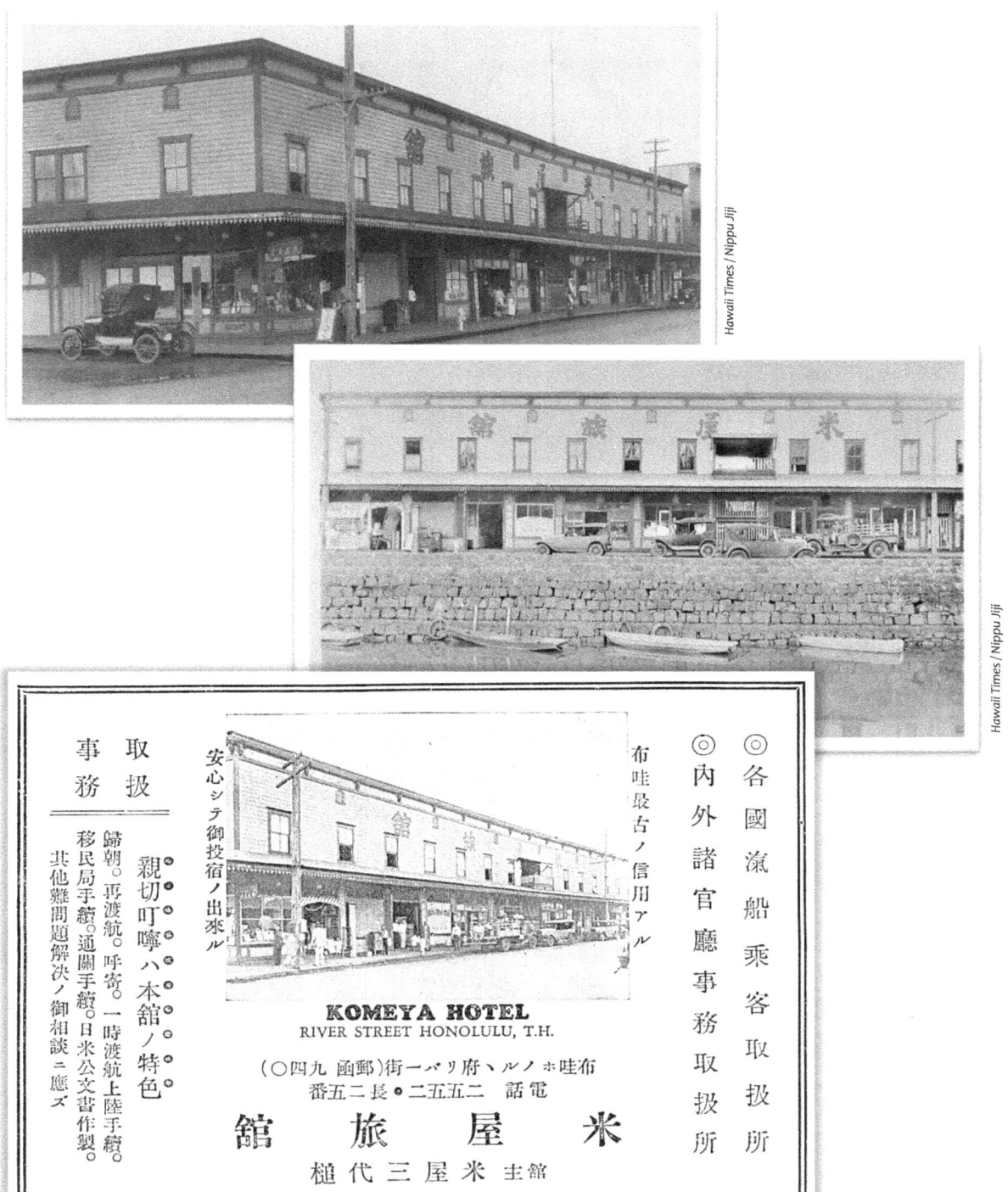

RIVER-PAUAHI APARTMENTS

1155 River
1981
Architect / Builder: Walter Leong Associates / Ken Nakamura

These two 4-story buildings with 40 one-bedroom units and 8 two-bedroom units were built for $2.6M in 1981 by developer George Fan as part of the city's affordable housing initiative for Block A of the Pauahi Urban Renewal Project. It replaced a rundown 2-story wooden apartment building (1189 River Street) that was built sometime after 1906.

By 2014 the apartment building was in disrepair and even included a liquor store with a hidden gambling room. It was purchased by the Ahe Group who spent $3M renovating the building, including converting the liquor store into a manager's office and following the city's affordability requirements.

At one time this was known as the "Teddi Duncan Apartments", named for a Chinatown activist who died while waiting for new housing.

These two buildings stood on the site before the 1900 fire and were built between 1897 and 1899 on newly reclaimed land – this site was in the middle of Nuʻuanu Stream before the 1896 rerouting project.

W.C. Achi's Hawaii Land Company built this building in 1898 on the mauka/waikiki corner of River and Pauahi streets. Less than two years later it burned in the 1900 fire.

William Charles Achi

…was a lawyer, politician, and land developer of Chinese and Hawaiian descent. Born in 1858, he was a great grandson of Puou, one of the warriors of King Kamehameha.

Achi studied law in the office of William Castle and was admitted to the Hawaiian courts in 1887. He was elected to the Legislature in 1897 and was one of the first Territorial senators.

He formed the Hawaii Land Company for the special benefit of Native Hawaiians, with the objective of encouraging them to save their earnings and put them into paying investments. By 1901 the company had five hundred member-stockholders who had purchased stock for $10.

In addition to the building at River and Pauahi, the company also built a brick business block of five stores at the ewa-makai corner of King and Maunakea streets, fifteen houses on School Street, a 3-story building in Kapalama, a 2-story building on Punchbowl Street, plus many other smaller buildings. They also had stock in several sugar plantations.

All excess monies after paying liabilities were reinvested in more real estate and buildings to increase stockholder dividends. The company lost over $100,000 in rent due to the 1900 Chinatown fire.

Achi died in 1928 after being hit by a streetcar on King Street – a similar fate had befallen his father who was killed by a horse-drawn tram about 30 years before.

SMITH STREET

Originally called Alanui Kamika, or Smith's Lane, it was named for the pastor of Kaumakapili Church, Lowell Smith, whose house and school were just makai of Beretania Street opposite the church. After the 1886 fire it was widened and straightened and extended to King Street, replacing the nearby private Meek Street. It was sometimes called Konia Street until 1900, and it was extended from King Street to Queen (Nimitz) Street in 1917 through the old Honolulu Iron Works property.

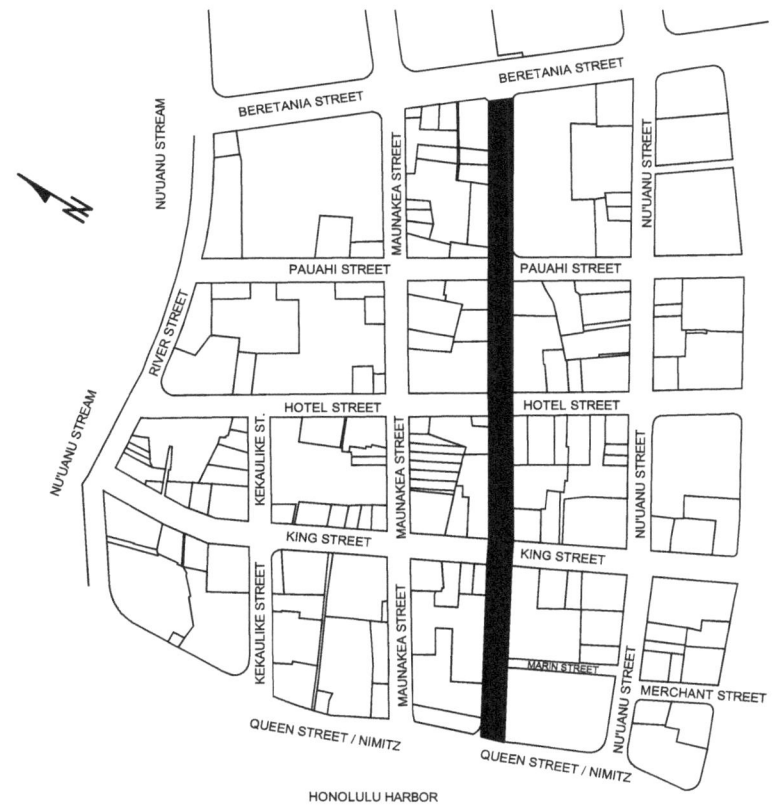

MARIN TOWER

800 Smith, 60 N. Nimitz
1994
Architect / Builder: Architects Hawaii Ltd / Fletcher-Pacific

Originally called the Smith-Maunakea Housing Project, Marin Tower is a $38M, 28-story, 250-foot public housing tower with 234 units, 425 parking spaces and nearly 14,000 square feet of commercial space built for the City of Honolulu Department of Housing and Community Development. Construction began in 1992 and finished in 1994.

It is built on the homesite of Don Francisco de Paula Marín and the site of the Honolulu Iron Works.

Don Francisco de Paula Marín

Born in Spain in 1774 and known as "Manini" by the Hawaiians, Don Francisco was a Spanish Army deserter who came to Hawaii in 1793 or 1794 and was fluent in Spanish, French, English, and Hawaiian. His knowledge of languages and Western military weapons led to him becoming a friend, advisor, and even physician to King Kamehameha I.

Manini built the first coral stone building in Hawaii in 1809 – a storehouse for King Kamehameha I's valuables. He was one of the most colorful characters in early post-contact Hawaii and had four wives and at least 23 children that we know of.

In 1810 his Portuguese stonemason son-in-law, Antonio Ferreira, built his 2-story coral house called "America". The site also had several outbuildings of thatch and adobe construction plus extensive gardens. Marín was the first to cultivate many plants now common to Hawaii – pineapples, oranges, mangos, grapes, melons, lemons, corn, avocados, peppers, coffee, roses, and perhaps even rice.

Manini also made the first wine, brandy, rum, and beer in Hawaii. Vineyard Street is named after the site of his grape orchard (where Zippy's restaurant sits today). A skeleton believed to be the remains of Don Francisco de Paula Marín was discovered during the archaeological investigations for the Marín Tower in 1992.

Honolulu Fish Market & Harbor Waterfront

Immediately makai of the present-day Marin Tower, and in the middle of what is now Nimitz Boulevard, was the longtime home of the Honolulu Fish Market.

First constructed in 1855, it was replaced by a new market on Alakea Street and the old market was burned in 1895 as a sanitary precaution during the Cholera epidemic.

In 1896 a dredger working near the old fish market turned up two carved Hawaiian idols made of Kauwila wood.

C. Brewer & Co. built a large 2-story brick warehouse on the site in 1897 that had to be relocated to the other side of Queen Street during the 1904 widening.

The Dakin Fire Insurance Map from 1891 shows the Fish Market as well as the 1848 Custom House and 1882 A.F. Cooke Warehouse on the makai side of Queen Street.

The street was widened in 1904 and again in 1950 and is now called Nimitz Boulevard. Smith Street was extended to Queen Street in 1917.

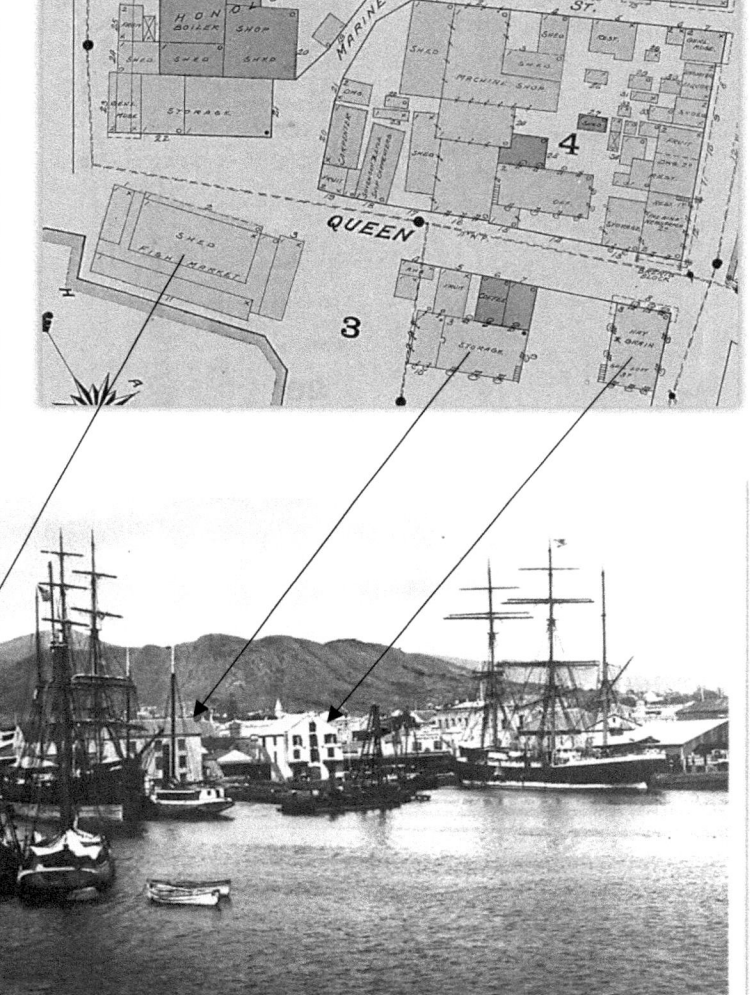

This photograph was taken from a ship in the harbor in late 1885 or early 1886

HONOLULU CHINATOWN

THE HONOLULU FISH MARKET.

Queer and Curious Edibles---Rare Products of the Briny Deep.

DESCRIPTION OF THE NEW MARKET

By the demolition of the old Fish Market, which will probably soon take place, Honolulu loses another one of her oldest landmarks. The building, or attenuated series of shanties, now used as a fish market was completed in 1855. Previous to that time the area between C. Brewer & Co.'s and the store of M. W. McChesney & Sons was utilized for the sale of all kinds of fish, and the building now occupied by C. Brewer & Co. was divided into stalls for the sale of vegetables, tobacco, bananas, etc. After a continuous use of 36 years, during which time the old kamaainas figured prominently, it became evident that the old building was too small for the rapidly growing city, and an appropriation was made by the Legislature of 1888 of $25,000 for the erection of a new market building.

The old market is situated a few rods beyond Brewer's wharf, its position being readily discerned on account of the usual string of hacks standing near by. On entering the market on the left hand side the visitor sees a meat stall over which a Chinaman presides. Next to this Mr. Mahoe, who has for several years past been part and parcel of the everyday life of the market, has three tables. In the first he has for sale all varieties of fresh fish; in the second he has fresh salmon, and in the third, every other day, fresh meat for disposal. Mr. Mahoe has grown old and well off in the business, and there is no more sociable and genial character in the place.

On the Ewa side of the walk are four Mongolians and one native, vendors of fresh meat. A bitter rivalry has existed since the native made his debut. The Hawaiian is a fluent speaker and would win over customers from his rivals' tables, consequently the Chinese are down on him. On passing these stalls the visitor comes to another Chinese stall, where fresh fish is sold, especially mullet. It is here that eels and other fish, for which the Portuguese have a great liking, are procured. The fish are all caught in the harbor. Adjoining this on the same side are several native women, who have for sale dried fish of every description.

Prominent among these dried articles are some very rare fish, which are brought by our coasters from the other islands. For instance, the aku, which comes from Kona, is a favorite dish with the Hawaiians, and sells at fifty cents apiece. The hee or squid is also bought here dried for the same price. These fish when broiled are excellent articles of diet. The wana or sea-eggs, fresh from the sea, can be procured at this stall on Saturdays only.

The next stand, at present vacant, was formerly occupied by John Kaulahea, a compositor by trade, but who in the dullness of the trade had deserted his avocation in the belief that he would make his fortune in the salmon trade. Unfortunately for him he has since failed. Continuing, another fresh fish stand greets the view. It is here that the moi is obtainable---a fish of a white color, which if cooked in ti leaves is very sweet, and is preferred by the natives to the sweetest of mullet. It is caught with line and bait, even in the harbor, but not so good as when caught in the blue seas. The awa and awaaua from ponds and salt water, the milu and hilu and other rare fish peculiar, it is said by old natives, to Hawaiian waters, are also for sale in that stand.

The next stalls on the same side are presided over by a syndicate, with Mr. Pekelo at the head. Lobsters, mullets, flying fish, fresh crabs, oio, uhu and another variety of fish are disposed of. The prices of the finny tribe vary in accordance with the times. Molokai furnishes for the greater part articles for these stalls. Dried fish, cut and dried on the spot, are in great abundance. Mr. Pekelo has made his fortune at the business, and increases his hoard with every shining hour.

Turning the corner on the route to the exit fresh fish stands again greet the view, some of which are presided over by a combination of young Hawaiians, their fish being of the same assortment as the last-mentioned stalls. Here a rather glib talker often lures the purchaser from the other stands and before he or she knows what they are doing the fish is forced upon them.

The Hawaiians are well acquainted with the fact that a plausible talker, with winning ways and abundant smiles, is generally able to sell you anything whether you wish it or not. Further on is a Chinese fresh fish stand, where for the most part mullet and crabs, and sometimes eels caught in the harbor, are exchanged for Kalakaua coin. Still another fresh meat market adjoins this stand. On the opposite side, going back on the left hand, are four fresh meat stands, presided over by the lads of the Flowery Kingdom.

Mr. C. B. Maile, who may be rated in the thousands, has a mortgage on the next tables, having for disposal dried meats and fish of every description, salt junk, sea-weed, etc., prices for the fish ranging from fifty cents to $1.50 apiece. On Saturday afternoons a native woman takes charge of one of his tables with fresh periwinkles, pipipis, ake and limu or seaweed. They are for the most part from Kauai and from Koolau. Manoel, a Portuguese who has had a salmon stand for several years past, still holds sway. Native women have stands on special days on either side of him, with oopus and shrimps cooked in ti leaves, which are considered delicious. Vendors of pig cooked in the ground and sweet potatoes cooked the same way frequent the inner stands on Saturdays only.

It may be interesting to note here how the rare fish are baited by natives. The aku, for which Kona, Hawaii, and Waianae, on this island, are famous, are caught in the deep blue sea. The method is as follows: The fishermen are aware of the close proximity of the fish by the sight of birds hovering over a certain spot on the ocean. They row near and affix a mother-of-pearl in the shape of a hook to a line which is dropped into the water; they then paddle as fast as they can. When the fish see the glitter they follow it and swallow the pearl, being thenof course hauled in. Uhu is a frequenter of the coral indentations far out. They are lured from their hiding places by a mixture of shrimps and taro. The fish is rare and sells from 50c. to $1.50. Squids are either spiked or caught with shells. Lobsters are dived for and when caught are turned over face to face. When placed in that position they will neither stir nor attempt to get away. Native Hawaiians are at home in the blue sea and are oblivious to the presence of the monsters of the deep.

THE NEW MARKET.

A contract was recently made with Theo. H. Davies & Co. to furnish a new iron market building to cover a space 240 by 145 feet; price delivered in Honolulu $14,215. The contract has been filled and an iron building now adorns the esplanade, at the foot of Alakea street, consisting of a centre span 55 feet wide and two side spans 37 feet 6 inches each, with a projecting veranda of 7 feet 6 inches all around the building. It has ample capacity for 100 stalls and is well lighted by means of two skylights on the roof of each span extending nearly the whole length of the building. The building is an ornament to the town, commodious and convenient for its purpose. To complete the building, including interior fittings, will require $19,000. It is to be hoped work on the interior of the new market will soon be commenced, and the old market, which is an eyesore, abandoned and demolished to make room for more stately architecture.

Evening Bulletin, August 8, 1891

Honolulu Iron Works

Established in 1852, the Honolulu Iron Works were manufacturers of "sugar mills, sugar machinery, steam boilers, rivetted steel pipe, steel tanks, etc." They were agents for several large manufacturing companies and were dealers in engineering and plumbing supplies, oils, greases, iron, steel, valves, and fittings. They also supplied ironwork for ship repairs.

They exported the equipment for complete sugar cane factories to such places as Louisiana, Cuba, Puerto Rico, Mexico, Taiwan, and the Philippines. They employed upwards of 500 workers and built over 200 sugar cane mills as well as refineries and alcohol distilleries.

The site contained numerous buildings housing the foundry, machine shops, workshops, smithy, boiler shops and company offices, and extended all the way to Nuʻuanu Street. In 1900 they relocated to Kakaako where One Waterfront Plaza is today.

> *"In Queen Street I found and visited the Honolulu Iron Works, of which it may be said that among the industries which occupy the time and attention of the business men of this town, none contribute more to the progress of the Islands' interests than this. Every requisite for the repair of large iron ships and steamers is always in stock and such work is accomplished with great dispatch; but the building of sugar mills and machinery connected therewith, is what has chiefly occupied the company for some years."*

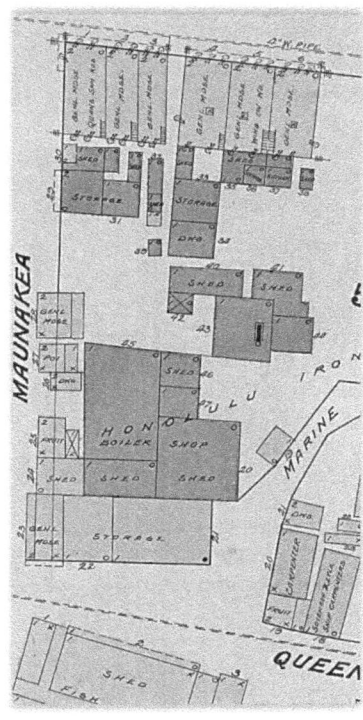

1891

Smith Street was extended through the old Honolulu Iron Works site from King Street to Queen Street (now Nimitz Highway) in 1917.

For over 30 years the popular Tasty Broiler restaurant was on the ewa/mauka corner of Smith and Queen streets.

It was owned by Hideo Naito and was famous for lobster, and a complete prime rib dinner was only $2.

The building extended completely across the block and was built in 1940 out of concrete and concrete blocks on the site of the old C. Brewer & Company warehouse.

HONOLULU IRON WORKS (SITE)

26 N. Queen (Nimitz), 801 Smith, 800 Nu'uanu
(1914)
Architect / Builder: Ripley & Davis (1914) / Spalding Construction (1914)

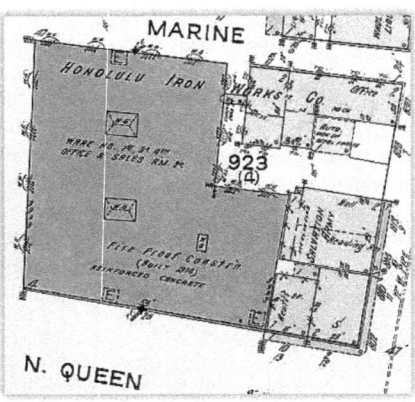

It's hard to imagine but at one time the second largest building in all of Hawaii was where this parking lot is today. Designed by Ripley & Davis and built in 1914 for the Honolulu Iron Works Company, it was a huge 4-story concrete warehouse and showroom measuring 163' on Smith Street, 159' on Queen (Nimitz) Street, and 125' on Marin Street.

Originally planned to be a 3-story building, they added a 4th story before starting construction. The first floor was occupied by the ironware department and general delivery rooms, the second floor contained a huge equipment showroom, and the third and fourth floors were warehouse storerooms.

Every floor had 24,000 square feet of floor space served by 3 elevators.

It was constructed using the patented Kahn system for reinforced concrete, with civil and constructing engineer Axel Stockelback as the local representative.

Honolulu Iron Works put the building up for sale in 1958 and it became the offices and storerooms for the Fisher Corporation, renamed in 1967 to Fisher-Hawaii. When they moved to the Mapunapuna Industrial Park in 1972 the building was purchased by Pacific Century Financial Corp, the holding company for the Bank of Hawaii, and it became known as the Bank of Hawaii Annex Building.

In 1994 Bankoh Corporation hired Stringer Tusher & Associates to design a 21-story 250-foot-tall tower with 280,000 square feet of office space but they had to back out since banking charters did not allow for the development of non-bank commercial property.

The building was demolished in 1998 by Rons Construction and turned into a 90-space "interim" parking lot that is still there 24 years later. JPI in Dallas and Intracorp in San Diego both proposed building luxury apartment towers on the site, but it was finally sold to the Luke family of Hawaii National Bank as an investment in 2004 for $5.5M.

SAILOR JERRY'S TATTOO SHOP

1033 Smith
c.1906-1914
Architect / Builder: unknown

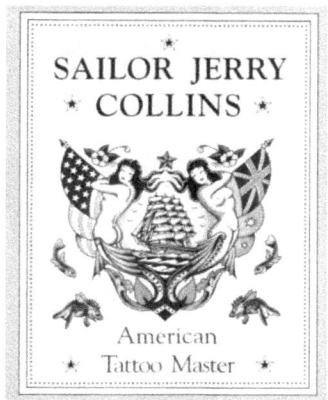

This building was added to the back of 49 N. Hotel Street sometime between 1906 and 1914. Its most famous occupant was Norman K. Collins, known throughout the world as the legendary tattoo artist "Sailor Jerry". Although he worked in the Hotel Street area since the 1930's in several different locations, this was the last location of his shop from 1960 until his death 1973.

Born Norman Keith Collins in Reno, Nevada in 1911, he grew up in Northern California, hopped freight trains across the country, and early on learned the traditional hand-pricking tattoo method. He learned how to use a tattoo machine in Chicago by practicing on drunks from Skid Row.

He enlisted in the Navy and moved to Hawaii in the 1930's. He created iconic designs featuring beautiful girls, ships, eagles, and hearts that were known for their rich colors. He was one of the first American artists to include Asian imagery, and one of the first to use single-use needles. This was *the* place for sailors going to Hotel Street to get "stewed, screwed and tattooed".

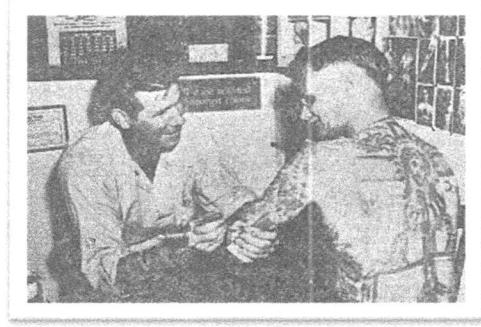

In addition to giving island tours as skipper of a large schooner, he also played saxophone in a dance band and hosted a talk radio program on KTRG as "Old Ironsides".

One of his protégés, Mike Malone, took over the shop for the next 25 years, and in 1999 established Sailor Jerry Ltd to market Sailor Jerry's artwork on all sorts of merchandise and clothing, including Sailor Jerry Rum.

The shop and part of the parking lot was the site of Harbor Master Captain John Meek's 2-story coral house built in 1847. From Marblehead, Massachusetts, Meek first came to Hawaii in 1809 and was one of the founding members of the A.F. & A.M. Order of Free Masons, and the "Lodge le Progres de l'Oceanie" met here for 35 years. The house was demolished sometime after 1878 and Meek Street ran through the site by 1884.

MENDONÇA MAKAI

1040 Smith
1901
Architect / Builder: Oliver Traphagen / Hawaiian Engineering & Construction Company

Often called the "Mendonça Makai Building", it is actually the mauka end of the much larger Mendonça building on Smith Street that was built in 1901 and extended all the way from here from King Street.

The rest of the building is still extant but was heavily remodeled in 1930 by James Mason Young of Pacific Engineering Company. Although the roofline was changed, the window spacing remained the same, and if you look really closely you can see a faint outline of the former window that was between the two buildings.

In 1995 this building was seized by US Marshalls for harboring drug activity at the notorious Club Escalator and it was subsequently bought by the City and County of Honolulu and renovated in 2000.

The Hawaii Heritage Center moved here in 2005. They are an all-volunteer 501(c)(3) non-profit organization founded in 1980 to support efforts to educate, preserve, and perpetuate knowledge of the history, heritage, and culture of the diverse ethnic cultural groups in Hawaii.

In addition to displays of historical donated materials showcasing Hawaii's multi-cultural heritage, they also display artifacts discovered in Chinatown during construction activities.

The center offers regular 2-hour walking tours of Chinatown which include an introductory orientation, a guided tour of their museum exhibits and Chinatown historic and cultural sites, plus sampling of food at five different shops.

LITTLE VILLAGE NOODLE HOUSE

1113 Smith
1895
Architect / Builder: Hop Hing

1900

Believe it or not, there was supposed to be a French Church on this site. This particular piece of land was called Kalanikāhua and in 1829 it was given to the Roman Catholic Church of the Hawaiian Islands by King Kamehameha III in an effort to show religious tolerance to all faiths.

> *"Those who represent the Catholic benevolence in these islands are mostly French and British subjects; and those who represent the Protestant benevolence are mostly American citizens. The lands claimed by these respective sects of Christians are claimed for eleemosynary purposes. They must receive equal favor under the 4th part of the act to organize the executive departments, which declares that the same civil rights of protection shall be extended by this Government to each.*
>
> *The object of encouraging religious denominations is to benefit the native race by extending to them the blessings of Christianity and education which these two sects of missionaries profess benevolently and gratuitously to devote themselves to instilling."*

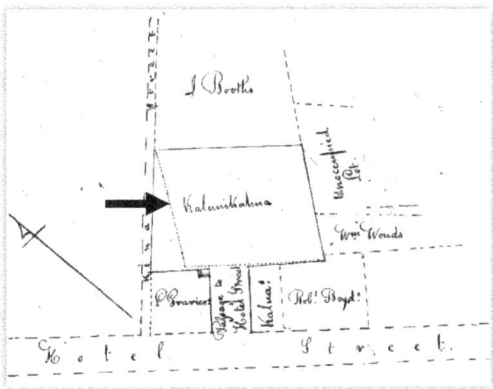

Although originally granted with the specific condition "that there be erected thereon a church to be administered by a priest of the French Nation", it never happened, and it was known as the "French Mission" site for many years.

The current building was built by Hop Hing in 1895, and some of the first businesses here were the Wing Ton Sang carpenter shop in 1900 and the Yee Lung Tai Company in 1905. It housed an aquarium store in 1933, and was altered by the Honolulu Redevelopment Authority in 1971.

It became the Little Village Noodle Shop in 2001, described at the time as "one of the few restaurants with an aesthetic that isn't Hong Kong modern or Maunakea Street drab".

SUN YUN WO (SITE)

1122 Smith
(1901-1977)
Architect / Builder: unknown

This courtyard is the site of Sun Yun Wo, one of Honolulu's premier Chinese restaurants for nearly 60 years.

Founded by Hee Cho, Quong Ming, Kan Wing Chew, and Chang Kim in 1901, it was housed in a two-and-a-half-story wooden building that could seat 250 people.

They specialized in large banquets with nine-course dinners and their featured dish was Kai See Min (Fried Chicken Noodles).

It was also THE place for business people to meet and finalize deals. It was here in 1922 that fifteen Chinese businessmen met to sign the charter application for Liberty Bank. In 1925, Chun Sing of C.Q. Yee Hop celebrated his 51st birthday here with 250 guests and 20,000 firecrackers, and a year later C.K. Ai's 61st birthday included all City Mill employees and families enjoying a nine-course Chinese feast.

Perhaps the largest birthday celebration here was for Lee Lup, president of Lee Lup & Co. in 1928. The 300 guests were treated to a 10-course Chinese feast and an amazing display of pictorial fireworks and pyrotechnics. A special stand was erected on top of the building that was nowhere near tall enough for the initial string of firecrackers, and above this was:

"…a huge Oriental good luck hieroglyph carved in green relief, above the lucky sign was a large bundle of a mysterious something, above the unknown quantity was a rectangular square conveying a message of congratulation whose letters were made of firecrackers and bombs.

Above the message was a temple room in which stood three two-foot figures, representing the three Chinese deities of fortune, bedecked in all their glory, like the picturesque actors one sees on the Chinese stage. Above the temple room were two gigantic monograms, inscribing in crimson letters the Chinese words, 'fook' and 'sau', meaning prosperity and posterity."

More than 2,000 people gathered in the closed-off street to watch the fireworks which lasted for over half an hour. As the final bomb exploded the good-luck sign caught fire and gave forth a huge shower of green embers and the mysterious bundle suddenly opened and revealed a small paper pagoda with shooting skyrockets and crackling flames which floated down to the street while the deities "blazed into heaven with crimson glory".

In 1959 the restaurant was sold and renamed Tim Tim Chop Suey. It became The Moon Palace in 1964 and Season Chop Suey in 1969. A disastrous sanitation inspection report that found live rats in the dining room forced the restaurant to close in 1974. It was briefly His Place, a Christian outreach center for "alcoholics, drug addicts, prostitutes and street people", but was demolished in 1977 by developer Bob Gerell as part of his large-scale restoration of the adjacent Mendonça and Tan Sing buildings.

TAN SING BUILDING

1124-1128 Smith
1920
Architect / Builder: Kerr & Pettit / Z. Sugihara Co.

Architect's sketch, 1920

Although the parapet says "1926" this building was constructed for J.P. Mendonça in 1920 at a cost of $25,900. Designed by H.L. Kerr and E.C. Pettit, it was built of lava stone by Z. Sugihara and has two downstairs storefronts, a large second floor for offices, plus a full basement.

For over forty years this was headquarters of the Sun Chung Kwock Bo (New China Daily Press) newspaper. Said to be the oldest Chinese newspaper at the time and the mouthpiece of the Chinese Constitutionalist Party, it was known as the "Anti-Sun" paper since they were in direct opposition to Sun Yat-sen and the Chinese Nationalist Party. Their composing room had more than 4,000 characters in regular use, compared to only 26 letters on a standard English-language linotype printing press. The Chinese typewriter has 7,792 characters.

On October 17, 1928, they caused a near riot by raising the old five-bar Chinese flag on the flagpole which attracted a large crowd of Nationalist sympathizers who fired thousands of firecrackers at the building and threatened to enter and tear down the offending flag. Luckily, the police arrived to restore order and disperse the crowd.

Seventy thousand rounds of firecrackers were fired off for the newspaper's 30th anniversary in 1929.

In 1943 they published the book *China's First Lady, Mme. Chiang Kai-shek* to raise money for Chinese refugees.

Tan Sing was a society of Chinese actors, singers and musicians founded in 1926. They provided musical entertainment for many feasts, festivals and events including staged dramas from Chinese history like *The Romance of the Poisoned Arrow* and *The Yellow Jacket*.

In the 1940's the second floor was home to the Camp Rooms brothel, one of about a dozen in this area of Chinatown. Eight women worked here under madam Mrs. Rebecca Paakonia.

The land was vacant for twenty years after the 1900 fire. In 1891 and 1899 there was a large horse shoeing parlor here that would have been built sometime after the 1886 fire. Before 1886 there were a couple of 1-story dwellings on the site.

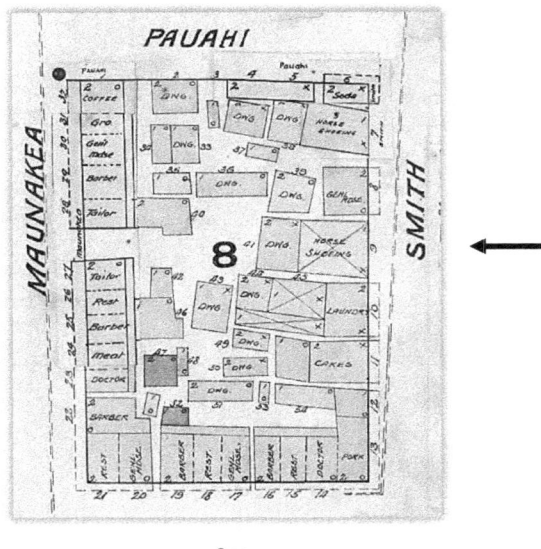

1899

The building here today was restored in 1982 by Mouse Builders under the direction of Honolulu architect Spencer Leineweber.

Zenkichi Sugihara was born in Hiroshima-Ken, Japan, and went to Kaua'i in 1890 with his wife Taki to work on a sugar plantation near Kapaa. When their three-year contract was finished, they moved to Honolulu where he partnered with Risuke Miyata in the contracting firm of R. Miyata & Company. In April 1915, shortly before Miyata's death, he bought the company and renamed it to Z. Sugihara & Company.

In addition to this building plus many houses, he also built the Japanese Hospital in 1917, known today as the Kuakini Medical Center. He was also president of the Honolulu Building and Lumber Company, Ltd. In 1925 he retired from the Z. Sugihara Company and turned it over to his son Edwin.

1125-1141 SMITH / 45 N. PAUAHI (SITE)

A parking lot today, at least three buildings have stood on this site. In 1885 there was a very large 2-story wooden Chinese lodging building here that would have burned down in the 1886 fire.

The building in this photograph was built between 1886 and 1891 and housed a general merchandise store, a barber, a restaurant, and a bakery.

It was burned along with a large portion of Block 11 on January 19, 1900 by the Board of Health.

The most recent building on the site was built c.1906 with ground floor shops and second story tenement housing. Starting in the 1930's there were numerous arrests here for bootlegging and moonshine (okolehao), opium, robbery, suicide, and gambling.

After years of landlord neglect the city condemned the building in 1975. This led to years of legal wrangling, vocal intervention by the People Against Chinatown Evictions (P.A.C.E.), and even a suspicious fire before the building was finally demolished in 1980.

This stone wall is the oldest historical remnant in Chinatown.

Completely covered up with buildings and shacks by 1900, it was rediscovered in the cleanup after the Great Fire of 1900.

No one at the time knew its origins, but it was allowed to remain since it was thought to be an old landmark used for land claim boundaries.

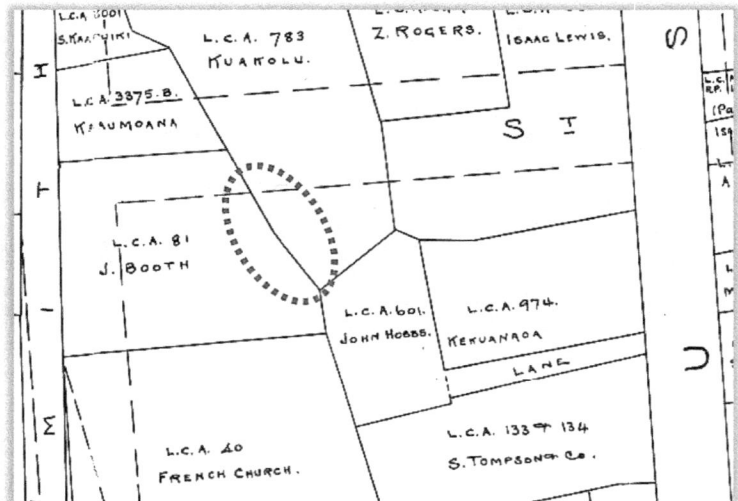

It turns out the wall was part of the border enclosure of the Kuakolu land claim (LCA 783) and is first referenced in 1848. But it might even date to way before that since the name Kuakolo can be translated as "five generations". If so, this stone wall could easily date to the 1600's or earlier.

1130 SMITH (SITE)

1130 Smith
1920
Architect / Builder: A.W. Heen / George M. Yamada

This little stone building that used to be next to the Tan Sing Building was designed by architect A W. Heen who designed miniature golf courses and also worked with Vladimir Ossipoff and Kenneth W. Roehrig on one of the designs for the Hawaii State Capitol.

L. L. McCandless, owner; A. W. Heen, architect; George M. Yamada, builder; stone and concrete store building; Smith street near Pauahi: $3000.

He was born **Afong Waianueanue Heen** in Kaʻanapali, Lāhainā, Maui in 1884. From 1920 to 1925 he was the County Architect for the island of Hawaii. He left in 1925 to open his own practice and designed the Mauna Kea Lodge of Foresters in Hilo (1924), Niumalu Hotel (1926), Kalihi Standard School (1928), Mid-Pacific Curio Shoppe (1929), Natatorium Public Bath House (1930), and the Waialua Fire Station (1932).

In 1930 Heen teamed up with Henry Inn of Fong Inn to buy the Wee Golf Course on Seaside Avenue in Waikiki. Heen designed the Palama Wee Golf Course (1930) and also donated the plans for the miniature golf course at Kalaupapa.

"Al" Heen was the Superintendent of Buildings for the City and County of Honolulu from 1931 to 1940. Returning to private practice after World War II, he designed the Hauula Beach Pavilion (1947), Kamehameha Girls School (1947 with C.W. Dickey), Aina Haina Elementary School (1950), Lihue Airport Terminal Building (1950), Washington Intermediate School (1951), Hawaii State Capital (1952, not used), Niu Valley Middle School (1954), Hilo Hawaiian Village (1955), and the University High School (1956, with Ernest Hara).

This little lava rock building might have been his first design, and it has housed a variety of businesses including car spring repair, wholesale grocery, real estate, watch repair, pool hall, bargain center, and barber shop.

It was demolished sometime after 1966.

1143-1151 SMITH / 46-50 PAUAHI (SITE)

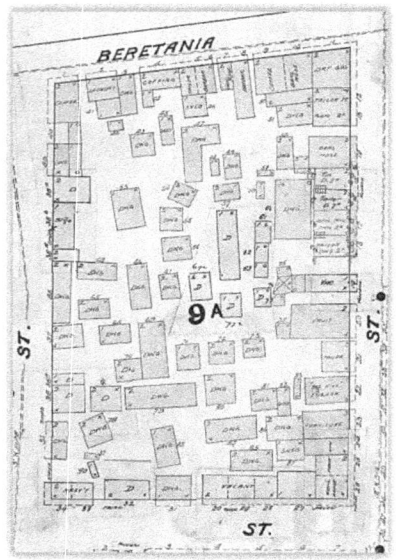

The 1899 Dakin Fire Insurance Map from 1899 shows this large open area to be filled with what the Board of Health called "filth-ridden and plague-infected" one- and two-story wooden dwellings.

In the late 1800's before the days of the "Iwilei Stockade" (later demolished for the Dole Cannery) this block was the location of most of Honolulu's houses of prostitution, known as "yoshiwaras". The name comes from the fabled Tokyo red-light district established in 1617.

The photograph below is the mauka-waikiki corner, taken just before the entire block was deliberately burned by the Board of Health on January 12, 1900.

The controlled burn started at the corner with these buildings and the firemen worked across the rest of the block against the prevailing wind.

After the fire this side of the block remained mostly vacant, becoming a "Children's Park" in 1911 and a surface parking lot in 1952.

In the 1960's the parking lot was known as "the gigantic urinal" due to problems with vagrants and drug users, a problem which still exists to a certain extent today.

After nearly twenty years of planning studies, in 2003 the parking lot was converted into an underground municipal parking garage with an open park on the surface.

This site was untouched in the 1886 fire and was the homesite of S. Kaapuiki before 1850, the residence of T. Silva in 1869, and Manuel Perry's lodging house in 1888.

Immediately after the 1900 fire a 2-story wooden building was constructed at the mauka-waikiki corner that housed a Japanese Hotel and a coffin shop. By 1914 there was a printing shop on the first floor, a plumbing shop in 1927, and a restaurant in 1955. But its most interesting history occurred during World War II.

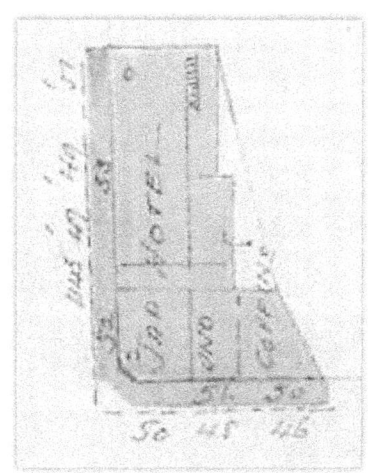

By the early 1940's the building was owned by Lee Yau Chong of the Wing Coffee Company whose coffee roasting plant was next door at 1153 Smith Street.

After the Iwilei houses were shut down, prostitution moved back into this area in a big way. At one time there were over a dozen brothels located within a block of Pauahi and Smith streets, and the second floor of this building became known as the Rex Rooms.

Molly O'Brian was the landlady/madam with five women working for her, mostly from the mainland.

One of her workers was the most famous of them all –

Jean O'Hara

Known as the notorius "Honolulu Harlot", O'Hara wrote and published a scandalous account of her time in Honolulu and particularly her troubles and interactions with the local police who were in charge of regulating this officially illegal activity.

The massive influx of wartime sailors created an enormous demand for sex services, and local officials thought that by allowing and containing such businesses to one area (Chinatown) that it would somehow protect the local women and their daughters from all those lusty males.

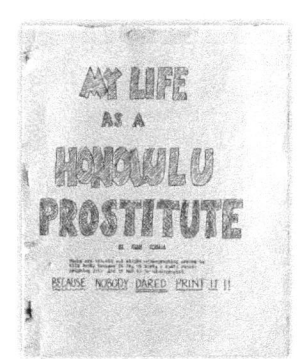

The sex workers had to be registered with the Chief of Police, undergo regular health checks, and were not to be seen outside of Chinatown (and certainly not in the "more respectable" areas like Waikiki).

Jean O'Hara is credited with inventing an assembly-line format that dramatically reduced the amount of time needed to prepare and provide the services which were carefully timed. The going rate? $3 for 3 minutes.

Everyone involved made an unbelievable amount of money – the girls, the madam, the landlord, and the local jewelry and finery shops who courted their business. Taxes to the government, and the police too, with official fees and undoubtedly a lot of under-the-counter payments.

In 1951, William Bradford Huie wrote the best-seller *The Revolt of Mamie Stover* which was turned into a movie in 1956 directed by Raoul Walsh and starring Jane Russell. Approximately 90% of the exterior scenes were filmed on location around Honolulu, with beach scenes at Waikiki and shipboard scenes shot aboard the Matson freighter *Hawaiian Educator*. The studio claimed the character was entirely fictional, but it is essentially the story of Jean O'Hara.

GOLDEN HARVEST THEATRE

1152 Smith
1980
Architect / Builder: Alan Leong / National Construction and Management Corp.

Used as a church today, Golden Harvest Ltd built this building in 1980 as a twin-screen movie theater to feature "the finest Chinese movies". It had a total seating capacity of 470.

In addition to owning movie theaters, Golden Harvest was the Hong Kong film studio that made Bruce Lee famous. The first two movies shown here were *The Sword* starring Hsu Chieh and Chen Shao Chiu, and *The Young Master* starring Jackie Chan.

The Golden Harvest theater specialized in Chinese action and martial arts films and was the last ethnic movie theater in Honolulu, closing in 1995.

In 1997 the building was purchased by Trinity Christian Center, affiliated with Trinity Broadcasting Network, to be converted into a broadcasting center and virtual-reality theater for biblical films.

The first building on this site was a schoolhouse built by Lowell Smith in 1837 for $486. Church services for Kaumakapili Church ("the native church") were held here before the large adobe and thatch church building was built on the other side of Beretania Street in 1839.

As this block was unaffected by the 1886 fire, this photograph from 1900 might show the original 1837 building. The gabled wing on the left was added sometime between 1891 and 1899, perhaps in 1895 when the Board of Education changed the curriculum from a native school to an English school. This building and all of Block 9 was burned on January 16, 1900, by the Board of Health.

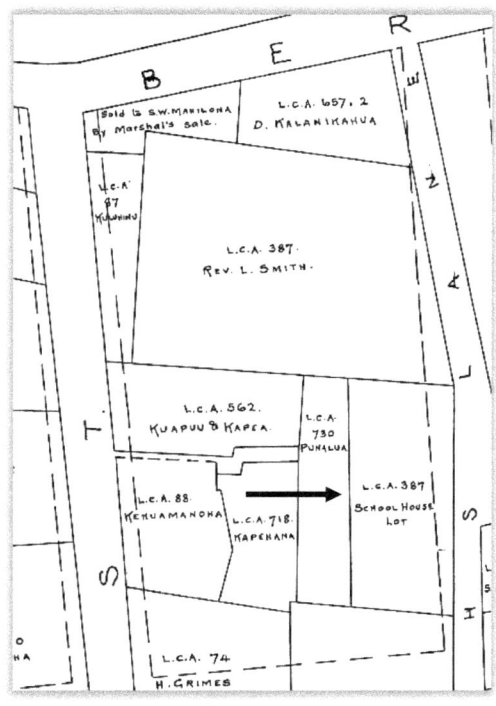

Reverend Lowell Smith was born in Heath, Massachusetts in 1802 and became an ordained minister in 1832. He came to Hawaii in 1832 aboard the ship *Mentor* after a voyage of 161 days.

Initially stationed at Molokai, in 1836 he became the first superintendent of Kawaiaha'o School and for thirty years was the pastor of Kaumakapili Church.

His adobe house was located in the large tract just mauka of the school, and across the street from Kaumakapili Church.

After lying vacant for over twenty years after the 1900 fire, this site became the home of Acme Auto Supply in 1924. They provided tire services, vulcanizing, and automobile repair here for over 40 years.

The buildings were designed by local Japanese architect Hego Fuchino (designer of the Oahu Theater in 1928).

The owner of Acme Auto Supply, **Yuen Yim**, was born in 1880 in Kwangtung, China. He was also Chairman of the Territorial Kuomintang, president of the Liberty News and the Chinese Laborer's Guild, and a director of the Wah Mun Chinese School.

HONOLULU CHINATOWN

1153-1155 SMITH (SITE)

(Fogerty Building / Wing Coffee)
(c.1927-1952)
Architect / Builder: unknown

From circa 1927 to 1952 there was a 2-story stone building at this address that was the offices and roasting facility for Wing Coffee before they moved around the corner to Pauahi Street in 1947.

In addition to grinding coffee here, Wing also supplied provisions for the US Fleet at Pearl Harbor in the 1940's. A typical delivery to the USS *Tennessee* battleship consisted of 1,500 pounds of pears, 4,000 pounds of oranges, and 10,000 pounds of potatoes.

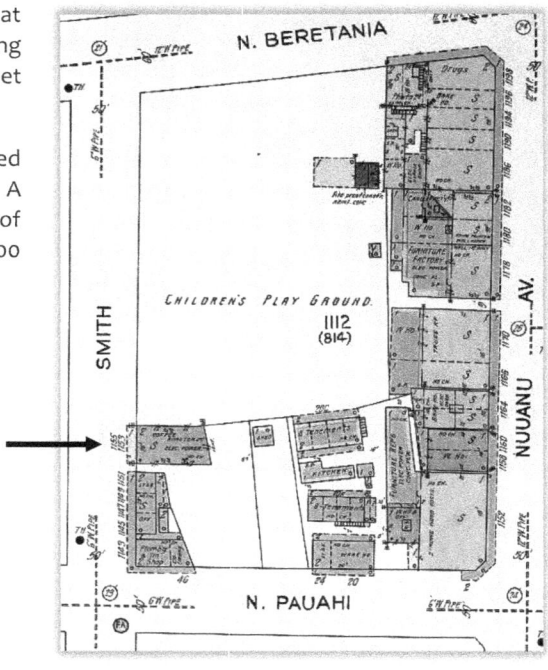

After Wing relocated to Pauahi Street, Mrs. Pansy Lum ran the Sun Jun Hing Oriental Art Goods store here until 1951 with the Hawaiian Togs clothing makers were on the second floor.

The city purchased the property and demolished the building in 1952 for the Smith-Beretania Parking Lot, which turned into the Smith-Beretania Park with underground parking in 2003.

There was a 2-story wooden dwelling on the site in 1891, and a larger one was here in 1899.

As early as 1869 the residences of Mrs. Maholona and Ah Chong were also in this general vicinity.

The 1886 fire did not reach these properties, but they were all burned by the Board of Health along with the rest of the block on January 12, 1900.

1159 SMITH (SITE)

Kobayashi Ryokan (Kobayashi Hotel)
(1892)
Architect / Builder: unknown

Not all pre-1900 Chinatown buildings were "rat-infested shanties" as evidenced by this rather nice Japanese Hotel on the waikiki side of Smith Street about halfway between Pauahi and Beretania streets.

The 10-room hotel was opened by Unosuke Kobayashi in 1892 to accommodate the growing number of Japanese immigrants coming to Honolulu. He was originally from Jigozen mura village, now called Hatsukaichi City, in Hiroshima prefecture.

Although the Board of Health said they originally wanted to save this building during the controlled burn of Block 10 on January 12, 1900, the fire managed to break through the back and side walls and the building quickly came crashing down in a wall of flames.

No trace remains today – the site became part of the Children's Playground in 1911, the Smith-Beretania Parking Lot in 1951, and finally the Smith-Beretania Park and underground municipal parking facility in 2003.

After the fire, Mr. Kobayashi opened a new hotel in Palama, moving to 250 N. Beretania in 1903 and building a 52-room hotel that was doubled in size in 1967. The family acquired the Waikiki Grand Hotel in 1963 and closed the Kobayashi hotel in 1982. The new American Savings Bank headquarters building is currently on the old hotel site.

Kobayashi's nephew, Kanae, was later president of Hawaiian Pacific Resorts, one of the largest hotel chains in the islands. The family still operates Kobayashi Travel Service and Polynesian Hospitality companies.

BE BOP HOTEL

1160-1166 Smith
1949
Architect / Builder: unknown

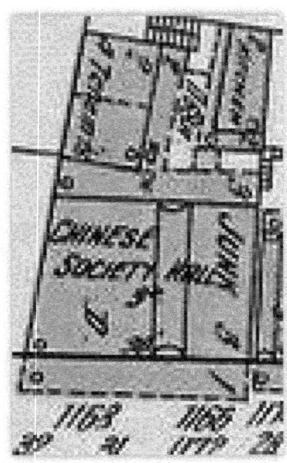

Sanborn Fire Insurance Map (1914)

In 1949 Chong Kam Sing replaced a 3-story frame building with this 3-story concrete and block building.

The previous wooden building was constructed in 1904 for the Quon on Kwock, a 175-member trade organization for Chinese cooks and waiters founded in 1901 by a group of wealthy young Chinese businessmen.

From the old Sanborn Fire Insurance Maps it appears to have been nearly identical to the current building. It cost $8,000 to construct in 1904 and was officially opened for Chinese New Year with "thousands of dollars to be spent on noise" along with a parade led by a Chinese dragon.

> *"All last night a Chinese band was stationed on the imposing balcony of the structure while hundreds of Chinese stood about the street near the building listening to its weird music. Occasionally there were firecrackers exploding. The whole front of the new three-story building was lighted with electric lights and lanterns, draped in American and Chinese colors and really presented a very gay scene."*

They had hoped to also set off a huge firecracker containing 100,000 smaller firecrackers, but delivery was delayed due to the Russo-Japanese War.

In 1927 the Oahu Kuomintang (Chinese Nationalist Party, founded by Sun Yat-sen) met regularly on the second floor, and Mr. Chong at one point was the society's president.

During World War II the building was known as the New Bungalow Hotel, one of many brothels in the area catering to sailors and servicemen. The photograph show sailors lining up to wait for their turn upstairs.

The new 1949 building did not have a much better reputation. It was initially called the Be Bop Hotel and later the Golden Wall Hotel. It was on the police watch list and was raided at various times for the selling of heroin and obscene pictures, and it was also known as a heavily barricaded gambling house.

This building was previously on the site and was built sometime before 1891. It was burned along with the rest of the block by the Board of Health on January 16, 1900.

Chong Kam Sing

… was born in Honolulu in 1882 and was a well-known realtor and merchant. He built the Golden Wall Theater (formerly at School and Nuʻuanu) and also developed the Kailua Coconut Grove residential subdivision. He was a member of the Oahu Kuomintang and a close friend of Dr. Sun Yat-sen, Dr. Sun Fo, and other prominent Chinese government officials. He was manager of the Liberty News Chinese newspaper and past president of Quon On Kwock, Lung Doo, Chung Sing Tong and Lung Kong Kung Shaw societies.

HONOLULU AUTO SUPPLY SERVICE STATION

1178-1190 Smith
1928
Architect / Builder: unknown

This was the Honolulu Auto Supply Service Station in 1928, managed by Izumi Chikasuye. They were a large automobile repair shop that also sold batteries, oil, and gasoline. Honolulu Auto Supply was the local agent for Chandler cars and Dunlop tires.

It replaced a wagon-making shop built after the 1900 fire and 1-story wooden tenement housing built by 1914.

By the 1950's this was a pretty rough place known as Be-bopper's Rendezvous – poker, dice, bootlegging, profanity, heroin, theft, assault, stabbing, even breaking a bottle over someone's head in the presence of the police! It was one of several places in Chinatown officially declared by the military to be off-limits to servicemen.

Here are two views of the buildings formerly on this site, constructed between 1891 and 1899 and later burned along with the rest of the block on January 16, 1900 by the Board of Health.

BUILDINGS BY DATE

Daily Bulletin (DB), Department of Planning & Permitting (DPP), *Evening Bulletin* (EB), *Honolulu Advertiser* (HA), *Honolulu Daily Press* (HDP), *Hawaiian Gazette* (HG), *Honolulu Republican* (HR), *Hawaiian Star* (HS), *Honolulu Star-Bulletin* (HSB), *Pacific Commercial Advertiser* (PCA), *The Independent* (TI)

#	Street	Building Name	Year	Source	TMK
1-9	N. King	Robinson Building / 1 N. King	1864	1863-10-01 PCA	17002039
1118-1120	Nuʻuanu	Paiko Block / Lai Fong	1880	1880-08-04 HG	17003064
24	N. Hotel		1886	1886-07-28 DB	17003057
1-11	N. Hotel	Cosmopolitan Saloon	1886	1886-07-13 PCA	17003007
21-25	N. Hotel	Club Hubba Hubba	1886	1886-07-24 EB	17003083
35-39	N. Hotel	Swing Club, Bar 35	1886	1886-08-04 DB	17003004
36-42	N. King	United Chinese Society Building	1886/1954	1886-02-04 HDP, 1954-11-15 HA	17003002
69	N. King	Yim Quon Buiding (1/3) (Smith & Kings Bar)	1886	1886-08-17 DB	17002045
75	N. King	Yim Quon Building (1/3)	1886	1886-08-17 DB	17002009
83	N. King	Yim Quon Building (1/3) / Yuen Chong Building	1886/1939	1886-08-17 DB	17002008
1006-1022	Nuʻuanu	Aseu Building (Nuʻuanu Court)	1886	1886-09-21 HG	17003001
1024-1026	Nuʻuanu	Aswan Building	1886	1886-09-21 HG	17003006
1028-1044	Nuʻuanu	Uyeda Building	1886/1891	1886-09-21 HG	17003009
2-20	N. Hotel	Encore Saloon Building	1887	1887-03-01 HG	17003056
2-4	S. King	Pacific Saloon / Flores Building	1887	1886-09-21 HG	21002042
2	S. Hotel	Perry Block	1888	1888-09-14 DB	21030017
1113	Smith	Little Village Noodle	1895	1895-01-04 HS	17003059
922-928	Nuʻuanu	Irwin Block / Nippu Jiji / Hawaii Times	1897	1897-01-02 HA	17002040
40-50	N. Hotel	Lee Wai Building (Lucky Belly)	1897/1901/1980	1899-07-03 TI, 1901-11-02 HA	17003059
124-134	N. King	Hop Sing Building	1900	1900-09-25 HR	17003019
1021-1043	Maunakea	Chee Wo Tong	1901	1901-05-17 HR	17003084
1034-1036	Maunakea	Y. Anin Block (part)	1901	1901-06-15 HS	17003076
54-74	N. Hotel	Joseph P. Mendonça	1901	1901-04-13 HA	17003051
76	N. King	Mendonça makai	1901/1930	1901-11-30 PCA / Sanborn	17003010
1036-1040	Smith	Hawaii Heritage Center / (Medonca makai)	1901/2000	1901-11-30 PCA	17003015

Address	Street	Building	Date	Reference	ID
142	N. King	Shun Lung Building / Arita Store	1901	1901-03-21 HR	17003028
108-120	N. King	Y. Anin Block (part)	1901	1901-06-15 HS	17003018, 17003090, 17003092
165-169	N. King	Winston Block	1901	1901-04-160 HR, 1901-06-13 HS	17002029
1162-1164	Nuʻuanu	Pegge Hopper Gallery	c.1901-1906	Sanborn	17004008
1142-1152	Nuʻuanu	C. Ahi / Fong Inn Building (Stack Bldg)	1901/2004	1901-03-21 HR	17004001
146-154	N. King	Tanaka Brothers Building	1902	1953-08-05 HA	17003028
902-910	Maunakea	M. Kawahara Building	1902, 1911-1912	1902-03-18 HA, 1911-06-05 HS, 1912-07-20 HSB	17002011
83-89	N. Beretania	Hai On Tong Building	c.1902	1902-04-17 PCA	17004018
32-34-36	N. Hotel	Risque Theatre	c.1902	1902-08-18 HS	17003058
53-59-63	N. Beretania	Honolulu Auto Supply	1903	1903-01-18 PCA	17004021
1113-1123	Nuʻuanu	McLean Block	1903	parapet, 1904-02-04 HS	21030016
15-19	N. Hotel	Maria Bonita / Union Bar	1904	1904-05-07 EB	17003006
145	N. King	Oahu Market	1904	1904-06-08 HS	17002034
178-182	N. King	Ching Lum Block	1904	1904-01-08 HA	17003030
158-174	N. King	Arrow Hardware Building / Chang Building	1905	1905-03-06 EB	17003066
175-185	N. King	Armstrong Building	1905	1905-08-27 HA	17002028
1158-1160	Nuʻuanu	Kimura Building	1905	1905-05-20 EB	17004009
119-133	N. King	CQ Yee Hop Market	1906 / 1951	1906-03-10 HS, 1951-07-24 HSB	17002021
1031-1033	Smith	Sailor Jerry Building	c.1906-1914	Sanborn	17003097
61-75	N. Hotel	Araujo Building	1907/ 1953/ 2000	1908-01-24 HS, 1953-07-25 HSB	17003015
1152	Maunakea	T. Sumida Liquor Store	1909/1916	1909-05-05 HS	17004028
136-138	N. King	L. Ah Leong Building	1909	parapet, 1909-09-11 EB	17003075
1-19	N. Pauahi	L.L. McCandless Block	1910	1910-04-01 HS	17003063
29-31	N. Hotel	Independent Theater	1911	1911-04-06 HS	17003005
1129	Nuʻuanu	Pantheon Bar	1911	1911-06-28 EB	21030018
1149-1153	Maunakea	Hawaii Hochi / Y. Anin Building	1912/1948	1912-12-09 HA, 1948-09-23 HSB	17004011
51-55	N. Hotel	Mendonça 1913	1913	1913-03-08 HSB	17003016
73-79	N. Beretania	Arita Building	1914	1914-08-12 HA	17004019
2	N. King	Hocking Building	1914/1916	1914-07-23 HA, 1916-04-28 HSB	17003001

Address	Street	Name	Year	Source	ID
1159	Maunakea	Chinese Chamber of Commerce / Tsung Tsin	1916	1916-02-01 HA	17004013
922-942	Maunakea	J.H. Schnack	1916	1915-10-14 HSB	17002025
31	N. Pauahi	Wing Coffee	1917	1917-02-10 HSB	17003094
923	Nuʻuanu	Wing Wo Tai	1917	1917-02-10 HA	21020037
1126-1134	Nuʻuanu	Love's Bakery	1917	1917-02-10 HSB	17003062
905	Kekaulike	Sperry Flour Building	1919	1919-09-03 HA, Sanborn	17002016
948	Maunakea	CQ Yee Hop Warehouse and Dormitory	1919	1919-06-26 HA	17002013
950-954	Maunakea	Hawaiian Mercantile	1917	1918 DPP, 1917-10-19 HSB	17002024
1124-1128	Smith	Mendonça / Tan Sing Society Building	1920	1920-02-18 HA, 1920-05-12 HA	17003098
171-175	N. Beretania	Fong Building	1923	Sanborn	17004036
25-31	N. King	Honolulu Trust Building	1923/1998	1923-03-02 HA	17002038
915-937	Kekaulike	Service Cold Storage Building	1924	1924-07-17 HSB	17002017, 17002018
1130-1136	Maunakea	Lum Yip Kee Building	1926	1926-07-17 HSB	17003049
102	N. Hotel	Siu Building	1926	1926-11-13 HSB, Sanborn	17003037
1138-1140	Maunakea	Sumida Building	1927	1926-10-20 HSB	17003048
1178-1190	Smith	Honolulu Auto Supply Service Station	1928	1928-04-19 HA	17004021
942	Kekaulike	Holau Market	1936	1936-07-29 HSB, Sanborn	17002026
1125-1127	Maunakea	Wing Sing Wo Building	1937	1937-10-01 HSB	17003052
119-131	N. Hotel	Lum Yip Kee Building	1937	1936-10-31 HA	17003025
103-115	N. Hotel	Wo Fat Restaurant	1938	1938-03-10 HA	17003026
1160-1164	Smith	Be Bop Hotel	1950	1950-08-12 HSB, 1948 DPP	17004024
1165-1169	Maunakea	Kam Chong Wong Building	1952	Sanborn	17004016
99	N. King	Liberty Bank / American Savings Bank	1952	Sanborn	17002007
928	Kekaulike	928 Kekaulike	1953	Sanborn	17002026
1021-1023	Smith	Central Pacific Bank	1953	Sanborn	17003003
50	N. King	Central Pacific Bank	1955	1955-04-21 HA	17003081
1010	Maunakea	Kwai Chan Trust Building	1956/1995	1956-12-05 HSB, 1995-11-17 HA	17003017
1001-1017	Maunakea	Lee & Young Building	1957	1957-02-17 HA	17003012
110	N. Hotel	Yee Yee Tong Building / Consuelo Foundation	1957	1957-08-18 HA	17003050
1159	Nuʻuanu	Marks Garage	1957	1957-11-0 HA	21003020
1026-1028	Kekaulike	Ying Leong Look Funn Building	1961/1994	1961-09-08 HSB, 1993-09-06 HSB	17003035

1032-1038	Kekaulike	Sam Chew Lau Building	1963/1994	1963-11-19 HA	17003034
62-64	N. Pauahi	Char Hung Sut Building	1963	1963-02-28 HSB	17004010
1022-1024	Kekaulike	City Villa	1964/1994	1964-07-17-HSB, 1994 DPP	17003036
1190	Nuʻuanu	Kokusai/Empress Theater	1964	1964-11-27 HA	17004005
159	N. Hotel	Lung Doo Building	1965	1965-06-29 HSB	17003033
158-190	N. Hotel	Winston Hale	1965/1981	1965-05-07 HSB, 1981-08-31 HA	17003044
111	N. King	C.Q. Yee Hop Plaza	1965	1965-02-20 HA	17002023
1155-1157	Maunakea	K.C. Siu Building	1965	1965-03-29 HSB, parapet	17004012
135	N. King	Yee Hop Market	1966	1966-09-30 HSB	17002019
155-157	N. King	Chun's Meat Market	1966	1966-01-28 HSB	17002033
1161	Maunakea	Loo Chow Liquor Store	1968	1968-03-20 HA	17004013
80-88	N. King	Lum Yip Kee Building	1968	1968-05-14 HA	17003011
1125	River	Komeya Apartments	1970	1970-02-25 HA	17003045
100	N. Beretania	Chinatown Cultural Plaza	1974	1974-06-13 HSB	17005019
1152	Smith	Golden Harvest Theater / New Life Church	1980	1980-11-12 HSB	17004025
1155	River	River-Pauahi Apartments	1981	1980-06-22 HA	17004034
60	N. Beretania	Honolulu Tower	1982	1982-03-26 HSB	17005011
1166-1182	Nuʻuanu	Smith-Beretania Apartments	1983	1993-10-16 HSB	17004007
167	N. Pauahi	Hale Kupuna Pauahi	1985	1985-06-22 HA	17003038
101-163	N. Beretania	Hale Pauahi (Hale Lahui, Hale Oʻpili)	1987	1987-06-28 HSB	17004030
158-162	N. Hotel	Yew Char Building	1987	1987-02-26 HA	17003042
171	N. Pauahi	Pauahi Recreation Center	1987	1987-12-03 HA	17003099
1112	Maunakea	Maunakea Marketplace	1989	1988-07-09 HSB	17003096
152	N. Hotel	Maunakea Marketplace	1989	1988-07-09 HSB	17003096
116-128	N. Hotel	Maunakea Marketplace	1989	1988-07-09 HSB	17003096
45	N. King	Hawaii National Bank	1989	1988-07-31 HSB	17002036
1212	Nuʻuanu	Honolulu Park Place	1990	1991-01-06 HA	17005001
1017-1051	Nuʻuanu	Chinatown Gateway Plaza	1990	1990-04-08 HA	21002038
65-69	N. Beretania	Roberts Building	1991	1991-04-20 HA	17004020
175	N. Hotel	Chinatown Manor	1994	1994-11-01 HSB	17003032
60	N. Nimitz	Marin Tower	1994	1994-02-06 HA	17002004
1039	Kekaulike	Kekaulike Courtyards	1997	1997-03-19 HSB	17003020
1016	Maunakea	Kekaulike Courtyards	1997	1997-03-19 HSB	17003020
51-79	N. Pauahi	Wang Building	1997	1997-07-23 HA	17003055
79	N. Hotel	Dan Liu Building (Police Station)	2000	2000-05-18 HSB	17003014

SOURCES & ACKNOWLEDGEMENTS

Bishop Museum Archives
        p.10, 220, 258, 323, 327, 340 – Rockwood-Barrere Map
        p.125 – Kaumakapili Church Organ
        p.264 – EC Winston Block (sign)
        p.308 – Asahi Theater
        p.369 – 1884 Love's Bakery Building
        p.117 – Maunakea Street makai from near Hotel Street
        p.119 – Maunakea Street mauka from Hotel Street
        p.394 – Liberty Theater

C.S. Wo & Company: p.228

Dakin Fire Insurance Maps (1885, 1891, 1899, 1906)
        p.154, 155, 156, 163, 167, 170, 171, 174, 181, 183, 184, 185, 194, 197, 201, 220, 227, 230, 233, 241, 247, 258, 252, 260, 269, 273, 278, 280, 293, 295, 296, 298, 306, 310, 315, 317, 325, 328, 331, 333, 338, 342, 346, 367, 381, 384, 404, 414, 421, 423, 430, 434, 435

Hawaii Department of Accounting and General Services: p. 91, 225, 437

Hawaii State Archives:
p. 10, 13, 14, 17, 18, 19, 20, 22, 31, 37, 38, 42, 43, 44, 45, 46, 47, 48, 49, 93, 94, 95, 96, 97, 98, 99, 100, 102, 103, 104, 105, 106, 107, 108, 111, 113, 114, 115, 117, 119, 122, 123, 124, 125, 126, 127, 128, 131, 132, 135, 156, 170, 190, 191, 195, 196, 201, 211, 212, 215, 216, 219, 220, 222, 223, 224, 227, 246, 247, 248, 251, 252, 253, 255, 258, 260, 262, 263, 264, 266, 272, 275, 278, 280, 285, 298, 299, 300, 302, 303, 306, 307, 310, 311, 312, 313, 314, 315, 316, 317, 320, 321, 322, 325, 326, 328, 329, 339, 342, 347, 352, 354, 359, 360, 362, 363, 367, 368, 371, 372, 374, 377, 379, 380, 383, 384, 386, 389, 390, 391, 392, 393, 397, 400, 401, 403, 404, 405, 406, 408, 413, 416, 417, 421, 427, 431, 432, 434, 436, 438, 439, 441, 442, back cover

Hawaii State Archives, Historic Buildings Task Force:
p. 58, 132, 147, 152, 153, 162, 203, 262, 283, 330, 337, 343, 407, 424, 433

Hawaii State Archives, Nancy Bannick Collection: p.126, 134, 184, 186, 236, 269, 345, 428, 431

Hawaii State Historic Preservation Division: p.179

Hawaii Times Photo Archives Foundation, Nippu Jiji Photo Archives: Copyright holder: Hawaii Times Photo Archives Foundation; digitization: Densho; and bilingual metadata: Hoover Institution Library & Archives and National Museum of Japanese History; https://hojishinbun.hoover.org. From the Scenery-Hawaii Collection:
        p.112 – Pauahi Street, SH1465.007
        p.122 – Honolulu Auto Supply, SH951.002
        p.183 – Miyako An Hotel: Today's Kagetsu Restaurant, SH1235.001
        p.186 – Fukuju Dining Hall on the Corner of Hotel and River Streets, SH894.001
        p.198 – Holau Market, SH943.001
        p.272 – Kawahara Building, SH1110.001
        p.284 – S. Ozaki, SH1358.001
        p.305 – Horse Drawn Carriages in Front of Old Sumida Building, SH1478.002
        p.305 – Exterior of the Old Sumida Building, SH1478.001
        p.396 – Iida Suisando, SH1083.003 and SH1083.004

p.398 – B.K. Yamamoto Building, SH1636.001 and SH1636.002
p.415 – Komeya Hotel, SH1165.002 and SH1165.003

Hawaiian Historical Society: p.53, 173, 382

Hawaii National Bank: p.226

Honolulu Police Department: p.162

Isaiah W. Tabor (1880): p.92, 101, 135, 142, 354, 358

Kamaka Hawaii, Inc.: p.21

Lion Fire Insurance Map (1879): p.17

Newspapers: *Daily Herald, Daily Honolulu Press, Evening Bulletin, Hawaiian Gazette, Hawaiian Star, Honolulu Advertiser, Honolulu Republican, Honolulu Star Bulletin, The Independent, Pacific Commercial Advertiser, Polynesian*

Paul Emmert / Library of Congress (1854): p.246, 323, 324, 327, 346, 381, 395

Ryan Kawailani Ozawa: p.254

Saltwater People Historical Society: p.193

Sanborn Fire Insurance Map (1914): p.60, 130, 167, 172, 176, 194, 201, 204, 205, 314, 316, 394, 405, 406, 409, 413, 424, 438, 440

Tony Grillo, Artistic Mindz Photography, Hawaii Lion Dance Association: p.61

Thrum's Hawaiian Annual: p.13, 79, 84

Tony Dierckins, Zenith City Press, Maryanne C. Norton: p.85

Thanks to the many intrepid and unknown newspaper reporters and chroniclers who have documented the history of Chinatown through the years, including Stephen Reynolds, Gorham Gilman, Warren Goodale, Richard Greer, Nancy Bannick, Don Hibbard, Bob Sigall, Stanley Solamillo, Wendy Tolleson, Peter Young, Carter Churchfield, and many many others, and especially all the uncredited archivists who labored long to digitize the thousands of historical newspapers, maps, photographs, and other primary sources that were so invaluable to this research.

Thanks to Dawn Chang, William Yu, and Beth Iwata for assistance with Hawaiian, Chinese, and Japanese translations.

Thanks to Adam Jansen along with Ron, Diane, and Troy at the Hawaii State Archives.

Thanks to Kay Ueda and Dawn Webb at the Hawaii Times Photo Archives Foundation.

Thanks to DeSoto Brown and Krystal Kakimoto at the Bishop Museum Archives.

And thanks to the Historic Hawaii Foundation for their tireless efforts saving places that matter.

THE AUTHOR

Trained as a licensed site civil engineer, Gary R. Coover has long had a keen interest in history and the built environment, and especially in those who have done the designing and building.

When Gary was much younger he enjoyed working on 1,000-piece jigsaw puzzles but little did he realize at the time that these same skills would apply to historical research. The pattern recognition is similar except the pieces are scattered all over the place, some will be missing, some won't fit, and then there is the multidimensional aspect of different pieces fitting different places at different times.

He has previously rediscovered the histories and works of several long-lost architects and has identified the builders and construction dates for over a thousand buildings in Texas and Arkansas.

Gary's Historic Downtown Fayetteville Walking Tour and Virtual Marker Program won a 2017 Preservation Award from Preservation Arkansas for its innovative use of QR codes to enhance the visitor experience with additional information and historical photographs.

A featured presenter in HGTV's "Dream Drives" and "If Walls Could Talk" television programs, and lecturer for many years in the Historic Neighborhoods series at the Rice University School of Continuing Studies, he also created the Historic Neighborhoods Photography Contest in conjunction with Houston FotoFest as well as the controversial "Godzilla Award" for demolished structures that was featured in *Preservation* Magazine.

A former Historic District Chairman and preservation society board member, Gary now lives in Honolulu and can often be found wandering around imagining historical Honolulu and Chinatown.

INDEX

A

Achi, William C., 416
Achuck, 208, 209, 216
Afong, 26, 82, 208, 209, 216, 236, 247, 432
Ala Moana Center, 55, 266
Alfie's Pub, 330
Allied Builders System, 282
Aloha Building Company, 197
AM Partners, 159, 161
Anchor Saloon, 82, 211, 212, 329, 336, 337, 338, 339
Apau, Kepoʻolele, 183
Araujo Building, 159
Armstrong Building, 80, 265
Arrow Hardware, 260
Asahi / Oahu Theater, 307
Aseu Building, 75, 79, 217, 341, 342, 348
Aswan, 348
Aswan Building, 82, 223, 346

B

B.K. Yamamoto Building, 71, 308
Babcock, Captain William, 322
Baker, Thomas J., 68
Bank Building & Equipment Corporation, 225
Bannick, Nancy, 55, 56, 57, 58, 59
Be Bop Hotel, 439
Beretania Follies, 129
Beretania Street, 120
Beretania Theater, 54, 129
Bickerton Block, 78, 136
Biltright Shoe Repair, 400
Booth, Joseph, 207
Brenig Block, 319, 323, 324
Brenig, Charles, 323
Brito, Cesar L., 22, 232, 248
Brown Derby, 383
Buffum's Hall, 141
Burlesque, 53, 54, 129, 136, 137, 147, 180, 292, 309
Burrows, S.D., 69, 360, 364

C

C. Ahi Building, 76
C.Q. Yee Hop, 70, 74, 84, 124, 126, 189, 193, 220, 244, 247, 249, 252, 275, 276
C.Q. Yee Hop Cold Storage & Dormitory, 275
C.Q. Yee Hop Market, 249
C.Q. Yee Hop Plaza, 74, 84, 244, 247, 252
C.S. Wo & Sons, 226
Caranave, John J., 323, 324
Cavanagh, C., 139, 341, *See* Kavanagh, C.
Cayton, Herbert Cohen, 295, 296, 363
Central Pacific Bank, 71, 84, 228, 230, 278, 395
Century Construction, 69, 278, 282, 283, 313
Chan, Charlie, 186
Chang Apana, 186
Chang, Luke Aseu, 343
Char Hung Sut, 404
Char, Y.T., 23, 69, 157, 165, 167, 212, 213, 236, 294, 369
Char, Yew, 182, 280
Charles Pankow Associates, 122
Chee Wo Tong Building, 287
China Engine Company No.5, 299
Chinatown Cultural Plaza, 60, 74, 128
Chinatown Gateway Plaza, 59, 74, 76, 344
Chinatown Manor, 59, 74, 183
Chinatown Police Station, 161
Chinese Bazaar, 371
Chinese Engine House, 49, 72
Chinese Exclusion Act, 17
Chinese Immigration, 16
Chinese Language & Names, 26
Chinese Theatre, 173
Ching Lum, 269
Ching Lum Block, 268
Ching Pui, 236
Ching, Calvin, 221, 249
Ching, W.S., 165, 294
Chong Kam Sing, 440
Chong Sum Wing, 402
Chong, Pang, 70, 121, 124, 127, 184, 190, 249, 252, 397
Chun, Ellery & Ethyl, 224
Chun, Kim Chow, 342
Chung Kun Ai, 191
City Mill, 70, 180, 190, 191, 196, 200, 217, 226, 227, 254, 427
City Villa Apartments, 202
Club Hubba Hubba, 78, 136, 137, 138
Colburn, John F., 49, 82, 246, 247, 271
Colusa Building, 80, 163, 164, 170, 175, 265

Command Construction Co., 125
Commercial Hotel, 394
Cook Plaque, 198
Cooke Warehouse, 319, 420
Cooke, A. Frank, 319
Cosmopolitan Saloon, 78, 351
Custom House, 72, 319, 420
Cykler, Emil F., 189

D

Daniel Mann Johnson & Mendenhall, 128, 394, 411
Davis, Isaac, 10, 322
Davis, Louis E., 81, 367
Dias, Augusto, 21, 22, 373
Dickey, Charles W., 70, 80, 81, 230, 241, 397
Dimond, Charles Kaimana, 175
Dole, James D., 15
Dole, Sanford B., 15, 141, 231

E

E.C. Winston Block, 263
Edison, Thomas, 14, 51, 206, 211, 230, 232, 233, 248
Ellis, E.W., 162, 275
Emmeluth & Co., 325
Emmert, Paul, 326, 380
Emory & Webb, 71, 273, 336
Emory, Walter L., 71, 273, 336
Empire Saloon, 77, 133, 134
Empress Theater, 387
Encore Saloon, 78, 85, 357

F

Filipino Immigration, 23
Fishel Building, 126
Flores Building, 85, 339, 340
Fong Building, 81, 131, 307
Fong Hing, 321
Fong Inn, 374
Fong Inn Building, 373
Fuchino, Hego, 71, 197, 307, 308, 436

G

George J. Oda Contracting Company, 171
Gerell, Bob, 58, 79, 154, 296, 355, 427
Glade Show Club, 178
Golden Harvest Theatre, 435
Goo Kim, 288, 363, 364

Goto, M.K., 197, 213
Goto, Tatsuo, 199
Gratz, Leslie N., 220
Gravier Lane, 250
Gravier, Louis, 249
Great Māhele, 11, 14
Grimes, E.&H., 323

H

Hai On Tong Building, 70, 127
Hale Pauahi, 59, 130, 408
Hara, Ernest, 71, 228, 230, 278, 432
Harbor Village, 59, 74, 411
Harbor Village Apartments, 411
Harrison, Fred, 72, 299, 365
Hawaii Hochi / y. Anin Building, 302
Hawaii National Bank, 225
Hawaiian Ballasting Company, 72, 217, 231, 232, 261, 367, 401
Hawaiian Chinese News Company, 18
Hawaiian Contracting Co., 189
Hawaiian Dredging & Construction Company, 74, 128, 176, 183, 189, 286, 344, 411
Hawaiian Engineering & Construction Company, 73, 154, 231, 232, 425
Heuck, Theodore C., 74, 207, 208, 215, 238
Hirano Brothers, 413
Historic Buildings Task Force, 57
HMS *Blonde*, 89, 207, 332
Ho'oliliamanu, 37
Hocking Building, 57, 72, 81, 156, 217, 218, 224, 341
Hocking, Alfred, 30, 218
Hoffman Café, 133
Hoffschlaeger Building, 80, 82, 337, 338, 356
Hogan, George, 171
Holau Market, 71, 197, 199
Holt Block, 78, 383, 385
Honolulu Auto Supply Building, 70, 121
Honolulu Auto Supply Service Station, 441
Honolulu Iron Works, 38, 47, 78, 81, 226, 236, 418, 419, 422, 423
Honolulu Park Place, 396
Honolulu Park Place Condominium, 60, 396
Honolulu Restaurant, 324
Honolulu Sake Brewery, 300
Honolulu Tower, 60, 76, 122
Honolulu Trust Company, 220
Hop Sing Building, 251
Horn, Frederick, 238
Hotel Street, 132

Hsi, Peter, 74, 128, 244, 252
Hu, Gilman K.M., 125

I

Ichiki, Masaji, 199
Independent Theater, 140
Inter-Island Steam Navaigation Company, 329
Inter-Island Steam Navigation Company, 215, 329, 412
Iolani Palace, 78, 82, 86, 207, 335, 390
Irwin Block, 70, 76, 81, 86, 126, 331, 335
Irwin, William G., 334
Island Steam Navigation Company, 198, 329, 411, 412
Izui, I., 271

J

J.H. Schnack Building, 71, 273
J.M. Oat & Co., 319
James Robinson, 215
Japanese Immigration, 19
Johnson, Samuel, 207, 208
Jones, Paul D., 75, 164
Joseph P. Mendonça Building, 154

K

K. Fukumura, Solomon K., 271
K.C. Siu Building, 306
K.C. Wong Building, 312
Kajioka Okada & Partners, 130, 407, 408
Kamehameha I, 10, 11, 12, 19, 391, 419
Katsey Block, 83, 228, 230
Kaumakapili Church, 41, 49, 69, 70, 72, 86, 121, 122, 123, 299, 346, 360, 381, 396, 397, 418, 435, 436
Kavanagh, C, 75
Kawahara, Masao, 272
Keali'imaika'i, 10
Kekaulike Courtyards, 59, 74, 176, 201, 249, 283, 286
Kekaulike Street, 188
Keli'imaika'i, 322
Kenn, Solomon F., 75, 150, 298
Kerr, H.L., 69, 76, 153, 231, 232, 235, 242, 255, 283, 286, 290, 373, 399, 428
King Market, 55, 70, 74, 243, 252
King Street, 206
Kobayashi Hotel, 438
Kokusai Theater, 387
Komeya Apartments, 413
Komeya, Myozuchi, 413

Korean Immigration, 23
Kuihelani, 220, 238, 322
Kukui Plaza, 59, 394
Kwai Chan Trust Building, 282

L

L. Ah Leong, 243, 253
L.L. McCandless Block, 399
Lacayo Architects, 320
Lacayo, Norman, 59, 76, 122, 331, 344, 396
Ladd & Co., 322
Lai Fong, 364
Lai Fong Building, 360
Law & Wilson, 249
Lawrence, Robert, 208, 215, 383
Lee & Young Building, 69, 71, 230, 278
Lee Fai, 260
Lee Let Building, 261
Lee Wai, 152, 251
Lemmon Freeth Haines & Jones, 184, 337
Liberty Bank, 80, 233, 236, 237, 241, 296, 387, 427
Liberty Hall, 38, 85, 169, 209, 245
Liberty Theater, 389
Lincoln, George W., 77
Lishman, Robert, 77, 86, 133
Little Village Noodle House, 426
Liu, Daniel Siu Chong, 161
Loncke, Captain Frank J., 198
Loncke, Mary Ellen Holau Freudenberg Leslie, 198
Loo-Chow Building, 84, 311
Love's Bakery, 72, 81, 82, 336, 367, 368
Lovejoy & Company, 329, 330
Lucas Brothers, 271
Lucas, George, 78, 136, 139, 226, 233, 236, 337, 351, 352, 357, 361, 383
Lum Yip Kee, 296
Lum Yip Kee Building, 58, 81, 84, 131, 171, 235, 295, 296, 298, 307
Lung Doo Building, 87, 181
Lusitana Society, 22

M

M. Kawahara Building, 271
Machado, Lena, 197, 199, 209
Marin Tower, 11, 59, 419
Marin, Don Francisco, 419
Marin, Don Francisco de Paula, 11, 15, 238, 247, 419, 423
Marks Building, 377

Marks Garage, 377
Marks, Alfred Lester, 377
Marshall and Wildes, 322
Matsumoto, Kikutaro, 73, 217
Maunakea Hale, 316
Maunakea Marketplace, 58, 59, 79, 85, 170, 175, 291, 292, 293, 403
Maunakea Street, 270
Maxey, John, 326
Mayhew, E.E., 79, 221
McCandless, L.L., 76, 265, 268, 276, 377, 399
McLean Block, 72, 84, 365
McTighe, Thomas, 248
Meek Street, 145, 229, 418
Mellen, George, 267
Melville, Herman, 13
Mendonça & Selig Building, 75, 139
Mendonça Building, 57, 58, 72, 73, 76, 79, 84, 85, 87, 153, 155, 242, 294, 413
Mendonça Makai, 231, 425
Mendonça, Joseph P., 158
Mitsunaga & Associates, 176, 286
Miyamoto, Koichiro, 266
Miyata, Risuke, 79, 88, 253, 254, 429
Montgomery, Isaac, 85, 238, 245
Mossman, Captain Thomas, 209
Mouse Builders, 79, 153, 170, 175, 273, 291, 301, 355, 429
Murphy's Bar and Grill, 328
Musashiya the Shirtmaker, 266
Mutch, William, 80, 170, 173, 265, 298

N

National Hotel, 344
Nippu Jiji, 331
Nisei, 20
Nolte, Henry J., 320
Norrie, Edmund, 231, 232, 399
Nowlein, Captain Sam, 219
Nu'uanu Court, 320
Nu'uanu Street, 318
Nunes, Manuel, 21

O

O'Hara, Jean, 434
O'Tooles Irish Pub, 330
Oahu Hotel, 325
Oahu Lumber and Building Company, 268, 269
Oahu Market, 256

Oahu Theater, 71, 81, 131, 307, 308, 436
Old Corner, The, 320
On Tai BUilding, 376
Ossipoff, Vladimir, 80, 237, 241, 432
Ozaki, Sanshichi, 248, 285

P

Pacific Construction Corp., 130
Pacific Saloon, 82, 85, 339, 340, 376
Paiko Block, 360
Paiko, Manuel, 364
Palmer & Richardson, 80, 329, 330, 356
Palmer, Isaac A., 80, 326, 327, 353, 356
Pang Lum Mow, 301
Pang Lum Mow / Aloha Hotel, 297
Pantheon Bar, 370
Park Associates, 87, 128, 405
Pauahi Hale, 59, 405
Pauahi Kupuna Hale, 59, 406, 407
Pauahi Recreation Center, 408
Pauahi Street, 398
Peacock, Walter, 325, 351
Peacock, Walter C., 327, 352
Peasley, Captain Matt, 192
Pegge Hopper Gallery, 382
People Against Chinatown Evictions (PACE), 59, 297, 383
Perry Block, 79, 80, 82, 134, 327, 330, 353, 356
Perry, Jason, 21, 158, 353
Pidgin, 24
Portuguese Immigration, 21
Potter, Mark, 233, 234
Prince Hanalei, 179
Puerto Rican Immigration, 23
Punchard, George W., 320

Q

Queen Emma, 391
Queen Emma Hall, 389
Queen's Court, 320
Quong Sam Kee Building, 77, 82, 237

R

Redward, Fred H., 83, 86, 335
Reynolds, Stephen, 219, 224, 325, 326, 447
Ripley & Davis, 69, 81, 217, 367, 368, 401, 423
Ripley, Clinton B., 69, 70, 81, 212, 217, 331, 338, 367, 368, 401, 423

Risque Theatre, 141, 144
River Street, 410
River-Pauahi Apartments, 415
Roberts Building, 125
Robinson Building, 37, 69, 74, 207, 210, 211, 213, 215, 216, 338, 346, 385
Robinson, James, 207, 208, 213, 215, 383
Rooke, Dr. T.C.B., 390
Royal Annex, 325, 355
Royal Saloon, 57, 80, 86, 326, 327, 328, 330, 335, 340, 356
Russian Immigration, 23

S

S.M. Iida Store, 87
Saiki & Davenport, 81, 131, 162, 295, 298, 306, 307
Saiki, Masataro, 81, 131, 298, 307
Sailor Jerry's Tattoo Shop, 424
Sam Chew Lau Building, 87, 204
San Antonio Society, 22, 232
Santo, Jose do Espirito, 22
Sarnoff, Robert, 225
Schnack, John Henry, 273
Service Cold Storage Building, 193
Shiigi, Ichinojo, 183
Shun Lung Building, 255
Sinclair, Archibald, 82, 86, 331, 335
Siu Building, 81, 131, 162, 163, 303, 307
Smith Beretania Apartments, 59
Smith Street, 418
Smith, Lowell, 123, 418, 435, 436
Smith, Peter, 58, 79
Smith's Lane, 89, 145, 152, 418
Smith's Union Bar, 135
Soga, Yasutaro, 334
Sperry Flour Building, 74, 189
Su Wai, 161, 287
Sugahara, Richard, 150
Sugihara, Zenkichi, 79, 88, 254, 428, 429
Sumida Building, 58, 75, 81, 131, 298, 307
Sumida, Daizo, 300
Sumitomo Bank, 72, 76, 231, 232
Sun Yat-sen, 151, 158, 173, 191, 235, 266, 280, 285, 364, 428, 439, 440
Sun Yun Wo, 427
Swing Club, 54, 145, 146, 147, 148

T

T. Sumida Building, 304

T.R. Foster Building, 80, 82, 327, 329, 330, 356, 412
Tan Sing (Mendonca) Building, 58, 76, 79, 427, 428, 432
Tanaka Brothers Building, 258
The Old Corner, 321, 323
Thomas, E.B., 68, 82, 86, 221, 229, 230, 240, 246, 279, 281, 329, 330, 335, 337, 338, 339, 340, 346, 347, 349, 353, 368
Tom's Grill, 315
Town Construction, 84, 184, 202, 228, 235, 244, 252, 311
Traphagen, Oliver, 80, 84, 154, 231, 232, 352, 356, 365, 425
Tsugawa, James K., 59, 85, 122, 154, 170, 175, 291, 292, 293, 301, 340, 357, 403
Tsung Tsin Association Building, 310

U

United Chinese Society, 18, 31, 37, 69, 76, 79, 82, 87, 128, 149, 210, 221, 222, 223, 224, 226, 234, 235, 299, 331, 364
United Chinese Society Building, 221
Urban Renewal, 9, 59, 122, 185, 296, 305, 313, 395
Uyeda Building, 82, 349

V

VIGILANT, 191
Vincent, Charles W., 85, 245, 286

W

Walker & Redward, 326, 327
Walker, Thomas B., 77, 86, 331, 335
Walker-Moody Construction, 237
Wall, Charles J., 68, 86, 123
Wang Building, 85, 403
Webb, Marshall J., 71, 273
Wing Coffee Company, 401
Wing Sing Wo Building, 294
Wing Sing Wo Company, 154, 157, 158, 294, 369
Wing Wo Tai / Wing Wo Chan, 337
Wing Wo Tai Building, 336
Winston Block, 183, 184, 185, 186, 265, 413
Winston Hale, 59, 75, 84, 184, 185
Winston, E.C., 184, 263, 264
Wo Fat Building, 69, 165, 169
Wo Hop Hing Kee, 321
Wo, C.S., 227
Wolter, E.H.F., 327

Wong & Wong Associates, 128
Wong Kong Har Tong Society, 162, 163
Wong Kwai Building, 82
Wong Tai- hoon, 26
Wong Tze-Chun, 14
Wong, K.C., 304, 312
Woo, George, 202
Woo, S.B., 371
Wyllie, Robert Crichton, 380

Y

Y. Anin, 285
Y. Anin Block, 76, 242, 248, 254, 281, 286, 290
Yamada, George M., 72, 87, 153, 306, 355, 395, 432
Yamamoto, B.K., 397

Yashida, Z., 135
Yee Hop Market, 70, 84, 244, 252
Yee Yee Tong Building, 75, 163, 164, 170
Yew Char Building, 182
Yim Quon, 234
Yim Quon Building, 78, 233, 236
Ying Leong Look Funn Building, 87, 203
Young, Clifford, 87, 221
Young, Clifford F., 221
Young, James C.M., 87, 181, 203, 204
Young, John Mason, 87, 231, 232
Yuen Chong Building, 69, 236

Z

Z. Sugihara Company, 254

GEOGRAPHICAL INDEX & WALKING TOUR

(Refer to page numbers on properties, begin at any location)

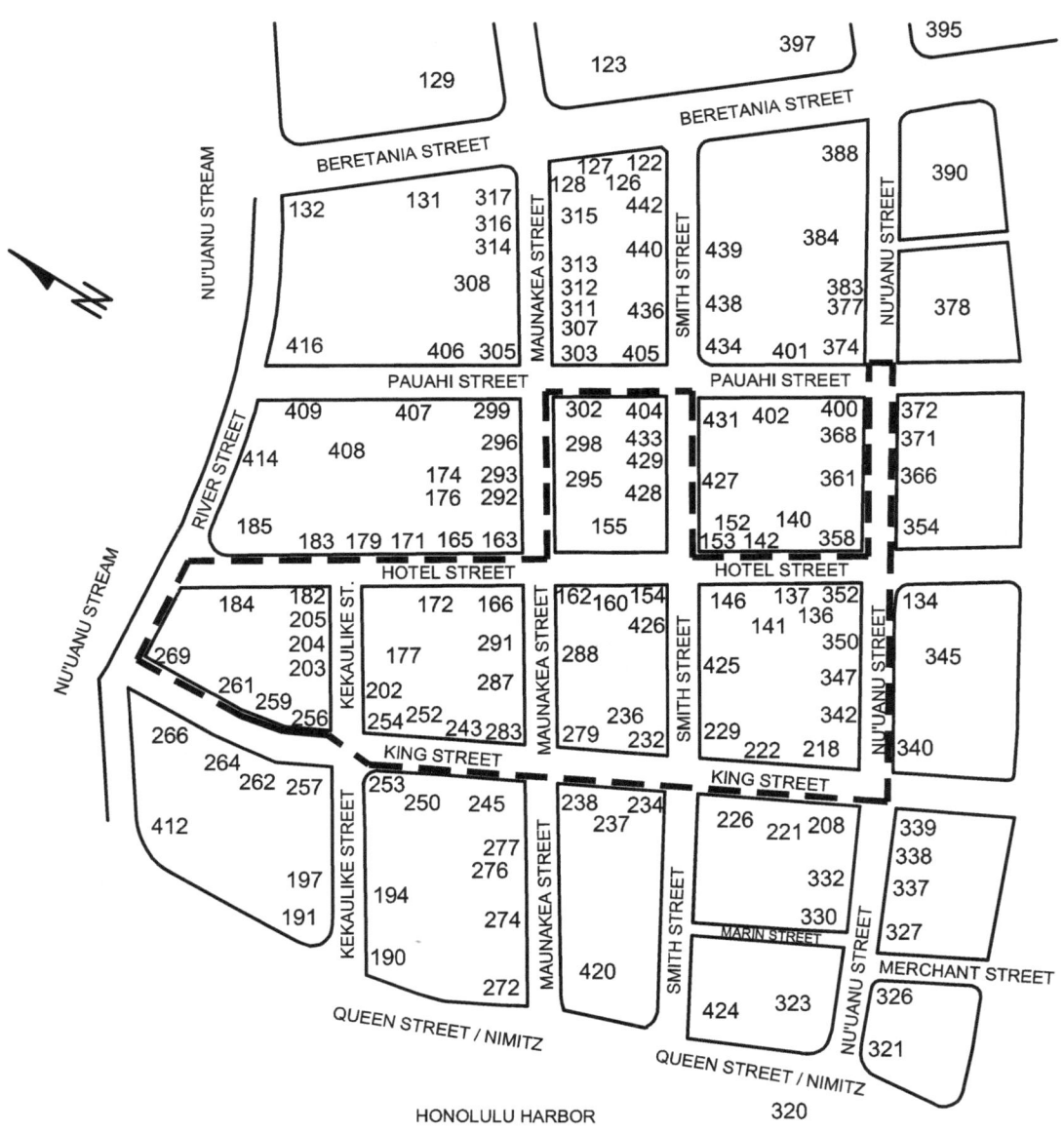

Obey all signs, watch for traffic, respect all properties

HONOLULU CHINATOWN

Available at Zazzle.com

www.ingramcontent.com/pod-product-compliance
Lightning Source LLC
Chambersburg PA
CBHW081124170426
43197CB00017B/2739